D1561858

THE BOXCAR BRIGADE

THE BOXCAR BRIGADE

Written By

MARY ELLEN ESTER

Mary Ellen Ester

A NOVEL

THIS BOOK IS HUMBLY DEDICATED TO:

My loving Father

Without whom there would be no story,

My beloved Husband

Without whom there would be no book,

My cherished Children

Without whom there would be no purpose.

Mary Ellen Ester FIBA

My most grateful thanks goes to the following people whose knowledge and time have been valuable to me beyond measure:

Henry Ester
Vaughn K. Neel
Mary E. Burton
Mildred (Auntie Mil) Weekley
Janet A. Wyse
Faye R. O'Dell
Margaret M. Gordon
Zane Walker
Thomas H. Snider, MD

The New London Public Library and Staff:

Carolyn Mench, Director
Janet Thomas
Cheryl Loescher
Sandra Snyder
Louieda Cumberledge
Mary Ann Fannin
Mary Noss

Louis M. Carratola, DDS and Staff:

Ruth Ann Cunningham
Carol Pondy
Pamela Howell
Debora Evans
Deborah Anderson
Deborah Myers
Marilyn Pheiffer
Mary Stieber
Kathleen Hanko

Irene (Peg) Ovenstone, M.D.
Freda (The Duchess) Bruce
Ruth J. (Ruthie) Chance
Linda and Robert Bender
Kenneth and Andrea Heimann
June and Charlie Krejcier
Dee and Frank Cooke
Bob and Barney Thomas
Nadene Sutherland
Betty Barker
H. S. Robinson

Huron County Agricultural Heritage:
Ralph F. Albright, President
Carl and Virginia Ruess
Midré
Peter Holick

The stories in this novel are based upon fact but may have been embellished to maintain continuity and readership. Some of the places and the names have been changed to assure privacy.

Chapter One

MA'AM SAYS

The sun was high in the sky before it cleared the rim of the mountain into this quiet, lush valley. A weathered log cabin set on the valley floor in a clearing near a river.

The Lansure family had lived here since 1754. James Clayton Lansure was born here in 1847. In 1877 he brought his bride, Mary Agnes Hobson, here to live. They added more rooms to the original cabin and put on the porch.

Sunday, November 16, 1897, dawned dry, clear and cold. Jimmy, known to all, stepped from the door into the cold air on the porch and paused at the steps. He turned up his collar to ward off the morning chill.

Jimmy Lansure was a stonemason by trade, but he was neither strong-looking or burly of stature that was expected of those who do that work.

He withstood the rigors of his occupation well and made a good living for his family. He was not tall but he was wiry and muscular. His red hair was thick, unruly and laced with white. His Van dyke-type goatee was red, white and wispy. Quick to smile and slow to anger, he enjoyed a good joke about anything.

Being a doting father and where possible, he would see to it his children got a bit more than was absolutely necessary.

He said, "Happy faces on a man's children is his wealth".

He gathered his around him often to tell a tale or spin a yarn.

Today was special. Jimmy's son, John Clellend, was five years old today. Although Johnny did not ask, everyone knew his childish wish was to have a dog of his own.

Jimmy knew where there were puppies for sale. The dry leaves swirled around his feet as he made his way up the road, into the trees, toward the village and the puppies.

Mary Agnes Hobson Lansure, also known as Ma'am, watched her husband walk down the road, turn the bend and disappear into the trees.

She moved from the window to the stove and continued the breakfast preparation.

Ma'am was a busy housewife and mother; also, she was Agnes, the local mid-wife. She was too tall and solid to be called girlish but her face was soft and warm. Her regal carriage and assured manner discouraged anyone from calling her 'Aggie.' Her eyes were caring, kind and reassuring. Her straight, black hair was thin and fine and she wore it in a soft coil at the back of her neck. The high forehead and long jaw was delicately split by her classic nose and dark, soulful eyes.

Ma'am turned the sizzling sausage and a delightful aroma filled the house.

Upstairs the children were dressing, all except two-year old Dudley, the youngest. He was trying noisily to escape from his cradle which stood nearby.

One by one her family came to the table and sat down.

Robert Bruce, age 16, was much like both of his parents. He was bookish and read everything he could put his hands on; but books around there were scarce. He was especially interested in American history, particularly Abraham Lincoln. He also worked part-time at the local feed mill.

"Morn'n Ma'am."

"Bruce", she nodded.

"Ma'am, I'm not going to church today. I think I have a new job."

"You have a job?"

"Not a full-time one."

"Where?"

"In the Kinley Mine."

"It's hard, dangerous work for a boy your age."

"I'm a man and it's no harder than buckin' wheat and barley sacks all day."

"Ummmm."

The conversation ended when little Dudley squealed impatiently for attention.

Leone Grace came into the kitchen. She was 19 and the sometime boss over her younger siblings. She was loud, abrasive and often frightening to them. If she brandished a wooden spoon, they would scurry away. Under it all, she was loving and kind.

"Morn'in Ma'am. Bruce."

"Leone, please see if Dudley is wet; he wants down."

"Your nappes soaked again? What will I do with you?" Leone lifted baby Dudley from his crib, hugged him and proceeded to change and dress him.

Rose Mary, age 9, and Louise Unice, age 13, jabbered their way to the table followed closely by little Seneca, age 4.

Rose was pretty, with black wavy hair, a bubbly nature and a healthy body.

Lu, on the other hand, had red hair and freckles, a quiet nature and was sickly.

Seneca Raindrop was an orphan Jimmy and Agnes took to raise as their own. To learn about Seneca, we go back in time about four years. . . . .

September in 1894 was the worst anyone could remember. It was damp, rainy and unseasonably cold.

Ross Greeley was a night switchman on the Buffalo, Rochester and Pittsburg Railroad. The BR&P ran through the village and switched cars to the siding there night and day.

One bad night that month while the train crew was switching and making up a train, Ross found an Indian girl in one of the boxcars.

She was about 16 years old, half-starved, burning up with fever and in the advanced stages of childbirth.

Ross sent the yard boy and a rig to fetch Agnes Lansure. Agnes was always expecting emergency calls and was ready.

The rig took them quickly to the railroad yards and Mr. Greeley.

"Thanks for coming, Agnes. Terrible night." He took her bag and helped her from the buggy.

"What kind of a problem you got here, Ross? This is a strange place for a birth'in," Ma'am declared.

"You will see. Over here. I don't know how long she's been here. This car has been here for a couple of days. She probably came here in that boxcar." He lead the way with a lantern to a car on a siding. He slid the boxcar door open and helped Agnes in. He scrambled in after her and held up the light.

In a corner, on a few scraps of straw, lay a pitifully undernourished Indian girl.

"More light, please. I will need hot water and blankets; she's in bad shape," Agnes informed Ross after a quick examination.

"Run to the hostler's shanty for water and there are some blankets and lanterns in the work caboose. Hurry, boy!" Ross called to his helper and rushed him on his way.

The Indian girl whimpered and opened her eyes. She was afraid.

''It's alright, don't be afraid, I'm here to help you. Do you understand me?'' Ma'am spoke softly to calm the sick girl.

The girl nodded but a birth contraction made her cry out.

Agnes was quick and efficient. She had delivered babies under adverse conditions but never in an unheated boxcar in the rain.

The boy returned with the supplies. Ross took them at the door and closed it to avoid the onlookers. He rigged more light overhead and covered the girl with blankets.

The poor wretch screamed again, then lay still. A trickle of water from the rain outside ran down the inside wall of the boxcar near her head. She saw it and smiled faintly.

At the same moment, Agnes held up the tiny baby to the light.

''It is a fine girl but a bit small.'' Agnes smiled. She rubbed the newborn with oil and wrapped it in a blanket.

''It's a girl!'' shouted Ross to the people gathered outside. Bad weather does not deter the curious.

Agnes placed the baby in the mother's arms. The frail woman had said nothing until now.

''Please, misses, come closer,'' she whispered and tried to raise her head. Agnes leaned closer.

''I know I'm done for. There's nobody to care for her. You take her, please. I'm a Seneca Indian Princess. Now, she is one too. We are the last of our tribe. Name her Seneca Raindrop so she knows who she is and so she will live with pride and dignity. Not as you find me here. Please, misses, I beg——''. Her voice faded away.

The tragic girl fell back, her head turned and she died. The questions Ross and Agnes had for her would never be answered.

Agnes stood up with the baby in her arms and spoke to Ross.

''You heard, Ross?'' she asked.

''Most of it, Agnes, but why call a baby Raindrop? Is that a name? You gonna take the little one home?'' asked Ross.

''You see that bit of water leaking in and running down the wall, there, by her? It's a custom among the Indians to name a baby at birth the first thing the mother sees. At this young'in's birth, her mama saw that raindrop trickling down the wall.'' Agnes snuggled the baby close.

''Imagine that. Never heard THAT before. What do we do now?'' puzzled Ross.

''You and the railroad can bury her. Put my fee to it. Lay her in Pine Grove. There's space to rest for a poor wretched soul like her. I'll take the baby with me 'til 'arrangements' can be made,'' instructed Agnes.

She waved greetings to the folks standing around in the rain while she and the baby climbed back into the buggy for the ride home.

At home she explained what had happened to her family. The baby was to remain there only until 'other arrangements' could be made. Agnes was having another child of her own in the spring.

Everyone pitched in, time passed and Seneca flourished. She cried very little and she ate well. Soon, she was woven into the fabric of their lives and loved by all. No talk of 'other arrangements' was ever made again. She grew rapidly. When Dudley was born, Agnes had two babies in diapers. No matter, Seneca was an accepted part of the family. She bares a striking resemblance to Ma'am and is never far from her skirts. . . . .

''Morn'n Ma'am,'' they all said together.

''Morn'in girls.''

''Ma'am, I don't want to go to Sunday school today. Mrs. Harper said if I go see her this morning, she will give me some extra floss for my hope chest,'' said Rose.

''Hopeless chest is more like it,'' quipped Bruce.

''Now, Bruce, don't discourage your sister's needlework. Lu, do you plan to take Johnny?''

''No, Ma'am, I don't. It's too far, he gets tired and I have to carry him and I don't feel like it. Where's pap?''

''He went to get the pu———,'' blurted Rose.

''Shu—————sh, Rose, don't spoil the surprise,'' cautioned Ma'am.

The girls snickered knowingly. Rose braided Seneca's hair.

John Clellend Lansure, age 5 today, marched into the kitchen and presented himself to his mother for inspection.

''My, my, don't we look proper,'' mused Ma'am.

He had dressed completely, if not correctly. His jacket was buttoned wrong, a stocking was wrinkled and falling, the shirttail was out in the back and one shoe was untied. He had made an effort to clean and dress himself and that was the important thing.

''You look just fine,'' praised Ma'am.

He beamed as Ma'am corrected his mistakes and smoothed his cowlick.

''Why you all slicked up so, somethin' special going on?'' Ma'am teased. He scooted up to the table and she placed his breakfast plate in front of him.

''It's my birthday, Ma'am, you didn't forget did you?'' exclaimed the wide-eyed boy between bites.

''Course not, I wouldn't forget THAT.'' She smiled and hugged the boy. ''Spose you don't want to go to Sunday school either?''

''Oh yes, I do. Li'l Dan and me, we're goin' together,'' declared Johnny.

''They can't walk that far alone.'' said Leone.

''Yes we can too,'' pouted Johnny.

''Why'd you make me always carry you before?'' quipped Lu.

''That was when I was little. Now I'm five and big,'' announced Johnny proudly.

''Oh, I see, now you're five you're big,'' said Ma'am.

''Uh huh,'' and cleaned his plate.

They finished breakfast and the girls cleared the table. Bruce went to his room to read and Ma'am tidied up.

The kitchen door burst open and in swirled Jonathan Daniel Lansure, the second and slammed the door behind him. No one turned a hair. He always made his entrances that way. Li'l Dan was first cousin and nephew to these Lansures. James and Johnathon, the first, were brothers.

Johnathon and his family lived on the other side of the hill but the two small boys used the path over the top. Li'l Dan and Johnny were about the same age and as soon as they could toddle, they went back and forth alone.

Li'l Dan was from March to November older than Johnny and the exact opposite. Dan was loud and wiggly. Johnny, on the other hand, was soft-spoken and calm. Li'l Dan leaped before he looked and Johnny thought it out carefully. Dan was quick, jerky and his attention span was short. Not Johnny; he was attentive and his movements were slow and steady; perhaps, because Johnny was left-eyed, left-footed and left-handed. Li'l Dan was not.

Regardless, Li'l Dan and Johnny were devoted friends and as close as brothers. If there was one, usually there was the other.

''Mornin', Aunt Agnes, happy birthday, Johnny,'' he yelled and scrambled up to the table beside Johnny.

''Mornin', Li'l Dan, you had your breakfast?'' asked Ma'am.

''Well yes, but somethin' sure smells good,'' he answered and sniffed the air.

''How 'bout a sausage sandwich?'' She wrapped the last piece of sausage in a slice of bread and handed it to him. The boy was always hungry.

''Yes ma'am, thanks,'' he yelled and grinned from ear to ear.

Between gulps he said, ''Come on Johnny, I got my copper.''

From her apron pocket, Ma'am took a coin and pressed it into Johnny's hand. She kissed him goodby, helped him with his coat and they were out the door.

The village was less than a mile away but the church was on the other side of town on Bradley Ridge. Not far for adults but a long walk for two small boys.

By the time they reached the bridge over the river this side of town, they were tired.

"Let's see if there are any frogs under the bridge," suggested Li'l Dan.

"All right."

Both boys went down the embankment to the water's edge.

"Ya know, Mr. Towns at the store has some new candy. It's got stripes," said Li'l Dan.

"Red stripes, like candy canes?"

"Naw, black and pink."

"Taste good?"

"I dunno; didn't have any yet."

"Cost a lot?"

"For a copper, ya get three."

"Three!", exclaimed Johnny.

"Ya want to get some?" Li'l Dan inquired.

"Them coppers is for the collection plate," reminded Johnny.

"I know, but if we spend only one, we still have one for Sunday school." He poked in the water with a stick he had found.

"Ma'm says the Lord knows when ya do bad things," warned Johnny. He squatted by the water and turned over a small stone.

"How does he? Does the church know how many coppers it DIDN'T get? Can he see us here?" Li'l Dan was perplexed.

"Dunno, but Ma'am says somethin' bad happens when ya don't mind The Lord or your Ma'am or Paap," Johnny explained and turned another rock.

"Like what?" Dan squatted by his friend and poked at a crayfish with a stick.

"I don't know." he said emphatically, "Just bad things."

"Ya mean, like the bogeyman will get ya, or maybe my Paap will wear me out with a corn stalk; like that?"

"Well, somethin' bad is sure to happen. We better go to church now." Johnny urged his friend on.

"Oh, well, guess we better," said Li'l Dan grudgingly.

The boys threw away the dirty, wet sticks and wiped their hands on their trousers. They made their way up to the road and into the village.

At Mr. Towns' general store, they paused, pressed their faces close to the glass and cupped their eyes to see in.

"See, there it is! See? Let's go in," exclaimed Li'l Dan.

''Ma'am says——'' hesitated Johnny.

''Yea, yea, I know, but if we spend only one copper we will still have one for the plate and we split the candy,'' urged Li'l Dan.

Both boys went into the store and directly to the candy counter.

''Morn'in boys, on your way to church?'' inquired Mr. Towns.

''Yep, but I want to show Johnny the new candy first,'' said Li'l Dan.

''I see, well, it's three for a penny. You want three or six? If you buy three, you will each have one and you can divide the third piece,'' explained the storekeeper.

One said no and other said yes at the same time. The boys stared at each other.

''Well, which is it, youngin's?''

''Come on, Johnny, just ONE copper,'' pleaded Li'l Dan.

''Well, I———''

''We'll take three, please,'' shouted Li'l Dan with glee and handed up his copper penny.

The storekeeper placed the divided candy into two tiny brown paper bags and gave each boy one.

Outside the store the boys paused on the sidewalk. Johnny was having serious misgivings about what they had done.

''I don't want to go to church, now,'' he said.

''Why, ya sick or somethin'?'' asked Li'l Dan stuffing candy into his mouth.

''No, but somethin' bad's gonna happen, sure.''

''Aw, you worry too much. Let's go back to the crick and play in the water. Eat your candy it's real good.''

Johnny took a bite of his candy but his heart wasn't in it. They walked in silence back to the bridge. At the water's edge they found more sticks and proceeded to poke at rocks, crayfish and bits of ice that formed around the edges.

''Ya think church is out by now?'' asked Johnny, after some time had passed. His sense of foreboding was growing.

''I 'spose ya wanna go home. Ya cold?'' asked Li'l Dan.

''Some——I just think we better.''

The boys trudged up to the road again and turned toward home. They had gone only a few steps when they heard a terrible noise. A sound they had never heard before and it was coming closer. Panicked, the boys dived into the ditch at the roadside—a boy on each side. They laid face down and held their breath. The huge MONSTER roared by. It threw leaves, stones, and made a cloud of dust. It bellowed HONK——HONK——OOGA——OOGA——HONK——HONK——HONK.

The terrified boys laid still for a moment more after it passed. They were soaked to the skin from the water in the ditch. Their paper bags fell apart and the candy melted.

They raised up and as soon as they could see each other, they scrambled to their feet and ran screaming toward home.

They turned the bend and Ma'am heard their screams. She snatched her shawl from the peg and ran to meet them.

They ran to Ma'am, clung to her skirts and they screamed their childish confessions to her. They played hooky from church, spent the copper penny, got dirty and now a MONSTER was going to eat them! They clung to her and promised never to do bad things again.

''All right—it's all right,'' Ma'am reassured them.

''The MONSTER is after us!'' they cried.

''There is no monster, hush, hush now.'' Ma'am tried to calm them.

At that moment, the monster roared around the bend and up the lane towards the screaming boys.

HONK, HONK, HONK, OOGA, OOGA, OOGA. The monster stopped and was silent except for a faint hissing sound. The boys screamed more.

''Hello, Mrs. Lansure,'' called the man who jumped to the ground. It was Roger Beasley, the local postmaster.

''Sorry I scared the children. Just took the mail to town and I'll be delivering the mail full time, now, in my new Stanley Steamer motor car.''

''Morn'in Mr. Beasley, the boys never saw a motor car before. They disobyed and they think it's a monster come to eat 'um.''

''It's no monster. Sure, it's noisy, an' all, but it gets me there fast. Come on boys, look her over, honk the horn, like this.'' He squeezed the rubber ball of the horn. HONK——HONK. The boys screamed again.

''Now, now. It won't hurt you, see,'' Mr. Beasley patted the brass horn.

The tearful boys peered, wet-eyed, from behind Ma'am's skirts. Slowly, they recovered from their fright and began to examine it.

''Come on, it won't hurt you, look, soft seats and shiny paint. Set up here on the seat,'' encouraged Mr. Beasley.

The boys gingerly touched the seats and climbed up. Soon they were inspecting it all over. Johnny was particularly interested in the steam boiler and how it worked. Li'l Dan poked and pinched it everywhere. Johnny asked how it moved without horses to pull it. Mr. Beasley was a patient man and answered all the questions. He listened to every word and it was then Johnny Lansure fell in love with the steam engine. A love affair that would change him and mold his life forever.

After a time, Johnny saw his father coming up the lane. He ran to meet him.

"Look, Paap, look, it's a Stanley Steamer motor car. See, no horses. It runs by itself. Steam makes it go. Mr. Beasley told me so."

Jimmy smiled at his excited son and patted his head.

At that moment a puppy stuck his head out from Jimmy's coat.

Johnny saw the dog and was too happy to speak. He looked up at his father and his eyes shown with delight and silent thanks.

Jimmy placed the warm squirming little bundle in Johnny's arms. The puppy was mostly black. He was short-haired, long-tailed and flop-eared. He had four white feet, a white throat and brown spots above his eyes. The dog was just mutt but to Johnny, he was the grand champion of all dogs.

The pup washed Johnny's face from hairline to chin. For them both, it was love at first lick. . . . . .

Chapter Two

THAT DARK PLACE

Johnny Lansure named his birthday puppy, Pude; pronounced Pood. No one knew where he got such a name or why he gave it to his dog. The two were inseparable.

The two good buddies were now three. Li'l Dan, Johnny and Pude roamed the woods and hills of the valley. They knew where the wild duck hid her nest and where the bees hid the honeycomb. They knew where the deer rested her fawn in the tall meadow grass on the valley floor. They knew the best sledding hill, swimming hole and trout stream.

The next five years passed quickly and the three grew strong and bright. Pude was not a big dog but his eyes were keen and his smell was accurate. Johnny and Li'l Dan learned from nature in the valley, from their families and from each other.

The boys spent many hours at the sawmill. They watched, bug-eyed, at the steam engine belching smoke and steam. The wide belts hummed and turned the great saws. The saw's glistening teeth gobbled trees of all sizes. Locomotives moved in and out of the valley, dragging long trains behind. The boys gaped, in wonder, at the huge machinery. Johnny's fascination for the steam engine grew stronger as the years passed. He trailed around after his father and did odd jobs for him but Johnny had no inclination to become a stonemason.

Bruce got the job at the Kinley Mine and worked steady. There were no child labor laws so children worked long hours, often under miserable conditions.

Johnny and Li'l Dan were given an opportunity to work in the mine, also. If one member of a family was employed by the mining company, other members were eligible to work, also.

Children were hired to gather the coal that fell from the coal hoppers along the rails inside the mine shafts. The coal was picked up, by hand, and placed in buckets and carried away. Clearing the rails and walkways of loose coal, cut down on derailments and accidents. It was backbreaking work. The hours were long and the working conditions were deplorable. The lure of 50¢-a-day wages was very attractive. Many children stood in line for hours, for the chance to earn such a sum.

Li'l Dan's aspirations were not as great as Johnny's. He wanted to be a miner like his father and talked of it often. He tried to persuade Johnny to do likewise. Li'l Dan knew it terrorized Johnny to venture but a few feet into the old abandoned mine where they played.

"Come on, Johnny, don't be scared. Nothin' to it. See, I'm not afraid," encouraged Li'l Dan.

"Naw, you go on, I'll wait out here in the sun. I don't like THAT DARK PLACE." Johnny hung back, nervously.

Time passed and Li'l Dan coaxed persistently to work in the mine. Finally, Johnny gave in. He did not want to work in the mine but he did not want to be labled afraid.

Ma'am bought Johnny a green dinner bucket like Bruce's. Li'l Dan had one of his father's. In those days, they were nearly all the same; Divided inside with a wire handle. Ma'am packed a healthy lunch in the new pail. Buckets in hand, the boys were off, with Bruce, for their first day at the mine.

Li'l Dan was exuberant and chattered incessantly as they walked along. Johnny was reluctant and quiet. Bruce noticed his brother's silence.

"You sure you want to go on with this?" Inquired Bruce.

"Sure he does," interrupted Li'l Dan. "Don't ya, Johnny?"

"I guess so." Johnny's answer was not reassuring.

At the mine, they met the foreman and were assigned a section of track to clear. Each child had a section and was explained the mine rules.

Li'l Dan and Johnny stashed their dinner buckets in a corner.

The whistle blew at 6:00 a. m. and the boys went to work. Each boy was given a container to fill with fallen coal and was told where to empty it. Johnny cleared the right side of the rails and Li'l Dan cleared the left side.

The coal cars moved in and out continuously. Clouds of dust and grit filled the air and breathing was sometimes difficult.

The 10 a. m. rest whistle blew and the tired boys dropped to the ground where they stood. After a moment or so, they moved to the wall, sat down and leaned heavily with their backs against it. The cars stopped, it was quiet and the dust settled.

The water boy passed the dipper and the boys drank eagerly. The miners were allowed a 15-minute-break twice a day, morning and afternoon.

''Whew, that's harder work than I thought it was,'' said Li'l Dan. He wiped his grimy, sweaty face on the sleeve of his shirt.

''It's the bending that get's me, right here.'' Johnny rubbed the small of his back with his left hand and tried to straighten his spine.

''We just ain't used to it yet. Tomorrow it will be better. It don't bother my Paap no more.'' Encouraged Li'l Dan.

Li'l Dan brought the dinner buckets from the stashed place, handed Johnny his and began to eat from his own.

''Don't you want something to eat? I'm starved.''

''I'm not hungry—just thirsty. This place gives me the dry mouth.'' Johnny took an apple from his bucket and hoped the juice would quench his thirst.

Too soon, the work whistle blew, again. The mine grew noisy, the cars rolled, the dust flew and the boys went back to work.

The coal cars were pulled by mules. Leverage was used to make the hawling easier and smoother. The cables and ropes were attached to the floor and ceiling of the mine by a series of pulleys.

The pulleys were fastened to the walls with huge iron bolts. The bolts creaked and groaned under the heavy weight.

The boys had been working a short time when a terrible metal-on-metal screeching was heard. Suddenly there was a loud CRACK. The floor cable snapped to the ceiling with an ominous TWANG, followed by a sickening thud. It all happened in an instant.

''Li'l Dan released his breath when the iron fragment hit his forehead and made no other sound. It hit him with such force, he was propelled backwards to the ground.

Johnny leaped over the rails to his friend. Li'l Dan lay on his back, his mouth agape and his eyes half closed. There was a deep purple indentation on his forehead above his nose. Johnny knew, without touching him, Li'l Dan was dead.

Johnny could not breathe. The horrible sight made him sick and he retched. He backed away until he was pressed tight to the mine wall.

The miners gathered around Li'l Dan's lifeless body and the mine's whistle screamed ACCIDENT. The people of the valley recognized the ACCIDENT warning whistle. They dropped what they were doing and ran toward the mine.

Johnny slid along the mine wall to the entrance. He retched again. There was nothing in his stomach to come up. Outside, he began to run. He ran as fast as his legs would carry him from that dark place. His forebodings and misgivings had come true.

He ran, cried, stumbled and fell. He scrambled to his feet only to fall again and again.

The branches stung his face and the brambles tore his clothes and skin. He ran and ran without aim or direction trying to escape his nightmare.

He stumbled and fell again but could not rise. He lay on the soft earth exhausted and sobbing. When he had no more tears, he fell into a deep sleep.

It was dusk when Johnny stirred. The dog was licking his face. Pude had found him.

"Awh, my Pudey, hi ya buddy, where'd you come from?" Johnny often talked to Pude and believed the dog understood every word. Johnny sat up and hugged his dog. For a moment, he had forgotten the calamity at the mine.

"Where we at, Pude? I never saw this place before. Me and Li'l Dan know this whole valley———Oh, Li'l Dan——. Johnny was jerked back to the horror at the mine.

He began to cry again and hugged his dog. "Li'l Dan is dead, I just know he's dead."

"Don't cry, Johnny, I'm here. It's alright, now. Don't cry. Over here on the stump." The voice was familiar, yet not familiar. It had a different quality. "You can see me but I'm in another place. It's nice here. Please, don't cry." Li'l Dan was sitting on a nearby stump.

Was it an apparition? Was Johnny dreaming?

"Li'l Dan! Zat really you?" Johnny whispered. He could hardly breathe, joy and fright was choking him.

Pude ran to the stump and jumped and barked excitedly. Li'l Dan extended his hand. The dog whimpered and was quiet.

Johnny stood up and walked toward his friend.

"How'd you do that? It is you—I can see you—Pude sees you, too." Exclaimed the startled boy.

"Don't touch me. Ya must'nt touch me. I'm different now. I'm in another place." Warned Li'l Dan. "I heard you cry and I knew you needed me so I came here. I brought Pude. He knows the way home. I knew you were lost."

"You're dead. I saw the pulley break and the bolt hit you. I saw it." I was sick and I ran. I ran from that dark place—I knew it was bad—just knew it." Tears ran down Johnny's face again.

"Please, don't cry, it's alright, now. I don't hurt. Nothing hurts here. If you ever need me again, look for me here. Go home, now, people are looking for you. Your Ma'am and Paap are worried." Li'l Dan's strange voice trailed off and he disappeared.

For a long time, Johnny stared at the stump. Was Li'l Dan real or had he dreamed the whole thing. He wasn't sure.

It was getting dark and Johnny had no idea where he was.

''How do we get home from here, Pude? I guess I'm lost.''

Pude barked as if he knew what Johnny said and ran off to the right into the woods. Johnny followed. After walking some distance, they came to a graveyard. It was the one behind the churchyard.

He had found a secret place on Bradley Hill, in the big pine forest. Maybe he could find it again, sometime.

Johnny knew he and Li'l Dan had never been up there. To reach the top, they had to pass through the graveyard. Those two gave graveyards a wide birth. That was a spooky place for the boys and if they came to one, they ran passed as fast as they could.

Johnny and Pude were nearing the center of the graveyard and were not afraid. They passed through calmly. At the big iron gates of the churchyard, they turned up the road toward home.

Rose and Lu were watching for Johnny. When he turned into the lane, they ran to meet him.

''Johnny, Johnny!'' They cried, together.

''Where you been? You alright? You look a fright!'' exclaimed Rose.

''We heard about Li'l Dan. Bruce said it was real bad. Your face is all scratched up. Ma'am and Paap are worried. That Pude ran off, too.'' said Lu.

''I'm fine—just tired. Pude's with me. We were—uh—in the woods—up on the ridge.'' Johnny tried to explain but couldn't.

The dog dashed out of the trees, barked happily and licked their hands.

''All this time? Supper's over and Paap and Bruce are out looking for you. We're 'sposed to go to Uncle Dan's and Aunt Rachel's to help out. They need us, now,'' said Rose.

The three went through the kitchen door and Johnny ran to his mother. Ma'am hugged him and stroked his hair.

''I'm so sorry, son, it just doesn't seem right. We have to believe it's part of the Lord's plan. Let me put something on those scratches. Rose, please bring me some salve. Sit here, son. Lu, fix him a plate of that stew, please. The young'in must be famished,'' directed Ma'am.

''No, thanks, Ma'am, I'm not hungery-just thirsty-I'd like some milk, that's all, I don't feel like eating. I'll get cleaned up. Aunt Rachel will need us,'' explained Johnny.

Ma'am spread ointment over the red welts on Johnny's face. He drank the milk Lu poured for him and went up stairs.

He's acting kind of funny, Ma'am, what's the matter with him?'' Inquired Lu.

''He's taking this pretty hard. He and Li'l Dan were real close. Just be patient. Different people grieve in different ways. He's grieving on the inside, that's why he can't eat,'' Ma'am told the girls.

Jimmy and Bruce were relieved to find Johnny safe at home when they returned. The family finished the chores, Ma'am filled a basket and they left the house.

The dirt path they took was so familiar to Johnny. He and Li'l Dan had explored it many times. He tried, in vain, to swallow the lump in his throat.

It was a short walk. Bruce carried Dudley and Jimmy carried Seneca. They soon arrived on the other side of the hill at Daniel's home.

The relatives greeted each other, hugged and cried. This was the first such tragedy in the clan.

Li'l Dan lay in the parlor, as was the custom. They all drew near to look at him.

Johnny clung to Bruce's hand and gulped back his body's urge to be sick. He was relieved to see the hideous purple mark on Li'l Dan's forehead was gone. Johnny did not know that the undertaker had hidden it well.

The dead child looked very little and pale against the stark white silk of his coffin. Everyone stood quietly and wept.

The house was full of people. Some filed in and out and offered condolences to Li'l Dan's family. Others stood in small clusters and talked in hushed tones.

Friends and neighbors brought food of all kinds. Ma'am brewed coffee and the girls served and washed the dishes. Dudley & Seneca played under the table.

Johnny went outside for air. The lump in his throat made breathing difficult.

Jimmy and Daniel were talking on the porch. Johnny stood by his father and his grieving uncle and tried to hold back the tears. Jimmy put his arm around his son and they held each other.

"Go ahead, ma' boy, crying is a good thing, at times. It sweeps the cobwebs from the soul. I know you hurt. This is a black day for us all. Where were you for so long? Bruce said he saw you backed up against the mine wall, after the accident. The next time he looked, you were gone. Here, sit by me." Both sat down on the porch step.

"I saw Li'l Dan fall. When I looked at him, I knew he was dead. I ran away. Far, to the top of Bradley Hill. To the big pine woods. When I couldn't run no more, I fell asleep. I was lost but Pude found me." Sobbed the unhappy boy.

Jimmy cradled his son in his arms. No words could comfort the child.

Johnny wanted to tell his father he had seen Li'l Dan on the stump but he could not. Perhaps it never happened. Maybe he dreamed the whole thing.

"When you die, do you go right up to heaven or do you wait 'til you're buried?" Asked the tearful boy.

''Well, as I know it, the soul-some call it the spirit-leaves as soon as you die. All that is buried is your remains-that is, your body.'' Jimmy explained.

''Does your, uh, spirit have a special place to go? Can it go anywhere? Can you see a spirit?''

''Son, I don't know, for sure, but I heard tell, once. You mind when Avery Peabody's brother, Sam, died, a while back? About two weeks later, a twister blew the tool shed in on old Avery and pinned him tight. Nobody believed Avery got out of that smashed building by himself or that he could have lived through it. He swore his BROTHER dug him out. They knew Sam was dead and buried two weeks before.

They could never shake old Avery's story and he stuck to it 'til he died. There are things we don't understand but that does'nt mean it can't happen or does'nt exist.'' Jimmy explained to his son.

Johnny listened attentively to his father. He stopped crying and felt relieved. Maybe it was Li'l Dan's spirit and not a dream. Johnny was comforted by his father's words and understanding.

Li'l Dan Lansure was laid to rest in the family plot, behind the church on Bradley Hill, the summer of 1902.

Chapter Three

JENNY

The next three years were a blur for Johnny. He did all the things expected of a boy aged 13. He went to school, helped his Ma'am and Paap and washed behind his ears. He attended cake walks, ice cream socials, husking bees, barn dances, barn raisings and barn burnings. He did his chores and minded his manners. Still the void in Johnny's heart left a hollow place within him and kept him depressed. He sorely missed his cousin.

He and Pude tried to find the piece of himself that was missing. They went to the secret place often. He sat on the stump and talked to the air, the trees and the grass. He called and pleaded but Li'l Dan never returned.

Strange, however, after each visit to the secret place and a talk to the air, trees, and grass, Johnny felt better. His heart was not as heavy and the routine of living was easier.

One day, in the spring of 1905, Johnny's life would change again.

Jimmy filled a wagon with corn, oats, wheat and barley and hitched the team. This was hauled to the mill, to be ground into corn meal, oat meal, wheat and barley flour. Also, obtained were stores of salt, bran and animal feed.

A wagon load was enough for six months in good weather and three months in bad weather. Bruce usually went along to help his father load and unload. It was a difficult, bumpy trip over rough roads. Johnny rarely went along but to spend time alone with his father, the trip was worthwhile.

Johnny had a strong attachment to his parents. An absent pat on the head or shoulder or a quick wink from Jimmy gave the boy security and approval.

A hug, a smile, a handful of raisins or a spoon to lick from Ma'am, gave him love and understanding. Equipped with these tools, Johnny was growing into a well-adjusted, forthright, intelligent youngster.

They jolted over the road, at a snail's pace, but eventually arrived at the gristmill.

There was the usual line of wagons waiting in turn. Jimmy reined up the team and they waited in their place.

The area was picturesque, nicely wooded and green. The huge mill stood to the right, on the river bank. The great paddle wheel creaked and splashed under the force of the water as it turned. To the left, in a grove of red oak trees, stood a neat, comfortable home.

Harvey Blair, the miller and his family lived here. His ancestors built the house and mill in the 1830s and it has been a family operation since.

''Hey, ya wanna climb trees?'' Came a voice from a nearby tree. ''I shoot marbles.'' The voice was calling to Johnny.

Sitting in the tree, with her legs dangling, was a scruffy, unkempt, dirty faced girl about 10 or 11. Her untidy blond hair was braided but one braid had slipped out and the ribbon was untied. Her stockings were torn, her apron was soiled and her high-top shoes were scuffed and unbuttoned.

''Do ya?'' she asked again.

''Go ahead, son, looks like we will be here for some time,'' said Jimmy.

Johnny climbed off the wagon and up the tree.

''I'm Jenny Blair. I live here. What's your name?''

''Johnny Lansure, we live up the other end of the valley. That's my Paap.''

The youngsters liked each other immediately. They laughed, talked and climbed trees. Jenny showed him around the house and barn. On top of the silo, they could see the whole valley below. They climbed to the rafters of the mill and watched the huge stones turn.

For the first time since Li'l Dan died, Johnny found a friend. Yes, she was a girl but she was different than any girl he had known. She was like a pal or a good egg. Yes, that was it, she was a good egg.

The time passed quickly. The wagons were unloaded and reloaded. It was time to go home.

''It was nice to meetcha—and your father. Will ya comeback?''

''Sure. Maybe ya could come see us, too.''

''I could get my brother to bring me 'bye.'' waved Jenny.

'' 'Bye.'' Johnny called over his shoulder and the wagon headed home.

''Sort of like that girl, don't you?'' Jimmy said, after some distance and a long silence.

''Uh, yea, sort of, she's different from other girls I know.''

"I see, different, huh? You mean she's like one of the fellas. She likes to do the things that you like to do. She's your chum, she's a good egg." Quizzed Jimmy, knowingly.

"Yes, like a chum. She sure is a good egg, she told me she likes to go barefooted and wade in the run." he said excitedly.

"Can you tie that!" exclained Jimmy, with a smile.

They rode the rest of the way home in silence. Each with his own thoughts. Johnny felt happy and he had much to think about.

Johnny could hardly wait to tell his mother about his newly found friend. The description he gave of Jenny was far different than the one his father gave of her. To Johnny, she was talkative, unafraid and fun, and she reminded him of Li'l Dan. To Jimmy, she was a ragtag tomboy and never destined to be otherwise. Ma'am hugged her son and was pleased at his enthusiasm. Perhaps her worry over his depression was unfounded. He hadn't been interested in much for a long time.

"If I see Mrs. Blair, at the store this week, I'll ask them to Sunday dinner. If it is that important to you," said Ma'am.

"Oh, yes, would you—please?" the boy beamed.

The dinner was a huge success. The two large families crowded around the table and chattered noisily. The Lansuer's were 9 and the Blair's were 8. Seating was difficult but they managed.

Ma'am and the girls made all Johnny's favorites since this was his special day. Ham and sweet potatoes, Hoppin' John, corn fritters with syrup, biscuits with peach butter and rhubarb pie.

The ham was baked slow, with brown sugar and cloves, surrounded by sweet potatoes.

Johnny liked the taste of Hopping John but he liked the name and story better. His Grandma Lansure told him the story. Long ago the early settlers would ask a guest to a meal by saying 'Hop in, John and have a bite to eat!'. It was simple fare of the day, but filling and tasty.

Hopping John was a flavorful combination of crisp bacon, onions, beans and rice. A good stick-to-the-ribs dish.

Corn fritters are a favorite, but the hit of the day was Ma'am's baking powder biscuits. They would take a prize but she never told her secret. Mr. Blair said if he put the recipe on his flour sacks, he'd sell more flour than anyone in the county. Ma'am was pleased at the compliment but declined. Johnny near burst his buttons, with pride for his mother.

The meal was topped with rhubarb pie specially for Johnny.

A Sunday dinner with family and friends is not a monumental event but Johnny Lansure will remember this one and refer back to it many times in his life.

After dinner, Johnny and Jenny explored all the places Johnny held dear. She saw his rock collection and his lead soldiers; the newborn calf of their milk cow, Daisy, and the stepping stones at the river ford. He showed her the apple trees, the berry bushes and the smoke house. From then on, their friendship grew.

They enjoyed each other in all things childlike, including the secret place. The years flew by. In winter, they went sledding on the hills, ice skating on the river and built snow forts. Sometimes they just sat by the fire and read Bronte and Browning, Longfellow, Stevenson and Kipling. They made fudge and popped corn. Pude was always nearby.

In summer, they went barefoot and swimming in their underdrawers. They climbed trees and explored the woods. They collected rocks, frogs and fishing worms and fished for trout, bass and chubs. Pude joined in but he was aging.

A change was taking place in the young people. The summer of 1907, the change in Jenny was most evident. She was not as eager to do all the childish things.

Her flour sack shape had changed. Her waist had nipped in and her hips and bust popped out. She was cleaner, neater, never shouted and would not go swimming in her underdrawers.

With Johnny, it was more subtle, except for the fact that he shot up to nearly six feet. He shaved more often but would never have a heavy beard. His voice cracked occasionally and had become a soft baritone.

By the spring of 1908, they had blossomed into a lovely young woman and a handsome young man.

Brother Bruce announced at the dinner table, that he was getting married. The family was delighted but puzzled since he had no steady girl, that anyone knew of and he was over twenty-seven. The delight turned to shock when he announced the bride-to-be was Grace Clark of Glenn Campbell.

She was Gracie to everyone and a very pretty Irish colleen of seventeen. She was bubbly and charming but to say her reputation was slightly tarnished, was a colossal understatement. Some folks called her a trollop.

"You wouldn't marry HER!" Exclaimed Leone.

"Now, I don't want you to start. I know what they say. I don't believe half of it and I don't care about the rest. She's a bit wild but she wants to settle down. She'll have me and that's what counts. Just remember, I'm no prize-already twenty-seven and a bent-over coal miner, besides, I love her.

"A bit wild, he says!" groaned Lu.

"I said, THAT'S ENOUGH!" Bruce growled through his teeth.

"All right, you two, that will do. You've made up your mind, then, son? You're sure? You thought it through, REAL GOOD?" asked the concerned father.

"Yes, sir, I have."

"Then, so be it. We will accept your choice and welcome."

Ma'am and the girls hugged him.

"It will be just fine, Bruce." Comforted his mother.

Where you gettin married? When is it? Ya gonna have a social? Asked the girls, together.

"We'd like Reverend Given to marry us in the church chapel. Nothin' fancy and no big doin's. Just the families and a couple of friends," said Bruce.

"That will be just right and afterwards we'll have cake and ice cream at the house. The girls and I can manage that for you." said Ma'am.

Everyone chattered and giggled in anticipation of the event.

The forthcoming marriage raised eyebrows among the townsfolk. If Bruce noticed the side glances or heard the whispers, he ignored them.

Bruce and Gracie were married April 8, 1908, in the church chapel. Afterwards, Ma'am served cake and the girls cranked out a tub of ice cream. Bruce beamed. Gracie was warm, friendly and soon accepted into the family and among the friends. The couple would move to Glenn Campbell to live. For Ma'am, it was bittersweet. Bruce was settling down with a wife and that was good but he was also, the first to leave the nest.

Pude laid on the big rug and watched the festivities. He was old.

At the party, Johnny was seeing Jenny for the first time. The pigtails were gone and she curled her hair with rags. Her face was soft and pink cheeked. Her hair was piled high on her head and held in place with a sprig of apple blossom. She was beautiful and the sight of her tugged at his heart string. The feelings were new.

Spring passed into summer. Johnny and Jenny spent much time together, but it wasn't like before. Now, they just sat and talked or read to each other.

Johnny talked of his dreams of becoming a railroader, an engineer on one of those huge iron locomotives that rolled in and out of town. How he would learn the railroad business from yard boy to engineer. He had big plans. Jenny listened attentively but there were times she thought his dreams were too great to be fulfilled. She cautioned him not to expect so much or he could be disappointed. Johnny would not be deterred. He had a dream and he would make it work. He knew he could.

In July, Pude took a turn for the worse. The vet said his hindquarters were gone and he should be put away. His grief was inconsolable. Once again Johnny was to loose a dear friend. The dog had to be put down but Johnny could not bring himself to kill his dear friend.

"I can't shoot him, Paap, I just can't!" declared the heartbroken boy, hugging his dog.

"I know, son, you make a place in the meadow and I will take care of it."

Jimmy performed his dreadful task and wrapped Pude in a blanket. They buried him on the valley floor where they once romped. Johnny was crushed. He hurried to his secret place for solace.

Jenny stopped at the house to see Johnny and Ma'am told her of the tragedy and that Johnny was out in the woods, somewhere. Jenny knew where and went to the secret place.

She found him. He was sitting, half hidden, in the tall meadow grass, hugging his knees. He was near his favorite stump. He smiled when she ran and dropped into the grass beside him.

"Oh, Johnny, I'm so sorry about your Pude, your mother told me. I'll miss him, too." She didn't know how to comfort him so she just patted his shoulder.

"I'm glad you found me. I need to talk to you. I'll sure miss that ole guy. We did everything together. Ma'am said he was my shadow. He never bit a soul and could hear me whistle half-a-mile away. He found me the first time I came here. I was lost." He tried to fight the tears.

Jenny leaned closer. They held each other and cried.

After a few minutes, they realized they were clinging to each other. They kissed. At first it was light and fleeting. As their passion grew, their kisses became more demanding and urgent as if struck by lightning, their youthful passion surged through their bodies. Their desires would not be stilled without complete release. They were out of control.

Their clumsy, grappling lovemaking left them exhausted and sweating. They lay spent, from the exertion, but filled with wonder, pleasure and bewilderment.

When Johnny regained his composure, he said, "Jenny, I er, we, I mean, that is, I'm sorry. I shouldn't have done that." He stammered.

"It wasn't just you, I wanted to as much as you did. It just happened."

"I know, but I should know better. It should not have happened. I got carried away—with everything. I'm sorry. I won't let it happen again, but I do like you—a lot."

"Oh, Johnny, I've loved you since we climbed the tree that first day. Didn't you know? Couldn't you tell?

"You LOVE me?" He seemed bewildered.

"Yes, you should know, after this, how I feel about you."

"I don't know what LOVE is, for sure. It's getting late—we better go." The conversation was closed and they started home.

Summer melted into fall with the usual excitement. It was barn dances, husking bees and harvest. Ma'am's garden was the best ever. She and the girls canned an abundance for the winter.

Ma'am delivered three more babies in the valley but no one noticed a change in Jenny.

One Sunday, early in October, Johnny and Jenny met after church, at the secret place.

"You looked kind of pale in church, today, you sick?" Johnny asked.

"Huh, no, I'm not sick but you and I have to talk, Johnny." She said, urgently.

"All right, shoot, what will we talk about today? You pick a subject." He said flippantly.

"Johnny, this is not a joke. We have to talk, seriously."

"You are in a strange mood, what is it?

"We have to talk—about us."

"About us, all right. I'm Johnny and you're Jenny. We Live in Richmond. I like rhubarb pie and strawberries make you itch———.

"Stop it! Stop it! That's not funny. I'm serious. I'm going to have a baby!" She blurted.

"You're WHAT?" Johnny looked as if he had been struck.

"I'm going to have your baby." She tried to stay calm.

"My baby—that's impossible—just that once—it can't be'." His voice was rising and she looked devastated.

"No siree, you're not going to trap me THAT way. I got plans—big plans—and they don't include kids. I'm not ready for a ball and chain. You know what I plan. Now, you tell me this. No siree, not me." His voice was harsh and his eyes were accusing. He was panicked.

Jenny stood frozen to the spot. Her eyes brimmed with tears. She had never seen Johnny like this before and couldn't believe what was happening. His words stung her like a whip. His hazel eyes flashed icy cold and hostile. She did not know the man that lashed out at her so unfairly. She fled from Johnny in tears and ran away from the secret place.

Johnny was shocked at his behavior and what he had said to Jenny. He was ashamed. Why did he hurt her so? He knew it was his baby and that it was all his fault. Why didn't he run after her and beg her forgiveness?

He did not know why and he was astonished at his cruelty. He dropped to the ground with guilt and recrimination.

If anyone noticed Jenny had not been around for a week, no one mentioned it.

Johnny had a week to think over the terrible thing he had done to Jenny. He thought it out, carefully and decided to go to Jenny and make amends. They would get married and he would go to work, with his father, as a mason.

While he was preparing to go to Jenny's, his father came into the house. Jimmy's face was ashen and his voice trembled.

''What is it, Jim?'' asked Ma'am.

''A terrible thing—terrible. I just came from Blair's Mill. I was at the general store when they sent word for a couple of us to come to the mill, on the run. It was awful. We had to climb up and help cut her down. Jenny hanged herself to a beam in the mill house.'' He sank into a chair and hid his face in his hands.

''May the good Lord preserve us.'' Ma'am whispered under her breath. She put her arms around the shaken man's shoulders.

All eyes were on Jimmy and no one noticed that Johnny sagged against the sink to keep from falling. He couldn't breathe and his mouth went dry. 'What have I done.' He thought.

His father spoke again. ''It was awful. No one knows why. She was always a happy girl. Well behaved, too, in spite of a bit tomboyish. Can't figure out what gets into young people, these days. Johnny, you know her about as well as anybody. Can you imagine why she would do a thing like that?'' Quizzed his father.

''No, I can't—I don't know.'' He lied. He was trying not to be sick.

''I'm sorry, son, I know how close you two were. Go hitch up my buggy, Minna Blair will need me, now.. Quickly, now, you can drive me.'' Said Ma'am. Johnny hitched the mare and they hurried to the mill.

While they rode, Johnny's agonizing secret was killing his soul. He knew why she did it and he wanted to tell Ma'am the whole story but he could not.

Johnny sleepwalked through the next few days. He was exhausted during the day and could not eat. At night, he laid in bed and stared at the ceiling or paced the floor.

They buried Jenny in the family's private plot near the mill. Johnny's torment was worse than grief. His guilt was soul-consuming. Nobody suspected she was pregnant so no one checked. Autopsies were performed when foul play was suspected but not in suicide cases.

Johnny was wasting away. He could not eat, he could not sleep and he coughed. Ma'am and Paap were very concerned.

At Thanksgiving, the plans were set. Johnny was being sent to Cushing, Oklahoma, to Ma'am's brother, Tom. The climate was dry and Johnny must have a change of surroundings, if he was to recover, according to old Doc ''Bones'' Brown.

If he was to arrive there, before the hard winter set in, he must start now. The arrangements were made and the tickets bought.

At the station, Johnny said 'Good-bye' to each member of his family, in turn and hugged them.

''Who you gonna swat with that wooden spoon when I'm gone.'' he teased and hugged Leone.

''You eat good and take care of that cough.'' she barked, as usual.

''Lu, I'll miss your cookin'. You're the best—next to Ma'am.''

''Place won't be the same without you. Be careful.'' Lu said.

''Rose, keep that scrapbook up to date. It's our history and we need it.'' He said.

''I will, Johnny, write to us—Ma'am will worry if she doesn't hear.'' Rose said.

''Sen, my Seneca. Keep up those studies. You are the smartest of us all and someday you will teach us a plenty.''

''Keep safe, brother.'' She hugged him.

''Duke, you look after your sisters. You are the only one left. You can have my gun and my bed.''

''Thanks, Johnny, but you aren't going to be gone that long are you?'' asked Duke.

''Paap, how far is it to Uncle Tom's place?'' Asked Johnny.

''The ticket agent said three days and nights. You change trains in Indianapolis, St. Louis and in Tulsa. Remember, if Tom isn't at the station when you get there, just wait. Son, I've taught you all I can, the rest is up to you. Remember, leave it better than you find it, in all things, keep your eyes open and your mouth shut and think positive. Come back safe.'' Jimmy hugged his son and slapped his back.

Ma'am touched his face and smoothed his hair. ''You go away a boy but you will come back a man. That is as it should be. You are my heart—keep it safe.'' Tears glistened in her eyes. She kissed his cheek, held him for a moment, then handed him his food basket.

''All Aboard.'' called the conductor and took part of Johnny's ticket. Jimmy tossed Johnny's valise onto the car platform and Johnny boarded the train. They waved and cried and the train pulled out. . . .

Chapter Four

OUT WEST

The trip west was to be a great adventure. Johnny was to learn, first hand, about the railroad. The sights, the sounds and the smells of it. He watched from the windows as the countryside passed by. There were big towns, small towns and hamlets. Travelers left the train and different ones came aboard. Johnny tried to imagine what was beyond his home valley but this spectacle far surpassed anything he could conjure. The windows of the passenger car was like Aladdin's lamp. Each pane of glass displayed a new wonder.

The day passed quickly and it was dusk before Johnny realized it. The conductor stoked the fire in the stove and lit the lamps that hung along the car's walls.

He stopped by Johnny's seat and said, "This your first trip on a train, son, where you from? What's your name?"

"Yes sir, Pennsylvania, Johnny Lansure, Sir."

"Johnny, you're pretty big to be called Johnny, aren't you?"

"Uh, yes, sir, JOHN Lansure, sir."

"That's BETTER. You're as big as a man—better have a man's name." The conductor winked at John, as if they had a secret between them and went on about his business. John, it was, from then on.

John lifted his food basket from the overhead rack and investigated the contents. He tore a piece from the bread loaf and folded it around a chunk of ham. He was hungry. Later, he had one of Ma'am's baking powder biscuits spread with peach butter and an apple.

It was a long while since he felt like eating or sleeping. He stretched his legs, leaned back on the seat and fell sound asleep.

The train bumped, jerked and clanked over the rails but he slept on. He awakened once to change positions then fell asleep again. The train rattled through the night.

At daybreak, it jerked to a halt, waking John.

"Change trains here! Change trains here! All Out! Indianapolis. Change for all points! Terre Haute, Evansville, Danville, Muncie and all points. All out!" the conductor chanted as he passed by.

John gathered his belongings and stepped off the train. People thronged the huge railroad station. John stared and gawked, it was a feast for his eyes and ears. After a while, he inquired of the station agent about his connecting train. He was given the gate number and time of departure. He had time for sight-seeing so he wandered around and tried not to miss a thing.

Near departure time, John went aboard. He found a seat and stashed his things.

"Board! All Aboard! St. Louis and points West! Board!" The conductor cried.

The train chugged west again. John watched the landscape pass. He pressed his face to the window glass each time the train rounded a curve so he could see the big engine puffing steam and rolling a great column of smoke from its stack. He had waited his whole life for this trip and dream. The countryside changed constantly. The day ran into evening. He ate from his basket, talked to a different conductor and stretched out and slept again.

He woke up early to shave and clean up in the men's room. He was a man, now, with a man's name. He thought of what the first conductor had said and he smiled.

"Next stop St. Louis! All out! St. Louis and all points! All out!

John gathered his things in readiness. The train hissed to a stop and again he found himself in another wonderland. There were more people, more noise and a larger station. The grandness of it all boggled his mind.

He checked departure time to Tulsa and went exploring. He made the most of the time between trains. He learned quickly and his confidence grew.

The conductor called again and the train rolled out of the station. The Missouri landscape was much like Pennsylvania and John found it comforting. Out of Joplin, the terrain changed dramatically. It was flat, with few trees and sandy soil. At Tulsa, the area was sunny and dry and one could see for miles in all directions. The clothing was different. There were Indians in moccasins and Orientals with long queues. The western twang made him listen carefully to understand. Many vendors hawked their wares. A Seneca Indian, who said he was dispelled from his home in the East, was selling 'worry stones', three for a penny. They were to be kept in a pocket for good luck and rubbed to chase away worry. The stones were the size of half dollars, smooth and with thumb size indentation on one side. John bought 5¢

worth which filled his pockets. By further questioning the old man, John learned there were very few Seneca left in the East and he told him about his sister Seneca until train time.

The train to Cushing was smaller than the previous trains and the passengers were not as fancy but the ride was just as fascinating., The train made many stops. When time permitted, John jumped down and walked along the train, inspecting the parts of the train as he went.

The engineer noticed him several times and was amused by John's careful but intense scrutiny of the train. He invited him up into the cab of the engine to have a look.

John was in heaven. He looked at all the shinny gages, levers and handles. Nothing could equal what he saw.

"Go ahead, put your hand on the throttle." The engineer pointed to a brighht brass handle protruding from the steel face of the big boiler.

John beamed, reached out with his left hand and grasped the cold brass. A feeling went through him like nothing before. He thought it was divine providence.

"You left-handed? The throttle is always used by the left hand. The Righties grab it with the right hand," mused the engineer.

"Yes and someday I'll be an engineer, like you," declared John. The moment his hand touched the throttle, his fate was sealed and he knew it. His dream would come true. At times like this, he even forgot his guilt.

The train was ready to move on and John went back to his seat. He would vividly remember the details of the inside of the locomotive cab.

Up to now, he had been too busy with his surroundings to think of Uncle Tom, Aunt Bea or his cousins. He had seen his uncle before but not his aunt or cousins.

At the station, John hoped he would recognize them. He stood on the platform and studied his surroundings.

Cushing was a cattle town. To the left were acres and acres of corrals, chutes and pens. To the right was the town, small and sleepy in the sun. Even in November, the sun was hot and it felt good on John's face. The town had the usual rudiments; a church, a school, an emporium, a hotel, a bank, a grain elevator and mill and assorted saloons.

A wagon load of men, nearby, called his name. He knew it was his family. Alex, 25, Sam, 23, Al, 21, Ben, 18, Mort, 14 and Uncle Tom had come to fetch him.

They greeted each other warmly and chattered all the way home in the wagon. It was about an hour's ride to the ranch but it passed quickly. Ben and John were close in age and they were to bunk together. Alex and Sam had wives and they all lived together in the big house on Uncle Tom's sprawling ranch.

John and Ben rode in the driver's seat with Uncle Tom and the others rode in the back. They had gone some distance when John asked, ''How many acres are there in your ranch?''

''The Bent Tee has about 2,000 acres. I sold some off when the boys got married, to increase the herd and enlarge the house.'' explained Uncle Tom.

''Whew ! That's huge!'' exclaimed John.

''That's not so big for these parts. A couple cattle men around here have half a million acres apiece, but this size serves me and mine just fine.''

''What's the Bent Tee,'' asked John.

''That's my brand, sort of a special name, a trademark, my sign. It's put on everything that belongs to me, like the cattle, horses, saddles, tack, equipment and guns, like this.'' He took a rifle in a leather sheath from under the seat and pointed to the brand burned into the sheath as well as the gun stock. The bent tee was just that, a T with a crooked top.

''The bent tee is for Tom. Why not H for Hobson?'' John inquired.

''When I came here, there were three ahead of me. Hadley with the Bar H, Harris with the Rocking H and Hubbard with the Lazy H. There were two Bs so a B for Beatrice was out, so I made it the bent tee.''

''Hey, fellas, it will be some job-'a-work to turn this tenderfoot into a ranch hand.'' Sam joked from the back of the wagon.

They all laughed and teased John good-naturedly and he enjoyed the fun. There was plenty of teasing and ribbing after that and the laughter was catching and healthy.

Alex's wife, Ruth, Sam's Netty, Cousin Bonny, age 16 and Aunt Beatrice waved to them from the great front porch when they drove in.

John liked his new found family and they made him feel comfortable and welcome.

He settled in easily. Uncle Tom and the cousins introduced him to ranch life. Aunt Bea saw to it that he ate well and kept up his laundry and mending. Bonny showed him her books, needlework, and her musical ability at the organ.

Life on a cattle ranch in Oklahoma was a far cry from life in the Pennsylvania hills. John enjoyed the difference and adapted quickly. He learned to ride and rope with only a few spills and rope burns. He ate well, slept well and filled out. Sometimes, when he forgot his troubles, he laughed and joked.

By Christmas time, he was just another 'hand'. Uncle Tom and the boys gave him his own western clothes for Christmas. They gave him a set of leather chaps, a pair of boots, a vest and a ten gallon Stetson. Bonny gave him a bright colored bandana for his neck and Aunt Bea made him an authentic western shirt. He was delighted.

He gave each of them an an Indian 'worry stone'. He told the story of his sister, Seneca, in detail, and about the old Indian selling stones in the railroad station. He explained how important it was to him to purchase anything the Indian was selling just to help him out, in the off chance he was a distant relative of Seneca, no matter how remote the possibility. The family found the story interesting and it gave the stones a special meaning to them.

John had graduated from tenderfoot to cowboy in just a few weeks. With his new clothes, he looked like a cowboy. His eastern accent gave him away but few people noticed.

Hard winter came in January and they hawled hay and water to the stock, cleaned stables and barns and mended tack and saddlery.

Other times, they sat by the fire and talked or sang songs while Bonny pumped and played the little organ. Everything was a great adventure to John and he was happy his Ma'am had sent him there. This was his first trip away from home and occasionally he suffered the pangs of homesickness which was natural, considering everything. He was usually kept too busy to brood.

Early March was calving time for the herd. The cows, invariably, dropped their calves in the last big blizzard of the spring. The ranchers are very harried at that time. The newborn calves must be up on their feet and dried in moments after birth or they will freeze to death. Hand drying wet squirming, kicking, calves, in a snow storm is messy, exhausting work. A healthy, big eyed, furry critter was worth the effort and was done all over the west to propagate the herds.

By the first of April, the spring roundup was over and John's homesickness grew worse. It was time for John to go home. Uncle Tom gave him ten dollars and wished him well. Aunt Bea and Bonny cried and the cousins stammered their goodbys. They packed his food basket and took him to the station. It was easier to wear his western clothes than to carry them, which he did. This decision would later prove to be a mistake.

He was anxious to get home but he had grown very fond of his western family and wondered if he would ever see them again. After tearful goodby hugs, his heart was heavy when he boarded the train to Tulsa and points East. . . . . . .

Chapter Five

AARON

Aboard the train, John stashed his belongings in the overhead rack and dropped heavily into the seat.

For reasons unknown to him, he was bone-weary. Maybe it was because he and the family had been up before dawn to catch the train or because his great western adventure had come to an end. In any case, he stretched out, pulled his ten-gallon hat down over his eyes and fell sound asleep.

About an hour later the train jerked him awake.

Up to now, John had paid little or no attention to the man seated opposite him, riding backwards.

The man was a coyote of the confidence game and a type completely unknown to John. The scoundrel was a natty dresser from his homburg to his spats. His plaid suit was mostly blue over a gray silk vest. A pearl stickpin held his cravat in place and a gold watch and chain hung from pocket to pocket on his vest. A small monogrammed leather case lay on the seat beside him.

John was too naive to perceive the confidence man had been studying him since he boarded the train.

"That was a nice nap you had; going far?" the man began the conversation. His mouth smiled but his eyes were cold and calculating.

"Yes sir, Pennsylvania," answered John.

"You look like a bright lad, would you be interested in a game of chance?" ventured the slicker.

"Game of chance?" John repeated the question.

"Yes, like this." His eyes gleamed at the thought of another chump to fleece.

He opened the small case at his side and it unfolded into a flat table-surface covered in green felt. The gyp-artist took three walnut shells and a dry bean from his vest pocket and placed them on the flat green cloth for John to see.

He deftly maneuvered the shells around and around making sure John saw which shell concealed the bean. He took his hands away and said,

"Now Laddy, where is the bean?"

"This one sir," John pointed to the correct one.

"Right you are—see how easy it is?" He lifted the shell and revealed the bean. He did the trick several times and of course, John found the bean each time.

"See—nothing to it. To make it a wee bit MORE interesting, would you care to make a small wager that you can find the bean again?" coaxed the chiseler. The 'mark' was hooked and then came the con.

"Ya do have a few coppers, don't ya, Laddy? A bit of mazuma—some scratch?"

"Yes, a little," John admitted.

"Ah, that's a fine Laddy, how would you like to wager a dollar?"

"A DOLLAR!" exclaimed John with surprise.

"A half, then?"

"No, I don't think——."

"A quarter then, ya do have a 25¢ piece, don't ya?" Urged the tin-horn.

John dug a coin from his pocket and the fancy dude slid the shells around. He allowed John to win a few times, then slowly, methodically proceeded to cheat the boy by hiding the bean or pea in the palm of his hand so it was under none of the shells.

Before the inexperienced boy knew what was happening to him, the unscrupulous thief had taken most of his money.

The con artist was careful to avoid the railroad conductor. When the train pulled into Tulsa, the crook made sure John boarded the wrong train out so John could not report what happened. The tin-horn was taking the same train to St. Louis as John was supposed to take but made sure John was not on it. He sent John northwest when his real destination was northeast.

John went aboard, stashed his things and settled down. He swore he would never be cheated again. He felt ignorant and stupid and paid little attention to the landscape slipping by. He was deep in thought and self-recrimination.

Night fell, the conductor lit the lamps and John picked at the food from his basket.

He mulled over his situation again and again. He had only $1.80 left and his tickets. Could he make it home on so little—he didn't know. He stared out of the window into the darkness. After a long while, the steady clicking of the wheels on the tracks lulled him to sleep and the train lumbered through the night.

"ALL OUT! LAST STOP! CHANGE TRAINS!" the conductor chanted several times.

Day was dawning and John stretched his stiff body.

"Hey there, young fella, I'll take your tickets now. Everytime I came to take them before, you were sound asleep."

"Here they are, sir." John handed his tickets to the conductor who thumbed through them and gasped.

"Where you bound for, son?"

"St. Louis and points east to Pennsylvania."

"You're traveling in the wrong direction for Pennsylvania! You're 100 miles into Kansas going north. My fault—sure should of waked you. Since it's my own doin', I won't charge you for the trip but the east bound conductor might."

"What do I do now?" John's heart sunk and an icy lump formed in the pit of his stomach.

"At the station in Dodge, you take the east bound to Great Bend. Be sure you ask the station agent how to make your connections—sorry, son and good luck."

"Thanks."

The conductor made his way down the aisle and John left the train.

In the Dodge City station, John explained his predicament to the station master.

"Don't that beat all! Them slickers do it every time! They took three marks this month already. You cowboys get it the most," he grinned knowingly.

"I'm NOT a cowboy, I'm from Pennsylvania. I was out visiting my uncle in Oklahoma and it's not funny."

"Sorry son, you're right and we do try to catch 'um but they manage to skitter around us anyway. To get you back on the right train east, take the noon local to Great Bend. There's not much there but it's the only way." The trainman looked at his watch. "That's about two hours from now. Kick your belongings under that bench, I'll look after them and you go out to the Old Fort. Have a look around and don't worry, I'll make sure you catch the east bound." The station master tried to reassure John and patted his shoulder.

Outside, John walked around Old Fort Dodge and found it very interesting but until he was back on the right train east, he was apprehensive and strangely uneasy. It was hot and crowded and people shoved and jostled him as they passed by.

After what John thought was a very long two hours, the east bound pulled in and stopped. He had retrieved his gear from under the bench, went aboard and found an empty seat. He tossed his valise into the overhead and sat down.

The train moved out and the conductor made his way down the aisle, taking tickets as he went. John gave his.

"The station master in Dodge told me about you, son, you're going to Pennsylvania, are ya?"

"Yes sir."

"Where's the rest of your tickets?" This part is good only to Great Bend."

"I had them here in this pocket." John patted his left shirt pocket.

"Get jostled at the Old Fort, did ya?"

"Yes, a couple of times. It was crowded in places."

"Sure, the pickpockets must be working there again and I thought we got rid of them. They get your tickets and redeem them for cash. I'm sorry, son, there is nothing at Great Bend but the river dock, water tipple, station and the stock pens. The boat stops every other week and the train stops once a week. After we pass, there's nothing for a week. You better get some sleep, you're gonna need it."

It was a long way to Great Bend and the train rumbled on through the night. John was in a fix and he knew it. He tried to sleep and did so, off and on, but it was not restful.

An hour before dawn, the train screeched and hissed into Great Bend. When it pulled out, a forlorn figure stood alone on the station platform with his bundles at his feet. John strained his eyes in all directions in the darkness to evaluate his surroundings. The morning breeze was cold and the smell of the stock yards hung heavy around him. Nothing was stirring except the cattle milling around in the pens. He carried his gear around the corral until he was upwind and sat down against a large post. Perhaps he dozed off. The next thing he knew, it was getting light.

He stretched his stiff body and scanned the horizon. To the north, the grass lands rolled on as far as the eye could see with nothing to break the monotony but a few jutting rocks or scrub trees here and there.

To the south, the great river glistened silver and black in the gray dawn.

The eastern sky was beginning to glow pink, yellow and gold. A speck, silhouetted on the lighted brilliance, grew larger as it moved westward toward John. Slowly, it grew large enough to see it was a heavily laden wagon pulled by a team of matched mules. It lurched and creaked over the trail. A trail too indiscernible to be called a road. The wagon drew nearer and John could see the driver was dressed completely in black except for his heavy leather boots which sheathed his legs to the knee. The lower trousers were stuffed into the tan boots and bloused out, full, at the knee. His long, heavy waistcoat covered a black sweater and shirt. The string tie around his neck fluttered in the chilly morning breeze. A wide-brimmed, shallow-crowned hat covered a shock of graying hair. From between the hat brim and a graying spade beard, the stranger's cornflower blue eyes peered intently at John.

"Whoa! Whoa!" called the man to his mules and reined the team to a stop.

"You need a job, son?" His eyes never left John's face. His voice was deep and resonant with an accent John had never heard.

"Yes sir, I do," John jumped to his feet and snatched the hat from his head.

"The work is hard and the pay is forty and found."

"I'm stronger than I look—I'll earn it, sir."

"Toss your bindle in the back and climb up." The man slid over and made room for John beside him.

"Yes sir, thank you." John tossed his belongings onto the loaded wagon and scrambled up to the seat.

The men rode without speaking. The wagon bumped and groaned over the trail and the team labored in the harness under their burden.

John wondered if he had done the right thing by accepting a job from a stranger and not knowing the kind of work he was to do. He had no fear of the man but of the uncertainty of the situation. His options were few to none so he settled back to observe the landscape around him.

John glanced at the man beside him from the corner of his eye, but tried not be obvious. Small talk was inappropriate but John felt all his questions would be answered in time.

The driver was fully aware John was examing him and let it pass.

They rode on and after what seemed like hours, the man spoke.

"What's your name—where you from—how did you get here?"

"John Lansure, sir, I'm from Pennsylvania. My folks sent me to my Uncle Tom's ranch in Cushing, Oklahoma for my health. I've been there since last fall and I'm homesick. I got hornswoggled and my pockets picked on the way home. I feel stupid but that's the truth." John was embarrassed.

"The truth is best. You don't look sick."

"I'm not now, sir. I'm fine."

"Got cheated, did ya? Happens to us all—ONCE. You know all about cattle ranching now?"

"Some, I learned a lot. My cousins and uncle taught me things. Sure was different from My home."

"You like ranch life?"

"It'll do but I want to be a railroad engineer soon as I'm old enough."

"How old are you?"

"Be 18 in the fall."

Again the man reined the mules to a stop.

"I'm Aaron Jacobs. My wife, Sarah and I own one thousand acres beginning there." He pointed to a huge boulder at the roadside. On it, chiseled in big letters, was J A C O B S. John wished to ask where the boulder came from and how it got there, but he thought better of it. Instead, he roared:

"Holy Joe! that thing must go two tons!"

"Three," the man stated flatly.

"We came here in '97 from St. Petersburg, Russia. It took us a year to get here. In the 1880's, my mother's brother came to this land and built a sod house. He had been exiled from Russia because he was a Jew who published radical literature. After he came here, the family received a few letters over the years, but no details. In time, the letters stopped and he was never heard from again. Shortly after Sarah and I married, we had to leave too. We had no place to go so we came here. We found Uncle Vladimir's remains in the sod house on his bed. He had probably been dead since the letters stopped coming. We have been here about 12 years come Passover. Up! Up! Sam—Dee Up-Up!" he shouted to the team. They strained in the harness.

Nothing more was said and soon the house came into view. The houses around here were low to the ground to escape the wind, pointed roofs to shed the snow and thatched with grass for warmth. Most had stone chimneys and porches. This one was similar but strangely different. It had twin roof peaks and between them rose a turret topped with a round, domed cupola that looked like a huge onion in the sun. John had seen pictures of these domes in Bruce's books. To the right of the house was a big barn with watering trough, windmill and hitching rail. To the left was a thatched lean-to on poles with no sides. Under it, sat three enormous iron kettles—the kind Ma'am used for apple butter and lard only bigger. All around the place were heavy wooden fences nailed to great posts.

Grass for thatching and stone for building was plentiful but timber was scarce and costly. It had to be hauled twenty miles from the river.

John was fascinated by the Jacobs' farm.

Aaron stopped the mules by the barn and John jumped down to tie them to the hitching rail. When Aaron stepped down, John was astonished at the man's size. He stood six feet three or four inches and was two hundred pounds of hard muscle. The men worked side by side as if they had always done so. The harness was unhooked and the wagon shafts dropped. The team was watered at the trough, led into their stalls, unharnessed and fed.

"We'll unload the wagon after we eat. Sarah will have something on the stove."

John followed Aaron into the house. The delightful smell of fresh bakery and roasting meat filled the kitchen.

"You can wash up there," Aaron pointed to the wash stand. Sarah came into the room. She smiled, went to her husband and hugged him. He kissed her cheek. She handed John a fresh towel.

"Sarah, this is John Lansure. He's going to help us out for a while. John, this is my wife, Sarah."

John mopped his wet face and hands with the towel, extended his hand and took hers.

"Hullo, Missus."

"How do you do—thank you for coming to help—please sit—both of you, the food is ready."

Her voice was soft and calm and she looked nothing like he pictured Aaron's wife would be. She was tall and shapely with black, wavy hair coiled on top of her head. A few threads of white shone here and there, mostly at the temples. Her skin was soft-looking and tanned but her face was remarkably unlined. Her eyes were blue—or were they green—they changed in the light as she moved. She stood straight and carried herself well. Next to Aaron's big frame, she looked small and doll-like.

At the table, the three made small talk about the house, the countryside and the weather. Aaron gave John the routine of the farm.

"We don't have a bunkhouse so you will sleep up there in the loft. We are up at sunup and you will eat here with us. We are usually ready for bed by dark but sometimes we read. You will have every Saturday off as it is our Sabath but you work on Sunday—that bother you, son?" Aaron eyed John carefully.

"No, sir, they won't miss me at church." John knew he should go to church but thought Ma'am would understand.

"The folks here abouts have a barn dance on Saturday night and all the young ones, like you, kick up their heels. You might find it interesting and make new friends. Use Samson or Delila when you wish."

"Samson or Delila—Who are they?" quizzed John.

"My mules, Sam and Dee. It's a long walk to town."

John got a big laugh out of that and for the first time, he saw Aaron grin from ear to ear, showing his beautiful even white teeth. Sarah enjoyed the joke and laughed happily.

"I break the Sabbath after prayers about once a month when I have to go for supplies. I don't enjoy it but God understands. Sometimes Sarah goes along but it is hard for both of us to go at the same time. Someone should be here to mind things. We need your help." Aaron finished his coffee and stood up.

"After we unload the wagon, I'll show you around the place then we will sleep early to be up early."

The men lugged the heavy bags of grain and feed into the barn and others to the pantry off the kitchen. One full wagon load brought enough supplies for a month for the animals and the table. This load also included a bolt of cloth, thread and new needles for Sarah. It was enough calico for two new dresses and curtains for the kitchen. Out of the remnants, Sarah would manage a doll dress or two for the neighbor's children and her collection which nearly filled the plate rail in the great room.

On the whole, the farmers this far out are self-sufficient with the help of the monthly supplies. The corn, grain, hay, sugar beets and sorghum was raised locally and for variety, the farmers traded and bartered with each other. One farmer had ducks and goats to spare; another had chickens and sheep, and so on.

The chores were done. Aaron, Sarah and John sat by the fire in the great room and talked over tea and cakes.

''Sarah, John tells me he was visiting family out Cushing way,'' said Aaron lighting his pipe.

John's throat constricted and he prayed Aaron would not tell he had been cheated.

''Oh, that so? Oklahoma is a long way from Pennsylvania. Tell us about your family.'' Sarah continued with the doll dress she was sewing on her lap.

''My father is a stonemason and my mother is a midwife. I have four sisters and two brothers. I'm next to the youngest boy. My sister, Seneca, is adopted. I was sent to my Uncle Tom's ranch for the dry climate to clear up my bronchitis. The whole family suffers with it off and on. I'm fine now.''

''What a nice family. Aaron and I have no children and as far as we know, there is no one left back in Russia.'' Sarah's voice trailed off and a deep melancholy covered her.

John was glad he did not have to explain why he was stranded. It was a very painful subject.

''Sarah will show you up and tomorrow I will explain your duties. Rest well, you will need your strength. Goodnight, son.'' Aaron tapped the ashes from his pipe into his leathery hand, tossed them into the fireplace and left the room.

Sarah took a coal oil lamp from the lamp shelf and lit it. She led John up the stairs to the loft room.

''Goodnight, John, if you need extra coverletts, look in that chest—at the foot of the bed.'' Sarah pointed it out and sat the lamp on the dresser.

''Goodnight, Missus, thank you.''

Sarah went back down stairs and John looked around the room in the dim lamp light. The rafters were exposed but the joints were snug and the room cozy. The bed and dresser were hand made and primitive but sturdy. A rope bed held a mattress stuffed with feathers, horse hair and corn husks. John undressed, snuffed the lamp and slipped between the coarse muslin sheets. The mattress was noisy when he moved but very comfortable and as soon as his weary head hit the pillow, he slept heavily.

When the smell of fresh bakery and boiled coffee stirred John, it was bright day. He jumped up, dressed quickly and made his bed. With the lamp in hand, he took the loft stairs, two at a time. He carefully placed the lamp on the shelf and presented himself to Aaron who was already finished breakfast.

''Good morning, sir, I think you will have to call me. I slept so well in that bed I would still be asleep if it wasn't for Missus's cooking.'' John was embarrassed for over-sleeping on his first day.

''Good morning, John, glad you slept well. Your breakfast is ready,'' called Sarah from the stove where she was cooking.

''Better eat up—we're late, son. The routine will come.'' Aaron stirred his coffee absently.

''Yes, sir.'' John took his seat at the table.

Sarah served breakfast and John hurried with his food but tried not to gulp. Aaron sipped his second cup of coffee and watched John eat.

''Thank you, Missus, that was some meal. You're almost as good a cook as my Ma'am.'' John took his plate and cup to the sink and Sarah smiled.

''Let's to it, son.''

''Yes, sir.''

Outside Aaron went directly to the lean-to where the three great kettles of water were boiling vigorously.

''I build fires under these pots early every Sunday morning and what you are about to see is a carefully-guarded secret and you tell no one. I keep broken-down, buzzard-bait type horses that can no longer work in the back corral. I buy all I can find from the local farmers here abouts but I never tell them why I want them. They wonder but they don't ask and you must not tell. Understand?''

''Yes, sir, I won't say anything,'' promised John.

''Good, now we bring out one of those horses.''

They brought out one and tied it to the corner post of the lean-to. Aaron picked up a twenty-pound sledge hammer that stood nearby and with all his strength, he struck the hapless animal between the eyes, crushing its skull, killing it instantly. It dropped like a stone to the ground.

John was so stunned, he stood rooted to the spot speechless.

''Come on, son, help me cut up this critter. The knives are there.'' He pointed to a box full of assorted knives, cleavers and saws.

''I know there is an easier way but powder and shot cost money and this is quick and painless,'' Aaron went on.

''I..uh..yes, sir.'' As soon as John could collect himself, he leaped to assist Aaron butcher the old horse.

They carved, chopped and sawed it apart and dropped the large chunks into the boiling kettles. The blood was caught on a canvas tarpaulin and later poured into pails and saved. Nothing was wasted. The work was strenuous and exhausting.

''Save the mane and tail, Sarah cleans, cuts and weaves it into bedding, pillows and dolls,'' instructed Aaron to John.

''Yes, sir.''

After about an hour the whole horse was cooking in the kettles. Aaron stirred the meat in the pots with a great paddle and poked it with a pitchfork. When the meat was partially cooked and no longer red, he said,

''THIS is my secret: SOOEEE—SOOEEE—SOOEEE!'' He screamed so loud, for a moment John was sure his ears were broken.

''SOOEEE—SOOEEE!'' Again he screamed. This time closer to the fence.

From over the rise, the whole earth began to tremble and the top of the hill seemed to move toward Aaron and John. It was the largest herd of hogs John had ever seen. There were hundreds of them—all sizes. They ran squealing and grunting toward them.

With the pitchfork, Aaron began tossing chunks of the horse meat over the fence to the hogs. John found another fork and the two men heaved the meat until the pots were empty and all the hogs had a share.

The noise was deafening and a great cloud of dust followed the herd. The hogs devoured the horse, hide, hair and bone and meat until there was nothing left. The din subsided and the hogs sauntered away. They eventually disappeared over the rise and all was quiet again.

Aaron mopped his sweating face with a red bandana.

''Now you know my secret. I raise the biggest and fattest hogs in the county. Feeding them a horse, along with their slop, adds to their health and growth and they don't root up the land as hogs usually do. I never have sick ones and my sows rarely eat a piglet—even an injured one. On occasion, I toss out a bucket or two of crushed coal when I can get it. The hogs eat it like candy. Coal is hard to come by out here. All this information was in my uncle's journal we found in the old sod house. It was written in Russian so if anybody found it, they couldn't read it. It was still a secret when Sarah and I found it.''

''Holy Pete! If that don't beat anything I ever saw.'' John dropped to his hunkers to rest and smooth his hair under his hat with his left hand.

"Remember, it's OUR secret. Where'd you learn to squat like that? I haven't seen anyone do it since I was in the army. The Serbs in my regiment could squat like that around a campfire for hours and rarely change positions. Always looked so painful to me," Aaron went on.

"I dunno, I've done it all my life—when I get tired. My Paap does it, too. Did your uncle raise hogs here too? I won't tell anybody. How many hogs do you have here?", John asked.

"We don't know. Depending on the time of year, between 800 and 1000 head. My brood sows will have twelve or fifteen in each litter and I have eight sows. I sell them off all the time, but it's still a lot of work. We fed them a horse today but tomorrow and the rest of the week we slop them. I mix their mash with corn and sorghum and some of the blood in the water from the butchered horse and milk if I have it to spare. The slop is mixed in a big drum I rigged on my mud sled so I can haul it summer and winter. The mule pulls the sled but it still has to be bailed into the troughs from the drum by the bucket and THAT, my boy, is hard work. The first week you will be too tired to eat and your hands will blister but soon you will get used to it. Still want to work here?" Again Aaron studied John's face.

John hesitated a moment and said,

"Sure, ya know I'm broke and stranded. Besides, I like it here. Missus' cookin' is almost as good as my Ma'am's. You and I get along and I learn from you. S'pose I'll get pretty tired at first, but I can do it—if ya still want me."

"You'll do. It's time for the evening meal—let's clean up."

Aaron wasn't much for words or flattery but John sensed his approval and felt comfortable.

The two men walked to the house in silence and entered the back door to the kitchen. Again the delicious aroma of cooking food filled the air. Sarah said,

"Your bowl and towel are there." She smiled and pointed to a SECOND wash bowl on the stand. Above it, hung from a peg on the wall, was John's own towel. He was delighted to know he had been accepted into the family.

"Thank you, Missus."

The two washed up side by side. John was content. The misgivings, homesickness and his hidden guilt faded a bit. He looked forward to the task at hand with Aaron and Sarah.

At mealtime they talked and learned about each other. They talked about the farm, hogs, Sarah's cooking and the weather. John spoke of his dreams of becoming a railroad engineer, his home and his family.

His hands, indeed, did blister and he dropped dead tired on his bed each night. However, he was never too tired to eat Sarah's cooking, although he did nod once or twice at the table.

Sarah would smile and Aaron would clear his throat and his eyes would twinkle. John would be embarrassed and they all would have a good laugh. Eventually he could get through his meals without falling asleep.

John worked at Aaron's side day after day and soon he could handle the day's chores by himself. At first, he was clumsy and awkward. Once he slipped carrying two pails of hog slop, fell face down in a puddle and came up with a dirty face and his clothes covered with mud and slop.

He was a sight. Aaron doubled over with laughter, threw his head back and waves of rich, baritone guffaws rolled through the air. It was the first time John ever heard Aaron belly laugh and it made John laugh too.

The days rolled into weeks. One afternoon, two riders came to the house, leading four old, worn-out horses.

''Afternoon, Seth—Max,'' Aaron greeted his visitors.

''Hello, Aaron.'' Seth Barnes owned a big spread about ten miles away.

''Hello, Mr. Jacobs.'' Max Rhinehart was Seth's top ranch hand.

''Tie the animals to the rail and come in. You want gold or stock?'' asked Aaron.

''I need six hogs. Two young sows and four shoats. Need them delivered too, if you're a mind. My stock wagon broke an axle and it isn't fixed yet. Can you do it?'' asked Seth.

''Guess I can. This is John Lansure. John, this is Seth Barnes and his top man, Max Rhinehart. John's helping me out. Friday be all right to bring the hogs? Sarah wants to get a few things in town so we will make a day of it.''

The men shook hands.

''Sure, Aaron, whenever you can,'' said Seth.

''You want the balance in gold—figure I still owe you,'' asked Aaron.

''No, if you deliver them, we call it square,'' insisted Seth.

The four men went into the kitchen where Sarah was cooking.

''Afternoon,'' she said and nodded to the men.

''Hello, Sarah,'' said Seth.

''Missus,'' said Max, and nodded.

Aaron took a jug from the shelf and poured some of the contents into four cups Sarah had placed on the table. He handed a cup to each man and raised one for himself.

''Mazeltoff,'' saluted Aaron.

The men drank the fragrant liquid. John gasped for breath. His eyes teared and the sticky, sweet fire burned all the way to his stomach. John was certain a swig of coal oil would burn less. He choked and coughed.

"Ugh—can't breathe—what is this?" John croaked.

"We call it slivovitz. It's a heavy type of wine or brandy Sarah makes whenever she can get the plums. We use it in our religious ceremonies and sometimes we take a nip just to ward off the chill," Aaron said with a twinkle in his eye.

"It burns all the way down but it sure does warm ya up fast!" exclaimed Max.

"Sarah, this is the best batch yet," said Seth, draining his cup.

"You say that every time, Seth. We call it 'The Recipe' because it's been in our family a long time. Plums are more plentiful now, than they used to be."

"It does warm ya up, for sure!" exclaimed John wiping his eyes.

The rest of the day was spent picking out the hogs that Seth wanted and soon another day was gone. For a Yankee boy from Pennsylvania, it was a whole new way of life. His guilt over Jenny and his homesickness never left the back of his mind but hard work and long hours helped dull his anxieties.

John and Max became good friends and they met every Saturday night at Preston's barn for the dance. It was the social event of the week and whole families came in wagons, carts and buggies to join the fun.

One night, while Max and John were outside the barn watching folks arrive for the dance, Max deftly rolled a handmade cigarette from his tobacco pouch.

"You want to roll one?" Max inquired, offering his pouch to John.

"Naw, thanks, they make me cough. I tried once with my cousins at the ranch."

Max struck a match on his jeans and puffed away on his smoke.

"What do you think of this part of the country, now that you are better acquainted?" Max asked.

"It's first rate, different than anything I've ever seen and not like my home town, but first rate. Good people are most the same anywhere, I guess. They may talk different and dress different but they are most the same," pondered John.

"Well—I don't know about that but I know where there is something you HAVEN'T seen—any place and there is NOTHING like it anywhere." Max looked around to be sure he could not be overheard.

"What's that?" John inquired loudly.

"Sh—quiet—not so loud," said Max in hushed tones and drew John nearer.

"Is it a secret or sumthin'?" asked John.

"Well, not exactly, but listen carefully. Ya mind the big yellow house at the edge of town? The one with the whitewashed fence and all the flowers?"

"Yes."

"Well, a giant lives there."

"A GIANT," cried John.

"Shhh—not so loud. Yea, a real giant, a black one, ta boot. The woman who owns the house keeps him around as her bodyguard—a real African."

"An African giant—naw."

"I swear it's the truth. They all came here a few years ago from the West. No one knows for sure, from where, but they all came together. Hannah, she owns the place and whueeee, what a looker! The African is called Big Sam and he sure is!" Max paused and ground out his cigarette butt with his boot.

"Big Sam has strange markings carved on his chest and neck that look like a chain or a snake and a big gold ring in his right ear. There's a handyman they call Cherry Pie. No one knows his real name. He wears a plaid tam with a fuzzy topknot on it and speaks with a brogue—an Englander—they say. Then there's a foreign girl. Hear tell she's sickly but nobody knows what ails her. And the GIRLS. Buddy, they got five of the most beautiful girls you ever saw! Ya can take your pick—for a price—of course. They all came here in a prairie schooner. Paid the Widow Bracken gold for the house. Later, they had a whole wagon train of furniture sent here from St. Louis. Been here ever since. Ya want to go see!" Max asked, catching his breath.

"Go see what, the giant?"

"No, silly, the girls in the house. It costs five bucks. The rules are: No drunks and ya have to take a bath first and they enforce the rules."

"Ya mean it's one of THOSE houses?" asked John.

"Course, what ya think it was, the Brethren Church!" Max said, snidely.

"How do you know so much about the place, you ever been there?"

"Naw, but I heard the other guys talk and it's mostly the swells that go there. I never had the price. Besides, anybody knows what goes on in there." Max was hedging and John could sense it.

"It's the giant—you're afraid of that giant, ain't ya?" John giggled.

"Am not and it's not funny, but I wouldn't go there on a bet!" declared Max.

"I would—if I had the money. I'd go just to see what it was like. There's nothing to be afraid of. Wouldn't ya like to see the giant up close and really see what goes on there? I can't, I'm saving for a train ticket home. I only spend a little each week." John said.

''You'd go there, would ya. Well, if the price is all that's holding ya, I'll fix ya. Come on, let's go in, the band is tuning up.'' The subject was closed.

The summer passed quickly for John but his homesickness returned when the harvest was done and the leaves began to turn.

John did his work but talked more and more about his family and home. The homesickness worsened when Ma'am wrote to him and said his sister, Lu, was getting married soon.

Aaron and Sarah had become very attached to John but knew he would be going away. To them, he had become the son they never had.

On a cold, rainy fall evening, while the three sat by the fire, Aaron spoke.

''Sarah, please bring some of your Recipe. I think it's time to ask John and tell him our story.'' Sarah brought the jug and three glasses and poured each one some slivovitz.

Aaron began by telling John they must travel back in time, to Russia, many years ago. . . . .

Aaron's parents were killed when he was twelve years old in a Jewish purge—one of many in Russia. He was adopted by a Cossack family who raised him in Orthodoxy. They never demanded he renounce Jewry but insisted he not practice it. He was given his adoptive family's name of Komorofsky and his original name of Yacobonova was set aside.

Aaron's adoptive father was a Commander in the Tzar's Cossack Life Guard. Eventually, this background led to Aaron's appointment into the Royal Guard Fusileers.

Later he was assigned to Krasnoe Selo, a large Russian military camp near St. Petersburg. With his knowledge of gunnery, he quickly rose to the rank of Captain.

Tzar Alexander III brought his son, the nineteen year old Tzarevich Nicholas, to the camp to learn ordnance. He was a good horseman but disliked guns and their noise. The Tzarevich had just been given the rank of Colonel by the Tzar and was assigned to Aaron for gunnery lessons. Nicholas was a bright student, usually, but could not concentrate on sighting, elevation or weighting because of the noise. All of which is necessary to fire a cannon. For better results, Aaron suggested the boy be taught the fundamentals in the quiet of the boy's apartment on the camp. It worked. He learned quickly and they became good friends.

Nicholas had other tutors, the strongest of which was Constantine Petrovich Pobedonostev. Although brilliant, he was violently Anti-Semetic. His prejudice also fell on the Catholic, Poles and the Moslems scattered over the empire.

For the time being, the bias did not harm the relationship between Aaron and Nicholas although some in power knew of his origin. Aaron did not hide his past nor did he make an issue of it. He watched Nicholas mature into an efficient tactician and competent fusileer. After he mastered the fundementals in the classroom, he was capable and comfortable on the firing range.

Nicholas was not born to be Tzar, Fate deemed it otherwise. He had an older brother named Alexander, who died in infancy and a younger brother, George, who died of tuberculosis in adolescence. From early on, Nicholas was groomed to be Tzar in spite of the fact his nature, personality and disposition were not conducive to the task. His grandfather and father were huge, imposing, swashbuckling, demanding and absolute Monarchs. Nicholas was none of these things. He was a slender youth of five feet seven inches with an open face and expressive, sad eyes. He was a reticent, timid loner who enjoyed reading, the arts and plays and hated the thought of combat and war.

He had one confidant and friend, his cousin, George V of England. He and George corresponded constantly, liked the same things and confided in each other. Nicohlas seldom listened to his ministers and usually dismissed or ignored them but he reguarded highly, his cousin's opinion and advice.

Nicholas kept his own council and generally suffered from melancholia but when depressed, he often consulted George. Young Nicholas had seen his grandfather, Alexander II torn to pieces by an assassin's bomb. Suffered terrible headaches, all his life, himself, from an assassin's glancing sword blow to his head in Otsu, Japan. He watched his father, Alexander III, die slowly of nephritis.

The dying Tzar gave formal blessings, for marriage, of his son, Nicholas II and Princess Alexandra Fedorovna, usually called Alex. On November 1, 1894, ten days after their betrothal, Alexander II died. Gentle Nicky's emotions were torn asunder. The agonizing grief of his father's death, the sweet joy of having Alex for his wife and the dreaded reality of becoming Tzar, all took it's toll.

After the normal mourning or 1 year, on May 26, 1896 he became Tzar.

At the age of twenty six Nicholas had become, His Imperial Majesty, Nicholas II, Tzar of all the Russias, Head of the House of Romanov and Monarch of his people. By his own admission, he did not want to be Tzar and had no idea how to become one.

Nicholas was a Russian in all things. When at his desk, he preferred peasent blouse, baggy breeches and soft leather boots. When on review, he wore the Cossack bright red tunic and karakul fur hat. For formal affairs, he wore his full dress regalia of cream and gold as Commander-In-Chief of the Russian armed forces.

One week after his father's funeral, on November 26, 1894, Nicholas and Alexandra were married. It was truly a marriage made in heaven. They were genuinely happy together and their family grew quickly.

Nicholas II, Tzar of Russia was quite another matter. He made it clear to all, he would follow his father's policies both for the House of Romanov and the Russian Empire. This would prove to be a fatal mistake.

Nicholas never mastered the technique of forceful, efficient management of his subordinates. The Tzar appointed all the ministers to the various government departments and could hire and fire at will, however, Nicholas gave them little supervision. Nicholas hated scenes and could not criticize or dismiss a man to his face. Instead, if one of the ministers transgressed, Nicholas would give him a friendly reception, comment gently and shake hands warmly. The next morning, he would send a letter, to the minister's office, regretfully asking for his resignation. This behavior added to the chaos in the government and nurtured the seeds of revolution among the Russian people.

The unrest in Russia was mounting steadily, year by year. George V of England, cousin and confidant of Nicholas, knew of the upheaval in Russia. He wrote to Nicholas and pleaded for him to alter his policies and observe more closely his problems of state. He implored his cousin to stop the religious persecution at once and urgently reinforce the Russian economy.

Up to that time, Nicholas was more interested in the external affairs of Russia. His efforts were to make peace between Russia and Austria, set rules and arbitration for war and settle the dispute between Austria and Serbia.

Nicholas appointed ministers to run the government departments and presumed they did so, however he did not investigate to make certain.

He was shocked by the letter from his cousin, George V. Upon investigation, he found most of his departments in shambles, the worst of which was religious affairs. Synagogues were closed or burned, Rabbis were murdered and their followers slain and scattered.

Nicholas quickly called Aaron into the palace for a conference. Aaron arrived at the Tzar's study door. It was ajar. Nicholas stood by the window and looked out into the October sleet and rain which coated the window pane.

Aaron took a few steps into the quiet, ornate room and hesitated.

"Aaron, my friend, please come in and close the door." The Tzar said quietly, without turning around.

"Your Majesty." Aaron saluted smartly and waited for Nicholas to turn and return the salute.

Nicholas turned slowly and saluted.

"Aaron, this as a visit between two old friends. It's been too long. You look well. Please, sit here." Nicholas pointed to a chair and Aaron sat uncomfortably on the edge of the seat. The Tzar looked tired but very much the same after seven years.

''For your own safety, my friend, you and your wife must leave Russia at once.''

''Leave Russia—I don't understand. I can't. . . . ,'' stammered Aaron.

''Some people have learned of your Jewish origin. Go tonight, a purge is at hand. This packet contains passports for you both, letters of transit and a years salary. Take only what you can carry on horseback. No valises, layer your clothing but take nothing that would indicate that you are traveling far. You know what can happen and I want you away safely before your name appears on their list. I can't promise my signature on these documents will protect you but you must try to go. It must look as if you are out pleasure riding or going to visit friends. Do you understand?'' The Tzar paused and gave the papers to Aaron.

''Yes, Sir.'' Aaron was astonished but accepted the pouch.

''Most importantly, you must NOT travel North or West. As I speak, the roads are being closed or, at best, being watched for those who wish to escape to safety. Go South or East. Yes, I know it will be hundreds of miles out of the way but safer. Few will be going in such a round about way. If you can get to the Black Sea you will be safe. Take boat passage to France, it would be the safest country and they accept our émigrés. Trust no one. Travel by night and rest in out-of-the-way places by day. The fewer people that know of your plans, the better. It would be best, for you to just disappear. You have been a good friend and I wish you God Speed.'' The men shook hands and the Tzar turned back to the window. The meeting was over. Aaron backed out slowly and closed the door.

Aaron hurried to give Sarah the shocking news. She had been very worried when Aaron had been summoned for an audience with the Tzar. In those times, a state summons usually meant trouble.

He explained what happened and showed her the packet of papers and money.

''But I can't travel now, what about our child?'' she cried and held her swollen belly. She was something over six months pregnant.

''I know that, Sarah, but it's go or die. The Tzar was emphatic about it.'' Aaron held Sarah in his arms to comfort her fears. He knew the task at hand was just short of impossible but dared not convey his fear to her.

Aaron did as the Tzar instructed and told only his aging, trusted servant, Felix Cossilov who looked more like someone's grandfather than a servant. In a knee-length black frock coat, his soft dark eyes peeked from behind white shaggy eyebrows, accentuated by long white hair and beard. He was always known to Aaron as Uncle Felix and had been with the Komorofsky family all of Aaron's boyhood. Since Aaron's parents were dead, he gave the family home to Uncle Felix and all that went with it. Aaron knew he would never return. He told Uncle Felix that nothing must change for two months. The routine, by the household servants must not change and after that time Aaron and Sarah would be away from Russia or dead. If Uncle Felix was pressured by anyone, he was to say the family had gone to visit friends and family in the Ural Mountains until the baby came and nothing more. Uncle Felix had his instructions and helped them sew their valuables into their clothing. Sarah wept at having to leave her mother's trunk and other family heirlooms behind. Uncle Felix picked two of the best horses, packed food for several days and hugged them. After tearful goodbys, Aaron and Sarah rode into the dark night to be as far away as possible by daybreak.

Sarah was unaccustomed to riding horseback and in her condition, the first night was terrible. Before dawn, they took shelter in a deserted barn and Sarah fell into an exhausted sleep without eating. They slept fitfully off and on all the next day and ate little. They clung to each other without words.

At full dark, they set off again. The first objective was to get out of their province as quickly as possible. The further away from their home the safer they would be. They hid by day and traveled by night. The border crossings were dreaded. People going and coming formed long lines and waited. The border guards examined their papers and searched their saddlebags. Fortunately their persons were not searched. Aaron was very imposing looking in his bright red uniform with fur hat and although the guard did not recognize the uniform of the Royal Guard, he was wise enough to realize Aaron was an important personage and allowed them to pass.

The ploy worked here but as they traveled further and further away from St. Petersburg and Moscow, the less and less important the uniform would be and the more suspicious people would become of any uniformed person.

This proved true at the next border crossing. They were about to be bodily searched when quick thinking Sarah pretended to faint and allowed her horse to run away across the border to safety. Aaron followed and the harried guards had too many agitated people crowding around to chase them and Aaron and Sarah got away again.

Sarah had been severely jerked when she allowed her horse to bolt at the crossing and was in great pain. She could go no further. It would be light soon and they had no shelter.

Some distance off the road, was a small church with a dense woods behind it. Aaron helped Sarah down, took the horses into the woods to hobble them out of sight.

He and Sarah went into the church and took seats on the side pew near an outside door; a precaution if they were forced to run. Aaron cradled her in his arms and she slept, perhaps they both did.

A gentle hand on Aaron's shoulder, awakened him with a start.

''Gently, my son, it's alright,'' said the elderly bearded priest, softly.

''My wife is ill and we came in here to rest,'' Aaron explained.

''Yes, I know, my servant told me the patrols are searching for an officer of the Royal Guard and his wife. You had a very close call. Quickly now, follow me.'' The priest moved a candle on the wall and a panel moved revealing a dark passage way. The priest lit a torch and the three moved along the musty passage and down two flights of stairs. At the bottom, the priest's servant was waiting.

''Nicholi put your horses in the stable at the back of the church. They have been fed and watered. He brought your saddlebags and these clothes.'' He handed Aaron and Sarah the clothes and they dressed quickly.

''The patrols are not looking for a priest or a nun traveling around doing God's work. The long habit will hide her condition and you will not be so conspicuous without the uniform. You should be reasonably safe through the next check point. It's the best I can do for you,'' the priest said simply.

''How can I thank you, Father, we are forever in your debt. You have risked your lives for us and we are not of this faith.'' Aaron spoke softly.

''I suspected as much when I found you here. A coin or two in the poor box will be help enough. May God be with you. It's dark and you must hurry.'' The priest made the sign of the cross for both Aaron and Sarah and left them.

Aaron dropped a handfull of gold coins into the poor box by the stable door and pressed one into the hand of the servant who was holding the horses.

Mounting the horses was difficult, specially for Sarah. The flowing cloth of the habits was cumbersome and awkward and she was very ill. After some maneuvering in the saddles, they rode away into the darkness.

They passed through the next road block without incident. The border guards gave little or no notice to religious orders and generally gave them a wide berth unless they suspected the travelers were Jews with forged papers.

Shelter was harder and harder to find in that sparsely populated region and the villages and homes were further and further apart. Aaron studied the map he kept concealed in his clothes.

Sarah knew there was something drastically wrong with her but up to then, she had said nothing to Aaron. When she could stand the pain no longer, she said, ''Please, Aaron, I have to stop. Under that bridge will do.'' She pointed to a low wooden bridge over a nearly dry river bed.

Aaron placed a blanket on the ground under the bridge and Sarah laid down to rest. He hobbled the horses nearby and sat down beside Sarah.

''What's wrong, Sarah, is it the baby? I know the riding is bad for you. I've been keeping the Ural Mountains on my left and if my calculations are right, we should be near Saratov. From there we go by boat down the Volga. You won't have to ride anymore.''

She nodded but said nothing. Aaron held her close and kissed her cheek. She was burning with fever. He knew she needed rest and a doctor. They slept.

At dusk, Aaron encouraged Sarah to eat something. She refused food but drank some water from the stream. At full dark, they were on their way again.

His estimates were correct. They reached the boat landing a bit before dawn. He inquired about boat passage from a passer-by and was told to move further along the wharf to a barge called the Victoria. The owners, Boris and Olga Vyrubova would take a passenger or two, if the price was right and they were scheduled to depart at dawn.

Aaron and Sarah found the Victoria and dismounted.

''Good morning. I understand you folks will take passengers. We would like to buy passage to Tzaritsyn. Sister Sarah is not used to riding horseback,'' Aaron said with a straight face. He hoped they would not notice Sarah's swollen shape under the flowing robes.

Boris Vyubova was a short, stout, unkempt man in his forties with a dirty beard and greasy trousers. Olga was a two hundred pounder with strong arms and a keen eye. With her dark hair tied back, she was much cleaner than her husband.

''Sometimes we do. That Nun looks sick to me,'' Boris said.

''She's just worn out. We have been up in the Ural back provinces and she needs to get home and rest,'' answered Aaron.

''Where's home?'' It was not idol curiosity from Boris, it was suspicious snooping.

''We are bound for Odessa but we have to get to Tzaritsyn first. Will you take us there?'' Aaron lied.

''Can you pay? Religious people never have money.'' Greed was showing on Boris' face.

''Yes, if it isn't too much,'' answered Aaron.

Olga stepped forward and pushed Boris aside in order to greet Aaron and Sarah.

''You folks come right aboard. We'd be glad to take you. Them horses go too?'' Olga was more pleasant than Boris.

''If we get boat passage, we won't need them and we will give them to you to pay our passage. You are right, we don't have much money.'' Aaron hoped the lie did not show on his face.

''Well, now, those are very handsome horses. Bring them aboard and we will talk,'' instructed Boris.

The barge had no cover for the horses but it did have hitching rail and feeding manger attached to a large cabin on the deck that was used for cargo and passengers.

Aaron and Boris continued to talk and Sarah dropped heavily onto a sack of grain to rest. Olga stood near and watched Sarah carefully. After a few minutes, she sat down beside Sarah and said, ''Missy, you can fool that Priest AND Boris but you can't fool ME . . . you are going to have a baby and you're in a bad way. Come with me.'' She took Sarah by the hand and ducked into the cabin door. ''Now you lie down there and let me see what's what. I've delivered more babies, human and animal, than I am years old and THAT'S considerable!''

Sarah was too sick to resist or argue and lay down, as ordered. After a quick examination Olga said, ''Uh huh, about seven months, I make it. You are feverish and there is something wrong, yes? Are you still feeling life?''

''I'm not sure, I've been riding most of the night. My horse jerked me a while back and it hurt me but the pain has gone now.''

''You're no nun and he's no priest I'll wager. Priests always have long beards and those grand expensive boots of yours don't belong to a poor nun. Oh, your secret is safe with me and Boris does what I tell him. You two are husband and wife and you're running away from something. No matter, you are safe on the barge and now you must sleep.'' Olga easily read the fear and desperation of Sarah's face. She covered Sarah with a course blanket and went out on deck to Boris and Aaron.

''Get up steam, Boris, it's full light and we should be in the drift before this,'' Olga ordered.

The boats use the currents, midstream, to save fuel and carry heavier loads down river. Traveling up stream required lighter loads and more fuel.

Boris stoked the boiler with wood and said, ''The priest says we can sell the horses and KEEP the money. D' you agree to that for their fare?'' Boris waited for Olga's approval.

''How far?''

''Tzaritsyn.''

''Tzaritsyn is it? Tzaritsyn is NOT your destination, I'll wager. You are émegrés headed West. You are not a priest and that nun is really your wife. She's very ill and about to deliver, too early, I'd guess. I will help her. You will be safe with Boris and me on the river. We will take the horses but not to sell. If you are discovered at Tzaritsyn, you may need them again. Boris! Steady as she goes!'' Olga hid her kind heart behind a mask of noisy blustering.

Boris jumped to steady the helm and Aaron went into the cabin to Sarah. Thinking she was asleep, he quietly removed the cumbersome priest's robes and replaced them with more suitable clothes from his bundle.

''I'm not asleep,'' Sarah said softly. ''Please sit here with me.''

''Shush, you're supposed to rest. Olga and Boris will take us to Tzaritsyn. She thinks you will have the baby too soon—how do you feel? The trip was too difficult for you. Oh, Sarah, what have I done to you?'' He held her close in his arms and wept.

Suddenly Sarah drew in her breath and shrieked with pain. Olga heard her cry out and rushed into the cabin.

''Out of here!'' She shouted and pushed Aaron out of the cabin. ''Go sit with Boris and leave this to me,'' she instructed Aaron.

Boris held the tiller firmly on course. Aaron sat nearby and stared at the river ahead. The river was black and foreboding. The October night was cold but dry with little or no wind. The barge slid quietly over the river bringing only the sound of water slapping on the hull mixed with the rhythmic chug of the steam engine.

Olga came out twice to draw water from the river but said nothing.

The barge moved on into the night. It would be three hundred miles to Tzaritsyn and another hundred to the Black Sea. Aaron and Sarah had traveled for weeks to reach Saratov and if nothing bad happened, it would take months to reach France.

Aaron mulled over his impossible plight. With his head in his hands, he sat motionless and stared into the night.

Time passed slowly and after what seemed like hours, Olga emerged from the cabin. She was disheveled and exhausted.

''Sir, what do I call you?'' Olga asked gruffly.

''Captian Aaron Komorofsky, at your service, Ma'am.'' Aaron jumped to his feet and saluted smartly.

''Easy Aaron Komorofsky, easy. None of that here, the river has eyes and ears. Your wife has delivered and if the bleeding stops, she will live. It was a bad birth and she was torn up inside. The child, a boy, had been dead for several days—maybe a week. I did all I could—now we wait. She will mend on the long trip down river. The trip is usually uneventful and when we put in for fuel, supplies and cargo, you two will stay undercover. We are well-known on the river and folks will pay little attention to us. It will be light soon. You must stay out of sight during the day light hours. Go into your wife and get some sleep.'' Olga wiped her face with her apron and dropped heavily onto a grain bag to rest.

''I—my wife—we thank you for all you've done. How will I ever repay your kindness?'' Grateful Aaron could not find the proper words to express his feelings.

''Oh, Sir, you will pay!'' She threw back her head and laughed loudly. Her jolly laugh sent shock waves into the still night.

Aaron disappeared into the cabin to Sarah and to sleep.

For the next few days, Sarah drifted in and out of feverish delirium. Aaron watched her closely. He covered her when she tossed the covers off and laid damp cloths on her burning face. Olga and Boris maneuvered their barge down river, as usual. Everything appeared normal.

Early evening of the forth day, Sarah opened her eyes and smiled at Aaron. They clung to each other. She had passed the crisis and would live.

''My love, I was so afraid——,'' Aaron whispered.

Shush, I just needed rest. Our son—I lost our son.'' Tears glistened in her eyes.

''We will have many sons, I promise.'' He believed she would recover in spite of Olga's predictions.

In the days that followed, during the trip to Tzaritsyn, Sarah regained her strength and health due largely to the blustering, bullying kindness of Olga. She fed them and ordered them about as childeren. Boris kept his distance.

They did not stop at Tzaritsyn but moved down river to a place where Olga and Boris had a friend with a larger boat that was necessary for the next leg of the trip.

After much vodka and loud bartering, Misha Agin, Boat Master and Trader, agreed to take Sarah and Aaron to Rastov, where he had friend with a boat to take them across the Sea of Azov and the Black Sea to Istanbul. It would be a long, long trip.

Saying goodby to Boris and Olga was more difficult than expected. Without a doubt, they had saved Sarah's life and had saved them both by hiding them from patrol boats and curious inspectors. Thanks was so puny for saving a life.

Sarah gave Olga the boots she admired and Boris was delighted with the gift of the horses. They were content and wished them God Speed.

The passenger's quarters aboard the Cathrine were larger than on the Victoria and the boat was larger but no cleaner. Captain Mish, as he was called, showed them to a cabin and explained they must remain indoors by day as before.

Captain Mish was nothing like Boris. He was older, tall and lean with a trim beard. His eyes were blue and his skin, weathered. His dark uniform was frayed but clean. He moved around the boat, attended to duty and barked orders to his three crewmen. The trip to Rostov would take about a week on the Catherine.

Sarah and Aaron settled in and kept to themselves by day and walked the decks by night.

At Rostov, Captain Mish presented Aaron and Sarah to Abdul Abanny, Captain of the schooner, Rising Star, bound for Istanbul. He said good-by and left them in Captian Abdul's care. The fare was great but Aaron paid it without comment.

Captain Abanny was a colorful Turk in a bright turban and flowing robes that only partially conceal the the gleaming scimitar which hung from his waist. He spoke many languages and knew the waterways well. The Captain assured Aaron and Sarah that they were safely away from Russia and need never hide again.

Aaron and Sarah could hardly believe their good fortune. Safe and free from years of fear and uncertainty. They gratefully took the opportunity to roam the decks freely day or night. They soaked up the sun and basked in the warm breezes. The sights and sounds of the new world they traveled through was fascinating. The trip across the Sea of Azov and the Black Sea was pleasant and restoring. The color came back to Sarah's cheeks and the worry lines faded from Aaron's face.

At Istanbul, Captain Abanny arranged passage for them on the French trader, Allard, bound for Marseille. He spoke enough French to negotiate a reasonable fare and accommodations.

This leg of the trip made Aaron and Sarah more apprehensive. The language barrier was enormous. They could not order food or drink, ask the time of day or chat with their fellow passengers. They never saw the Captain of the ship. A crewman escorted them and what baggage they carried, to their small cabin space and left them. Bells rang, the engine rumbled, the ship groaned and creaked but no one came.

The bunks were upper and lower but comfortable. Sarah was amazed to have running water in the tiny sink and used all manner of excuses to turn on the tap and draw water. After careful inspection of their cabin, they climbed into the bunks to sleep.

They were shocked awake by a loud pounding on the door. The same crewman who had escorted them in, stuck his head in the door, said a few words in French, pointed down the gangway and was gone. Aaron and Sarah dressed quickly and followed his directions down the passage.

At the end of the passage was a large dining room. People were lining up, cafeteria fashion, for meal time. The people chatted noisily in many different languages. Aaron and Sarah understood none. They observed twenty or so passengers and a few crewmen. All stood in line for the same plate of food and cup of coffee. Aaron and Sarah had no idea what they were eating but it was hot and filling and they cleaned their plates. The coffee was strong but palatable and the chunk of bread was specially delightful. It was hard and crusty on the outside and white and fluffy on the inside. Very different from the chewy, dark rye bread they were used to. It would become a favorite of Aaron's.

After meals, Aaron and Sarah walked the decks of the ship as did the other passengers. When they were in their quarters, they had time to talk of the future.

In the 1880s, Aaron's uncle Vladimir Kropotkin had gone to America. His address was Catharine, Kansas. The family had received a few letters from him then they stopped. For Aaron and Sarah, the distance to America seemed insurmountable. They had no idea where to find Catharine, Kansas, so going there was discounted.

The ship made two port stops in Greece and two in Italy. Sarah and Aaron watched with great interest, as the ship unloaded and re-loaded. They waved at the people on the docks and observed their wagons and coaches which moved in and out of the wharfs. Sarah was enchanted with their fashions and clothing. The ship moved on to Sicily and Sardinia and again the panorama was different. Each location had it's own colorful sights and sounds and the fashions were picturesque.

After the ship had cleared the coast of Sardinia, two men knocked on the door of Aaron's and Sarah's cabin. One, was the crewman familiar to them, the other was a stranger. He spoke passable Russian but was not Russian. He explained he was a Canadian, named Jacques Tu Lain, in search of émegrés to go from Marseille to Quebec and Montreal in Canada. He said the winter crossing would leave about one week after our landing at Marseille.

The Canadian government was offering minimal passage and free land to settlers.

"We have no clothing or supplies for a winter crossing," said Aaron.

"Your passage will include warm clothes for you both. What do you do for a living?" Inquired Jacques.

"I'm a horseman; rider, driver and trainer. Sarah is a seamstress and doll maker," answered Aaron.

"Excellent, the ladies will have need of her services and we need good horsemen. I suppose you can handle a four-up and a six-up? Wagon trains move out constantly, for the West and always need experienced drivers."

Aaron had seen coaches and wagons at the docks of several ports with multiple teams and guessed it to mean four-up and six-up but he said nothing. In Russia, the sledges, carts and wagons are drawn singly or troika—with one or three horses.

"Do you wish to join us in Marseille," asked Jacques.

"May we have time to talk it over?" Sarah inquired.

"Yes, of course, I will see you tomorrow." The two men left the cabin.

"What do you want to do?" Aaron cradled Sarah's face in his hands.

"Oh, Aaron, we have come SO far, already."

"I know you are right, but if we cross the ocean, we will be closer to America and Uncle Vlady's place."

"Do we have enough money to go on after we reach Canada?"

"I have no idea. If not, I will work for our passage. I'm a good teamster. What do you say—go or not?" He teased. He was making sport of his lack of knowledge of foreign drayage.

"We've come THIS far—might as well go on!" They clung to each other and laughed and cried.

Arrangements were made and in three days after they reached Marseille, they were on board the steamer, St. Clair, bound for Quebec and Montreal, Canada. Along with clothes, they were given a small book of translations.

This time, they shared cabin space with four more adults and a child. They were a French couple, their child, a boy of ten, the Frenchman's mother and brother. There were six bunks which left the child to share space with a family member. Conversation was impossible but communication was accomplished. With difficulty, Sarah and Aaron learned that an epidemic had taken all the other members of the Frenchman's family and they were going to Canada in search of a new life.

The crossing went smoothly until they passed the Azores. A storm came up and the winds and the seas raged.

All in the cabin were sea sick except Sarah. She cleaned away the vile vomit they tossed around indiscriminately, bathed their faces and comforted them. She propped open the cabin door for fresh air but there was little. Many of the passengers were ill and the air was fouled.

Aaron lay quietly on his bunk, his face the color of ashes. The other people in the cabin moaned and groaned and the child cried. Sarah carefully tended her charges.

On the morning of the third day, the tempest subsided and the seas calmed. Gradually, the sick recovered. Exhausted, Sarah dropped onto her bunk to sleep. She had made grateful friends.

Jacques Tu Lain stopped by the cabin to see how Sarah and Aaron and the other passengers had fared during the storm. The French family excitedly explained how Sarah had nursed them through their ordeal.

Jacques introduced them properly. Pierre and Mimi La Farge, his mother, Jozette, his brother, André and their young son, Jean-Pierre.

"They are very obliged to you and wish to repay the kindness," explained Jacques.

"It is not necessary. I'm sure they would have done the same if the circumstance was reversed, but there is something. You know we speak only Russian and they speak some English as well as French and we would be very grateful if they helped Aaron and me to learn."

Jacques spoke a few words to the French family. After some chatter, he said,

''They would be honored to teach you both. They also, wish to know where you are going when we reach Canada. They plan to winter in Montreal and go into the interior at first thaw. They have a prearranged place to winter and beg you to join them.''

Sarah and Aaron were astonished and delighted. It was an answer to their prayers and they accepted with pleasure. They hugged and the group was jubilant. . . . . . .

John was brought back to the present day of 1909 on the swine farm, by the sound of Aaron tapping his pipe on the stone fireplace. He emptied the bowl of ashes into his leathery hand and tossed them into the flame.

''We wintered with the La Farges' and studied French and English with them. For a living, I trained horses and Pierre taught languages in school, there. In the spring, I gave the papers, that entitled Sarah and me to Canadian land, to Pierre. With our land and his, he could raise his family and do well. Sarah taught Mimi and Jozette to sew, tat lace and make dolls. She's working on one now, like those on the shelf.'' Aaron explained and pointed to a long row of dolls on the wall shelf.

John had seen the twenty or so dolls before but paid little attention to them.

''Here is a Greek fruit seller; An Italian wine merchant; A Russian sailor; Tzar Nicolas and Alexandra; George V of England and William II of Germany, first cousins of the Royal Family. That's Olga and Boris, the Captains, Mich and Abanny; the La Farges; Jacques; Sarah's mother and mine and on her lap, is YOU.'' Aaron pointed, with a flourish, from the dolls on the shelf to the doll in Sarah's hands.

''After the danger had passed, we received a letter from Uncle Felix and soon after, he sent Sarah's trunk, some family heirlooms and Sarah's doll collection, along with a few pieces of linen and assorted cloth, ribbons and lace that Sarah prized.

Sarah had the most remarkable ability to remember details and colors that few notice and was able to reproduce them. She did all the dolls from memory and the Royal Family from photographs and tintypes. She had never seen the Royal Children, so she did them by age and imagination. Olga, born in 1895, was 12; Tatiana, born in 1897, was 10; Maria, born in 1899, was 8; Anastasia, born in 1901, was 6; Little Alexis, born in 1904, was an infant.'' Aaron's enthusiasm displayed his pride in Sarah's ability.

With uncanny accuracy, Sarah was putting the finishing touches on a miniature cowboy.

"Look in the left hand pocket of your likeness," Aaron suggested.

Sarah held up the doll and John placed his finger into the tiny pocket. He retrieved a small, smooth pebble.

"See that, Sarah made the doll left handed and it carries a worry stone, the same as you." Aaron and Sarah watched for John's reaction and were delighted when his face lit up and he beamed with pleasure.

The cowboy doll was about 10 inches tall and astonishingly exact. The hat, vest and chaps were made of soft leather. The trousers were denim and the most delightful of all, was the shirt. It was of the same material as the shirt John's Aunt Bea had made for him in Cushing, on the ranch.

"It's unbelievable—it's like looking in the mirror—but better! You do have a gift. It looks so real, it's scary, where did you find the shirt cloth?"

"I took a bit from the tail of your shirt once, when I washed it, where it wouldn't be seen." Sarah confessed, sheepishly.

"You did—I never missed it—can't tell it's gone—anywhere."

"If Sarah doesn't have the exact fabric or cloth, she waits 'til something close comes up, then she improvises. Some of these dolls took years to finish. The scimitar on Captain Abanny's robe took the longest. It was a watch fob belonging to a cutlery drummer who passed through here peddling his wears a few years back. Sarah plied him with her food and a generous supply of the 'Recipe' and he GAVE it to her." Aaron laughed and Sarah blushed.

"John, we've told you all this for a reason." Aaron grew solemn.

"What a story! An impossible trip but you made it. You are real pioneers!" John was genuinely proud of them.

"You know we are all alone, here," said Sarah, softly.

"We are getting old and we have no heirs. I need help on the farm already and will need more and more as time goes on. We've told you all about our past so you would better understand us—our customs and our religion. When Sarah lost our son, we lost our ability to have children, although we didn't know it, at that time. We have talked it over carefully and this is not a snap decision. We look upon you as the son we lost. We wish you to be our son, legally. We will draw up papers to make you our legally adopted son. You will be heir to all we have. Sarah's doll collection will be very valuable sometime. The farm, the animals and the land will keep you well, the balance of your life. If you decide to settle here with us, we will deed everything we own to you, legal and binding. Now, don't answer yet. Think on it—sleep on it—we will talk again, good night, Son." The conversation was closed and Aaron and Sarah left the room. She touched John's cheek on the way out.

John stared into the dying fire and mulled over all he had heard. Sleep on it—how could he sleep. He watched the glowing embers and remembered his ambition—his dream—to become a locomotive engineer. He thought of his home and family and about Aaron and Sarah who had become family to him. He thought of how they had struggled to come here to settle.

After sometime passed, exhaustion crept in and he needed to sleep. He crossed the dark room to the loft steps. He knew the way in the dark—he had done it many times without a lighted lamp. Once in bed, he fell into a troubled sleep.

The next day, the routine was the same and nothing was said about the evening's conversation.

It was Saturday and John's day off. As usual, Max picked him up for the dance at Preston's. John was unusually pre-occupied and the two men rode without speaking.

''I know you ain't much for words, John, but you haven't said a word since our 'Hello's', you got troubles?'' Max asked after a few miles down the road.

''Uh-oh, not exactly troubles—just got some thinking to do, sorry.'' John said absently.

''Come on, buddy, perk up, can't have any long faces at the dance. What'ud people think?'' Coaxed Max.

''Sure, okay, what's new with you?'' John tried to make conversation.

Max chattered on and on as they road. John nodded and grunted and tried to listen. After sometime passed, John spoke.

''I'll be going home soon.''

''What!'' You can't do THAT—it's October—winter's comin',''
shrieked Max.

''You helped me make up my mind, thanks.''

''I helped—how'd I do that?''

''You reminded me of my brother and home. My birthday's coming and I've never been away on my birthday—before—then there's Christmas—and my sister is getting married. I just have to GO HOME. I will miss you, buddy, you're first rate in my book.'' John put his hand on his friend's shoulder. For the first time in his life, Max Rhinehart was speechless. They rode on to Preston's Barn Dance in silence.

At the dance, John joked and laughed with the fellows, teased and kissed the girls and danced every dance. He knew this was his last Preston Barn Dance and the memories, he made, had to last.

On the ride home, Max said, ''You still going home soon?''

''Yes, I think I'll take next Monday's packet boat from Great Bend to Hutchinson. That way, I can catch the train, Eastbound, without backtracking. I looked into other ways, too, they said the Stage line still operates from Newton-El Dorado over the mountains to St. James-Rolla. I'll see which is cheaper. Then, it's a straight shot to St. Louis and points East.''

''Well, if you're positive you're going, I want to take you to the boat. How about staying the night with me and the boys, in the bunk house and lift a few. Mr. Barns allows us a bottle now and again for something special. I'll make sure you catch the boat on Monday—I promise.'' Max entreated his friend.

''It's a long way to the boat and I will need a ride. Tell ya what, if you pick me up Saturday, for the dance, I'll stay over with you and the boys. Sunday night you can take me to the boat that way you won't miss any work for Mr. Barns.'' John was grateful to his friend and it was agreed. The men rode on in silence. At Aaron's, the men said good night and Max turned his team toward home.

John went to bed quietly, as not to disturb Aaron and Sarah. He laid on his bed and stared at the rafters. How would he explain to these nice people how grateful he was to them or how attached to them he had become or how very much he had come to respect and like them both. How would he be able to refuse an offer most men can only dream of. They had suffered enough and he hated the thought of hurting them again. How could he explain his homesickness and his need to go home. He tossed and turned and eventually fell asleep.

The next day was Sunday and John and Aaron butchered a horse, as usual. They were too busy to talk but the question hung heavy between them.

After the evening meal, Aaron lit his pipe, went into the great room and placed another log on the fire. Sarah finished the dishes, hung her apron on the peg, took a doll from the shelf to work on and sat down in her chair.

John knew it was time to speak of his decision. He sat stiffly on the edge of the settee and began.

''You know I've been very happy here. I look to you as my second Ma'am and Paap. You've treated me like your son. What you offer is a dream-come-true to the right person. It's a big responsibility, too. You need some person with drive and imagination—a leader. I'm not like that. I've had only one dream in my life and you know what that is. I could never run this place the way it should be run. I appreciate your offer more than I can say but I'm not the one you want. I'm a dreamer, a story teller, an idler. You need a planner, an organizer and he will come to you, I'm sure. You need a man like Max, he was born to this life—it's second nature to him and he could do the job but not me. I'm sorry. If it's alright, I'll be heading home next Saturday. Max will pick me up for the dance and I'll stay over with him and he will take me to the boat.'' John was sweating profusely. That was the most difficult thing John ever had to do. He did not know where he found the words.

Sarah stood and touched his cheek, ''Yes, you are right, we will find another helper. We will NEVER find another son.''

"You won't change you mind, will you?" Aaron said resolutely. He took John's hand and held it in his own for a long moment. He tapped out his pipe and followed Sarah from the room.

The pain on their faces tore at John's heart. He choked back the lump in his throat and cried. When he gathered his composure, he went up the loft stairs to bed.

The week passed quickly as there was much to be done. Because he was leaving, a trip to the granary was important. They sheathed grass for thatch and fire, searched for firewood and put new shoes on the mules. John had grown very fond of Sampson and Delila. All this was done between butchering a horse and slopping the hogs.

Saturday came and John finished packing his grip. Sarah had washed and mended his clothes and gave him his likeness-doll to pack. He took another look around the loft room that had been his home for so long as to stamp it forever in his mind. He went down to the kitchen to join Aaron and Sarah for their last meal together.

The atmosphere was light and cheery as if all the crying had been done.

"I've packed your basket with all the things you like. Now eat your supper." Sarah smiled and placed the food on the table.

"Yes and a fruit jar of the 'Recipe' to ward off the chill—so she said." Aaron said with a wink.

"I will never forget you two and what you've done for me——I——"John's voice croaked.

"Now eat your food and smile, saddness hurts digestion—hand me another biscuit, please." Aaron interrupted John, trying to be jolly.

They ate in silence, but John's food stuck in his throat. He swallowed constantly, to dislodge the lump there.

"Sarah, three glasses and the jug, if you please, we must have a toast," Aaron said with a flourish, when they had finished eating. "A small sip will chase the night chill and send John off with good cheer," he went on.

Sarah filled the tiny glasses and they held them up for the toast.

"We will miss you, my son, God speed and may life be all that you expect! Za vashe zdorovye! L'Chaim!" Exclaimed Aaron.

The three drank the slivovitz in one gulp. John had forgotten how the sticky sweet liquid burned all the way down.

The wheels of Max's wagon crunched over the gravel lane and announced that departure time was at hand.

"Here's a hug for luck, John." Sarah stood on tiptoes and hugged his neck. John kissed her cheek and would remember she smelled of fresh starch, castile soap and vanilla.

"Goodby and thank you." He whispered in her ear.

Aaron flung his huge arms around John and kissed him on both cheeks, as a general rewarding a soldier. He smelled of fresh hay, pipe tobacco and slivovitz.

"Always wear dry socks and always tell the truth. If you ever change your mind—we are here.——." Aaron's voice trailed off. "Here's your pay and a little extra." Aaron handed John a small leather pouch.

"I wish I HAD been your son. I will always remember this place and you." He stuffed the pouch into his jeans.

John took his belongings and climbed onto the wagon with Max. He turned back when the wagon passed through the gate. Aaron and Sarah waved from the doorway. He waved back as long as he could make them out in the twilight.

Hot tears stung his eyes but he dared not allow his friend to see him cry. He never felt so alone. Max sensed the parting was sad and said nothing. The two men rode away from the farm without words.

Chapter Six

HANNAH'S HOUSE

After traveling several miles in silence John said, ''Max, you missed the turn at the fork.''

''No, I didn't miss it—we aren't going that way. Remember a while back, I told you about Hannah's House? Well, the boys and I've cooked up a surprise for you.''

''A surprise!—I don't feel like surprises tonight.'' John snapped.

''Aw, now don't get all riled up—we were going to have a party in the bunk house but figured OUR surprise would be better.'' Max tried to smooth John's feelings.

''I don't want any of your surprises!'' John barked.

''Yes you will, when you hear what we did.'' Max was delighted with the plan.

''Alright, out with it!'' John was losing his patience.

''We took up a collection for you!''

''For ME—what for?''

''You said you would go to Hannah's House if you had the price. Well, we got the price and took it there. Hannah said you would have a REAL good time on 8 dollars—that's how much we collected.''

''You did WHAT! You guys must be crazy to do that!'' John stormed.

''But you did say you would go if you had the price—remember?'' Max chided.

''Well, yes I did, but I don't feel like it tonight,'' hedged John.

''It's tonight or never ole' buddy, tomorrow you go away.'' Max reminded.

''How could you do that without asking me first? I thought you were my friends,'' John grunted angrily.

''It's all arranged. I'll drop you off there and pick you up. Some of the guys are already there—just to make sure you go IN. I'll take care of your bundles and be here when you come out. They didn't tell us how long you could stay for 8 dollars.'' Max teased his friend.

The thought of going to a whore house made the sweat bead on John's forehead. Max turned the wagon off the main road into the alley behind the train station to the edge of town. Hannah's house was large and stood out against the night sky.

Max pulled up and stopped alongside the white picket fence near the gate.

''Fine pal you are—go on—get out of here.'' John jumped down from the wagon seat and gestured to Max with his left hand.

Max grinned at John, urged the team on and drove away into the darkness.

John stood thoughtfully and studied the big house, the picket fence and the large circular driveway. There was something very grand about it. If you didn't know what it was, one would think it to be the residence of the mayor or the home of a successful business man.

John blushed red in the face at the thought of what Ma'am would say if she knew he was about to enter a whore house.

He tread the front porch steps slowly and turned to see if anyone was watching. Sure enough, two of the hands from the Barns spread were loafing at the hitching rail, trying to look inconspicuous.

At the door, he doffed his hat and mustered his courage. After all, it was 1909 and times had changed. A man of 17 could go in here if he wished.

He twisted the brass bell and waited.

Max had warned him Hannah had strict rules in her house and a 7 feet tall black giant to enforce them.

When the door was opened by the fearsome, half-naked giant, John was rooted to the spot by his terror. His predicated description was woefully inadequate. The big bouncer had a gold ring in one ear. His leather, sleeveless, open vest exposed strange scarrings on his body. The scars were chain-like and they circled his neck and waist, these were joined by a vertical scar chain that ran from his throat to his navel.

The giant grabbed John by the scruf of his neck, dragged him in and dropped him into a soft chair in a small, elaborate anteroom.

When the giant left the room, he turned at the heavily draped doorway, threw back his head and roared with laughter. The deafening sound shook the fancy chandelier on the ceiling and rattled the glassware on the tables. Still laughing, he disappeared behind the hanging.

Although John's friends had paid his way into this house he knew positively, they had never set foot inside themselves. It was the most elegant place John had ever seen. For that matter, it was more grand than anything he could imagine, such as a king's palace or a duke's castle. Naive boy that he was.

The upolstery, draperies and carpets were soft, velvety and plush. The room reeked of scents so delightful to him, he inhaled great gulps of air until it made him light-headed.

Hannah entered the room unnoticed and mused at the boy's childish antics.

''Hello, John. Your friends told me all about you. You're right on time, I like that. You can call me Hannah,'' she said softly.

She had startled him and John gaped at her.

''That IS your name, isn't it? John,'' she repeated.

John jumped to his feet.

''Uh, I, yes um, I mean it is ma'am, John Lansure, er, Miss Hannah.'' John was mortified by his stammering and he blushed beet red.

''It's alright, don't be shy, Hannah has picked a special girl for you. Hang you hat there and come along.'' She pointed to a nearby clothes rack and led him up a beautifully carved staircase.

John tried not to stare at her but failed. She looked like a queen to him, or as he believed a queen would look.

Her red hair fascinated him. His sister, Lu, had red hair but nothing like this color red. It was piled high on her head and was held in place with assorted jeweled combs and pins. In the lamplight, it sparkled gold and copper.

Her dress of pale green brocade was cinched so tight at the waist her creamy bosom bulged out at the top. The skirt was draped from front to back where it formed a bustle and under it were several pettycoats that rustled when she stepped. Her buckled silk slippers were heeled and the same pale shade of green as her dress.

John had never seen marabou feathers so he had no notion what comprised the white boa that covered her shoulders and fell nearly to the floor.

All sorts of gold, silver and pearl jewelry adorned her neck, hands and arms. At the end of the upstairs hall, she opened the door and ushered him in.

''John, this is Spanish Dee. Dee, this is John Lansure, he's all yours.'' She smiled at them, stepped out and closed the door.

In the room, more of the mind-dulling perfume filled his nostrils and his brain. He couldn't find a place for his hands so he jammed them into his pockets. He was tongued-tied and he slid along the wall as to make more distance between them.

''Come on, don't be bashful.'' Her voice was soft with a trace of accent.

''Uh, er, yes ma'am.'' John took a few steps closer to the huge bed where she stood.

''I'll help you,'' she said gently.

She slowly but expertly undressed him, one piece of clothing at a time. She was careful to touch and caress each vulnerable place on his body.

While she worked, John could remember nothing or think of anything except the sweet smell of her hair, the heady perfume that surrounded him or the frenzy building inside him.

She gently directed him onto the fancy bed. The cool sheets had no affect on the fires that raged inside his body.

Suddenly he jumped off the bed. He had long since stopped being embarrassed about his erection. He was about to have a climax and was powerless to stop it.

''I'm going to—I'm about to I can't help—,'' John shuttered.

''Of course you are, go right ahead.'' She picked a towel from a nearby chair, draped it over his penis, pulled him close to her and held him.

He clung to her. All the wild fires exploded into an inferno. The dam broke and the flood of passion rolled over him in waves again and again until his knees buckled.

He was jerked back to his senses by a warm, sticky trickle running down his thigh. His sweating body was stuck to her flimsy negligee.

He jumped away, cowered in a corner and mopped at the drips with the towel he had managed to retrieve.

So deep was his humiliation, he wished silently for death. He could not look at her face. He had a completely uncontrolled ejaculation.

''I'm—I'm sorry,'' he mumbled and hung his head in shamed embarrassment.

''Shush, don't say that. There is nothing to be sorry about. That's natural and I expected it. All is prepared. Come.'' She took his hand and they crossed the big room to a heavy drapery which she pushed open.

There was another small room. Inside sat an oversized bathtub partially filled with fragrant warm water.

She touched the water, dropped her wrap and stepped in.

''Come on, come on. The water is just right. I made it very hot so it would be ready for us now. Get in—I'll wash you and you will wash me,'' she coaxed playfully.

The water was warm and soothing. Dee was gentle, comforting and reassuring.

John soon relaxed and the two of them laughed and splashed while they washed and stroked each other.

The young man's pleasure was beyond words and it was plain to see, he was falling in love with his wondrous teacher—child-man that he was.

She was twice his age but it was inconsequential, her body was frail but youthful and her long black hair hung over her shoulders. To love-struck John she was beautiful.

Except for the horrible tragedy of Jenny, John had no knowledge of the art of lovemaking or of the carnal pleasures of man. Spanish Dee would change that for the 17-year-old.

''May I ask you something?'' John inquired hesitantly.

''Of course,'' she knew what was coming, they all asked the same question.

''How did you—I mean—why did you—,'' he stuttered.

''How did a girl like me get into a place like this—is that it? Do you really care HOW I got here?'' This boy appeared more interested than most.

''Yes, I do—please tell me.'' To Dee, he seemed genuinely sincere.

''Alright, if you want to hear—I'll tell you. I was born Bedelia Consuelo Margarita Maria Vargas, near Seveille, Spain. My parents came to Mexico when I was a child. My father Eduardo, bred prize fighting bulls for the ring and export. I grew up in a hacienda near Chiuahua. At sixteen I married my childhood sweetheart Juan Jose Valdez. He joined my father in the family's cattle business along with my brothers, Miguel and Carlos. The business prospered and Juanio and I were very happy.

A couple of years later, my father received an order for ten bulls and forty cows. The herd was to be delivered to Kansas to a cattleman there, for mix-breeding to strengthen his herd of longhorns.

I begged to go along. My mother had died sometime ago and I did not want to be left alone. My family was very reluctant because I was carrying our first child. The trip was long and dangerous but eventually I was allowed to go.

The cattle drive was very exciting to me. I had my own horse to ride and a wagon for Juanio and me to sleep in. To me, it was another honeymoon. The countryside was lovely. The days were bright and full of excitement and the nights were dark, warm and full of love. My life was complete.

At the Cimarron River crossing, my life ended.

The rustlers attacked in the night. They killed my Juanio, my father, my brothers and shot or ran off the drovers.

Shooting was not ALL they did to me. After struggling with and being raped by four of them, I fell unconscious. I was not aware I had been shot twice.

Hannah's group accidently happened upon our grizzly scene at daybreak. I was barely alive but breathing. I had given birth to our stillborn child.

The sheriff of Twin Forks had forced them to move on and it was unsafe for them to wait for me to recover.

They buried my dead, gathered what was left of my belongings, made a place for me in their wagons, had Sam carry me there and took me along. My chances of survival were slim to none, in any case.

Faces, voices and sounds drifted in and out of my dreams; The thunder of a cattle stampede; gunfire and my own screaming voice; a black giant who carried me; a strange doctor; the earthy conversation of several women; jolting over the prairie in a wagon; a special calm voice and gentle touch. It all faded in and out while I fought to live. The bullets in my right chest had been deflected by my ribs and were close together. Cherry Pie simply cut them out but he could not fix a collapsed lung or the damage to my insides.

One day, I opened my eyes to Hannah's cool touch on my face. I was alive. They had saved my life. . . . .''

Abruptly, Dee wiped away the tears that had gathered in her eyes, swallowed the frog in her throat and grabbed two towels from the rack.

''Come on—get up I'm cold—the tub water is cold—let's get warm in bed.'' She handed a towel to John and they dried themselves and got into bed.

''What a miserable time you have had. I'm sorry I dredged up old wounds.'' John felt clumsy and intrusive. He drew her close to him.

''That was long, long ago in the past. My health has never been good since and I hated myself. I felt lonely and deserted, useless, used and DIRTY. When I found I would live, I prayed to die.

Hannah and the girls changed that. I was too weak to work but one day Hannah brought me a set of buttons to sew onto a blouse of hers. The girls brought me broken straps and split seams to mend. Little by little, I began to feel useful and needed. I became the house seamstress and sometimes I fixed their hair.

Many months later when I had recovered as well as I would, I asked Hannah if I could become one of the girls. She said she would be pleased to have me but wondered if I had the vigor the job required. She said a good GIRL had to be like a good race horse and have three things; Heart, Strength and Stamina. As you know I have none of those things. However she said, occasionally, a father would bring his young son in to be taught the ways or a green youngster would come in, like yourself. This was to be my job. Hannah knew no harm would come to me and Big Sam was always near. Although my condition was delicate, I'm well enough for that.

Cherry Pie did the best he knew how but he is not a REAL sawbones. He got his learn'n from back street knifings, barroom brawls and a revolution in his native Scotland. That hat he wears—with the topknot on it—he never takes off. The cloth is the tartan of his clan—sort of a family brand—so-to-speak. He doesn't talk much but he has been with Hannah for years. No one knows when he came or why he stays.'' Dee moved in John's arms. ''Now that's enough talk—you didn't come here to hear all this.''

''Yes, I did—I mean—I'm glad to hear—I'm glad to know all about this place and you. Everything interests me.'' John was pleased to hear the stories.

What about that big Giant. How did he become Hannah's bodyguard?'' John asked.

''Now that's a VERY long story—surely you don't want to hear that, too!''

''Yes I do—please tell me.'' John coaxed. He smoothed her hair and held her close.

''Hannah said Big Sam was a Christmas present from Cherry Pie years and years ago. We have to go back a long time to a Christmas Eve on the San Francisco waterfront, I don't know the year. . . . .''

The snow fell steadily on the water front streets of San Francisco in the 1880's. It was Christmas Eve and people moved about the streets, chatted and did last minute shopping.

Hannah's Place was the best brothel on the front. It was clean, the girls had no disease and she allowed no rough stuff.

Wildigan Spotsworth was Hannah Zopley's helper, right-hand, confidant and friend. He was always called Cherry Pie. He could cook, bake, chop wood, drive the team, lay a fire and when necessary, he set broken bones or stitched up cuts. No one knew why he was called Cherry Pie but it was worth your life to call him Wildigan Spotsworth. Few knew his name anyway and all called him Cherry Pie.

As usual, Cherry Pie carted the ashes to the trash bin in the alley around closing time at Hannah's.

Rummaging around in the trash was a skinny, half-grown black child of nine or ten. He had no coat and his shirt was tattered and dirty. His stove-pipe pants did not cover his scrawny legs and he was barefoot.

When the child saw Cherry Pie he bolted but could not escape the man's grasp. The boy, weak and thin, stopped struggling and began to tremble and whimper.

Cherry Pie realized the boy was half-starved and frightened. He talked to him but found he did not understand or speak English. The words the child spoke were of a language unknown to Cherry Pie. The man could not leave the starving child in the alley so he carried him into the kitchen at Hannah's.

At once, the boy huddled near the stove for warmth and continued to whimper.

In the kitchen, Ruby, one of Hannah's girls was making a pot of tea.

"Hurry Ruby, find Hannah, we've got a little problem here," urged Cherry Pie.

"I can see that—and smell him, too. The poor starved kid needs a bath." Ruby left her tea to steep and went to find Hannah.

Cherry Pie put some of the stew on the stove into a bowl and tried to feed the child with a spoon. The boy shrunk from him and would not eat.

"What have we here!" Hannah came into the kitchen.

"I found him digging in the garbage for food. Couldn't leave him out in the cold to freeze or starve—now could we? It be'in Christmas and all." Cherry Pie held up the stew on a spoon but the boy refused to eat.

"We won't hurt ya lad, have a bit of bread." Hannah smiled and her voice was soft and reassuring. She knelt on one knee and handed the boy a piece of bread from the table. She held it close to him. He snatched it from her hand, stuffed it all into his mouth and gobbled it down.

"Here—here—not so fast—you'll be sick," Hannah spoke quietly. She handed him another piece, this time she buttered it.

After much coaxing and talking, the boy's fears subsided. They managed to get him to eat the stew from the spoon. After three bowls of stew, half loaf of bread and a pitcher of milk, the exhausted child moved nearer the stove and huddled there. Hannah wondered silently, who would throw away a child.

"What are we going to do with him? We can't turn him out in this weather—look at his feet—they look frostbit' to me," said Hannah who moved in closer to examine the boy's feet.

"I could give him a bath and put him to sleep on the cot in the pantry. When I get him clean, I'll fix his feet," suggested Cherry Pie.

"Will ya look at that ragamuffin!" Exclaimed Ruby when she returned with two more of Hannah's girls; Sadie and Clara.

"A dirty ragamuffin at that," laughed Sadie.

"He's a pickaninny" scoffed Clara.

Fu Chow, the Chinese cook came into the kitchen with a tray piled high with dirty dishes for the sink and scolded all for invading his kitchen. He notified every one the kitchen was his domain and gave the distinct impression intruders needed his permission to enter. He looked disapprovingly at the child.

"Stop that! Girls, go about your business and leave this to me and Cherry Pie. Fu Chow, please bring a bath and towels," Hannah said sternly.

The girls sat down at the table to enjoy their tea and Fu Chow left the room, grumbling in Chinese. He understood English and could speak it but did so rarely.

"All right Cherry Pie, at least he can stay the night and tomorrow we will figure out what to do with him," she said thoughtfully. Something in the child's huge sad eyes tugged at Hannah's heart.

At Cherry Pie's urgings, the cowering child followed him into the pantry for his bath.

A few minutes passed and Cherry Pie shouted from the small room,

"Hannah! Hannah! Come quick!"

"I jumped a foot, Cherry Pie, what is it?" Hannah ran to the pantry.

"Will you look at THIS—did ya ever see such scars!" he said.

"Dear God, they look like they were put there—on purpose!" she said.

"They WERE—with a very sharp knife—when he was a baby—I'd guess." he said.

"Who would DO such a horrible thing to a baby," said Hannah at closer examination.

"I'll bet you money this young'in came from Africa on one of those ships in the harbor. They beat him and he jumped ship. His back has the whip marks. He must be a prince or king where he came from—why else would he be marked like that." Cherry Pie was fascinated by the scars that resembled a chain. One circled his throat and one circled his waist. The two were joined by one that ran vertically from neck to navel.

"No matter now, get him cleaned and into bed. One of your shirts will do for sleep. Tomorrow we will worry about clothes for him. Good-night Cherry Pie." Hannah left Cherry Pie to tend the child.

"Do you think he will try to run if I leave him alone here to sleep," Cherry Pie called after Hannah.

"If he runs—he runs, we can't hold him if he wants to go now can we," she called back.

Cherry Pie washed the dirty boy, dried him carefully, examined and treated his frostbitten feet—it wasn't serious. The shirt he gave the boy to sleep in dwarfed the child but it was warm. He tucked the urchin into bed, covered him carefully and as Cherry Pie watched, the child fell sound asleep.

Christmas Day dawned bright and sunny. The sun glistened on the new snow like tiny diamonds.

The boy slept soundly on his cot in the pantry. Cherry Pie built a warm fire in the cookstove and Fu Chow grumbled in Chinese while he beat the pancake batter. His long queue swung back and forth as he moved. Soon the kitchen warmed and smelled of perking coffee and sizzling bacon.

Hannah bounced into the kitchen. She was pretty in a white nightgown-negligee ensemble. It was made of flimsy white gauze, ruffled all over and trimmed in white lace and silk ribbons. The huge mandarin-style sleeves fell nearly to the floor and the negligee was open down the front but tied at the waist.

Her long red hair fell loosely over her shoulders and she smelled of soap, talcum powder and face cream. Hannah was bathed but not made up and was quite beautiful. She threw her arms around Cherry Pie and kissed him with a loud smack.

''Merry Christmas, ya ole horsethief,'' she jammed a tiny box into his hand, ''this is for your hat. How do you like my new outfit—the girls had it made special for me—pretty, huh?'' She spun around on her toes, threw up her arms and in the bright sunlight from the windows, she looked like a white angel floating from heaven.

''You are a bonny lass, ma' girl, bonny. Me thanks ta' ya.'' He blushed to his hairline at her kiss and sat down at the table to open his gift.

The child came out of the pantry unnoticed. When Hannah spun around in the sunlight he ran to her, dropped to the floor on his knees, kissed her feet and the hem of her dress.

''Malaika, Malaika, Malaika,'' he chanted, over and over again.

''Here now get up, we will have none of this,'' Hannah said softly. She lifted the boy from the floor, sat down in her rocker by the stove and took him onto her lap.

''What do you think of THAT—I guess the child likes me.'' She rocked and patted the orphan.

''Aye, he does that. Wonder what he's say'in—strange words. Guess we will never know. . . . Oh!'' Cherry Pie's eyes grew large when he opened the box.

''It's made out of GOLD wire—in the shape of your Scotland.'' Hannah was proud of her gift to her friend. ''The ruby hanging on it is worth the exact fare to Scotland. If you ever want to go home you will always have passage money.''

''Me soul it's that grand. I can pin it on—it has a clasp and all.—It's—I'm—thank'y'.'' Tears glistened in his eyes and words failed him.

Fu Chow served the food as the girls came into the kitchen. Ruby, Sadie, and Clara chatted amiably with Molly and Zoe and all sat around the table. They examined Cherry Pie's gift and talked about the child who snuggled on Hannah's lap.

''He's so thin,'' said Zoe.

''You gonn'a keep that ragamuffin?'' asked Ruby.

''What will you do with a child—HERE!'' exclaimed Irish Molly.

"At least he's clean now," said Sadie.

"He's still a pickaninny," sniffed haughty Clara.

"I hadn't decided what to do with him 'til you all came in here. Now I know. I'm going to keep him. He likes me and I always wanted a child of my own—which I can never have—so he's mine. He likes Cherry Pie and he will learn to know you." Hannah stated flatly.

Fu Chow growled in Chinese and cleared the table but not before Hannah stuffed a hearty meal into the child on her lap.

"He's still a pickaninny!" Clara had to make the remark again.

"That's enough! I will keep him. This boy is now my adopted son and if any of you can't face that—you can move on. If you stay, he's to be treated like family, cared for and helped in all things. I will teach him his letters and his numbers and you all will help. Be surprised how good you will feel when you think of some one other than yourselves. He will learn the manly things from Cherry Pie and Fu Chow will teach him the necessaries of the kitchen," Hannah decreed.

A wave of Chinese grumbling went up at the sink as expected but Fu Chow's bark was worse than his bite. The other members of the group murmured among themselves but agreed to comply.

"There's something else. No one except ourselves must know he is here—for his own safety. He will remain away from the front rooms and you tell no one. Now, THIS," Hannah carefully removed the child's shirt and exposed his whipped back and the strange scars on his body.

"Holy Jesus," Ruby caught her breath and swore in her rough way.

"Mother of God," Zoe said under her breath.

"Saint's preserve us," Molly said in her Irish brogue.

"Poor darlin' little pickaninny," Clara drooled in her best Southern drawl.

"Who would treat even a Nigger boy that way!" Sadie was horrified.

"Those marks were cut into his flesh when he was a very tiny baby—maybe newborn. He was marked this way because he's special; A prince or king, that way there could be no mistake. To us he may be just a deserted, forlorn waif but some place in this world, he's very important." Cherry Pie explained the scars the best way he knew how.

"Do you all understand why we must keep him our secret? If he did come from a ship in the harbor, someone may be looking for him. I will not allow them to take him back to be whipped and starved, is that clear?" Hannah was resolute.

The girls touched and gawked at the boy. He huddled closer to Hannah but appeared accustomed to the probing. It had been done before.

"Cherry Pie, you surely gave Hannah a A CHRISTMAS PRESENT this time!" joked Ruby in her coarse way.

They had a good laugh and scurried around to find proper clothing for the new addition to the family. The boy said nothing except the word Malaika which sounded like Ma-lee-ka. He repeated it again and again and watched Hannah closely.

The most difficult problem with the boy would be communication. Hannah would tap her chest with her hand and repeat her name over and over and hoped the child would understand. She made the same gesture with Cherry Pie and Fu Chow with little or no response.

A few days later, in one of those learning sessions, the boy tapped his chest and said, ''Beegasaam.'' He repeated the word and the gesture.

''Glory be, he understands! Beegasaam—you are pretty small to be Big Sam—but if that is your name, Big Sam it is. Hannah was delighted he understood and had great hopes for his ability to learn.

The years passed quickly and Sam learned his letters and numbers. Cherry Pie and the girls read to him and helped him with the simple tasks of life. He responded well and quickly. Hannah often read him stories from the bible.

One day, while he was thumbing through the pages, Sam became very excited and pointed to a picture in the book.

''Malaika, Malaika!'' He exclaimed enthusiastically.

Cherry Pie came into the kitchen with a load of firewood and heard Sam shout.

''What is it, Sam?''

''Malaika—Miss Hannah is Malaika.'' He exclaimed and pointed to the two ascending angels drifting in the clouds, on the page.

''Well, don't that beat all! You thought Hannah was an ANGEL FROM HEAVEN!''

''Miss Hannah protect me—save me from Cap'n Eli—she won't let NOBODY hurt me.''

When Sam learned enough English to be understood, he told about the missionaries who taught him of the Angels who protect us.

He and his mother were kidnapped and his father was killed. They were taken from the village and sold to Arab traders.

Sam's father was a king of the Watusi tribe and Sam was born a prince. To mark his status, the cuttings were made into his flesh at birth, assuring the line of succession.

When they were taken Sam guessed he was about five years old.

On the ship, his mother was made servant to the Arab captain and the sailors who used and abused her. After many months, Sam's mother tried to stab one of the sailors who raped her. She was too weak to succeed and the sailor killed her.

Big Sam was sold from an Egyptian slave market to a Portuguese sea captain as a cabin boy who considered him an oddity, a freak and whipped him just to see the boy flinch. He was fed only at the captain's whim and never enough.

When the ship dropped anchor in the San Francisco harbor, Sam waited his chance and came ashore. He wandered around the streets and alleys for several days before Cherry Pie found him.

Ten years later, Sam had grown to almost seven feet. He was well-muscled, lean and hard. He worked around Hannah's house. He helped Cherry Pie, ran errands for the girls, carried heavy loads for Fu Chow and made sure all the men who patronized Hannah's House did so with gentlemanly good grace. At no time was he far from Hannah. He was classically overprotective of Hannah and all who knew him, were aware of it and found him interesting and quaint. However, strangers found him imposing even menacing.

One night a group of noisy, unruly foreign sailors stomped into Hannah's bent on rowdyism. One demanded Hannah's attentions and grabbed her. She expertly slid from his grasp and encouraged him to accept one of the other girls. He gripped her shoulder roughly and his fingers dug into her soft flesh. She jerked away. His fingers tore away several pieces of her dress and his fingernails left three bloody scratches on her skin.

Big Sam raged. His body stiffened and his muscles twitched as a tiger prepares to spring.

Sam raised the man over his head and jammed the sailor's body over his huge knee. The sailor's spine snapped as easily as a small twig. He died instantly. A hush fell over the place as all stood stupefied. Sam allowed the dead man to slide from his knee to the floor in a heap. Hannah was the first to move.

"Get Sam out of here and go get Duffy," Hannah whispered to Cherry Pie, who ushered him out the back way.

Duffy Boggs was the cop on the beat she had been paying protection money for years. He managed to keep her in business and out of trouble by overlooking small problems.

The sailors carried the dead one out and in a foreign language, indicated they would return with help.

Hannah called the girls to clear the house by pretending it was closing time.

When Cherry Pie returned with Duffy, he had explained the situation.

"Ya've done it this time lass. Even I can't fix a killin'." He cupped her chin with his hand and kissed her cheek while he examined the gouges on her shoulder.

"Ya got to help me Duf, Sam's my son. He didn't mean to kill that man but you know how he is sometimes." Hannah pressed a roll of bills into his hand. She was visibly shaken.

"I know lass, I know but the sailor is from that Greek ship in the harbor and the captain will want answers," explained Duffy. He studied the money in his hand.

"We will leave—that's it, we will pack up and leave town," stammered Hannah.

"Tell ya what, the harbor master is me third cousin. Can ya be gone from here in three days? I can delay the investigation for three days—that's all. Cherry Pie, take this money and go buy two of the biggest wagons you can find. That's the best I can do for ya, lass. God speed." The big man had been secretly in love with Hannah for years.

"Duffy Boggs you're an ole fraud. Under all that bluster beats a heart of gold. Thank you my friend." Hannah hugged his neck and kissed his cheek.

"Gwan now, off with ya—times a waste'n." The big policeman blushed to his hat.

"Well, ya heard the man—get busy! Cherry Pie, see if Fu Chow wants to join us, if so take him with you to help bring the wagons. Girls, who wants to go or stay? You have a choice. I've no idea where we are going or how far but we are headed East. You can take one trunk apiece—no more—now git!" Hannah regained her composure and barked the orders. All scurried.

Everyone agreed to go and in three days the wagons rolled out heaped high with furniture, trunks, food and people. Fu Chow grumbled in Chinese for a hundred miles at having to leave his cook stove behind. . . . .

Spanish Dee stirred in John's arms and he was brought back to the present day.

"You know the rest, they found me and we came here. I'm the only one of the original girls left. Some died, others married and the rest just drifted away. Cherry Pie and Fu Chow are old but Hannah is ageless. Now I'm not going to do any more talking—come here." Spanish Dee drew him to her.

Their bodies were warm and John felt his inner coals begin to glow brighter and brighter. Dee felt it too. With her lips close to his she whispered, "If you want to make love to a woman, first you have to taste her, like this." She kissed him gently, explored his lips with hers and followed each curve with her tongue. John responded instantly by grabbing her urgently. He kissed her hard and his body demanded hers.

"No, no not yet, you have to taste ME now and learn to control yourself. Now, taste me like I showed you." she insisted and drew away slightly.

He leaned over and kissed her awkardly at first, again and again, gaining more confidence each time.

"See how easy it is?" she breathed between his kisses. "Now taste my cheeks, eyes and ears. Like this." Her parted lips caressed his skin and her cool tongue left moist traces.

John convulsed and quivered with delightful excitement. The exquisite pleasure was beyond all fantasy.

Not yet! It's your turn to taste me," she scolded playfully.

John complied and soon learned there was almost as much fun in tasting as there was in being tasted.

By the time the two had sampled each other to the navel, John was again fighting to keep control.

Dee nibbled her way up John's thigh to his groin. When the palpitating boy groaned with impending ecstasy she knew it was time. She quickly covered his body with hers and allowed him to slip deep within her.

He engulfed her with searching lips and hands. His frenzied rapture coursed through his body. Three convulsive thrusts and it was done. The passion died and they lay spent in each others arms.

She shifted her weight from his body. When she stirred he whispered,

"I love you," and fell into a satisfied sleep.

John slept less than an hour but awakened completely rested and refreshed. He reached for Dee in the big bed. She was gone. He sat bolt upright.

"Here I am," she said softly.

She was seated at her dressing table brushing her beautiful black hair.

John crossed the room to her. He kissed the top of her head and whispered in her ear, "You are wonderful!"

"Of course I am," she said facetiously.

The old adage repeated again, "The schoolboy falls in love with the teacher."

"Bathe quickly and we'll eat. Sam brought fresh water and food while you slept. Afterwards, I'll see what you have learned and teach you the rest."

He washed hurriedly and she continued to brush her hair. Both were quiet.

John and Dee sat at a small table by the window to eat.

"You hungry?" she asked.

"Starved," was the quick answer.

They ate bread and cheese with red wine in silence.

"John, you asked about me—how I came to be here. Why did you ask? Do you really care? Most people don't,—they look down on us. We are considered riffraff—lowlife—a nuisance to the town. They don't care if we live or die. Respectable people snub us and those who pay to come here treat us like dirt. They don't seem to know or care that we are just ordinary people with mothers and fathers and family. We have feelings—we can suffer too. You are different from those that usually come to me.'' Dee sipped the wine thoughtfully.

''I asked because I do care. I'm interested in you, this house and the people in it. My Paap says there is usually a reason for everything that happens—if you just take time to look for it. Don't judge a man 'til you've walked a mile in his shoes. That applies to most everything.'' John's pride in his father was very apparent. He finished his food and wiped his mouth with his napkin.

''You are very nice, John Lansure, well brought up too. How did you come to this place?'' Dee was careful not to appear inquisitive.

''It was a going away present from my friends. I leave here for home in the morning. I said I would come here if I had the price and they chipped in. I should've kept my big mouth shut—nearly lost my nerve at the door. Dee I'm not a bit sorry I came. You are wonderful—I love you.'' John was self-conscious.

''Of course you do—silly boy—the student always fall for the teacher.''

''You're making fun of me.''

''A little. You must not be so serious. You have never had a woman before have you, John.'' She was amused but not ridiculing.

''Yes I have—no I haven't—not exactly—not like this.'' John stuttered with embarrassment, ''There was a girl back home but it wasn't like this.''

John's heart sank every time he remembered Jenny. His guilt never let him rest and his face revealed his anguish.

''What's the matter, you two have a fight or something?''

''Yes and she died. It was my fault.'' John remembered.

''I'm sorry I mentioned it, it's none of my business but I doubt it's your fault. Sometimes it helps to talk. Do you want to tell me about it?'' Dee asked.

For the first time since the tragedy happened, John had someone to tell the heartbreaking tale. No one but John himself knew the true reason why Jenny Blair took her own life.

Before he realized what was happening, John poured out the tragic story of Jenny to Spanish Dee. He told how he and Jenny had been childhood sweethearts and had no secrets from each other. How he planned to go from their village and become a railroader. He had no desire to be a miner like his brother Bruce, or a stonemason like his father. She also knew he would not be deterred.

One day when Jenny knew it would no longer be a secret, she told John she was carrying his child. John disclosed to Dee his panic and his denial. How he shouted at Jenny and denied the child was his when he knew full well it was his. How he accused Jenny of trying to trap him and keep him from his railroad dream. And how pitiful she looked when his contemptible words crushed her spirit and broke her heart. Jenny never answered his untrue, unfair tirade. Tears of grief and disbelief ran down her cheeks and she fled from him in dispair.

John was shocked at his hateful ability to unleash such an untrue venomous tongue-lashing. It was several days before his panic passed and he could think out the problem.

John made up his mind to return to Jenny's and beg her forgiveness and ask her to marry him. He would take back all those terrible words he had said and reassure her he loved her very much.

Before he could return to Jenny's, John's father, Jimmy, told his son they must have a talk. Jimmy had just returned from Blair's Mill and had terrible news. They had found Jenny's body hanging from a rafter in the mill. Jenny had hanged herself.

"Oh, Madre Dios," Dee sighed under her breath and crossed herself.

"See, I told you it was my fault." John's guilt choked him and his eyes stung with tears. The old agony was back.

"I couldn't eat—I got sick—I wanted to die. My family did not understand what was wrong with me and I could not bring myself to tell them. If anyone knew or suspected Jenny's condition, nothing was said. My Ma'am and Paap worried about my poor health and decided to send me to a drier climate away from our damp valley. My favorite Uncle Tom, lived in Cushing, Oklahoma. The climate was dry and ranch life was healthy. I regained my health but eventually I grew homesick. On the way home some mishaps landed me at the railhead flat broke. Aaron Jacobs came along and hired me and I've been there since spring." John hung his head under the secret burden he bore.

"You can't go on blaming yourself. We've all done things we're sorry for, sometimes we hurt the people we love most. You tried to make things right. Are you going to continue to punish yourself because you were too late? How could you know she might do something like that? God will forgive Jenny but you must forgive yourself if you expect to survive. It's done and you can't change any of it. You have to accept it, forgive yourself and never make the same mistake again. If you don't, you will be a mental cripple all your life. Learn from it, don't be hasty, think before you speak and try not to judge others to harshly. A great man once said, "That which does not take my life, gives me strength." Come now this is too sad. We are here to enjoy so come to bed. Show me what you have learned.'' Dee closed the subject and her mood turned to frivolity.

''I can't—not just now,'' John hesitated.

''Yes you can. You are young and strong and you will.'' She urged him onto the bed and drew him close to her. ''We will taste each other again.'' She had infinite persuasion. Soon it was love and be loved. All else was blotted out.

John's fingers were no longer clumsy on her skin but light, caressing and tender. When the time was right—and he knew when—he covered her body with his. They joined as one and their rhythmic motion gave yet another added dimension to John's ecstasy. It brought new rapturous sensations from deep within him. Again the fingers of ice and fire clawed at his insides releasing waves of passionate frenzy. The thrusts and it was done. He lay heaving and spent. Soon he slept.

He awakened and searched for her. She was standing by the window.

''Hurry now, I've let you sleep too long. It will be light soon and you must go. You learned well and you will not forget.'' She helped him with his clothes.

''I'll be back again,'' he promised as he dressed.

Spanish Dee did not answer because she knew he would not return. The learning is but once.

They kissed 'goodbye' and she watched him disappear down the stairs. She saw the boy come in and the man go out. He was different somehow, a special man with a special destiny but she would never know what a profound influence she would have on his future.

At the foot of the stairs, Hannah was waiting.

''Ah John, I will see you out but before you go, lift a cup with Hannah, will ya?'' She poured two cups of steaming coffee from a pot on the tray in the anteroom, laced them with a blood colored liquid from a decanter, also on the tray and handed one to John.

''Umm that's good, tastes like cherries, and hits the spot, thank you.'' John drank enthusiastically.

''It's just a little sloe gin but since I don't allow booze, I tell them it's Miss Hannah's Revitaliz'en Tonic. It sure gives the fancies to a cup of java.'' Hannah's throaty laughter was infectious. They returned the empty cups to the tray.

''Come along.'' Hannah handed him his hat and stepped out on the porch with John. She drew in a great breath of the fall air and said, ''I love the early morning. It's a new beginning every day. It's a new beginning for you too, John. The learning can only be done once. The water runs under the bridge once—so to speak. Now you put what you've learned to use. You practice and remember.''

John blushed red. Hannah noticed and cupped his chin in her fingers and went on. ''You remember all that Spanish Dee taught you but NEVER come here again.'' She held his chin and kissed his cheek lightly.

''NEVER come back! Why? I thought this place was a —'' exclaimed a shocked John.

''You're right it is,'' interrupted Hannah, ''but it is not for you. We taught you all we can and now you must move on. This place is for rowdies, field hands and n'er-do-wells. You are not one of them. Put what you have learned to use where and when your life demands but don't come back here. Your life is ahead of you. Sure, you'll make mistakes, we all do, but learn from them boy, learn from them. It says somewhere, ''Give me the courage to change the things I must, the strength to accept the things I can't change and the wisdom to tell the difference''. or somethin' like that—you get my mean'in?'' Hannah was suddenly flustered by her inappropriate philosophic emoting.

''I guess I do but I will never forget you, Big Sam or this place. I have special feelings for Spanish Dee and I told her I'd be back.'' John insisted.

''Dee understands how you feel and she knows you won't be back,'' Hannah assured him.

''I will always have special feelings for her.'' John was strangely sad.

''We know you will and Dee would say 'Via Con Dios, John, where ever you go.'' Hannah kissed his cheek again, stepped into the house and closed the door behind her.

John made his way to the road and turned to have one last long look at Hannah's House. He felt an inexplicable loss. He had given little but gained much from those genuinely propitious people who lived in that wholly unlikely place.

Could the old adage be true? 'Sometimes even a dunghill sprouts a rosebush'?

John knew he would never return and why. He was serene, complete and a man. Spanish Dee taught him to be a man in more ways than one. His carnal appetite had been honed to a fine edge and he could face Jenny's tragic death with understanding. He would learn to live with it and perhaps in time, come to terms with his guilt.

In his lifetime, John would not forget a gift from friends that became a treasure.

Chapter Seven

HOME FOR CHRISTMAS

John walked away from Hannah's house with mixed emotions and a strange thoughtfulness. He was a man and a better human being for having gone there. The world is full of learnings and lessons. John had but scratched the surface and his life changed over and over in only a few months.

Max's team and wagon waited at the end of the alley and John nudged his sleeping friend in the wagon bed.

"Max wake up, Max." John shook his friend.

"Where you been all this time?" quizzed the sleepy man. "I came here TWICE before this," he scolded.

"I've been right here—all the time."

"All this time! What you been doin' 'til this hour? You haven't the strength—I mean—so long!—"

"It's not like you think. I met a girl and we talked a lot." John interrupted.

"Talked—you talked! We sent you in there to—to—."

"Well, that too. But the talk was the most important—to me anyway."

"Wait 'til I tell the guys—you talked—they'll kill me!" Max spurred up the team and they moved down the alley and out of town.

"They are interesting people. They are not like what you hear at all. If the guys had been there—they would know what it's like. They've NEVER been there—have they?" Jack asked.

"Earl has—he's the only one and he won't tell us anything about it. That's the truth. Everybody knows a little bit about Hannah, Big Sam,

Cherry Pie and the girls but nobody knows any details—like where they came from or who they really are. Earl won't tell about Big Sam or Hannah or maybe he doesn't know anything. I 'spose you won't tell either—'sat it?''

''That's it. It's an interesting place run by interesting people who do interesting things. Unless you go—you will never know and maybe not even then. That's the way it is.'' John could never explain Hannah's house to anyone or did he wish to.

The two men fell silent but for different reasons. Max was disappointed not to hear the details and John was full to running over with his pleasure and thoughts.

At the river dock, Max reined up and waited. They were early for the boat.

John dug into his food basket and came up with the mason jar of Sarah's Recipe.

''My friend, have a swig with me. It will be long—if ever we meet again. You were a comfort to me when I was homesick to death. I will miss your nonsense and your wisdom.'' John handed the opened glass jar to Max who drank choked and coughed.

''It burns all the way down but there is something comforting about it.'' Max observed.

''Sure is. Sarah will never know how comforting it REALLY is. Keep well. If you ever come East look me up. The latch will always be out for you.'' John took a swig from his jar and replaced it in the basket.

The boat arrived and the dock came alive with activity.

The men shook hands and thumped each other on the back.

The whistle screamed. John went up the plank and found a place for his bindle. He waved to his friend and the boat moved away from the dock.

The paddle wheel interested John and soon he was talking to crew members who allowed him to examine the huge engines that turned them. It was a great mystery to the young man how the operation worked. How the wood burned making a hot fire to heat a great boiler full of water into steam that hissed along the pipes to make pressure enough to turn the great wheel. He learned very quickly.

The time passed quickly and again the deafening sound of the whistle announced their arrival at Hutchinson. John thanked the crew for their help and kindness, took his belongings and went ashore.

John looked around the town, found the stage office and bought a ticket to Newton.

He had time to kill before his stage departed. He stashed his bindle under a bench in the stage office and went out to look around the town.

Hutchinson was not big but it was the halfway mark between Great Bend and Wichita and growing fast. The river, the railroad and the stage line made it a busy hub.

John could have taken the train from here but decided a trip on a stage might be interesting and he could learn from it. It may be the last chance he would ever have to ride the stage. Besides, Aaron warned him never to pass up an opportunity or a chance to do or learn something different. Sometimes it would be successful; sometimes it would not. In both cases you would learn and that is life.

He made his way along the street and took in the sights. Thinking of Aaron made him remember the pouch he had jammed into his pocket when he left them. It was still there. A busy street is no place to show a pouch of money. John had learned that bitter lesson.

He ducked between two buildings and away from prying eyes. He retrieved the pouch, loosened the ties and poured the coins into his hand. Gold! More gold than a king's ransom. Two-four-six-John counted sixteen coins in all. Six were United States mint but six were different—they were Russian coin.

John was struck dumb. He held a fortune in his hand. When Aaron gave him the pouch, he told John it was his pay and a bit more, but John paid little attention. A bit more! Aaron and Sarah had given him wealth no matter that he did not stay to be their son. Did he mean so much that they would share their gold with him? He steadied himself by leaning on the rough board building. He felt giddy and lightheaded. John wasn't given to swooning but this was a new experience. He gathered his composure and stepped out into the busy street.

He searched up and down the row of buildings until he found a sign that read ASSAY OFFICE. If anyone could explain his gold, it would be the assayer.

He made his way to the assay office and went in.

It smelled of metal and chemicals and a man of forty or so, turned from his work and said, "Something I can do for ya?"

"Yes sir, I have these gold coins and I need you to tell me about them." John said.

"Saint's alive boy, that's a fortune! Ya didn't steal it, did ya?" The man asked.

"No I did not! It's my pay and a gift from friends. I never saw gold coins like these before and these came from Russia." John explains.

The two men study the coins. After a moment, the assayer began to speak.

"These two are twenty dollar double eagles, these four are ten dollar eagles and these are five dollar half eagles. Boy! That's a round hundred dollars! As for these other ones, I've never seen them before. Just a minute." He said. The assayer placed one of the Russian coins on a small scale on his work bench. He placed a ten dollar eagle on the other balance tray and they balanced perfectly. The Russian coin was larger but weighed the same.

"They weigh the same as our ten dollar eagle. If you want to sell them, I'll give you ten dollars apiece for them." The assayer handed John his coins.

"Oh, I don't want to SELL them, I just wondered what they were worth. I told you they were a gift and I never saw gold coins of any kind." Do I owe you something for your time—I appreciate your telling me about them." John explained.

"Naw, but if you ever want to sell them, remember me." The man said.

"Thank you very much for your help and I sure will." John could see no reason to tell the man he was leaving town with a lengthy explanation.

Outside he headed toward the stage office. The realization that he was a man of property had not fully sunk in.

At the designated time, he was ready to board the coach.

"Young fella! Ya want to ride up here with me?" called the stagecoach driver from up top.

"Sure, thanks," John scrambled up after his bindle and dropped onto the seat beside the driver.

"Can you handle a Henry?" Asked the driver who pointed to the rifle in a sheath attached to the kick board of the coach near their feet.

"Never have, just a Winchester and a Remington on the ranch," answered John.

"That 'ill do. The old Chief died and the young bucks are feel'in their oats. Been hit-en-run fights on the farmers other side of station Number 2. We get passed there, we'll be all right." The driver explained.

"Aiee Up—Aiee-Up!" Shouted the driver. He cracked his long whip near the ear of the lead horse. "Get up there Mose, Ike, get up there!" The coach lurched forward, the six-up strained in the harness and the carriage rolled out of town.

The road was rutted and dusty and the teams threw dirt and pebbles onto John and the driver. The conveyance was a wheeled bucking bronco that leaped and jolted over the rough road. After ten minutes on the hard wooden seat, John knew he had made a colossal mistake. He held onto the careening contraption for dear life. Escape was in the foreseeable future but not imminent.

He observed the driver who expertly directed the horses and called them by name. If one dared to lag or misstep he swore a blue streak and snapped the whip over it's head.

After watching for some time, John asked, "You never hit the horses with the whip, why not?"

''What! Whip Ole Mose! Never! He's a lead horse, ya never whip a good lead horse. They have real good ears and answer to my voice calls. Whipping a good horse breaks it's spirit. When that's gone they're plum no good fer nuthin'! Why, Ole Mose can hear me lift the whip from the whip-socket of the rig and he knows just what to do. Watch his ears now, he knows we are talking about him.'' The driver explained.

The coach clattered on. At the top of a particularly long hill, the driver rested the horses for five minutes to allow them to catch their breath. The horses stomped, switched and chafed at the bit but precisely at the end of five minutes, in unison, they leaned into the harness and again the coach leaped ahead with no instructions from the driver. They knew what to do and when to do it. They were well-trained, intelligent horses.

''See what I mean, Ole Mose is real smart. What he and Ike does, the others do too.'' The driver was proud of his animals.

It was too noisy for further conversation so John fell silent and clutched the seat handles to stay aboard. He wondered if the glass jar of Sarah's Recipe could survive the trip and silently vowed never to ride shotgun again at any price for Wells-Fargo. For every mile he traveled on the stage was one more reason to travel by rail.

At station 2, they stopped. John was not sure his legs would hold him when he climbed down. It was a ten-minute stop and the passengers were herded into the station for hot coffee. The ''necessary'' was out back. John found standing was a pleasure after the circulation in his legs returned.

A fresh six-up of horses was hitched to the coach and the passengers took their seats. John climbed up on top with the driver and they moved out again.

''Aiee Up! Joe, Tom, Aiee Up! The driver shouted and cracked his whip over their heads. These horses were as well-trained as the others.

''Keep a sharp eye out Sonny, from here on it could get tricky. The next ten or twelve miles are trouble spots.'' The driver instructed John.

''Yes sir, I will.'' John said.

The terrain was rolling and stony but not wooded. Visibility was good in all directions. Far in the distance was a low mountain range. John scanned the land carefully.

''If we get across the river to those hills we make it. Newton is just beyond the hills,'' the driver shouted.

John was apprehensive about an Indian attack but resolved to take what came.

The trail was all but impassable. Sinkholes and boulders, ruts and quagmires barred the way at every turn but there were no Indians.

The teams dragged the squeaky coach over the ground. The fall rains had flooded the river ford but the driver slowly inched the team and carriage across. With great expertise, the driver and horses clamored up the opposite bank and stretched out on the run. Up the hills and down to Newton there were no Indians. Relief was written on all the faces when the coach clanked to a stop at the stage office in Newton.

John took his belongings from the coach top and much to his surprise the glass jar was unbroken. He thanked the stage driver and made his way to the railroad station up the street.

John was in luck, the night rattler for St. Louis was due in at sundown.

Somehow the towns and people looked different than they did on the west bound trip. He was no longer the starry-eyed boy who made the trip less than a year ago. So much had happened to him. He was still interested in everything but somehow less astonished at what he saw and learned.

Across the street from the station was a big building with a sign that read EMPORIUM. He crossed over and went in. After all, Christmas was coming and he had money.

He made his selections carefully but quickly. Something nice for Ma'am and Paap, Bruce and Gracie, Leone, Rose and Lu and Dudley and Seneca. For himself, he selected a gold railroad watch and chain. It was beautifully carved and engraved with a snap-open face. A railroad man must have a railroad watch and Hamilton made the best or so he was told.

He had the salesclerk wrap his parcels carefully and then tie them into a bundle he could carry. He had spent sixty dollars and change from his fortune. Up to now he had never been able to buy anything for his family and was pleased he could do so now. He paid the man and crossed back to the train station. It was nearing departure time and almost sundown.

He went aboard and put everything in the overhead rack except his food basket. He was hungry and enjoyed a drink of Sarah's Recipe with his ham and biscuits.

The trip to St. Louis was long and tiresome but John was undaunted. He studied the land, the trainmen and slept when he could. He watched the people come and go from the train and talked to the conductor who cheerfully answered dozens of his questions. He guarded his belongings and kept tabs on his money pouch. He had learned the bitter lesson well.

In St. Louis, he changed trains. There was time so he wandered around the station but he was carefull not to be jostled. The same Seneca Indian was selling worry stones and remembered John. They talked and John bought a handfull of the stones.

At the designated time he went aboard the train for Indianapolis and points East. He ate and slept and studied the right-of-way along the tracks. He was homesick. The greener the country side the more homesick he became. He was certain he could smell the big pine trees that passed in his view from the train window.

There was little time to make his connections in Indianapolis so he stretched his legs and was off again. Pittsburgh was the last leg of his long journey.

John's family was expecting him this week but which day was unknown. He stood for a long moment on the station platform of his beloved hometown. His eyes followed the tops of the familiar hills that rimmed his valley. He took in great gulps of air. The morning breeze smelled of pine, burning leaves and HOME.

''Mornin'n Mr. Greeley.'' John called to the station master.

''Why John Lansure I hardly know you, you're a man full growed. Haven't seen ya for quite a spell.'' The man extended his hand and John took it warmly.

''I've been away for nearly a year—out West.'' John explained.

''Well, welcome home, son.'' Mr. Greeley was pleased to see him.

''Thank you sir.'' John was happy to be home.

John gathered his belongings and headed up the road and home. The November morning was sunny but brisk. The dry leaves swirled around his feet and rustled in the trees. He walked faster and his head pounded. At the bend he could see his house. Home! What a magnificent word HOME.

Ma'am came onto the porch. She had seen him through the kitchen window, snatched her shawl from the peg and went to meet him.

He dropped his bindle and ran to meet her. He snatched her up in his arms kissed her and swung her around off her feet.

''Oh Johnny, my John, how I've missed you,'' she cried and happy tears stung her eyes.

''Ma'am, it's so good to be home—hey, you've lost weight, he said and put her back on her feet.

''Nothing of the kind, it's you, you're just stronger and taller too. Let me look at you.'' ma'am said.

Her boy had come back a man. He stood an inch less than six feet tall and the skinny kid was a hard-muscled completely filled-out, tanned and lean man.

His sisters ran to him in turn and hugged and kissed him. They squealed their delight at having him home again. Dudley hugged his brother and carried his bindle into the house.

''Look who's all knees and elbows, you've grown kid.'' John teased his brother.

''They call me Duke now, I got a part-time job at Mr. Town's store,'' explained the embarrassed boy.

"That's great Duke, they call me John now," John encouraged his brother. "Duke where's Paap?" John asked.

"He's husking at Walt Brown's, the whole town is helping. He just left. At noon the girls and I will be taking food to them. You will see him then," said Ma'am.

For the next several hours John talked of his trip and ate Ma'am's cooking. He told where he had been and what he had done and seen. The girls asked all kinds of questions and Duke hung on every word.

The baskets of food were loaded and the family climbed aboard the wagon for Brown's farm. By now, the ravenous corn huskers were ready to devour the food.

On the way John studied his sisters. Only Seneca was quiet and thoughtful.

"Sen, my Seneca, you doing your studies?" John asked.

"She's an A student," chided Leone.

"A's huh, I told you, you were the smartest of us all." Teased John.

"She can make biscuits almost as good as Ma'am's" declared Rose.

Seneca beamed at the attention she received but was very shy and said nothing.

"Rose, you still keeping up the family bible and scrap book and your journal?" That's important you know," encouraged John.

"Oh yes, she scribbles in that thing most every day," said Leone.

"Leone, you got a beau yet?" John inquired.

"Yes, she's sweet on that Murray Hurd but he won't give her the time of day," teased Rose.

"Stop that, she'll get a beau when she's ready," insisted Lu.

"Duke what you do at the store?" John asked of his brother.

"I sweep up mostly. Put things on the shelves and run errands. What ever Mr. Town wants me to do. It keeps me in spending money and guitar strings.

"You still plink around on that old thing, do ya? I learned a few cords myself on the guitar from the cousins out west and Bonny taught me a few cords on the organ."

"Who's Bonny?" Duke asked.

"Why your cousin Bonny Hobson, of course." John was surprised but understood since Duke had never met them.

"I'd rather have a banjo. I learned on Blair Hill's. He plays the accordion too." Duke also enjoyed the guitar and played it often.

The wagon arrived at the Brown's and John's family joined in the festivities. John went to his father. They hugged each other and tears glistened in Jimmy Lansure's eyes but they did not speak. A pat on the head or a wink from Jimmy was all the reassurance John needed from his father. The feelings between them were deep and needed no words. After some moments Jimmy said, "good to see you, son."

"Home never looked so good! Oh, Paap, have I got yarns to tell." John said.

"You and I will talk and speak of it." Jimmy was very proud of his John. The boy had gone away and the man had returned. Jimmy was eager to hear about the adventures.

John was greeted by all his friends and there were sideways glances from the girls around the village. Now John Lansure was a very eligible bachelor. He had been away a long time and had traveled far. To the towns folk travel meant learning, learning meant education and education meant wealth.

At seventeen he had done more and seen more than most people here about. Besides he was very handsome in a darkly quiet way. His body was strong and healthy now. His straight black hair was shiny and his hazel eyes were expressive and penetrating.

If his birthdate was unknown, an astrologer and some people would know by looking at his eyes that he was a Scorpio born November 16 and that year of 1909, he was 17.

The husking bee was huge success and the Brown's corn crib was filled for the winter. The food the ladies brought was laid out and soon devoured by the hungry huskers. When the corn was husked and the food eaten, the fiddler struck his bow and the dancing began.

John danced with the local girls and his sisters danced with the boys. Except for Louisa who stood in a corner and stared lovingly at her betrothed, Tom Montgomery. Their wedding would be soon.

When all were exhausted, the men took their sleepy children and tired families home. The husking bee usually announced the end of harvest.

The next weeks were busy ones at the Lansures. Lu's wedding and Christmas heaped chores upon on the family and they loved it. All the while, the girls begged John to see the contents of his packages but he held firm.

"Those boxes contain Christmas for all of you but you can't have them until Christmas—except for one. I have a wedding present for Lu—that is, if I get a custard pie for supper!" He teased his sister. Lu was the pie baker of the family.

"Oh, we'll make you a custard pie—won't we Lu!" squealed his sisters.

"Sure John, all you can eat," assured Lu.

John went to his room and shortly returned with a box and gave it to Lu.

She opened the box and began to cry. John held up three yards of beautiful white lace for her wedding veil. The girls giggled and felt the lovely material. Louisa hugged her brother's neck and cried her thanks to him.

''Oh John, it's grand indeed,'' said Ma'am, ''It will make a fine wedding veil.''

''See, it's real FRENCH lace,'' cooed Rose, after careful examination.

''Must 'ta cost a pretty penny,'' growled Leone, and fingered the cloth.

''I will weave a bayberry and fir garland to go on it,'' stated Seneca. ''The whole wedding will be Christmasey. We will have the greenest, tallest Christmas tree in the country. Seneca, Leone and I will make decorations and wreathes and string garlands. John, you and Bruce will find the tree and Duke, you find a big Yule Log for the fireplace. We will make fruitcake, shortbread and gingerbread and mull the cider!'' Rose was so excited and eager.

''Seems like a lot of work to me—all this goin's on and hoopla,'' grumbled Leone. She always grumbled but worked harder than anyone and loved every minute of it.

At noon on December 24, 1909, Louisa Lansure and Thomas N. Montgomery were married in the church chapel by Reverend Givin. After the ceremony, Jimmy and Agnes Lansure held open house at their home for a few close friends and relatives. They served shortbreads, fruitcake, gingerbread, dried fruit and nuts, doughnuts, mulled cider and hot coffee. It was a happy time.

Before the ceremony, in private, John had given his sister, Lu, the gold earrings he had for her as a Christmas present. She wore them with love and pride. She was a radiant bride. Seneca had woven evergreen and bayberry sprigs into a halo of Christmas red and green for her veil. Her dress was of white broadcloth and there had been enough lace leftover from the veil to make trimmings for the dress. Lu's flaming red hair appeared even redder against all that white but the freckles on her face had been carefully covered with face powder. Ma'am and the girls had made her traveling cloak and hood of forest green wool with a muff to match. She had always been frail and sickly but today she looked well and happy and pretty as a princess.

Tom on the other hand, was a tall ungainly man who continually looked uncomfortable. He appeared anxious and constantly fidgeted with his starched collar and fingered his new belt buckle that John had given him for Christmas. He was content only when Lu was by his side.

By late afternoon the festivities were over and most had gone away. Tom's best man and friend Milton Brass, brought the rig around to the front door. Milt would drive the bride and groom to their home a few miles away. They left in a hail of rice and the clatter of old shoes and cans tied to the buggy. Under the heavy blankets, he had placed a hot brick on the floor boards to keep them warm and comfortable for the ride.

Every one was happy yet sad; one had flown the nest.

It had been sifting lightly all day but now it was snowing heavily.

Bruce and Gracie stayed over for Christmas and all was well with the family.

Ma'am and the girls tidied up and Bruce brought in wood for the fireplace. Duke stirred the fire around the Yule Log and Jimmy lit his pipe. John brought out the gifts he had for his family. He hunkered down in the middle of the floor as he often did and said, "Before I begin, I have to tell you how I got the money to buy all this. You know I went to Uncle Tom's and got stranded in Kansas, now I will tell you how it happened." John began his story.

He told them of the cardsharp and the shell game and of the pickpockets. He told how Aaron hired him and what they did on the swine farm. He explained how Aaron and Sarah fled from Russia and why they wanted to adopt him. And how he found the fortune in money and rubles in the pouch they gave him. He also explained the fluid in the mason jar.

He did not mention Hannah's House or what happened there but later, when the time was right, he would tell his father and Duke in private, at least part of the story.

"What a yarn! It reads like one of those penny dreadfuls I've seen at the store," exclaimed Duke.

"They really wanted to ADOPT you?" asked Rose.

"Maybe the "Ancient One" was a member of MY family," stated Seneca, referring to the old Indian in the station, who sold the worry stones.

"You were just lucky that's all, you could have come to some bad end out there all alone," Leone was grumbling again.

"Good people are good people no matter who or where they are. I'm happy for you son." Ma'am understood.

"Sure would like to meet the Jacobs—sound like fine folks. That Indian man too," Jimmy said, lighting his pipe for the third time. He never could keep his pipe lit.

"First of all, this is for all you ladies. I told the clerk I wanted enough dress calico for six dresses. He said I needed twenty four yards so I took the whole bolt of twenty five yards and six yards of assorted colored ribbon for trim. You may choose which color." John loosed several yards from the bolt, spread it for all to see and tossed the ribbons about.

The ladies shrieked their pleasure, gathered around the fabric and ribbons to touch and examine it. It was pretty and soft. The background was a light shade of tan or cream and was covered with tiny flowers. Any of the ribbons matched the flowers. The ladies were delighted and divided the ribbon among themselves. Each selected her favorite color.

''I'll start with you Duke, since you are the youngest. By the way, I'll need to borrow my rifle back from you—just for hunting season—that be alright with you?'' John handed him a box.

''Sure okay—thanks, John.'' Duke stammered and took the box.

The box contained a pocket watch and chain and a worry stone. Not an expensive watch but a perfectly functional one.

From behind the Christmas tree, John took a banjo that he had been hiding. It was secondhand but sound. John handed it to his brother.

''You get this too, kid.''

Duke's eyes popped and he grinned from ear to ear. He lunged to hug his big brother and nearly knocked John off his haunches.

Duke fled up the stairs to his room so his family could not see him cry for joy at such wonderful gifts.

''Now you, Sen, my Seneca. This is the latest thing to go with your pretty handwriting.''

The box contained a fountain pen, a worry stone and a lovely pair of gold earrings. She held her prizes in her hand for a long moment and began to cry for joy.

''Like this, Sen; unscrew the top, pull down on this little lever and release it. That fills the pen from the inkwell, then you write.'' John placed it in her hand.

She was speechless and sobbed openly. She hugged John's neck and clung to him.

''Now, now, this is no time to cry—this is a happy time.'' Jimmy took Seneca from John's arms and comforted her in his.

''Oh Paap, they are the grandest presents I've ever had,'' cried Seneca.

''Now, if ya all are gonna cry and carry on, I'm not gonna give ya anything more.'' John scolded his family in jest.

''Oh John, I won't cry, I promise,'' begged Rose.

John rummaged through the stack of presents and said, ''Rose, I don't find anything for a Rose. Who's she?'' he teased and pretended to have nothing.

A shocked expression came over Rose's face. John quickly handed her his gift. He could see it was no joke to her.

''Oh John, I thought you forgot me,'' she whispered.

''Forget you—don't be dumb—I was just foolin'. I'd never forget my Rosie. Open the box.'' John teased.

''And don't call me Rosie,'' she scolded. ''Oh look Ma'am, a pen for me, too—and earrings! You didn't forget me.'' She cried and hung on his neck.

"Stop that, I told you to stop all that blubbering," John struggled to unlock himself from his sister's grip.

"John, those are tears of joy. They have never been given such grand gifts or did they ever expect to get them. Let them enjoy." Ma'am was the moderator for all.

"Leone, if you blubber all over me, I'll take them back—swear I will—even if you do have the most beautiful hair in the family." John gave Leone her box and she opened it carefully.

Inside was a matched set of mantilla-style tortoise shell combs, one for each side of the chestnut colored coil of long hair she wound on her head. Also, a pair of gold earrings and an worry stone.

Even old maidish, often coarse, gruff Leone choaked up and her eyes teared. "God Damn it John, now look what you've done! I need a hankie—give me a kiss-ya big brat, 'fore I swat ya, one." She sputtered and sniffed and left the room to find a handkerchief, after the kiss.

"I should never give you anything—for all the whacks I got from your wooden spoon." He swatted her rump lightly, as she passed him to leave the room.

"You're a bad one John Lansure, a real bad one," she called over her shoulder and escaped to the kitchen. Under it all, she adored her family.

"Come on, Gracie, it's your turn." He gave her a box.

"But John, you gave me dress material—I don't expect more." She opened the box and there were her gold earrings. She shrieked, cried and ran around the room and flung herself into John's arms.

"Here, here, Gracie—Bruce take care of this crazy woman, will you?" John thrust Gracie into Bruce's arms.

"I told you all if you carried on anymore I'd take everything back and I will—unless you all get into the kitchen and get me something to eat, scat, all of you," threatened John.

"John, we must go to church first. Afterwards, we will have a late supper. Don't be too hard on your sisters. Never have they had so much or been so happy. They can't find the words to tell you how they feel so they just cry." Ma'am understood everything and knew John was teasing.

"This is for you, mother." John opened the box and laid the black, beautifully woven, fine Alpaca shawl around her shoulders. "The clerk told me that the wool came from an animal in Peru."

"It's so grand John, so soft and warm." She fingered the cloth and hugged it to her. Her eyes filled.

"Now, don't you start, too." John put his arms around his mother and held her close. "You get a worry stone and earrings, too." John gave her a small box.

Agnes Lansure clung to her shawl and rocked in her chair by the fire. She had no words to express her pleasure of the gifts or of her pride in her son.

"Come on Dad, Bruce, get your boxes, it will soon be time for church." He gave Bruce a worry stone, a book on the life and times of Abraham Lincoln and a serviceable but not fancy, watch and chain.

"Damn, John, I feel bad. I have nothing for you and you gave us so much. How'd you know about this special edition? It's very hard to find. Never owned a watch in my life. Thank you, brother." Bruce's voice cracked.

"The clerk told me—glad you like it." John asked.

Jimmy Lansure opened the box to find a beautiful black brocade and wool vest of the highest quality, elegantly detailed down to the mother-of-pearl buttons.

"My son, you remembered! All my life I've wanted a fancy vest. Never thought I'd see the day. Agnes would ya look at this!" Jimmy's voice cracked and he cleared his throat.

"This is to go with it, Paap." John gave his father a smaller box. "I knew you had nothing to hang a watch and chain from."

Jimmy opened the little box and sank into his chair. He looked lovingly at his son but words failed him. The gold watch was beautifully carved with a snap-open face similar to John's.

"Now, we've had our Christmas and it's time to go to church for the real purpose of Christmas. Duke, hitch up Ole Stoney and we will take the sleigh. Bruce, there are two hot bricks on the stove—put them on the floor boards of the sleigh. Leone, you and the girls bring the blankets. I'll bank the fire so it holds 'til later," Jimmy said to his family. Each did his task and dressed warmly.

The family bundled up and crowded into the sleigh for church. The evening was still and dark and the snow fell steadily. Duke hung an extra row of bells on Ole Stoney and the sound carried far. The family sang Christmas carols and hymns while the horse clomped through the snow up to his hocks.

If John Lansure could be happier it was not possible. He was able to give to his family as he never could before. The sights and sounds of this Christmas marked John's memory and for years to come he would look back on it with loving thoughts and happy memories.

At the church, Duke covered Ole Stoney with a blanket and the family went inside.

All the candles were lighted and they flickered brightly. The church smelled of pine boughs and candle wax. Most of the village was present.

The Lansures greeted the Reverend and their friends, found their pew and sat down. John could not remember when it was different.

The organ boomed, the choir sang and the Reverend spoke. Every Christmas, John and his family came to Christmas Eve service, here, his entire life but this was the one he would remember. He always felt better after church; restored, stronger and up-lifted.

On the way home they sang, laughed and huddled under the blankets. The snow fell on their clothes and stuck to their eyelashes. The cold pinked their cheeks and nipped their noses. Their spirits soared. The bells on Ole Stoney sounded and resounded and echoed up and down the valley.

If these family ties could be measured as wealth, King Midas would not have the price.

At home again, the family ate a quiet supper, talked of the days events, examined their costly gifts and soon trudged off to bed.

The balance of the winter was a contented one for John. He hunted with his brother and roamed the hills. He spent time at the "quiet place." The clearing appeared smaller to John. The mountain laurel was encroaching from the edges and young trees sprung up here and there. The soft, tender grasses of his youth had turned to stalks of hay and weeds. He studied the decaying stump where he had last seen his beloved L'l Dan. He never appeared again although John always felt better for having gone there.

He studied the family bible and journal with Rose.

He talked to Seneca about her intentions to teach Indian children language and art and that she expected to earn a scholarship to college. Something no family member had ever done.

It was difficult to talk to Leone. She preached to her younger sibblings: "Wash behind your ears; wear clean underwear; go to church; save your money; write to your Ma'am and Paap; behave yourself." John listened to his sister. He knew she had his best interest at heart and Leone was Leone.

He spent many long hours talking and listening to his father. Mentally, he catalogued in his mind the helpful hints and advise from his father's wide variety of life's stories. Simple gems of wisdom to be used as guides. For instance; always leave it better than you find it. Never judge a man unless you have walked a mile in his shoes. That which does not take my life—gives me strength. Give your word and keep it. Make your handshake your bond. Tell the truth. Judge all men on merit—not on hearsay. Be kind to your elders, children and animals. Look before you leap. Keep silent and thought dumb rather than speak and erase all doubt. Believe nothing you hear and only half of what you see. Never a borrower or a lender be. If it isn't broken, don't mend it. Save a dime—save a dollar. It's not what you earn but what you save. If you tell a secret—it isn't. Work hard—sleep well. Charity begins at home. Envy and greed are pockets of the same shroud. If you can't take the heat—keep away from the stove. Always remember, there are doers, the never-doers and the undoers. If you won't pull—get out of the harness. Never tell a lie and always keep a confidence.

Jimmy Lansure passed his principles on to his sons as his father had passed them on to him.

"Remember, son, the only thing a man ever really owns is his good name. A man has to have a set of rules to live by. A pattern by which to plan his life. A code of do's and don'ts. Then comes the hard part. After the code is set, a real man lives by his code. There is nothing worse than a man who knows the principles but does not live by them. I know it is hard to do but that is the right of it." Jimmy did not preach to his sons and daughters but he made sure they understood the code and expected them to abide by it.

"Even the best men waver, slip and fall, it can happen to any of us and we all make mistakes, that's alright so long as we don't repeat them. Do your best son, do your best. None can ask more."

John applied his father's code to himself and patterned his life accordingly. He had already learned mistakes are allowed if a lesson is learned and if the best effort was made. Let go, forgive yourself and go on.

John's time with his mother was precious and rare. That winter he drove her in the buggy to three deliveries. Two were normal, healthy babies and one was premature and stillborn.

He waited with the families and observed the anxiety, impatience and pleasure that surrounded the birth of a child.

He watched Ma'am's gentle, calm and composure stave off all situations. A panicky husband awaiting his first born. A frightened young mother having her first child and the hysteria that comes with a stillborn.

"I just can't get used to it. The grief, despair and agony of a still birth. It's times like these that I think maybe I should have been a dollar-a-day garment dressmaker. When a seam splits it can be repaired. When a child dies everyone is torn apart." Ma'am said quietly as they rode along toward home in the buggy.

"You and I both know, you would not be content to just sit and sew." John said.

"S'pose you are right but I'd suffer less." Ma'am said solemnly.

"Maybe so, but any one can sew. How many can deliver a set of twin babies? How many have you delivered?" John inquired of his mother.

"Three sets so far, all alive and well. Except for the Elliots, they lost one of theirs in the flu epidemic of '92. Bad year for sickness, that. I guess when the feet are put upon the course there is no changing it. What about you son, I see you reading that technical book on Airbrakes, Couplings and Signals. You getting ready to set out again and find your own way?" John's mother's face expressed her pride and her pain. She knew John's going was for good this time, to seek his dream.

''Yes Ma'am, as soon as the weather breaks, I'm going. I understand they are hiring new men on the Baltimore and Ohio through the Cumberland Gap. Ed Ridgley said the best place to sign up was at Cumberland, MD. The B&O runs east and west from there. Some of his family got jobs there and they never railroaded before. I think I have the same chance. Mr. Greeley, at the station, loaned me the book after I explained that I expected to be a railroad engineer. He said my chances would be better if I had some know-how about railroading. You know what else he said? He said any white family that would take in an Indian baby to raise as their own deserves the best of everything and that he was proud to lend me the book as long as I need it. Ma'am, why won't they forget that? Seneca Raindrop Lansure is as much a sister to me as my own and you and Paap treat us all alike. Why do they remember just that. She came to us only minutes old—that makes her ours—for ever.'' John said, thoughtfully.

''Different my son, it's the DIFFERENT. If your skin color is different, your language is different, your religion is different, your home is different, some folks feel that the different ones are the enemy. It's not that folks are bad, they just don't understand that different is not harmful. Just the same, to be different is to be scorned, ridiculed and often persecuted. Whenever possible son, try to right that wrong. Be helpful, tolerant and understanding. It never harms and good can come of it.'' Ma'am patted John's arm while they rode along.

They fell silent and rode the final mile without speaking. John had to ponder his mother's words.

The winter of 1909 and '10 was snowy but not bitter. The family spent their evenings by the fire. Ma'am and Paap rocked in their chairs, she embroidered and he tapped his foot to the music. John and Duke strummed the guitar and banjo and the girls sang songs. They popped corn and mulled cider and Jimmy tried to keep his pipe lit.

March, 1910 came in like a lamb. The ice and snow melted and it rained. In the middle of the month, Ma'am and Paap gathered their brood for one more Sunday dinner family get-together before John was to leave.

Bruce and Gracie and Tom and Lu arrived early. The house came alive with talk and laughter and smelled of meat roasting and pastery baking. The ladies bustled in the kitchen. The table looked delightfully inviting. Seneca had made the center piece of Pine. The men gathered by the fire in the great room and finished what was left of Sarah's Recipe. Tom brought out his fiddle and the men tuned up the guitar and banjo. Bruce banged the pie pan which was often used as a percussion instrument in family group concerts, such as these. Jimmy puffed on his pipe which had gone out again.

After several tunes and much laughter, Ma'am called the family to table. Jimmy said Grace and thanked the Lord for food, family and forgiveness. He prayed for John's health and safety on his long journey and he thanked God for his bounty and for his loving family.

After prayers, the food was served and they ate with gusto.

John was certain it was the best meal he would ever have but he often felt that way when Ma'am and his sisters cooked a meal.

By evening, the party was over. Bruce and Gracie and Tom and Lu said tearful good-bys and went to their homes. It would be a long time before they would see each other again.

Ma'am and the girls packed his clean underware and sox, two shirts, two pairs of pants and a sweater. He wore his only suit and vest. His bindle was not much and it fit into the old grip with room to spare.

Jimmy gave John a straight razor and strop and said, "A man needs his own toilet articles. I've had these since I was your age. Were'nt used much, I've worn a Van Dyke most of my life. Today, clean-shaven's the thing. Now give me a penny so's the blade won't sever our ties. That's an old wives' tale but I heed it." John gave his father a penny and they all laughed.

Seneca brought the black silk string tie she made for John and hung it around his neck. "A man is well-groomed if he has on a necktie. Black goes with everything and silk won't wrinkle much." She kissed his cheek.

Duke gave his brother a shaving mug and brush with a bar of fine soap.

"I knew Paap planned to give you the razor and you would need a cup and brush. Mr. Town gave me a discount." Duke blushed red in the face.

"For years, I've been telling you to wipe your nose—well here's something to do it with!" Leone roared and gave John two white linen handkerchiefs each hand sewn and embroidered with the letter L.

Ma'am gave John her mother's leather-bound traveling bible. Grandma Hobson brought it from England when she came to this country as a child.

"Keep it close to you son. Refer to it. It will help you make decisions and soothe the hurts. It will fit in any pocket or if necessary, down the top of your sock if you don't have a pocket." Ma'am said with love and good humor.

"Thank you, all of you. I don't know what to say. You've fixed me up so good, I'll go right out of here in style. Which reminds me. I want to say our good-byes tonight. I'm up over the road very early tomorrow and there's no need for you all to stand in the cold at the station. Duke can help me with my truck and we'll walk. I'm not much for words but I think you know how comfortin' it's been to be home with you. So long as a man has roots somewhere, he can go any place and do anything 'cause he knows somewhere in the world, there's home. This place and you are my roots and my strength. As long as I have you, I'll make it.'' He hugged his family, in turn and went up to bed.

Dawn was chilly but bright. John shaved and dressed leisurely as there was plenty of time. He knew Ma'am was cooking—he could smell the bacon frying. He went to the kitchen and kissed his mother.

''I thought I told——.'' He began.

''You didn't really think that I'd let you go on an empty stomach now did you?'' Ma'am interrupted.

''Mornin' John, at least we can see you up the lane.'' Growled Leone and the other family members gathered at the table.

''Wouldn't be right not to see you off,'' said Rose.

''The family ate together and chatted. After the meal, John closed his grip and said his good-byes. The family cried and waved from the porch. John looked back and waved until he turned the bend in the road and they were out of sight.

Duke lugged the grip and at the station, John bought his tickets and they said good-bye.

The train arrived. John tossed his grip onto the train platform and stepped up after it. The train unloaded, reloaded and pulled out. John waved to Duke as far as he could see him. John took his grip inside and found a seat. His family had seen him off on his pathway to destiny. His feet had been placed upon the course and naught could change it. . . .

Chapter Eight

A MAN AND HIS TRAINS

John watched from his window seat while the train rumbled from the foot hills of the Allegheny Mountains up the Laurel Hills to Somerset then over the Big Savage to Cumberland, Md. The Applachian Mountain country was lush, green and beautiful with great heaps of grist for the mill of the poet and painter.

John marveled at what he saw and talked about it with the conductor. After some time, John told him where he was bound and why. The conductor suggested John leave the train in the yards and go directly to the Baltimore & Ohio Railroad yard office. He would be sent there, in any case, to apply for a job and there was no point to a double-back.

When the train stopped in the yards to take on coal and water, John thanked the conductor for his help and left the train.

It was late in the afternoon and time for crews to change shifts in the yards. John watched while the switching crew kicked cars and made up trains. The place teemed with activity. He dragged his valise around and absorbed the sights, sounds and smells of railroading. He sat down on it to watch a host'ler drop the ashes from one of the resting locomotives.

John was noticed by a railroader near by. David Wellington Stanton was a seasoned, long distance, freight train, locomotive engineer and was known to all as Big Davey. He stood six-four and weighed two hundred, plus. His grey eyes were soft but keen as an eagle's and they missed nothing. He was the epitome of a railroad head hogger or hog head, in his porched cap, pin stripped cover-alls and red bandana.

''What you doin' around here boy, you lost? Can be dangerous if you're not careful.'' Big Davey spoke gently to John.

''No sir, I'm not lost. I've come here to get a job. I've never seen a yards this big before and I was just looking around. I'm going to be an engineer someday. My name's John Lansure-nice to meet you.'' John held out his hand and the big man took it.

''John Lansure, is it? Well, D. W. Stanton but you can call me Davey. You're going to be an engineer are ya? Right away, I expect.'' Davey could not resist the urge to tease the inexperienced boy.

''Yes sir, soon as possible.'' John was determined.'' What do you do here, sir?''

Big Davey leaned back and roared with laughter. His booming voice ricocheted around the rail yards.

''Son, I can see you are long on eager but short on know-how. Have ya got a place to stay?'' Davey liked the boy.

''No sir, I just got into town.''

''Tell ya what let's do. You come with me. We'll get ya a place to stay and some supper then we will talk. The Riley's keep a clean house and the grub is second to none. Come along, son.'' Big Davey put a big strong arm over John's shoulders and they walked from the rail yards to the street beyond.

As they walked along, John told Big Davey of his dreams of being a railroad engineer and that he would be 18 in November. Big Davey was easy to talk to like his Paap and soon John was pouring out his heart and dreams.

''We may have a problem with that, son,'' Davey said, after a while.

''With what, sir?'' John asked.

''Your age boy, ya have to be full 18 to sign up for the road. Otherwise, all ya get is yard work and the dirty jobs, at that. Don't fret none, we'll see what we can do about it.''

John's face fell but his hopes were high.

At the boarding house, Davey introduced John around to the other men there.

''This is John Lansure and he plans to railroad with us.'' John beamed and to the Riley's, Davey said, ''This is Mike Riley, he's Irish and can lick ANY man in a fair fight. If you don't believe me—ask HIMSELF! And this fair damsel is his lovely wife, Gretchen, she's German and will feed you an awful lot of cabbage but her apple strudel melts your heart. When you gonna leave this Irish SCALAWAG and marry me?'' Davey teased Mike Riley in good humor and kissed Gretchen's cheek. It was all in fun because Davey had a wife somewhere.

''Nice to meet ya Sir, Ma'am.'' John shook their hands.

''Big Davey, zere's plenty of zupper but I won't have an empty room 'til Zaterday, next. Rodger Dice has been bumped to East end and his room will be empty zen. I can put up a cot in your room and you can bunk togezer 'til zen. Will zat be alright wiz you?'' Suggested Gretchen in her pleasant German accent. Her Ss sounded like Zs as did her th's.

''That will be just jake with us, ahy what, son? I only snore when I'm on my back.'' Every one laughed.

The Rileys called the boarders to table. Tonight, with Big Davey and John, they were twelve. Davey was right; corned beef and cabbage, boiled potatoes, creamed corn and hot biscuits. For dessert; apple strudel or canned peaches. The mounds of food quickly disappeared as the hungry men gorged themselves.

The railroaders laughed and talked shop while they ate. They hashed over the day's happenings and told jokes-some off-colored. Davey noticed the puzzled expression on John's face and asked, ''What's the trouble, John—John—John Wells, John Black, and John Beaty—there are just too many Johns around here—from now on, you will be Jack Lansure, do ya hear-Jack? Jack is nick for John anyway.'' All agreed and laughed.

''Now that is settled Jack Lansure, what's troubling you?''

''Sir, I listen very carefully to the men talking but I don't get it all. I know it isn't a different language but I don't understand it!'' Jack explained.

''Remember, I said you were short on know-how? Well, railroaders have a language all their own and that's only the thumbnail of the total you will have to learn. Railroad jargon is as much a part of them as their work. Before you can understand a railroader, ya have to learn his lingo. Now pay attention, Gretchen is taking breakfast orders.''

''John, do you want cackel berries on a raft or cluck and grunt?'' Gretchen asked of John Wells.

''Cluck and grunt please, some burnt punk and sweets,'' he answered.

''How about you, Mister Black?'' She asked the next man.

''I'll have corn grind and cow—my innards are growlin' again,'' said Black.

''Roll me some with burnt punk and grease,'' said Mr. Beatty.

''Did you hear what they said, Jack?'' asked Davey.

''Yes, I heard what they said but I don't understand.'' Jack (John) confessed.

''The first man that asked for cackel berries on a raft was asking for bacon and eggs. The second asked for cluck and grunt and burnt punk and sweets. He wants ham and eggs and toast and jelly. The next asked for cornmeal mush and milk because his stomach ulcer is acting up again. The last one, asked for her to roll him some with burnt punk and grease wants oatmeal and buttered toast. See how easy it is?'' Explained Big Davey to his wide-eyed friend.

''Holy cow, I'll have to learn a whole new language!'' Exclaimed Jack.

''Just keep your eyes and ears open and your mouth shut and it will all come to you in time. Now, it's time for bed,'' said Davey.

''Davey, what will you and Jack have for breakfast?'' Asked Gretchen.

''What do you say kid, you tell her for us,'' urged Davey.

''How about cluck and grunt with burnt punk and sweets. How'd I do?'' Jack was delighted to use the new language he was learning.

''Zat's good—ya did real good,'' said Gretchen.

''See, it's not so hard—you'll have it down pat 'fore ya know it,'' encouraged Davey.

''It's kind of fun. Does Gretchen know when we will be up in the morning?'' asked Jack.

''That's not exactly how it works son, breakfast is at 6:30 A.M. sharp and if your late, you're out of luck. Most crews mark up between 7 and 8, depending on the schedules. Mark up—that means sign in for a job. There are two basic groups of railroaders, those who prepare the railroad and those who operate it. In the first group you find track men, telegraph line men, machinists, section men and right-of-way men and others. In the other group there are engineers, fireman, brakemen, switchmen, telegraphers, yard clerks, inspectors, conductors and policemen and more. The wrecking crew is a unit by itself and contains all of the above. You gettin' the idea, son? I'll help you with the jargon and the ropes.''

''Whew, there is sure a lot to learn. I will need all the help I can get, thanks,'' answered Jack as they went up to bed.

''Son, are you sure—I mean real sure you want to join the Boxcar Brigade? It will lift ya up—knock ya down—break your heart and be the most rewarding thing you will ever do.'' Davey had to know if Jack was determined to make railroading a lifetime pursuit or just another job.

''Yes, sir, I'm real sure.'' Jack was definite.

''Jack did not sleep a wink and it was not because Big Davey snored like a buffalo but because hé was so excited about railroading. So far, it was way beyond his greatest expectations. More and more, he liked Big Davey and looked up to him. He enjoyed the railroaders and their language no matter that he didn't understand it. He was determined to learn. His spirit soared. His dream was coming true, bit by bit. He even enjoyed being called Jack.

The morning came bright and clear. The men finished whopping breakfasts at Gretchen's table. They thanked her, praised her cooking and left for work.

It was a nice day for a walk. The two men stepped the distance to the yard office quickly and went in.

Davey explained the situation to the Yard Master, Bill Darcey and after some words, Jack was hired.

"When Big Davey goes out on the run, you go along as a smoke's helper. When he's off, you work around the yard and barn helping the nut cracker with the tallow pot. When he don't need ya, ya run errands for the mud hop. You'll get 10 cents an hour to start and if ya make the grade, in 90 days you'll get 20. You can start with Big Davey on his run. All that agreeable to you?" the Station Master asked when he had finished his instructions.

"Yes sir, it is—you mean I'm hired—it sure is—thank you, SIR!" Jack could hardly breathe for the excitement.

"Sign your name here and from now on, you sign the markup board—over there." He pointed to a huge chalk board on the wall which was covered with crewmen's names and information.

J. C. Lansure scrawled his left-handed signature on the paper and from then on he was a railroader.

Jack and Davey thanked the man and left.

"Davey, I'm much obliged to you and I'm in your debt. Thanks and there is something I have to ask you."

"Not necessary, son. You have the makings and all ya needed was a start. Now what's the trouble?" Big Davey thumped Jack's back affectionately.

"About my orders, I heard them but I don't understand what I'm to do, besides learn firing from you. What do I do with a nut cracker and a tallow pot and what's a mud hop?" Jack quizzed his friend.

Big Davey roared with laughter. "Listen carefully, boy and I'll tell ya. The nut cracker is the head machinist of the black gang in the barn—the roundhouse, to you. He will give you an oil can—tallow pot—and you will grease everything that moves on the rolling stock—engines, tenders and cars. When he's finished with you, ya go to the mud hop—yard clerk and run errands for him. That can be anything from delivering train orders to train crews to sweeping up. You understand that? One more thing son, there is no drinking on the job. If you are caught drinking or you are drunk on the job, it's the sack and a black ball and no questions asked. That means your fired and no railroad in the country will hire ya. The reason the bosses are so severe is because you not only risk your own life but the lives of the other crew members. Railroading is a team effort. Each man does his particular job and pulls his own weight. A drunk can't. There is no place in this risky business for a drunkard."

"That doesn't bother me none, I'm not much of a drinker. I had some homemade slivovitz that a friend made. It was sweet and sticky but it burned all the way down."

"Oh sonny, don't get me wrong. I said you can't drink on the job but I never said ya couldn't have a drink after work or at home. Why, railroaders are notorious for their capacity to imbibe and they get tanked regular, but NEVER on the job. And stay away from the cheap tangle-foot, drink the good stuff. You gettin' all this, boy?" Davey was amused at Jack's seriousness.

"Yes sir, I am. I'd never hurt anybody on purpose and I'm not lookin' to get myself killed." Jack declared.

"Now that we got that settled, let's go to town. I don't mark up 'til morning and we have things to see to today. You got any work clothes, a shirt and tie won't do?" Davey said.

"No sir, I don't."

"For a dollar extry a week, Gretchen will do your laundry. You got any money?"

"Enough to last 'til pay day, if I'm careful." Jack left most of his money with Ma'am and brought only enough to live on temporarily.

"You will need two complete sets of work clothes; one on and one in the laundry; a pair of heavy leather gloves—gauntlets—and high topped shoes. If ya can't swing it, the local haberdasher is a friend and will trust ya 'til payday." Big Davey was attending to Jack's needs as a helpful, fatherly friend.

The two men walked to the clothing store and the obliging haberdasher outfitted Jack with all he needed. They took their parcels and started back to Riley's.

"Now that you are all fixed up, I have to get to the brass pounder and send a message to my little woman. I have to let her know that I'm not over on a curve somewhere. I have a place on Tygart Lake outside of Grafton on the west end. She's a good railroader's wife. She's used to serving over-done meals and I'm used to eating them. This is not a 9 to 5 job and we make the best of it. Usually, when I have a full day off, I deadhead home. She has learned not to panic for at least 24 hours but I'd better send her word." Until now, Davey had not said much about his family.

"Now let me see if I've got it. When you deadhead, you ride for free to home station, are not working and the brass pounder is the telegrapher. How'd I do?" Jack asked.

"You're learn'n, boy, you're learn'n!" encouraged Big Davey, "You go along, I'll see you at supper."

Davey cut up the alley to the railroad yards and Jack went to Riley's.

The next morning Jack was up early, shaved and dressed but he had not slept much. He scrutinized his image in the mirror and was pleased. In his new railroad garb, he looked the part. At last, he was a railroad man.

He and Davey ate huge breakfasts, joked about his new clothes and went to the yard office.

At the B&O yard office in Cumberland, Maryland, March 1910 John Clellend Lansure scrawled his left-handed signature on the markup board, J. C. Lansure, now known as Jack to his friends. It was the first of thousands of markups to follow for this fireman's apprentice and yard boy.

D. W. Stanton, Engineer, known to all as Big Davey, marked up and received his orders. He was head hogger on the long, heavy freight trains on the West End through the Gap to Parkersburg, W. Va. and back. He could read the rails, roadbed and right-of-way better than most engineers on the B&O, freight or passenger. He could hear a cracked rail by the sound it made when the engine passed over. He could recognize a dangerous rock formation along the right-of-way that was a potential land slide in wet weather and he could sense a weak pylon under a bridge span. He also knew instinctively when an engine's steam pipes needed reaming. When rust and scale collect and clog the steam pipes, violent, disastrous boiler explosions are imminent. It is possible to learn some things by observation and experience but the gift of instinct comes from within.

Davey's train was made up and his 'Iron Mistress' stood hissing on the main track pointing out of the yards. The big Baldwin was relatively new by locomotive standards, built around 1900. It was able to drag heavy trains over the Applachian Range.

"Come on son, ya have to learn to swing up on this iron hog whether she's stopped or moving; it's raining or dry; in good footing or bad," instructed Davey. "Remember, if she's moving to the right, use your right hand on the right bar. If she's moving to your left, use your left hand and the left bar. The momentum will swing you into the ladder. Hang on tight. One slip could cost you a leg or worse."

Jack grabbed the long gangway bar, swung up, climbed the iron ladder and dropped with a clang on the iron cab floor. Davey scrambled up after him.

"Holy cow! I thought hauling stones for my Paap made muscles, but hauling yourself up into the engine will build you up all over." Jack was surprised at the strength is required to pull himself up the ladder.

"Now, son, go down," urged Davey.

Jack turned around to back down and Davey stopped him.

"No, no, boy, ya grab the bars like this, facing out and slide down!" Davey dropped to the ground. "Now, you do it," Davey called up to Jack.

Jack looked down at Davey. It was a long drop to the ground. Jack grabbed the long gangway bars, lifted his feet and slid. He had not pushed off enough and the drop scraped his back painfully on the ladder steps. He grimaced and Davey noticed.

"Ya have to do it a couple of times 'til ya get the hang of it. You hurt bad?" Davey asked.

''No, just scraped a little.'' Jack would have said 'no' if all the skin was off his back. He vowed silently to do it right the next time, now that he knew there was a trick to it.

Davey's fireman arrived and the three men climbed into the cab.

''Jack, this here's Wally Barrigan, the best long haul Smoke in the business. Wally, this is Jack Lansure, he's to be your helper for a while,'' explained Davey.

''Glad to meet you, sir,'' Jack said and extended his hand.

''My helper, are you. You ever swing a ''Banjo'' before?'' The fireman asked and took Jack's hand.

Jack glanced pleadingly at Davey for help. He had no idea what Banjo meant in railroad jargon. Davey glanced at the big fireman's coal shovel that rested, half covered with coal in the tender's chute. Jack's eyes shot a grateful 'thank you' to Davey.

''No sir, I haven't but I can learn.'' Jack assured the fireman.

''Jack, you stand over there—out of the way and watch.'' Davey found Jack a corner near the fireman's seat box.

Wally was about 30 years old and built like an oak tree. Straight up and down from neck to thigh, short legs, long arms and hard muscles from head to toe.

Wally grabbed the huge coal shovel with both hands; one in the grip and one on the shaft and jammed it in to the coal pile. In one smooth motion, he heaved the full shovel out of the pile, swung his body around, stomped his left foot hard on the firebox door release and threw the shovel full of coal into the open firebox. Again, back to the coal pile, around onto the door release and in. Again and again in a rhythmic display of grace and strength. Over and over until the fiery stomach was gorged and each shovel full was placed exactly in it's designated spot for best efficiency. Task completed, Wally wiped his sweating face with a red bandana and smiled at Jack with a wink.

Jack was spellbound. The fireman had the grace, timing and balance of a tightrope walker and the strength of an ox. Jack hunkered down on his haunches, which he often did to rest and the fireman dropped onto the seat box.

''Holy jumpin' up if that don't beat all! Think I'll ever learn to do that?'' Jack exclaimed, excitedly.

''Sure, if you really want to learn, nothing much to it.'' Wally grinned at the green kid.

''Oh you will learn, alright. If you want to be a hogger, you will and learn it good. Every engineer is a Smoke first and a good one. You learn his job before you can learn mine. You will also learn to be a mud hop, a dolly flopper, a gandy dancer and a shack.'' Davey was positive.

''Oh, I'll learn all I can but do you think I will live long enough to learn all that!'' Jack was astonished at what he had seen and the men laughed at his naivete.

Jack observed carefully as Davey and Wally prepared the huge locomotive to roll and haul the long, heavy train out of the yards. Davey got the green, sounded his departure whistle and released the brakes. He eased the throttle over and the train moved but the big drivers slipped on the rails under the load.

''Some sand Wally, this is a heavy one,'' Davey instructed his fireman.

''Right,'' was the answer.

The sand dropped onto the rails gave the engine the traction it needed and the long, heavy train moved out of the yards into the countryside. The terrain was beautiful and wooded and more or less uphill for the next fifty miles thru the Gap. Jack watched carefully as the men worked the levers and gauges. The locomotive chugged and hissed and groaned and clanked up the grades, around the curves and over the bridges. The open firebox seared his face inside the cab and the cold March wind stung his face when he leaned out the gangway. Huge billows of smoke festooned up from the smokestack and trailed back along the train. Jack savored the sights, sounds and smells of the work he had chosen.

After a long while of observing, Wally handed the shovel to Jack. He staggered under the weight of the coal and fought to keep his footing. He was a very clumsy beginner. Jack was left-handed and all that he observed and learned had to be reversed. He tripped and stumbled, missed the firebox and spilled coal on the deck. The motion of the engine pitched and tossed him about and to swing the coal shovel and keep his footing was next to impossible. He faltered and slipped and was punched and gouged by every gauge and lever on the boiler face. The engine jerked and thrust him into a protruding lever that raised a noticable purple mouse above his left eye. In spite of his pummeling, he never complained, gave up or stopped.

Davey was delighted with the stouthearted lad and said, ''That's enough for now, ya did good.'' Davey beamed and thumped the boy's back.

Jack dropped to his haunches and mopped his face. ''It's harder to do than it looks.'' All three men had a good laugh.

Again, the men performed their work and Jack paid close attention.

The pretty mountain country reminded Jack of home and the trip into Parkersburg was exciting for the youth but uneventful.

Big Davey and Wally turned the train over to the yard crew and cut out at the yard office. The men roomed at a near-by once grand, now run down at the heel but clean, hotel called the Emporia.

They arranged for Jack to stay there and all went to their rooms to clean up. They agreed to meet later in the restaurant for food and drink.

At the supper table, Jack was introduced to the waitresses Fern and Edie and the barkeep, Ben. They laughed and joked about the day's run over their food. Finally Big Davey said, "Raise your glasses, Lads, I propose a toast to a new railroader. He thinks like a man and works like the Devil!" Davey was indeed, proud of Jack.

They clinked their glasses and Jack was embarrassed and blushed beet red. The food was finished and eventually they went up to bed.

Jack fell asleep at once.

In the morning, Jack was too paralized to move when he opened his eyes. Every joint and muscle cried out in rebellion. The purple lump over his eye had turned green and thumped with each of his heartbeats. Still he wouldn't have it any other way. As soon as he could move his stiff body off the bed, Jack whistled while he dressed. He looked forward to the day's happenings and he could not remember when he had been happier.

The trip back to Cumberland was not so grueling. Jack improved and was finding his sea legs. He spilled less coal and his confidence was growing.

"Now tomorrow, you report to the nut cracker. I'm off and I'm deadheading home. Get acquainted at Riley's and write your Maw." Big Davey thumped Jack's back. "Another thing, for a dollar extry a week Gretchen will pack ya a poke. If ya'd ruther, ya can eat in the crummy with Squawk, Shack, Smoke and me. Oh, yeah, the crummy is the caboose; the Squawk is the conductor; the Shack is the brakeman and you know Smoke. There's usually somethin' cookin' and we take turns or we time our meals with a water and coal stop. Suite yourself." Davey waved and went on down the street.

Back at Riley's, Jack asked Gretchen about the lunch arrangements. She said. "You have to have a dinner bucket or basket. You leave it on zee stair-steps at night and you pick it up in zee zame zpot in the morning. I make up zix already, you will be zeven. If you haven't a bucket, I'll find you zumezing. I make zandwiches of cold meatloaf, cold pork, cold beans, ham, eggs and roast-of-beef, when I can get it. I put mustard on everything except eggs-on them you get ketchup. You get cupcakes and cookies or pie if I have it. You get fruit in zeason and an orange when I'm flushed. If ya want a fruit jar of coffe or tea—zat, too. Does all zat zoot you?"

"You bet—sounds great." Jack was enthusiastic and was not a picky eater.

Gretchen smiled and pinched Jack's cheek. He blushed red and went up stairs.

He laid on his cot in the dim light and pondered all that had happened. Suddenly he remembered Davey's instructions. He got up and turned the lamp bright. He took a pad and pencil from his valise and sat down on the cot to write a letter to Ma'am and Paap. When he was finished, he folded the letter, turned out the lamp and fell on his cot to sleep.

The next morning he took the stairs—two at a time and gulped his breakfast. On his way out he asked Gretchen about the post and told her he had a letter to send.

"Geev to me—I will post it when I go to zee market. I will put it on your bill." She handed him his lunch in a badly battered but servicerable dinner bucket, similar to the one his brother Bruce carried in the mines. He thanked her; she pinched his cheek he blushed and hurried toward the yards.

At the yard office, Jack marked up and was told to go to the Barn and find a man called Zebadee Wells. Zeb was the head nut cracker and was to be Jack's boss.

Inside the roundhouse, Jack asked a man to point him out.

"Over there—in the tool cage—the big one is Zeb," the man said.

"Much obliged," said Jack and walked to the cage.

The tool cage was just that but sometimes it was called the Crib. It was a huge square, fenced and covered iron cage. The padlock that hung open from the only door was as big as a man's hand and two inches thick. The outside walls were covered with pigeonholes of all sizes and in the center, rows and rows of shelves and more pigeonholes. If the tool or parts was essential to repair a locomotive, tender or car, it was in this cage. If not, it was custom-built here.

For a long moment, Jack studied the interior of the barn. It was immense. The windows were grimy and shut out the light. It was cold, dank and dim; smelled of grease and oil, burning metal and charcoal smoke. The striking of metal upon metal was deafening. The workers clanked the metal and shouted to one another.

Zebadee Wells was huge. Jack had never seen hands that large on a man. Jack learned later that Zeb was the son of a blacksmith and learned to shape metal at an early age. Zeb was taller than Davey—at least 6′4″—and outweighed him by 100 pounds.

Jack moved toward the cage and said, "I was sent here to help the head nut cracker. My name is Jack Lansure."

"Put your bucket there and come with me." The big man's voice was gravelly and deep and it sounded like a croak as he pointed to a space on a shelf nearby.

"I'm Zeb Wells. This is where you will work. Every night the men bring their tools here to be put into the bins by you and in the morning, they will tell you what they need for the day's work. You will learn what the tools are called, what they are used for and where they are stored. If a man calls from his work station for a tool, you will take it to him. You will hear the call—sound carries well in here. If they need grease and oil, you get it from those barrels. The pigeonholes and bins are marked, so go along and learn where things are located. This is Rolly Hunter, he works here, too. If ya get stuck, he will help you out. Rolly, this is Jack Lansure.''

The two men shook hands and wandered into the maze of nuts and bolts, pliers and clamps and hammers and tongs. Jack followed Rolly around all morning and ran the tools, grease, oil and parts back and forth from the cage to the workers.

At the sound of the noon whistle, Jack dropped to his haunches.

''Doesn't anything in this place weigh less then ten pounds?'' Jack growled.

''Ya get used to it. Big engines have big parts and need big tools,'' Rolly said with a grin and gave Jack his dinner bucket.

''Thanks. You been here long?'' Jack asked and opened his lunch.

''About a month. It's the first descent paying job I've had all winter. Besides myself, I have a wife and baby to feed.'' Rolly was grateful and uncomplaining.

''Sorry, Rolly, I shouldn't pop off like that.'' Jack felt guilty.

''You really will get used to it. Do you work full time.'' Rolly asked.

''Yes. When I'm not here I am a fireman's apprentice and I go out on the West End freight run with D. W. Stanton.'' Jack answered.

''Oh, I heard of him—he's the best.'' Rolly said.

The two men fell silent and ate their food. Soon the whistle blew and all went back to work in the dirt, smoke and noise.

By quitting time, Jack was ready to drop. The awful noise sapped his strength more than the work. He thanked Rolly for his help, marked off and went home to Riley's. He was filthy dirty and had to clean up but he was too tired to eat. He fell on his cot dead to the world.

About 9:00 PM Big Davey returned to the room. In one hand he carried a glass of milk and a sandwich. In the other, he carried a stack of books and papers. Jack opened one eye and stretched.

''Evenin' son, Gretchen said you didn't eat supper so she made ya a sandwich.''

''Thanks, I'm starved,'' Jack ate hungrily.

''These are for you. Read them good, it will help ya later. How'd ya make out with the Black Gang? Hard work, ahy what?'' the big man grinned good-naturedly.

''Not too bad but the noise gets me. A guy named Rolly was a big help. I'm pretty stiff but Rolly says I'll get used to it. COUPLING-BRAKING-SWITCHING-FIRING were the titles of the books. Thanks Davey, this is just what I need,'' Jack said having read the book and pamphlet titles aloud.

"The next 90 days are important. Read and study all you can. Pay attention, ask questions and learn. Apply yourself—you're a quick, bright lad, it will come easy to you." Davey wanted Jack to succeed and encouraged him.

"Thank you Davey, I will. The sandwich is good. I was too bushed to eat earlier."

"It's a backbreaker, for sure, but you will get used to it. You need to know what goes on in the Barn and in 90 days, it's over. After you pass your tests you will be a fireman and on the road full time. To sleep son, morning is pushing." Davey undressed to his long-johns and dropped heavily onto his bed. Almost at once he began to snore.

Jack put the books and papers on the floor beside his cot, snuffed the lamp and stretched out to sleep.

The next three months passed quickly. Jack worked, ate and slept railroading. His body hardened to the tasks. His mind absorbed pages and pages of written material and the activity around him. His blistered hands toughened and in general, he matured. Rolly helped him in the Barn and Davey and Smoke taught him how to run an engine. They frowned when he was careless and laughed when he was outrageous. He took his hard-knocks and his teasing with good humor. Jack was given full time status at the end of the trial period and passed his tests. In November of 1910, he became a fireman and was assigned to a yard switching crew.

He fired the little switch engines in the yards with a man named Orrin Platt. Orrin had a keen eye and a surgeon's touch on the throttle. He could kick and bump cars with an artist's precision. Not enough kick and they rolled a few feet and stopped. Too much kick and they banged and slammed into the trains. A good depth perception was imperative. Jack was eager to learn how it was done.

In the spring of 1911, at Big Davey's request, Jack was sent back to fire for him on the long distance freight. Jack was delighted and the old friends were together again. Jack learned the road and the towns and villages along the way. We waved at the people and they waved back. When they waved back, especially the children, it gave him a sense of belonging and inner warmth that he could not explain.

It reminded him of his youth. When he and Li'l Dan trod the ties and hung around the station. A comfortable, pleasant feeling nudged his inners.

Jack and Big Davey did every thing together. Aside from their work, Jack and Davey spent much time together. In the summer, they would often swim and fish at Davey's home on Tygart Lake. In the winter they would hunt or set by the open fire and tell yarns and hash over their work. Davey's wife, Rebecca—sometimes called Becky—was a tiny, shy woman who devoted her whole life to Big Davey. They had no children. She cooked, cleaned, gardened and waited. Waited for her Davey to come home, as did all the families of railroad men. She enjoyed having company, especially Jack and learned his favorite foods and cooked for him. After a good meal, Jack corded the piano, Davey strummed the guitar and Becky sang.

Their camaraderie lasted for a year then Jack was bumped to Middle Local. He preferred to stay with Davey but a man goes where he is sent. Jack took his bump without grumbling. A man with seniority had priority—those are the regulations—he can bump any man for his job if the other has less seniority.

On the last run with Davey, Jack said his goodbys in Cumberland and Parkersburg. He had become quite attached to all he knew. To him, they were like family.

At his last breakfast at Riley's, his co-workers shook his hand and wished him well.

"Take care of yourself," said one.

"Watch those curves," said another.

"Look for the green," was heard.

"Thank you all. You're a great bunch of guys and I won't forget how you helped me get started." Jack could feel himself begin to choke and hoped no one noticed.

"I kees your cheek and you come back to us." Gretchen was tearful and cried into her apron.

"Thank you, Gretchen, I will miss you." Jack kissed her hair on the top of her head.

"You are a natural, Laddy. You've done it and we are proud of you." Mike Riley said in his inimitable Irish way, sniffed and wiped his nose on his sleeve while he pumped Jack's hand affectionately.

Big Davey grabbed Jack in a bear hug and nearly squeezed the breath out of him. "My boy, you are like the son I never had. You're quick, bright, honest and hardworking—that's more than a lot of us can say." Everybody laughed at Davey's words and all agreed.

"Come along, I'll walk ya to the yards, I'm off today." The two men waved goodby and left Riley's.

"I haven't got the words to tell you how I will miss you or how obliged I am for everything you have taught me. In many ways, you are like my Paap." Jack choked again.

"For you to say I'm like your Pa is all the thanks I need. You're a good fireman and in a few months you will be a great engineer. Watch, listen and learn. You're young and healthy and the whole world is at your feet. Local is good work. No long hours and off every night. Get to know the fellas at both ends. Make friends and get yourself a tootsie. You're old enough to handle one now." Big Davey's eyes twinkled.

''I don't have time for girls and I wouldn't know where to look for a tootsie and I wouldn't know one if I saw her,'' Jack confessed and blushed.

''Go into any saloon near any railroad yards and THEY will find YOU, specially if ya put a fiver on the bar. Watch yourself, those gals can drink ya under the table and steal your lucre, ta boot. Drink the good stuff sparingly and watch your poke,'' were Davey's instructions.

''What am I going to do when you aren't around to mother me.'' Jack teased Davey.

''Go along now, and let me hear from you once in a while.'' Davey clasped Jack's hand in both of his and held it for a moment, then turned on his heel and walked away.

Chapter Nine

THE ICE HOUSE

At the yard office, he was told the engineer he was to fire for was Ira Morris. Jack was to deadhead to Oakland, mark up at the yard office and report to Ira tomorrow morning. He was told to deadhead on the morning passenger headed to Clarksburg and the crew was expecting him. No one rides the trains without orders.

He located the train in the yards, tossed his valise into the cab and climbed in. The crew asked if he would like to ride the caboose but he preferred to ride in the cab.

Shortly after noon the train arrived in Oakland. Jack thanked the crew for the lift and reported to the yard office. He marked up, passed the time of day with the local railroaders in the office, introduced himself and asked about lodgings.

''Hattie More has the best grub but her beds aren't that good,'' said one man.

''Yeah, but it's clean and cheap,'' said another.

''That will be first rate with me, thanks,'' said Jack.

''Walk the tracks to the first cross-street and turn left. It's the big house with the swing on the porch. Hattie's always around some place,'' said another man in the office.

''I'm much obliged to you fellas and I'll see you again. I report to work tomorrow for Ira Morris.''

''He's a good hogger—does everything by the book, good luck,'' said another.

''Thanks again, gents.'' Jack gave them one of his left-handed, two fingered salutes and left the office.

He walked along the tracks to the cross street and scanned his surroundings. To the left was the residential area and to the right was the business district. Those little towns along the railroad were primarily the same. Oakland's population was about 1400 souls, give or take a few. It was a sleepy mountain crossroads and railroad layover.

He had no trouble finding Hattie More's Boarding and Rooming House. On the front porch, he turned the handle on the brass door bell.

"You lookin' for me?" Hattie called from the corner of the house.

"I'm looking for Misses More."

"I'm Hattie More." She was a big woman with a pleasent face and dark hair. She wiped her hands on her apron.

"I'm a railroader—names Lansure—I need room and board. The guys at the yard office said yours is the best place in town," Jack explained.

"I got a back room with the morning sun. That's a dollar a day for board and room. It's 25 cents for the room, alone or 75 cents a day for board, alone. Linen change once a week. A dollar a week extra and I do your laundry and another dollar a week for a packed pail. Pick your needs and I'll show you the room," she stuck out her hand to Jack and he took it in his.

Jack followed her into the big house and up the stairs.

"There are three other men on this floor and you share the bath. Lights out at eleven and no drinkin!" she said and opened the door to the room.

It was small but light and Jack liked it. There was a dresser and chifforobe, a straight backed chair and the bed looked sturdy if not soft. Hattie opened one the two windows and a cool breeze fluttered the lace curtians.

"This will be just fine and I'll take everything—bed, board, laundry and pail. I'm not much for tea and I like my Java hot, light and sweet. Other than that, I eat everything. Can I move in now?" He dropped his heavy valise to the floor.

"If you've got a week in advance, the room is yours," she declared.

"That comes to nine dollars a week—I'll pay you ten against the time I might be a little short." Jack knew he would never be short he made $2.40 a day but was happy to have a nice room. The lodgings were well worth the price and Jack had made a new friend. Hattie beamed happily.

"Thank you——what do I call you? She jammed the folded bills into her apron pocket.

"Jack Lansure."

"Well, Jack Lansure, call me Hattie. We eat at six and six and the noon meal is when I fix it—sorry, you're too late today." She smiled .impishly.

"That's alright. I want to go up town and look around—sort of get my bearings. I'll be back before six," He said.

They went down stairs together and he left the house.

The village square was quiet in the afternoon sun. In an hour's time, he had gone completely around and studied it all. There was Butler's Hardware, Allen's Dry Goods, The Bank and Trust, Murphy's Saddle and Tack Shop, Walt's Diner, the drug store, haberdashery, meat market and grocery, Simm's Barber and Beauty Parlor. Ollin's Ready-To-Wear, the feed mill and a very pretty stone church. There was a police station, fire house, and 2 saloons near the railroad station down the block.

Jack went into Walt's Diner and slid onto a stool.

"Hello, Mate, what will you have?" Walt was a stout man with a ruddy face in a white apron.

"Ya got any custard pie?" Jack asked.

"Sure do—fresh today." Walt answered.

"I'll have a wedge and a cup of java—hot, light and sweet." Jack gave his order.

"You're a railroader, aren't ya? I can tell by the way you order. A railroader never asks for coffee—always java. I'm Walt Barry, retired ship's cook and I own this place." He wiped his greasy hands on his apron and extended one over the counter to Jack who took it.

"I'm Jack Lansure, how are you?"

Walt placed Jack's order in front of him. He drew himself a cup of coffee from the steaming urn, carried it around the counter and sat down on a stool next to Jack.

"This time of day business is slow and I clean up. You're new around here aren't you? The railroad seems to be growing—that's good for my business."

"Yes, I'll be fireman for Ira Morris on the local here," Jack ate his food.
"I know him. He comes in here once in a while—lives around here, I think. Well, better get back to work." Walt finished his coffee and went behind the counter to wipe up.

"That's mighty good custard pie and the java was just the way I like it. Your wife bake it?"

"Thanks mate, all that comes over the counter here, I make. I was married to the sea for twenty years and now I'm married to this place but I have no wife. I keep a room at Hattie More's for Sundays and Holidays but I keep a hammock in the storeroom in case I need to bunk out," Walt explained.

"I just took a room there. Bet you've got stories to tell. I'll see you again." Jack dropped a few coins on the counter and went out the door. He liked the interesting man.

"Nice ta meet ya, come in again and I'll tell ya some." Walt called, as Jack left the diner.

Jack walked back to More's Boarding House in the warm, late afternoon sun. Somehow he no longer felt strange or alone. He remembered his Paap's words 'Good people are found every where if you just look'. Leaving Riley's and Big Davey was less painful now.

At the boarding house, the men were gathering for the evening meal. They were lounging on the steps and the porch railing. Jack counted six including himself. He introduced himself around and shook their hands. They spoke of Hattie's cooking. Another said the tap beer at Al's Saloon was a bargain at 2 cents a glass. They spoke of the weather, the high cost of living and politics. The men made Jack feel comfortable and welcome.

The dinner bell hung on a cord from top of the staircase in the big hall. It was a large cow bell and Hattie delighted in shaking it vigorously. The din could be heard three doors away. She said it not only called the folks to dinner but it woke them from a sound sleep and saved her many steps.

The men found their places at the table and Jack took the last open chair. They talked and ate ravenously. They talked among themselves and joked with Hattie while she served the huge platters of food.

One by one they finished, excused themselves and drifted to their rooms.

Jack was stuffed also and he said, "Miss Hattie, that was some meal! You're a good cook."

"Just Hattie, Jack, just Hattie. I like to see a man with an appetite. Don't forget—breakfast at six sharp."

"I'll be up," he assured her and went up to bed. He planned to read, then sleep.

Jack was awakened by the sun streaming through his windows. He washed, shaved and dressed quickly and the scent of Bay Rum filled the room. He glanced at himself in the mirror. He was looking for flaws in his appearance; a turned up collar, shaving knicks or a loose button. He was not aware that he had become a very handsome man. His hair was jet black and shiny and he combed it straight back without a part. His expressive hazel eyes flashed green or blue or even black when he was angry—which wasn't often. He stood a half inch less than six feet, was long boned and lean. He had good teeth and a ready smile. The fingers of his hands were long and straight more like the hands of a skilled surgeon than a railroader. His skin was surprisingly fair for a man with black hair. He was left-eyed, left-footed and noticeably left-handed. He was soft-spoken, unassuming and slow to anger. His manner was quiet and calm but he was keen-eyed and very observant.

People liked him and he liked people. He made friends where ever he went but he had no—what you call—close friend except Big Davy, whom he looked upon like a father.

Jack was a loner at heart. He enjoyed a walk in the air with the wind in the trees and the sound of the birds all around or to sit under a tree and read or think. Those quiet times restored and refreshed him as it did as a boy in the 'quiet place.' They allowed him to collect his thoughts and make plans. Jack Lansure was a man.

He found nothing wrong with his image in the mirror, took his hat and gauntlets and left the room.

Jack dropped down the stairs two at a time, bounced into the dining room, found his chair and sat down.

"Morn'in Jack, you sleep okay on that bed?" Hattie asked while she sat Jack's ham and eggs and coffee before him.

"Um—smells good—sure did—like a log! How are you, Hattie?"

He chatted with the other men and soon all were off to work. On his way out, Hattie handed him his lunch.

"I packed your lunch in this salt bag but you better get a pail. The hardware has nice ones. Don't drop it! I put your java in a glass fruit jar," she cautioned.

"Thank you. I'll get a pail and I'll be careful of the glass," Jack teased.

Jack walked up the tracks to the yard office by stepping on the crossties. In the office, he marked up and asked for Ira Morris. He was told the local was westbound on track 10. He made his way there and called up to the engineer in the cab.

"I'm looking for Ira Morris—my name's Lansure—I'm his smoke."

"Come on up—I'm Morris. You ready to roll?" He motioned Jack up into the cab.

"Yes sir, I am glad to meet you—I'm Jack Lansure," he said and extended his hand.

"Jack," he said and took Jack's hand and pumped it. "Most call me Ike. I do all this by the book and if you do, we will get along fine," and waved his arm around in the cab.

"Yes sir, by the book."

"Stash your gear in the seat box and lets get to it."

Ike Morris was all business and Jack knew it. The two men made ready to move out and waited for the green signal. When the red turned to green, the train moved out of town.

Ike was thorough and efficient and Jack was impressed. Ike did everything by the book and Jack was careful not to make a mistake. He followed instructions to the letter and kept the steam exactly at the ordered level. Ike's manner was different from Big Davey but the expertise was there. The trip to Clarksburg went without incident.

As they neared Clarksburg and the train moved slowly along the village park or green, Jack appeared to be looking for something there.

''You looking for something?'' Ike inquired.

''Yes, a girl in a blue picture hat. She often sits in the park on a bench and we wave to her,'' Jack explained.

''You know her?''

''Nope, she's just someone to wave to and she is nearly always here. Besides, I like her hat.'' Jack stated flatly.

The two men scanned all the benches as the train moved along. About halfway through the park, she was there. They waved and she waved back.

''That her?'' quizzed Ike.

''Yep, that's her. Pretty hat, she always wears it.'' Jack waved.

The two men went back to their gauges and the business of railroading. The park or green ran from the edge of town to the village square. The train tracks passed along the south perimeter of the park directly into the yards, two blocks south of the square.

''Maybe you can meet her, now that you layover here,'' Ike said after a long silence.

''I don't think so. She's not one of those tootsies that hang around the saloons. She looks like a nice girl to me and I try to steer clear of personal entanglements. I'm studing for my engineer's and I'm never in one place long enough to settle down. The tootsies do me fine—no ties—no questions and no problems. The girl in the blue picture hat is just someone nice to wave to when I pass through here, that's all.'' Jack was emphatic and the subject was closed.

Ike and Jack went back to the work of running the engine and soon the train was in for the night and the men were finished.

''The Ralston Hotel has rooms but the food isn't much. You can get a sandwich and coffee at the bar but there is no lunchroom. Want to try it?'' inquired Ike.

''Sure, that's Jake with me.'' Jack agreed.

The Ralston had a big lobby, small rooms and noisy plumbing but it was cover for the night and Jack was satisfied. He settled in and for the the next few weeks, it was his home-away-from-home.

Ike and Jack worked well together and for Jack, it was interesting and exciting. He watched, listened and learned.

The weather was unseasonably wet. It rained a bit nearly every day. The tree-covered, high-walled banks along the right-of-way were waterlogged and unpredictable.

Landslides were frequent in those mountains but in wet weather, it was particularly dangerous. A whole mountain side could fall onto the tracks without warning and cause disastrous train wrecks and derailments.

So it was that day. A huge pile of mud, rocks, trees and grass fell onto the tracks and was as high as a two story building.

When Jack's local rounded Crow's Point, there was no place to go but into the slide. The engine buried her boiler up to the windows but it did not blow or turn over. She stuck fast and the sudden stop caused the train to telescope and toss the cars in all directions along the tracks. The tender flew into the cab and caused the huge, loose iron plates of the engine floor to fly up and pin both men against the firebox and front windows. It happened in an instant and they had no time to jump to safety.

The sound of grinding steel and splintering wood stopped suddenly and a deathly silence prevailed. A slight hissing of the steam in the boiler was heard faintly, nothing else.

After some time passed, voices were heard along side the engine. The other crew members were not seriously injured and had arrived from the caboose to help Jack and Ike. All were bumped and bruised and one had a broken arm.

"They didn't have time to jump so they must still be in there some place," said one.

"The cab is nearly gone, where can they be?" said another.

"We have to look for um, they might still be alive in there." They slogged up the mud pile to the top of the boiler to uncover the front windows and broke them out.

"Over here, I found Ike, I think he's dead," called one man.

Indeed, Ike was badly crushed. The search went on in the fireman's side for Jack. After some time of careful digging, a worker called, "Over here, he's wedged in a space between the plate and the firebox. I can only see his head and he's covered with blood."

"Is he dead?" called someone.

"I can't tell. Help me dig him out—I need a crowbar!" The man was very excited. He tore the broken window completely out of its frame. With help, he lifted Jack's limp body from the wreckage.

"I'm no saw-bones but Jack's bad hurt, if not dead. His face is a bloody mess and I don't think he's breathing."

They laid Jack on a makeshift litter and slogged down the mud slide to solid ground being careful not to jostle or drop him.

"Any of you hear the wrecker whistle? I expect they will send the wrecker and the Big Hook from Parkersburg since it's closer. That means, the wrecker will be coming in from the other side of the slide. How about one of you guys keep'n watch on top of what's left of the cab. Shack, how bad is your arm? Guess I'm the only one who's all in one piece and I'm a little shaky,'' confessed the Flop. (A Dolly Flopper is a switchman and the Shack is a brakeman).

''It's broke between the elbow and shoulder. I got slammed into the stove in the caboose. Could be worse—it's not through the skin—but it hurts like a son-of-a-bitch.'' swore the shack.

''Here she comes!'' called the man on the cab roof.

''Bout time, they will have the Doc and I bet the Cinder Dicks will be all over this place.''

The railroad police inspectors (Cinder Dicks) will want to know why the gandy dancers (track men) did not recognize this impending slide.

The wrecking train edged up to the landslide and the crew of twenty or so scrambled over the mud pile to the crippled engine and train. The doctor went right to the injured men who all sat around on the ground near Jack and Ike.

''How many hurt?'' he asked and opened his bag to work.

''Three thumped and bloody, one broken arm and two dead,'' he answered.

The doctor examined the broken arm quickly and when the man howled at his touch, he said, ''I can't set it here but I'll brace it and give you a spoon full of laudanum for the pain. I'll clean and bandage the rest of you. I'll need your help to get the clothes off these dead men, down to their underware, before rigor mortis sets in,'' were the doctor's instructions. while he examined Ike.

''Is he dead, Doc?'' asked one of the men.

''Yes, son, he is. Help me undress him,'' he said after a preliminary examination.

''How about Jack, here?'' He asked again.

''It looks like his head is crushed. There is a deep gash under his left cheekbone, one at his hairline between his eyes and there's bleeding in his chest near his right shoulder. He's probably smashed inside but I'd need more equipment to tell for sure. It will be hours before we leave here and we must get these men out of this heat.'' The kindly doctor explained.

A crowd had gathered and someone said, ''There's an old ice house and lake beyond those trees, about three hundred yards or so, you could take them there.'' The man pointed the way.

''That will do nicely. Couple of you lads lend a hand here and cart them over there,'' the doctor directed.

Four men lugged their sad cargo to the ice house and went in. It was refreshingly cool after the late day summer heat. The floor of the building was stacked high with ice blocks of all sizes that were carefully covered with sawdust and canvas.

The men uncovered two very large blocks, carefully placed the nearly naked dead men on the ice and covered them with canvas. Their job done, they went back to the wrecked train.

At the train wreck, crews worked feverishly to clear the tracks and right the cars. The work would continue through the night until all was cleared away and the repairs made.

The two dead men had been in the cold ice house since about four o'clock. It was now about midnight and a faint groan was heard coming from under the canvas. Jack Lansure was alive! He began to shiver violently because his body was chilled to the bone. He tried to move but the pain was excruciating. His head and face throbbed with each heartbeat and the pain in his shoulder ran down to his fingers. The rest of his body was stiff and cramped while his head and face began to bleed again. He rolled his tongue around in his swollen mouth and found several bits of broken teeth.

He tried to raise himself to a sitting position but found he was completely covered with a heavy, damp canvas. He was naked to his underwear-bottoms and the cold, wet canvas added to his discomfort. He threw off the canvas and forced himself to sit upright. He spat out the pieces of his broken teeth and upon further inspection, he found one was loose and two were broken off. The damage was to his upper jaw. His fingers traced the gaping, half-moon shaped gash on his cheek and found it bleeding again. The gash on his forehead was causing the blood to drip down his nose and drop off.

He sat there a few seconds longer because he could not remember anything.

It came back to him in a jerk. LANDSLIDE! No time to jump and everything went black. Somehow he had survived the wreck but how did he get into that old ice house. Where was the wreck and the crew? Ike—where's Ike?

When his eyes could focus in the darkness, he tried to observe his surroundings. He was freezing cold and shook uncontrollably. When his legs would support him, he slid off the ice block and tried to brush the sawdust from his back. It was dank-smelling and itchy.

He felt along the ice blocks and found Ike. Jack knew the instant he touched him that he was dead. He found no one else.

He had to escape from that cold tomb and find the train and crew. He was naked and cold and decided a wet, stiff canvas was better than no clothing at all. He wrapped himself in the canvas, found the door and went out into the night.

The night air was chilly but far warmer than the ice house. Jack was grateful and looked around. He could see the small lake in front of him but was not sure which direction to take. Should he go left or right? He could not see the lights or hear the noise of the wreck on the right-of-way to his right because a small rise and a stand of trees blocked his vision.

Being left-handed, he went to the left and the wrong way.

His progress was slow and painful and there was not much of a path. The rough terrain hurt his feet and the briars and brambles scratched and tore at his flesh. The canvas was stiff and unyielding and did not cover where it was needed.

After walking and stumbling halfway around the lake, he was jerked suddenly by his neck and thrown violently to the ground on his back. He had walked under a rope clothes line and hung himself. When he regained his senses, he realized he was covered with several pieces of cloth and his Adam's apple throbbed. His weight snapped the line and the clothes fell with him.

Clothes! Something to cover himself. What luck! He searched the articles that fell near him. They were long johns—not the tops or bottoms but full ones. They were all sizes from baby size to some that would fit Big Davey. He found a pair near his size, removed his own and climbed into fresh dry ones. What a pleasure to cover his cold bleeding body.

He was in someone's door yard and but a few steps from a huge bank barn. That meant shelter for the night and a warm bed in the hayloft. He went in quietly being careful not to frighten the animals who could sound alarm. None seemed to notice as he made his way to the loft ladder and climbed up.

The hay smelled sweet and clean. He made himself a bed, covered his tired body and fell into a deep, exhausted sleep.

When he stirred his body seared with pain. He opened his eyes to bright daylight and his face was about eight inches from the sweetist little face he had ever seen who was peering at him through the rungs of the loft ladder.

She was about four years old with big eyes and long dark braids that fell from her neat white skullcap.

''Are thee dead? Thee are very bloody.'' She was not afraid and her huge eyes studied his face.

''No, I'm not dead but I am banged up, some.'' He raised himself to one elbow.

''Why are thee wearing my sister's underdrawers? Are thee a robber?''

''No, I'm not a robber and I didn't know these were your SISTER'S johns.'' He exclaimed and examined them closer.

''Are thee a hobo from the tracks?'' She questioned him.

''No, I'm a railroader and we had a wreck.'' He tried to be patient with her. ''What are you doing up here?''

''I came to feed Maudie,'' was the reply. The child studied him carefully.

''Who's Maudie? Jack asked.

''That's Maudie, over there,'' she pointed, a few feet away to a beautiful three colored cat nursing four tiny kittens. ''She had her babies here and I came to bring her this.'' She held up a small pail of milk.

''Oh, I see, THAT'S Maudie. Well come up and feed her, I won't bite you.'' He tried to assure her.

''My sister will be very sad that thee took her underdrawers. We only have two—one on and one in.'' She stated flatly and proceeded to feed the cat.

''What does that mean—one on and one in?'' He asked the child.

''Thee are not very smart, are thee? Everybody knows THAT,'' she was indignant but adorable. ''Thee better come into the house and 'splain.'' She backed down the ladder and Jack followed.

When Jack reached the floor he felt dizzy. The door opened and in came a strange looking man followed by several women, all sizes and dressed alike. Jack took a step toward them but fell unconscious on the barn floor.

When Jack regained consciousness, he was in a warm bed. He had been washed clean all over, his arm was in a sling and his gashed face had been stitched and bandaged.

Around the bed stood eight women, all dressed alike with the strange man from the barn. At Jack's left side stood his little friend from the loft.

''Who are you and where is this place?'' Jack tried to sit up but the pain stopped him.

''Welcome back to us friend, we feared for thy life but our prayers were answered.'' The man spoke softly. ''I'm Wilbur Hays and these ladies are my daughters'' He started with the eldest and named them. ''This is Saphire, Emerald, Garnet, Pearl, Ruby, Jade, Opal and Crystal. They are my jewels. And what do they call thee? He asked politely.

''I'm Jack Lansure, Sir, I was in a train wreck—I think—hid in the barn—but I don't know how I got in here.'' Jack was puzzled and his head ached.

''Say hello and welcome to our friend Jack Lansure, girls,'' the man instructed the women and they all chattered welcome together.

''And what's your name my pretty little friend?'' Jack smiled and touched the child's long braid that fell on her shoulder.

Fertiga, that means, The End. We had to SOAK thee in the tub to get thee clean—thee were that dirty!'' The little one was astonished at Jack's miserable condition.

''Ferty, that's not a very nice way to speak to a guest,'' Wilbur gently scolded the child. The other girls giggled and whispered among themselves.

''But papa, it's true. Shaphire scrubbed him with a brush and Emerald held him up so he wouldn't drown—right in that tub.'' she pointed to a large metal tub that set in the corner of the room. She was emphatic.

"Shush, now, child, we must not tire our guest. Ruby, please bring the soup." Wilbur was gentle and soft-spoken with his family.

"And Pearl had to burn HIS underdrawers in the stove!" Ferty was persistent.

Jack's embarrassment was full-blown when he suddenly realized he was stark-naked under the bed covers. He blushed to his ears.

"I'm sorry to be a burden and I thank you for all that you have done. I'll be going now." He tried to lift his sore body.

"There, there, Friend, thee must stay quiet and rest so thy wounds will heal. Thee have been here since yesterday and although Jade is an expert seamstress, thy stitches are fresh. Now have some soup then rest." Wilbur explained and Ruby offered Jack the soup. The girls eagerly helped him rise to a sitting position and fluffed his pillows.

"Umm, this is great soup, thank you Ruby. Which one of you is Jade?"

"I'm Jade," said the prettiest girl of all.

'I'm obliged to you for sewing me up. As for the bath——."

"Rest thyself Friend, I was there to see to thy personal needs," Wilbur interrupted, "it was all quite proper besides my jewels are aware of the biological differences between men and women."

The subject was closed and Jack's embarrassment subsided. The girls giggled but Ferty would not let it rest.

"But thee were very dirty and bloody—black and blue, too," she insisted.

"Ferty, that will be quite enough." Wilbur was gentle but firm. "Thee must forgive Fertiga, she has never really had a mother's hand. My dear wife gave her that name when she was born. It means finished or the end in Dutch. Rachel was very ill and three months later she went to her reward. Thy have observed we are Quakers. I am the iceman of these parts. My daughters and I cut ice and store it in the ice house in the winter and in the summer, we deliver it to the folks here about. We heard about the train wreck. Two dead and several injured, I understand," explained the kindly man.

"Not exactly as you can see, I'm NOT dead, they just thought I was. There was a landslide and no time to jump. That's all I remember until I woke up in your ice house." Jack finished his soup. "I must get word to the crew before they scare my Ma'am and Paap with news of my death." Jack's voice pleaded urgency.

"Calm thy self Friend, as soon as we were certain thee were out of danger, I went to the wreck and told them thee were with us but in grave condition. They were disbelieving until several went with me to the ice house and found thee gone. I told them of thy injuries and assured them, thee were in capable hands. We are to care for thee until thee are healed enough to travel, at which time we are to take thee to the train station in Rosemont where thee will take the passenger train to Clarksburg. Now thee must sleep.''

Wilbur had arranged everything and Jack was confident in his new friend but very tired. Wilbur's daughters fawned over Jack. One girl drew the bedroom window shades, one helped remove the pillows to allow him to recline and several smoothed his bed clothes. All but Jade, she demurely lowered her eyes and hung back.

In his lifetime, he had never seen so many girls with love-starved hungry eyes. The way they stared at him made him feel as if he was 'the last pork chop on the plate' and were about to pounce on him. He reasoned, there must be no eligible Quaker men around otherwise they would pay no attention to a total stranger. Jack was too sleepy to think further and closed his eyes.

''May I stay and watch him sleep? I promise to be very quiet,'' begged Ferty.

''Thee may NOT!'' Saphire took Ferty by the shoulder and gently but firmly marched her out of the room. The other girls followed and she closed the door.

Jack fell into a deep sleep.

When he awakened again it was still daylight but all was quiet. His injuries hurt less but his bladder was bursting. His eyes searched the room for a Thunder Mug, White Owl, Chamber Pot or whatever it's called, to relieve himself. It was there under the edge of his bed. He dragged himself out of bed and since he was naked, he prayed no one would open the door until he was finished.

After he was blissfully relieved, he crawled back into the covers to sleep again.

He was wakened by Ferty's voice by his bed.

''Mr. Jack, thy breakfast is ready and we are here,'' she said loudly.

All the girls came in and bustled around him. They helped him sit up, fluffed his pillows, brought him hot water in a pitcher and bowl for shaving and each had an article of clothing for him to wear.

''They are father's clothes—not Emerald's,'' Ferty said at the top of her voice.

''Shush Ferty, he must eat first—shave later,'' directed Saphire.

''I must change thy bandages and see to thy stitches,'' Jade said softly.

''These clothes will fit thee and when thee are strong enough, thee will get up a few hours at a time,'' was Emerald's advice and all placed the clothing on the bed.

''Ruby cooked the eggs but Opal scraped the toast, they won't ever let me help,'' pouted Ferty.

''Ferty, with so many to learn from, before long, you will be an expert.'' Jack patted her shoulder.

''Expert! I'll be expert! Expert!'' Ferty shouted, ''What's expert, Crystal?'' She asked her older sister.

''Never mind Ferty, run along.'' Crystal ushered the child from the room.

''Thee must excuse Ferty, she's just a baby.'' Jade set a small pan of warm water and a towel on the dresser with a roll of clean bandages. ''I may have to soak the bandages to get them off. I'll try not to pain thee.''

''Ferty's as cute as a button. Go ahead, I'll try not to holler,'' Jack could not resist the urge to tease her.

Jack studied Jade as she carefully removed the soiled bandages, cleaned the wounds and applied fresh ones.

Her face was creamy white with dark brows and lashes over calm gray eyes. Her long dark hair was braided into one thick braid which hung down the center of her back. The strings of her skullcap swung loose along her neck.

She dressed his wounds with gentle steady fingers and when she was completed she said, ''Thee are healing nicely. Did I hurt thee?''

''Not a bit, thanks.'' He said.

''Are thee up to getting dressed for a while and moving around some?'' She asked.

''You bet! It would be good to stand up again. Last time, I was pretty wobbly.''

''Outside everyone—allow Mr. Lansure to shave and dress,'' Jade always spoke softly.

The girls giggled and left the room.

Jack slid into his underwear and stood painfully to his feet. His bruised body was sore but healing. His first glimpse into the mirror was a shocker. His own mother would not recognize him. His black and blue puffy eyes had turned a sickly green and his left jaw was twice the normal size. He washed himself and shaved what he could. It hurt him most to raise his right arm. He managed to dress and opened the bedroom door.

The girls were waiting to show him about the place. Ferty took Jack by the hand and the expedition was happily underway. They showed him the big house, room by room. In the barn was the milk cow called Buttermilk, a pet sheep called Elmer and a coop full of chickens. The team of horses that pulled the ice wagon were huge Percherons called Ezekiel and Mortakai—Zeke and Mort—also plowed the garden and hauled sawdust for the icehouse.

The girls chatted about everything. They told Jack how they cut and hauled the ice blocks into the icehouse for storage and how it was delivered in the summer. Few people had iceboxes but most had spring houses, where they kept their perishables and a large block of ice there, would last about a month even in the hottest weather. Saphire, Emerald and Opal helped their father in the ice business and Garnet and Pearl kept house. Ruby and Crystal did the cooking and Jade was the seamstress. All helped with the chores and the garden.

When Jack sat down on the porch swing to rest the girls began with the questions.

''Where do thee come from,'' asked one.

''Tell us about the railroad,'' urged another.

''Do thee have a wife?'' said someone.

''How old are thee?'' asked Ferty, of course.

''Whoa! One at a time! I come from Pennsylvania—near Du Bois. I'm a railroad smoke—a fireman—I'm not married and Ferty, I'm old enough to be your Papa.'' He pulled Ferty up on the porch swing beside him.

''How old is THAT?'' inquired the precocious child.

''Ferty it's time for thy nap.'' Saphire gathered the child up in her strong arms and went inside the house.

''Please, tell us about the railroad, we have never taken a ride on one,'' said Crystal and sat down in Ferty's place beside Jack, on the swing. ''We hear them go by in the distance, that's all.''

''Well, the fireman keeps fire in the box to keep it moving. The hogger, the engineer, keeps it on the tracks and moving ahead. The rest of the crew keep it together. That's about all there is to it.'' There was no simpler way to explain the functions of the railroad to those sheltered girls but he tried and they seemed satisfied.

''That's enough now, Jack must go back to bed,'' Saphire ruled the roost and all went unside.

For the next three days Jack ate and slept and his wounds mended. The girls competed for Jack's attention, each in her own way, except Jade, she stayed apart.

The evening of the third day Jade removed the stitches from Jack's face and examined the cuts.

''Thee are healing well. Tomorrow thee will go away, do thee wish bandages on or not,'' she asked.

''My face looks like plowed ground but the air is good for healing, so if you please, leave them off. Jade, I will always remember you,'' he said softly and kissed her cheek.

''Thee are from another world from mine and thee will soon forget,'' she said, simply.

The next morning the girls and Wilbur drove him in a surrey to the Rosemont station. The station agent had received Jack's orders and relayed them. Jack was told to report to the company doctor and would receive further orders on the other end. The train was in and ready to board.

Jack tossed Ferty into the air and kissed her cheek.

''Now thee must kiss my sisters!'' Ferty shouted at the top of her voice.

''By all means, I will! Thank you Saphire, for the bath——'' He didn't have time to finish. Saphire grabbed him in her huge strong arms and kissed him soundy. He staggered to keep his footing under her weight.

''Emerald, sorry about your underwear,'' he whispered and kissed her cheek.'' She hugged him and kissed his cheek.

''Garnet and Pearl, thank you for keeping my bed and room clean.'' He kissed their cheeks, in turn.

''Ruby you make the best soup!'' He kissed her cheek also.

Opal and Crystal, thank you for reading to me when I was unconscious—I heard you.'' He kissed their cheeks.

''Wilbur, I'm ever in your debt, thank you,'' Jack extended his hand and Wilbur took it, ''You sure I don't owe you something.''

''Ney Friend, it was a pleasure for me and mine to have thee as our guest. Our door is always open wide to thee.'' Wilbur pumped Jack's hand.

The conductor called ''All Aboard—All Aboard!''

Jack took Jade into his arms and kissed her gently on the lips and whispered, ''I'll always remember you.''

Jack stepped onto the train and it moved slowly away from the platform. They all waved until they could no longer see each other. . . . .

Chapter Ten

THE GIRL IN THE BLUE PICTURE HAT

Jack was to report to the yard office in Clarksburg and pick up his orders. When they arrived there and the train moved slowly along the edge of the park, Jack searched for a glimpse of the 'Girl In The Blue Picture Hat'. There she was sitting on a bench, as usual.

Jack waved vigorously at her from the passenger car window but she waved back absently. She had no idea the man in the window was the same man she waved to as a crew member on the locomotive. She went back to the book she had been reading and Jack felt strangely disappointed. Why would he feel that way? He did not know her yet he had odd feelings about it. Maybe it was his street clothes or perhaps his bruised face. Could not be that, they had never seen each other up close, only passing in the distance.

The train pulled into the Clarksburg station and Jack went to the agent for his orders. He was to continue on to Parkersburg and the company offices, to see the doctor. After a complete physical examination and with the doctor's approval, Jack was to mark off and go home for thirty days recovery furlough.

He went back aboard the train and it moved on.

It was early evening when the train rolled into Parkersburg. Jack took a cheap hotel room near the station, had a double shot of rye with a beer chaser and went up to bed. He paid no attention to the stares from the room clerk and bar tender about his injured face.

The next morning Jack reported early to the railroad offices. He was directed to Doctor Brundage and Associates. He was stripped to his long johns, ushered from room to room and poked, prodded and pricked. He was examined by an assortment of doctors and nurses—then told to dress and return to the main office and wait.

Back at the offices, Jack stepped to the caged inner office.

"I'm finished with the doctors and they sent me here." Jack spoke to the man behind the iron bars.

"Oh yes, Mr. Lansure, it will be sometime until we hear the results. Will you have a seat in the waiting room please." Said the pleasant man.

"Lansure—you J. C. Lansure?" Called a man from the back of the caged area.

"Yes Sir, I am." Jack answered.

The man stood up from his desk with a stack of papers in his hand and moved toward Jack at the cage. "According to this, you are up for your engineer's exams," he said.

"Yes I am." Jack stated.

"You can take them here and now if you want to since you were in a wreck and missed the usual date. It will be a while before the doctor's report is ready and you have to—," Before he could finish Jack interrupted.

"Yes I do!" Jack was excited.

"Come around that swinging door." The man pointed to his right and Jack's left.

They seated him at a long table facing the wall and dropped a stack of papers in front of him. "We won't disturb you until you are finished but we close at five o'clock. Everything you need is here—paper, pencils and such."

The man turned and walked back to his desk.

Jack had no way of knowing that he had missed the exams although he had been expecting them soon. At that moment, he was not so sure it was the right time. He had hoped he would be given last minute preparation time to study. He could feel the sweat standing on his upper lip and his mouth was dry. He took the first page from the stack and began.

After several hours he put down his pencil, stretched his cramped body and looked at his watch; 4:10 P M and two pages to go. About half an hour later he finished.

His bottom was paralyzed, his eyes burned and his brain felt numb. He dragged himself to his feet.

"Ah, Mr. Lansure, you are finished. We have the doctor's report. He said your cheek was crushed but it saved your skull which was not fractured. Your right shoulder was torn but nothing broken. Your are healing well and the doctor who stitched you up should be commended. You are free to go home and recover. The results of your exams will be sent directly to your home." The man said.

"Thank you for all your help. I can go directly home from here for thirty days?" Jack inquired.

"Sure can, you're lucky to be alive. You can deadhead tomorrow or take the packetboat upriver tonight. Here is your pay and your furlough papers. Oh I almost forgot—." He disappeared behind the cage and suddenly reappeared through the swinging doors that Jack had gone through earlier.

"D. W. Stanton left this valise for you. He said there was a note in it for you. Well, goodbye and good luck." The man extended his hand and Jack took it. "The trolly outside will take you directly to the riverfront, if you want to take the boat." The man explained.

"I'm much obliged, thanks." Big Davey was always there when Jack needed him. The 'doctor' who stitched up his face was a little slip of a girl about 17 years old and as long as Jack had a face, he would remember Jade.

Jack dragged his heavy valise outside. He hopped a slow-moving trolly in front of the building and jumped off at the docks.

He bought a ticket on the packetboat and walked up the gangway. He dropped his grip onto the deck and leaned over the railing. It was good to stand after all the day's sitting.

The trip upriver was restful for Jack and he had time to think and mull over the events of the past few weeks and ponder the future. For a long while, he watched the boat slip quietly over the dark water and studied the lights on the shore as they passed by. Later he found a seat inside and stretched out to snooze.

Suddenly he remembered the note in the valise. Jack rummaged around in the grip and came up with Big Davey's letter. Scrawled on the back of a printed railroad order form were these words:

> 'Glad you're alive Laddie, the lesson you learned I could never teach you. Hattie and the Gang send regards. Greet you on your return.'
>
> D W Stanton

Hattie had packed all his needs and his laundry was fresh. Jack was constantly reminded of his father's words; 'Good people are everywhere.' He dozed off.

The packetboat's shrieking horn announced their arrival at Pittsburg and Jack was jerked awake. All disembarked from the Ohio River and Jack bought another ticket for the Allegheny River to Kittanning. About sunup, they arrived there. At Kittanning, he deadheaded on the night freight to Plumville. For the last leg of his trip he hitched a ride home on a wagon load of melons.

Jack stood in the warm morning air at the end of the lane to his home. How beautiful it was—HOME. The leaves had gone from green to gold, orange, red and brown. The air smelled of pine and burning leaves.

Would there ever be a better place for him than this valley? He thought not.

He looked at his watch; 8:00 AM and Ma'am would be cooking breakfast.

And so it was, Ma'am had seen Jack arrive from the kitchen window. She moved the skillet of ham and eggs from the heat and ran to meet him.

They saw each other at the same instant and ran together. He held his mother in his arms and stroked her hair. She clung to him while hot tears of joy stung her eyes.

Soon all the family came to greet Jack. After much hugging and crying and dozens of questions about the wreck and his injuries, the family sat down to breakfast together, for the first time in years.

He told them about the wreck, the Quaker family that nursed him and his injuries. They brought him up to date on the family affairs and the news in the village.

''John, I'm so happy that you will be here for my wedding. I marry John Rice on October 1,'' Rose announced happily.

''Marry! What does Paap say? You old enough? Who's John Rice?'' shouted Jack who was unprepared for the declaration.

''Yes married. He's from Dixonville, he works steady and they approve.'' Rose said quietly and blushed to her ears.

''Well in that case—sure it's what you want—go ahead. That way you don't have to worry about being an Old Maid!'' Jack hugged his sister and pinched her cheek. He could not resist the chance to tease her.

Jack's visit to his home was revitalizing and happy. Friends and relatives came and went. He tramped the hills and explored old haunts. Memories flooded back—some good and some bad but he was a man and accepted the bitter with the sweet.

His mother and sisters stuffed him with his favorite foods and chattered incessantly.

He walked and talked with his father and brother.

When the day of the wedding arrived, all of Jack's bruises had disappeared. All that remained were two thin, red lines. One ran straight from his hairline to his right eyebrow and the other was a crescent-shaped red line on his left cheek. His dental work would be done later but was not apparent.

Rose was a lovely bride in peach and white. Lu had given Rose her own white wedding veil and with some alterations and Seneca's artistic touch, it looked brand new.

The groom was red-faced and nervous. He stood first on one foot and then the other and had no idea what to do with his hands.

After the ceremony at the chapel and the festivities at the house, the bride and groom were to be taken to Dixonville to their home.

On their way out, Jack pressed several folded bills into John Rice's hand and whispered, "Take good care of my best gal, won't ya?"

After all had gone home and the house was quiet, Jack sat at the kitchen table and stirred his coffee, thoughtfully.

Jimmy poured himself a cup and sat down beside his son. His pipe had gone out again.

"When do you have to leave, son?" Jimmy asked.

"I have to mark up on the 15th. so I figured to light out on the 10th. or 11th." Jack answered.

"That soon? It's a trial on a man when his young'uns strike out on their own. Makes ME feel old." Jimmy lit his pipe again.

Seneca came into the kitchen and said, "Mr. Beesely left this on the porch while we were at the church, I think. It's addressed to you, John." Seneca handed the letter to Jack.

"Keerusalum! It must be my test results! You open it, Sen, I'm too shaky!"

"It's from the Baltimore and Ohio Railroad." She said, opened the letter and read:

Dear Sir:

This is to inform you that you have successfully completed all exams and tests required to progress from Railroad Fireman to Railroad Engineer. . . . .

Before she could read further Jack gave a cowboy's yell and threw Seneca up into the air. "Eeee hah! I did it! Read the rest, quick!" Jack said.

Seneca read more of the letter:

. . . . We further advise, that of this date your rate of pay will be duly adjusted to your new status. You will receive additional orders upon your return to work following your recovery furlough.

Yours truly,

T. Wells Barrett, Road Superintendent

"Paap! I did it! I'm a railroad Engineer!" Jack leaped around and shouted like an excited schoolboy, "I can't believe I PASSED that awful test! Wheeee!"

Jack's boyhood dream had come true and like everything else, it had it's price. Jack celebrated with his family and prepared to return to work. On October 10, 1913, Jack left his family to return to his place in the world. It was a sad parting for all. He said goodbye to his family at home and Duke walked him to the train station.

Jack hugged Duke and said, "Keep your back to the wind, kid."

"One train-wreck in a lifetime is enough, hear?" Was Duke's reply. "And write now and then."

Jack just smiled and tossed his valise onto the train platform and stepped up. The train pulled out and Jack was on his way to the Cumberland.

News travels fast along the railroad and by the time Jack had reached the yard office that evening, everyone knew about the wreck and his promotion to engineer.

The men noisily congratulated him, pumped his hand and thumped his back. The number dummy—yard clerk—smiled from ear to ear when he handed Jack his orders. "Did ya know they gave you Ike Morris's run? It says so right here!" The man pointed to the orders.

"That can't be! They wouldn't DO that!" Jack was horrified.

"Yes they DID. Guess they figured you'd do better than anybody, you bein' his smoke and all. Now that you're a hogger—seems the natural thing 'ta do," was the man's point of view. "You pick up the engine and crew at Oakland as usual the morning of the 15th," he went on.

Jack felt dazed. He stuffed his orders into his pocket and made his way through the group of railroad men. He thanked them for their interest in him and went outside. He had to think over the strange turn of events and talk with Big Davey.

Jack made his way to Riley's Boarding House, found Gretchen and asked to stay the night. He said he was to go tomorrow to Oakland and the local run.

"Of course you will stay wiz us. I will put a cot in Big Davey's room for you. He will be here later." She cupped her hands on his face and examined his scars. "My poor boy, what have zay done to you! Enough of zat come, I will make up your bed. After you rest—zupper as usual. Rest on Davey's bed for now." Gretchen dragged Jack upstairs to Davey's room and sat him on the bed.

Jack was pleased that Riley's Place and Gretchen had changed very little since he had been gone. He was comfortable. He kicked off his shoes, stretched out on the bed and fell sound asleep.

The clang of the dinner bell jolted Jack awake. He washed up, dropped down the staircase, two steps at a time and bounded into the dining room. Davey and the men were there.

"Davey I'm that glad to see you! Thanks for getting my bindle to me. I didn't hear you come into the room." Jack pumped Davey's hand. The men were happy to see him.

"Hear me! I could have torn the house down around you and ya would'nt 'ove heard me! Ya never moved a muscle the whole time I washed, shaved and dressed, ya were that dead to the world. Surviving an awful wreck takes a toll on a man that nobody sees. It leaves deeper scars than the ones that show. Part of that toll is exhaustion. In time it will pass. Now my boy, what's next?" Big Davey understood those things.

"Davey, there is something that I don't understand. My orders say I'm to pick up my engine and crew at Oakland and run the local. Davey, that's the run I just came off of—it's Ike Morris' run. It must be a mistake." The entire idea was painful to Jack.

The meal was finished, the men drifted away and Jack and Davey were alone.

"Now hear me, Laddie. It is not a mistake and it is not personal, it's business. The company lost an engineer, now you are an engineer and they need an engineer there. It's that simple."

"But Davey————"

"No buts about it. Railroadin' is like the army. Ya get your orders and ya do it the best you can. You got that, Laddie? Oh I know it hurts to lose a side-kick but this business is full of hurts. Remember Jack, I asked you if you were real sure you wanted to join this 'smoke and steel menagerie'—this 'pony wheel parade'—'this boxcar brigade'—didn't I? Well, this is just one of the trials and there will be more. Ya have to look at it from ALL angles then go on." Big Davey was fatherly but emphatic.

"Ya mean when somebody dies, they just move on?" The thought was incredible to Jack.

"That's exactly what I mean Laddie and the sooner ya learn it the better." Davey stirred his cold coffee, absentmindedly.

Gretchen had long since cleared the table while Jack and Davey talked.

"Come on, ya must sleep on big problems. Things always look better after a good night's sleep." Davey suggested.

The two men went up to bed.

The morning routine was the same as usual and Jack and Davey walked to the yards together.

"You might as well deadhead with me. Ya won't get there any faster on the passenger," Davey said.

"I hoped you'd ask—I like that better." Time with Davey was important to Jack.

The freight run to Clarksburg was uneventful. When they neared the town and the park, Jack began to search for the 'Girl In The Blue Picture Hat'.

"You still watch for that lassie?" Davey asked Jack.

"Sure do. I don't know why but I do." Jack confessed.

"You're gonna be around here a lot, why don't ya look her up?" Davey suggested.

"Naw, she's not my cup of tea." Jack sounded flippant but he simply could not put her into any category that was familiar to him. She was definitely not an end-of-track trollop.

In the Clarksburg yards, the two men said their goodbyes and Jack walked to town and the Ralston Hotel to get settled in.

"Heed my words Laddie and you will do fine. You have the makens'. Don't forget, Becky and I expect you for Christmas. Davey called from the cab window.

"Could'nt have made it this far without you. I'll be there." Jack gave Davey his two-fingered, left-handed salute and watched Davey's freight train roll out of the yards.

Jack checked in at the Ralston Hotel, put his clothes in the room and went up town to eat. A sandwich at the hotel bar was fine once in a while but today Jack preferred a meal.

The main street was lined with assorted stores and shops. Jack found a homey looking restaurant. It was a mom-and-pop operation where the food was usually good.

He took a stool at the counter and scanned the menu; Beef and boiled potatoes; pork chops and apple sauce; sauerkraut and wieners——that's the one he selected.

"Take your order, Mister?" Asked a plump lady of about forty who stood in front of him, behind the counter.

"Put two dogs on a load of hay and let 'um ride; a side of rabbit hash, punk and grease with java, light and sweet." was Jack's order.

"A number #3 with a side of coleslaw," she called to the kitchen. "Coffee and bread go with the meal," she said to Jack and wrote it on the pad, "You railroaders sure do have a way of speakin'. My man and I had to learn a whole new language to run this place." She placed his table service and a glass of water in front of him and smiled.

"If the food is as good as the service, I'll be back," Jack said and winked at the busy waitress.

He was disappointed when told there was no more custard pie.

"That goes first around here, the most of it goes with the lunch crowd and by supper, there is none left," the woman explained.

Jack paid his check, left a generous tip and went out into the night air. He walked back to the hotel, bought a newspaper and went up to bed.

Germany had swallowed up those little countries and Great Britain had declared war. The news was ominous in the fall of 1914. It was a year of great change and happenings in the world and in Jack's life.

Fall fell into winter without incident. Jack had become good friends with his crew and memorized each little idiosyncrasy of his locomotive. After a few weeks, he knew all her foibles and weaknesses as well as her strength and abilities. He had a gentle hand on the throttle and kicked cars with a surgeon's precision; too hard a kick, broke equipment and lost time; not hard enough forced a repeat kick and that wasted time and time was money.

Jack was serious about his work and soon earned the respect of his crew men as well as the management.

He became a familiar face to the other railroaders. He was quick to smile, slow to anger and darkly handsome. He was a man's man but the ladies adored him. When the urge prevailed, there was a lady of easy virtue to satisfy his needs. His passion was frequent but fleeting. His loving was casual, non-commital and without involvement. His carnal appetite was great and he ate often. He patronized the local saloons, bought his needs from the local stores and became a respected member of the community.

One snowy night in mid-December, Jack walked into the apothecary and drug store to purchase various toilet articles and select a small gift for Becky Stanton by way of a 'thank you' for his Christmas invitation. Jack's sister Leone, had pounded his manners into him at the end of a wooden spoon and he learned them well.

Jack made his purchase of Bay Rum, mug soap and a styptic pencil and paid the clerk. The selection of Becky's gift would take longer. He browsed over a table loaded with beautifully packaged Christmas selections.

There was assorted boxes of candy, packaged talcum powder, bottled toilet water and a variety of sachets. He sniffed the scents of lavender, rose, lilly and sandalwood sachets and made his selection. It was envelope-shaped, lavender-scented and large enough to scent a few handkerchiefs or an entire drawer of ladies unmentionables.

Jack glanced up and there she stood on the opposite side of the table. It was 'The Girl In the Blue Picture Hat'. He was riveted to the floor. Their eyes met and a strange ripple coursed through his body. When his legs would move, he went quickly around the table to her.

"It's you—you're her! I know you are her—it's you!" Jack stammered foolishly.

"I am who?" she said softly.

"You're the girl in the blue picture hat!" He exclaimed, "The one I always wave to in the park! I'm the railroader on the train!" Looking into her huge, brown eyes made him feel like a weak-kneed, cotton-mouthed, stumble bum and the ripples of delight spread again and again. It was a sensation he had never experienced before. He struggled to regain his composure and erase his red face.

"Oh, is that so? Which one are you, I wave to them all," she said softly and her gaze never left his face.

"I'm the engineer on the local. I was on the through freight before that." Her huge eyes studied him, thoughtfully.

"Are you the left-handed one who salutes?" She asked and smiled.

"Yea, that's me!" He was flustered and wanted to kick himself for acting like a ridiculous schoolboy.

"I see you are doing your Christmas shopping." She said and pointed to the sachet in his hand.

"Yes, I'm invited away for Christmas and this for the lady of the house." He had no idea why he blurted that out.

"Nice choice," she said simply and moved away from him along the table.

"Miss, may I walk with you?" He blurted again but tried to remain calm.

"If you like, after I've paid for this," she said and looked for a clerk.

"Oh yes——sure—I have to pay too." He had forgotten what he was doing there.

With packages in hand they went out into the snowy evening. She pulled the fur collar of her long dark wool cape up around her ears and cheeks. He buttoned his overcoat and took her elbow.

It was cold but not windy and the snow fell softly upon them in large flakes.

"I live up by the park," she said and as they walked, the snow crunched under their feet.

"I stay at the Ralston but I'm from Pennsylvania." She was easy to talk to and he soon regained his composure.

"You in town every day?" She asked.

"I am now. I had a wreck and then I got my engineer's papers, a while back."

"It must have been a bad one—I see your scars," she said with concern.

"Yes, a BAD one. It killed my friend and busted me up good."

"It is very dangerous work isn't it?" She didn't expect an answer.

"You always lived here, ah—a—I don't know your name. I'm Jack Lansure."

"Em Butterfield."

"Em?" He repeated.

"Yes, that's for Emmaline Abigail Butterfield—much too long." She explained.

"You live here with your family? I have a big family in Pa." They walked along.

"My father's dead. I live here with my mother, Momori and Uncle Peter." She said.

"I'm sad to hear that. Who's Momori? Jack asked.

"That's short for Mother Mariah. That's the best I could do when I was small. Momori and Uncle Peter have been with my parents since they married and before that, they were with my father's family. We came here in 1905 from Atlanta, Georgia. Father was a cotton and fruit broker. He died suddenly the next year and my mother hasn't been well since." She stopped in front of a huge ornate home.

"I didn't mean to snoop." Jack apologized.

"It's alright. I haven't had anyone to talk to for along time. Do I talk too much?" She asked.

"Oh no, please go on!" Jack said.

"Well, you see me in the park nearly every day. I 'take-the-air' in the afternoon when my mother takes her nap. She has heart trouble and is bedridden. I seldom go out in the evening without Uncle Peter but tonight he is down with the grippe. I was at the apothecary for medicine for him and mother. I'm happy for your company." She was'nt giggly or coquettish like the other girls Jack had known.

"You sure have had a dish full, haven't you? I've often wondered about you, seein' you in the park all this time. I did a lot of guessing but I wasn't even close." Jack admitted.

"Why do you call me 'the girl in the blue picture hat'?" Em asked.

"Because you are. The guys and I always looked for you in the hat. We were happy when you were there and disappointed when you were'nt. It was a kind of game we played. Never thought I'd get to meet you. I was struck dumb when I saw you in the store." Jack confessed.

"It's my favorite hat. It keeps me warm in winter and shades me in the summer. I must go in now." She said softly.

"May I call on you—tomorrow—we must talk more." Jack asked.

"If you like—say about seven?" She offered her hand and Jack took it.

She walked up the snowy path to the great stone steps of the porch and stepped to the door. She turned, waved to Jack and went inside.

Jack felt nine feet tall and light as a feather. His behavior was baffling especially to himself. He walked back to the hotel quickly but felt none of the cold or the snow that fell upon him.

The next night about seven he twisted the huge, ornate brass bell on Em's front door.

Momori opened the door and showed Jack into the great hallway. He could sense her mild disapproval.

"I'm Jack Lansure. I've come to call on Miss Butterfield." He doffed his hat and coat and stood holding them.

"I'll tell her you are here." Momori scrutinized him carefully without smiling and hung his hat and coat on the halltree.

The house was stately and grand. The great wooden staircase curved down from the upper floor with grace and elegance.

Emmaline popped out of a doorway down the hall and said, "I'm so glad you could come!" She held out her hand to Jack and he took it. "I hope you like good music. I have a new recording of Enrico Caruso singing Pagliacci. Momori, we will have tea in the library, please." Em led Jack into the room down the hall.

Jack had no idea who Enrico Caruso could be and he wasn't much on tea but he said nothing. In the room, the walls were covered with shelves full of books and the heavy leather furniture looked comfortable and inviting. An open fire danced and crackled in the fireplace and beside it stood a Gramophone on an ornate cabinet. Em began to crank the handle on the Gramophone and said, "Some people are not interested in opera or it's music. I'm glad you are."

"I like music but I never heard opera," he admitted.

"All the better! If you really like it and are willing to learn, I'll teach you all I know about it. Through a friend in the East, I have gathered a collection of operas, symphonies and works of the great masters. Books are fine but the Gramophone has been the greatest help to those of us who enjoy great music." She went on.

She placed the needle arm on the waxing and the music boomed from the great horn.

Suddenly there was a throbbing in the pit of Jack's stomach and it slowly traveled up to the back of his neck and caused his hair to stand on end. It was a delightful sensation. The machine was a wonder to the country boy from the hills of Pennsylvania.

"Isn't his voice marvelous?" She asked over the sound.

"Yes, who is he?" Jack called back.

Em rummaged through a stack of papers on a table and handed one sheet to Jack.

"This will tell you about Caruso," she said loudly.

Jack read the paper and Em cranked the machine again. The paper said, 'Enrico Caruso, street singer turned opera tenor and star. The greatest voice ever heard. His range and power has never been equaled. He makes audiences cry with Pagliacci and hiss with Faust. He can sing anything by Puccini, Rossini or Verdi and by most others.'

"That's quite a write-up!" Jack shouted just as the sound stopped. "Sorry," he said and they both laughed.

"What do you think? Isn't he amazing? Want to hear more?" She cranked the machine and the sound filled the room.

The music was very moving to Jack and the second time was more enjoyable. The quality was hollow and scratchy, yet astonishing for the time and Jack found it pleasant and satisfying.

"Do you REALLY like it or are you just being polite?" She searched his face with her big brown eyes.

"Yes, I really do. I never heard opera or Caruso before but I enjoyed it." He said truthfully.

"Oh I'm so happy—I have so much to show you!" She was excited.

Momori came into the room with the tea tray and placed it on a table near Jack.

"Thank you Momori, we will serve ourselves." Em said to the black companion.

Momori said nothing, nodded and left the room. She studied Jack from head to toe.

"What have I done, that lady seems to dislike me for some reason." Jack said.

"Pay no attention to Momori, she and Uncle Peter have been protecting me from unknown dangers all my life. She means no harm. Come, we will have tea. I know most men don't care for tea but I make it special. We learned it in school but without Miss Mateland's approval." She poured the tea and took a heavy crystal decanter from a small table in the corner. Without measuring, she splashed a generous amount into each cup of tea.

"Umm smells good!" Jack enjoyed the aroma of the amber colored liquid.

"It's called Amaretto, it's made from almonds and comes from Italy. It does wonders for a cup of tea and is even better in coffee." She gave Jack a cup of the tea mixture. "The story goes, that a man died and left his wife and children penniless except for the grove of almond trees. Having nothing else, the widow concocted a liqueur extracted from the almonds and sold it locally. It became an international success and she could provide for her children. I love a success story." She admitted.

"It's delicious!" Jack said after several sips. "How can it be a girl from the South has no southern drawl. I like the sound of your voice but the accent is strange to me and that's quiet a story." Jack said.

''It's because I spent most of my life in boarding school. My father traveled the world and mother traveled with him. At eight, I was sent to Miss Emiley Waterford's Preparatory School for Young Ladies in Connecticut. When I was twelve, I went to Miss Matilda Mateland's Conservatory of Fine Arts in New York then two years of college in Vermont. I graduated two years ago and came home to live. I lost my accent long ago—Miss Waterford saw to that. Now, I have what they call a down-East accent—a broad A sound, most in these parts think it strange. My books and music come from friends in the East who send me the latest editions. Enough of that—how about a symphony? Mozart is always good,'' she said while she dug through the pile of disks.

Anything she suggested was fine with Jack, he could bearly contain his enthusiasm. Emmaline had opened an entirely new world for Jack. She played one recording after another and before they realized it, the evening was over. Jack looked at his watch: 10:10 PM., where had the time gone?

''I didn't mean to over-stay my welcome. It was so interesting I forgot the time.'' Jack knew he shouldn't stay longer.

''Will you come back? I rarely have anyone to play them for. There is much more.'' Em asked.

''I want to but I'll be away over Christmas. I'm going up to Tygart Lake to visit my friend Davey and his wife, Becky. May I come when I get back?'' Jack explained.

''Oh yes, the lady you bought the sachet for.'' she smiled knowingly.

''THAT reminds me!'' Em followed Jack from the room to the hall tree. He rummaged through the pockets until he found a fancy wrapped package.

''I bought this for your Christmas but now it's for this nice evening. You showed me things that I never knew existed and I'm grateful. Thank you.'' Jack placed the package in her hands.

''How thoughtful of you. It's been years since anyone has given me a present. May I open it now or do I have to wait until Christmas?'' She was pleased and child-like.

Jack blushed to his hairline. ''Open it now.'' Jack had purchased it at the store earlier this evening, on his way to visit Em.

She carefully unwrapped the sachet and said, ''I'm so happy you bought one for me. It's a lasting gift any woman would be proud to have. It's my favorite shade of blue. Thank you.'' Em was pleased.

''Your welcome, besides, you are 'the girl in the blue picture hat,' remember?'' Jack said.

Em's sachet was round, blue and smelled of lilies and the ribbon and lace work was the same. Becky's was similar but lavender scented and envelope-shaped.

Jack took her hand in his and said, ''I'll be away but I'll see you right after the first of the year. Thank you for tonight.''

''You're welcome and thank you for this.'' She inhaled deeply the fragrance of her gift. ''See you soon.''

Jack slid into his overcoat and went out into the night. Em watched from the window as he disappeared into the darkness.

Davey was at Tygart Lake station to meet Jack.

''Laddie, you're a sight for sore eyes! What have ya been up to lately?'' Davey gave Jack a big bear hug.

''Davey, I'm that glad to see you!'' The men thumped each other on the back.

''I got ta tell ya! Something very special happened to me.'' Jack was excited.

''Well tell me while we ride along, Becky's waiting dinner. Since we have all this snow and Becky loves to sleigh ride, I rented this sleigh rig for a couple of days. Get under that bear rug and we will talk as we ride. Up! Mose, Up! Now Laddie, tell me the news.'' Davey headed the horse toward home through the snow-covered hills.

''Davey, you remember 'the girl in the blue picture hat? I met her by accident in the drug store!'' Jack began.

''Sure ya did—by accident.'' Davey teased.

''It's true—I swear! I went in to buy something for Becky and there she was! We talked and she let me walk home with her!'' Jack was excited.

''Gwan! Ya walked her home, it was love at first sight and ya lived happily ever after!'' Davey could not resist poking fun at his young, awestruck friend.

''Davey, you're makin' fun of me and it isn't like that at all! She's one year younger than I am but seems older and a whole lot smarter. She's been educated in the best schools and has shown me things I didn't know existed! I heard Operas and Symphonies on her Gramophone! Enrico Caruso's voice sent chills up my spine! Have YOU ever heard a symphony orchestra! I don't have words to describe it! And Davey, she knows all about the great painters! And books—she has a whole room full of them! My brother, Bruce, would get crazy with all those books!'' Jack's voice had risen and he flung his arms about, wildly.

''Easy boy, easy! You really like that longhair stuff, do you?'' Asked Davey.

''Davey, it's a whole new world for me.'' Jack admitted.

''A Gramophone I got—but none of that longhair stuff! Now Alexander's Ragtime Band—that's the ticket!'' Davey insisted.

''You really got a Gramophone—the kind ya crank up?'' Jack could hardly believe his ears.

''Sure do, gave it to Becky on our 15th or was it our 18th wedding anniversary?'' Davey scratched his head to think. ''Becky's got several of those recordings—Auld Lang Syne, Jeannie With The Light Brown Hair and The Blue Danube.'' Davey went on.

''YOU have a Gramophone? I can't believe it! Yippee!'' Jack gave a cowboy yell. He was filled with anticipation.

By the time Jack and Davey arrived at the lovely home by the lake, Becky had the meal ready to serve. The home was a log cabin style but with all the modern day accruements. The house was big, yet it sat in a grove of snow covered pine trees that towered above it's roof.

Becky waved from the front porch and Davey put the horse in the shed.

''Oh Jack, I'm so glad you could come! Davey's like a kid at Christmas and your being here is like an extra gift. Come in! Come in!'' She reached for Jack and he snatched her up in his arms and swung her off her feet.

''Keeruslam! Becky you don't weigh more than a cake of soap! My left leg is heavier than you are!'' Jack teased.

It was true, Rebecca Kathleen Russell Stanton had a large name but a tiny frame. She hennaed her graying, dark hair to diminish the aging and soften her lined skin. The effect was startling. The large thatch of auburn hair on top of her tiny body gave her a doll-like quality. She was pleasant, understanding and fun and Jack was very fond of her, as he was of his friend, Davey.

''Put me down! Put me down, ya big ox!'' She laughed and kissed his cheek. ''You'll muss me all up before dinner!'' She was very fond of Jack as she would be of a son. ''Come on in, dinner is ready.''

The three sat down to a delicious meal and Davey raised his wine glass. ''To the three of us: 'May we be in Heaven a week before the Devil knows we've died'!''

''Here! Here!'' Jack said and they clinked glasses.

At the end of the meal Jack said, ''Rebecca, you are almost as good a cook as my Ma'am! One thing for sure is better. How do you make everything LOOK so nice! It's too pretty to eat.''

''David is gone a lot so I practice,'' she said simply.

''Didn't seem to hurt your appetite none, Laddie,'' Davey teased, ''Ya ate everything but the plate! Come on you two, let's up over that mountain in the sleigh. We'll do scullery later.'' Davey suggested.

''That's a great idea but Becky, how do you put up with this 'ole horsethief?'' Jack sassed back.

"Cause he looked like a grizzly bear and I love animals!" Her eyes twinkled and she laughed. The banter went on.

The three bundled up in heavy clothing, snuggled under the bearskin in the sleigh and pointed the horse up the road. They laughed and sang while the sleigh bells sounded their passing. The people waved and dogs barked. It was a carefree happy time for all. When the poor horse was quite exhausted, they went home.

At home they sat by the fire, sipped buttered rum, played the Gramophone, danced and talked. The memories of this time would follow Jack forever.

Jack and Davey tramped the snowy hills and prowled the leafless woods. Both men were at home in the forest.

Christmas Eve found them in a near-by church for services. It reminded Jack of his family and home.

When Jack, Davey and Becky returned home, they sat beside a roaring fire and talked more. They talked about the War in Europe, politics, family and railroading.

"Becky, you're a good sport to put up with us so I brought you something." Jack retrieved a package he had stashed under the sofa.

"Thank you for having me here and Merry Christmas." He gave her the package and kissed her cheek.

"Why Jack, aren't you the thoughtful one! Look David, a gift for me!"

"That's real nice of ya, Laddie, women make an awful lot out of such things." Davey said, thoughtfully.

"Oh it's lovely! Umm, it smells of lavender and spice thank you, Jack, I'll keep it in my drawer among my 'specials'." Becky was very pleased. "I think I'll go up to bed, I'm sure you two have lots to talk about." She left the room.

"I have something for you too 'grizzly bear'!" Jack couldn't let that pass. "Remember, I told you my sister is a Seneca Indian Princess?" Jack took Davy's hand in his and placed in his palm, a small stone. "This stone is a Seneca Indian Worry Stone. The Indians believe these stones have special power and will protect those who carry them. They are carefully hollowed out and polished and given to friends and relatives. When you are sad or worried, rub the stone. The Indians believe everything dies sooner or later but never rocks or stones which are just moved around from place to place and exist for ever. Often the good spirits hide in stones to escape bad spirits. Keep it in your pocket and it will keep you safe—or so the story goes." Jack explained to his friend.

"Yes Jack, I do remember about your sister. Thank you, I'll keep it with me. That's some story, Laddie. The Indians really believe it protects them?'' Davey rolled the stone over and over in his palm and examined it carefully.

The men talked on and on into the night. By the time the fire had gone completely out, Jack and Davey had revamped the entire railroad system—twice.

''The most dangerous thing about the railroad today, is a split rail. Until they come up with better steel, it will be the biggest widow-maker.'' Big Davey was adamant.

Jack knew it was true. The rails were affected by heat, cold, over-load, twisting, buckling and crumbling. Better steel was the answer.

Eventually the men went to bed.

Christmas Day, Becky laid out a feast for the two men. Jack had never eaten Roast Goose a la Orange, Raisin Dressing, Plum Pudding with Glaze or Chocolate Mousse but he was familiar with mashed potatoes, gravy and candied yams! Jack ate as if he had just come off a chain gang. Davey teased Jack but he also ate whopping portions.

The table decorations were beautiful and the food was outstanding. Becky had planned for weeks to make this Christmas very special.

The time flew by and soon it was time to go. Jack stood on the train platform and hugged his friend. ''Big Davey Stanton, I will always owe you more than I can ever pay. If ever a man had a friend—you're it.'' Jack was desperately choking back his tears.

''Laddie, I can still see you! Stumblin' around in the Cumberland yards with sky-high hopes and as green as grass but now, you are like the son Becky and I never had. Keep the wind at your back and go with God.'' The two men hugged and Jack boarded the train. He stood on the train step and watched until Davey was out of sight on the platform.

Jack had dozens of acquaintances but only one close friend. He missed him already. . . . .

The trip back to Clarksburg was uneventful but everything had a festive air. At the Hotel Ralston, the huge Christmas tree filled the lobby with the delightful scent of pine. Everyone greeted Jack warmly and reminded him of the New Years Eve party being held in the hotel's bar and lobby.

Jack thought of asking Emmaline but dismissed it. The place would be full of raucous railroaders and painted chippies. Besides, Jack told Em he would see her after the first of the year.

Indeed the party was noisy and gay. The people ate, danced and laughed. At midnight, they banged on the tables, blew whistles and threw confetti and streamers.

The women dragged the men onto the dance floor and Jack was no exception. They drank and danced into the night.

Later, Jack went upstairs with Mabel for instant gratifacation. He could have taken Sadie or Ida but Mabel was the least noisy and the cleaner of the lot. After tonight, he would not remember her face or her name, so unattached was his sex drive and he preferred it that way. . . .

At work he was busier than usual. He made up trains that carried more coal, ore, grain and lumber. The tentacles of the European War had reached this place. 1915 would be more historic than Jack could ever imagine.

He spent at least two evenings a week with Em and more when he could. The time spent with her was very special to him. They had become good friends and she was a better teacher of the Arts than any professor. She played the great music on the Gramophone and read to him of the Masters of music, writing and painting. Jack absorbed like a sponge and hung on every sound he heard and all that she read. He eventually wore a dent in the soft leather couch where he sat to hear her teachings.

They listened to the works of Bach, Beethoven and Chopin; of Handel and Mozart; of Rimsky-Korsakov, Tchaikovsky and Wagner. She read to him of Alcott, Balzac, Beńet and Carroll; of Cooper, Crane and Dumas; of Gray, Grimm, Melville and Longfellow. He learned of Audubon, Cellini and Van Gogh; and of Remington, Goya and Toulouse-Lautrec. Jack's appetite for the Arts was great and Emmaline delighted in feeding him.

Abruptly, they were shocked into the reality of the time when the newspaper headlines screamed 'Lusitania Sunk'. The date was May 7, 1915.

By June 1st, his job was very demanding. More and more trains were made up and the talk indicated War was imminent.

Jack spent as much of his free time as possible with Em but their meetings were down to two a week and often less. Usually very observant but now preoccupied with work, Jack failed to notice that Em had developed a slight cough. By midsummer, her creamy skin had turned ashen and she lost weight.

At one of his visits to her home he said, "It looks like I may be bumped back to Cumberland and the East End."

"Oh I hope not! September is our Johnny Appleseed Festival and you MUST be here for that!" She was unusually distressed at the prospect of his transfer. She coughed gently.

"What's that?" Jack asked.

"It's a festival to honor Johnny Appleseed!" She explained.

"Who's he?" Jack had no idea.

"Why Johnny Appleseed was one of our great pioneers. His real name was John Chapman and he came from Massachusetts. He planted all the apple trees around here and in a large part of this country. He invented many va-

Jack, the Man and his Train

Blue Goose

400

ACY

406

407

Plymouth

Delphos

New London

Carey

Railroaders

Smoke Eaters

Engineer and Conductor

Ma'am and Paap

Aunt Leone

Perry and fuzzy friend

Hal takes Jake flying

Jake the hunter

Jack Rilla (Marrilla) Fan

Rilla and Perry

Hal and Rilla

"Rilla" at 27 years

"Rilla" at 33 years

Chief Jason

Jake and the Navy

Granddaughter, Great-Granddaughters, Grandma Fan

Jas and Hal

J.C.L.

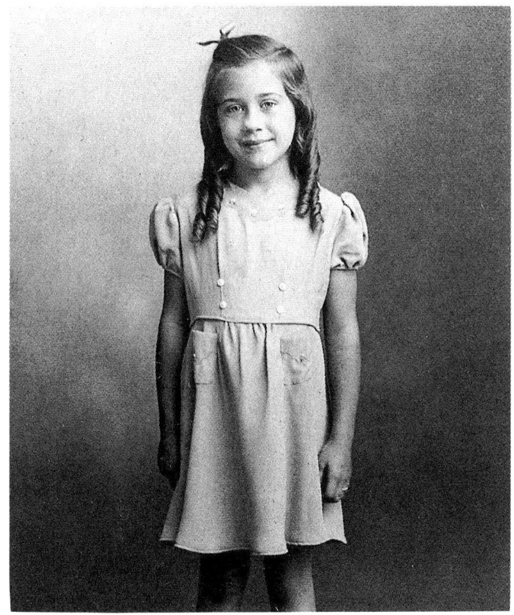

Jannell

Jack and Jannell

Jannell

Ross and Jannell

Perry, Rilla, Jack

Jack was a 32° Knight Templar

Rilla and Jack

Perry and friend on the rifle range.

Perry in Navy

Perry and wife Enio

rieties of apples and planted orchards everywhere. Many are standing today. At the festival, the thing you do most is eat and drink. I get enough apple cider to last all year. If it can be cooked with apples-it's served there. Applesauce, applebutter, apple fritters, apple dumplings, apple cake, apple muffins, apple pie and anything else they can think of. Someone always comes up with a new recipe.''

''It sounds jake to me. I'll look forward to it if I'm not bumped too soon.'' Jack said.

''Oh you must come! It's the last festival before winter sets in!'' Jack did not notice the urgency in Em's voice or her increased coughing.

''Tell me some more about that Johnny fella.'' Jack asked.

''According to legend, he was born in the late seventeen hundreds in Leominster, Massachusetts Bay Colony. He was orphaned early in life and grew up sad and lonely. He was tall, skinny and poor. He loved apples and nature but apples were scarce and he believed that if there were to be apples for all, he must sow the seeds. Dressed in tatters, he tramped the country side with nothing but a sack full of seeds and saplings and his mother's bible. He would accept a half-penny in payment but preferred a pitcher of milk and honey. The treat sustained his body and pleased his palate. The beautiful Grimes Golden Apples grown around here now, are of his cultivation and cross-pollination.'' Em stopped speaking and began to cough. This time it was a bad spasm.

''Easy girl, sounds like you've caught a bad cold,'' Jack steadied her.

''Yes that's it—a bad cold.'' She made light of it and Jack had no idea that she was very ill.

''Will you come back again—real soon?'' She pleaded at the door.

''Sure, in a couple of days unless I'm bumped. The mines are at peak production and so are the mills. The company is workin' the tar out of us to get the coal and timber to the seaports and they are short of engineers and crews.'' Jack's preoccupation with his work kept him from noticing Em's failing health.

The next few weeks were hectic for Jack and his crew but he was not bumped.

The festival day arrived and Jack cut out early to call for Em. She was waiting on the porch and ran to meet him. They strolled the park.

Everything was decorated with gold, orange and green streamers. Colorful bunting hung from the doorways and around the tables that had been set up for the folks for eating all the goodies offered.

Jack and Em sampled everything and drank much cider. They walked around the square, talked and stuffed themselves with all manner of apple delicacies.

As they walked Jack held Em's elbow. The sun went down and the fall evening air turned chilly. Em began to shiver.

''Em you're shivering, are you cold?'' He was concerned.

''It's nothing. I'm just a bit tired. Could we start home?'' She coughed violently. Her face was pale and her eyes were sunken.

For the first time after all this while, Jack realized Emmaline was ill.

''I'm such a fool Em, walking you all over town this way. You are sick, aren't you? Tell me what's wrong, please'' Jack asked.

There was nothing to her, she was skin and bone and hollow cheeked. He was shocked, as if it had just happened and he had not seen the gradual decline.

Her knees buckled and she sagged against him. He lifted her up in his arms and with her head on his shoulder, Jack walked quickly to her home. He was strong and her wasted body weighed very little.

Momori and Uncle Peter were at the door to meet them.

''My poor chil', what happened? Take her into the library!'' Momori cried.

''We walked too much and she's tired.'' Jack carried her into the library and laid her on the soft leather couch.

Momori loosened her clothes and propped her head up with a pillow.

''How stupid of me to swoon like a mealy-mouthed school girl! I'm fine—just a bit tired.'' She coughed again.

''Uncle Peter, may we have some hot tea, please.'' Jack urged the man.

''Yes sir, right away sir''. Uncle Peter was worried too and left the room.

''Momori, does she have medicine for that cough?'' Jack inquired.

''Yes she does—I'll get it.'' Momori hurried out of the room.

''Don't fuss so, I'll be fine as soon as I rest a bit! Jack, please put something on the Gramophone—a symphony, I think.'' Em insisted.

''Sure if you are up to it.'' He searched her face. Jack cranked the machine and again the music filled the room.

Momori and Uncle Peter returned at the same time. Em took her medicine and Jack laced the tea with Amaretto from the decanter.

''Thank you both I'll be fine. Now go along.'' Em ushered Uncle Peter and Momori out of the room but she did not look well. The music stopped.

''I'll be going as soon as we finish our tea.'' Jack assured them.

''Nonsense! We will have more music!'' Em insisted.

''Not tonight—you have had enough excitement for one day.'' Jack was gentle but firm.

''When will I see you again,'' she asked.

''As soon as I see my new orders, I'll let you know.''

"New orders—have you been bumped? Her voice had risen and she looked terrified.

"Yes but I didn't want to ruin our day at the festival. I report the day after tomorrow. I leave tonight on the through freight." He tried to be kind.

"Oh my God, when will I ever see you again!" She was distraught. "I'll NEVER see you again!" she cried.

"Hey take it easy, gal! I've been bumped to the other end—I didn't DIE!" He tried to make a joke.

"Don't say that—don't EVER say that!" She looked so panicked.

"It was only a JOKE, Em, I'm sorry." It was not funny to her and Jack was unnerved at her response. "In two or three months I'll be back, maybe on the West End. We never know where we will be sent. They put us where they need us." Jack explained.

"Two or three MONTHS! That's a lifetime! Anything can happen!" Her fear was out of proportion and Jack did not understand it.

"Em that's not long. I'll be back before ya know it." He tried to console her.

'I HATE to think of you going away. You are such an important part of my life." She suddenly realized she was making too much of the matter and her attitude changed to frivolity, "Who will I play the recordings for?"

Jack wondered at her child-like behavior. It was so unlike her usually levelheaded personality.

"Take care of that cold and I'll see you sooner than you think." He patted her hand.

"Keep safe and come back soon." She touched his cheek for a moment and her eyes brimmed with tears. Jack choked back the lump in his throat.

In the hall, Momori helped him with his coat.

"Mr. Jack, you know Emmaline is bad sick don't ya?" She whispered.

"I know she has a bad cold," he said.

"Dr. Morgan say she have the consumption and when the bad cough'n come—she could bleed to death!" Tears ran down her face and her voice cracked. "She takes great stock in you—please, don't stay away too long!" She begged.

"Consumption! I don't believe it!" At once, her strange behavior fell into place and Jack understood.

"It's true, she's been poorly ever since she came home from school—worse lately." Momori mopped her face on her apron. "Her Mama done sapped all that po' chil's strength. She fetches and totes most all the time—'septen when she 'takes the air' in the park. Mrs. Butterfield's too near gone to know what she's done." Momori's body shook with grief.

"I'll come back as soon as I can Momori, I promise, but I'm being transfered away!" Jack explained.

"No! No! LORD have mercy!" She shook her graying head.

Jack went out into the night. His mind raced while he walked back to the hotel. How could he have spent all that time with Em and not notice she was ill? How could he not see she was losing weight? Why was he not aware that she crammed everything into a short time? Why such urgency to do things right now? Time—that's it—because time was the one thing that Emmaline had none of. She had known all these months, her days were few.

Jack's new job on the East End local was interesting and kept him busy but thoughts of Em filtered in.

War hung heavy over everything like a black cloud. Great Britain and France were desperate for supplies. Railroad men and crews worked around the clock to move the needed material.

Jack saw Davey whenever possible but their meetings were more and more infrequent. Both men worked long hours.

The weeks ran into months and the months passed quickly. The Holidays came and went and in February of 1916, Jack asked for a few days off.

His instincts told him to go see Emmaline. He deadheaded to Clarksburg and went directly to Em's home.

On the porch, his heart sunk. There on the door was a wreath draped in black. He twisted the bell and waited.

Momori answered the door and she and Uncle Peter welcomed him in.

"Oh Mr. Jack you came! She said you would! She just knew it!" Momori wept into her apron.

"Momori, what happened here? Is it Mrs. Butterfield? Where's Em?" The lump in the pit of Jack's stomach grew larger.

"Why, Mr. Jack I thought you knew! That's why you came!" Momori was flabbergasted at Jack's ignorance.

"Know what? I came to visit Em! Where is she?" Jack's ignorance turned to panic.

"My! My! It's Providence! That's what it is, Dee-vine Providence! He didn't KNOW about her but he came anyway!" Uncle Peter shook his head and shuffled down the hall.

"For Christ's sake, Momori, will you tell me what's going around here!" Jack hissed through his teeth and took her firmly by the shoulders.

"Oh, Mr. Jack—.

Before she could say more a strange, well-dressed man of about fifty, with graying hair and a Van Dyke beard came out of the library door down the hall.

"Mr. Lansure, will you come into the library please, I'm Oliver Blakely." Momori took Jack's hat and coat and Jack followed the man into the room.

"I'm sorry, son, that I'm the one to tell you." The man extended his hand and Jack took it.

"Tell me what? What's going on here?" Jack was disturbed and irritated.

"Please sit down." The man spoke gently and Jack sat on the sofa where he had many times before.

"My firm, Blakely, Pierse and Donnelly have been attorneys for the Butterfield family for many years and we are good friends. I watched Emmaline grow up. She was always a frail child———

"Where is Em?" Jack interrupted and demanded.

"Please! Let me finish. Emmaline came home from school with a serious illness. It has taken years for the symptoms to show up. The final stages began to appear in late summer in the form of a slight cough, with weight loss and pallor. Increased coughing spasms were deadly, they caused internal bleeding. Emmaline had such a fatal spasm and she will be laid to rest this afternoon." His voice trailed off and Jack jumped to his feet.

"It's not true—it can't be true—people live a long time that have consumption—she only had a cold!" Jack felt as if he had been kicked in the guts. He could not vomit because there was nothing in his stomach and he gulped back the urge to be sick. He did not want it to be true but down deep he knew it was.

Jack dropped onto the familiar sofa, put his head in his hands and cried softly.

"That's right, my boy, cry it out." The kindly man patted Jack's shoulder.

After some time Jack gathered his composure, wiped his face with his handkerchief and blew his nose.

"Here son, drink this." Mr. Blakely gave Jack a small glass of Ameretto to drink. Jack downed it in one gulp and made a face.

"It's better in tea." he said absently.

"Emmaline wanted me to give you this book of poems. She marked her favorites and left you a note." The man explained.

"Thank you very much. How is Mrs. Butterfield holding up?" Jack inquired.

"I suppose you would have no way of knowing that either. We laid her to rest one month ago today beside her husband at Willow Grove Cemetery. You know where that is—on the edge of town by the park. Will we see you there later?" He asked.

"Uh—I think—not sure." Jack was numb and disoriented. He took his book and went out into the hall where Momori was waiting with his hat and coat. She helped him into his things.

"Mr. Jack, Miss Emmaline threatened ta rawhide me if I toll but I just have ta toll ya. Miss Em loved ya with her whole heart. Oh she knew you didn't feel that way about her and that you two were jes' good friends but Mr. Jack, she LOVED you. You were the only bright spot in her life. She lived for your visits and sobbed like a chil' when you left. If'n ya HAD loved her—she wouldn't allowed it—she knew all along she was dyin'. You were the only thing that kept her alive this long. Bless you for that. When ya first came here, I worried you might bring harm to her but I was wrong. I will always be grateful to you for making her last days happy. The Grigri I place upon you will keep you safe until I die." She placed her index finger upon his forhead and mumbled an inaudible chant. When she finished, she said goodby and Jack thanked her and left.

Jack walked away from the house but turned at the end of the path to look back once more as if to imprint, forever, the house and it's memories in his mind.

As he walked along, he felt dazed and disconnected. He looked at his watch: 2:30 PM. If he hurried he could catch the Flyer, Eastbound. What about Emmaline's funeral? Jack hated funerals. He felt it was a paganistic ritual that should be abolished. It was tortuous for the living and insignificant to the dead. He could not bring himself to look upon her cold face, in death. Instead, he wished to remember her in life—as she was in their room filled with music and poetry.

He walked faster and caught the train East.

After riding a long while in stunned sorrow, he remembered the book in his overcoat pocket. It was a book of poems by Elizabeth Barrett Browning. Among the pages was a folded note from Emmaline. Tears blinded him as he read the words: 'My dear friend Jack, do not be sad. Know that the time we spent together with our Art, was the happiest time of my life. Enjoy what we had. Think of me when you eat an apple. Remember me when you hear a symphony, read a poem or see an opera. I will be there with you. I go from this world but I will be near you when the leaves rustle in the trees or when a soft breeze touches your cheek. You will find my favorite poems here and one of yours.'

Farewell, my friend,
Em

Jack hoped no one saw his agony. She had enclosed the poem IF, from the ancient writings of Omar Khayyam. He unfolded the paper and began to read. There seemed to be no end to his tears. He brushed them aside and tried to read the words again:

IF

IF you can keep your head when all about you
Are losing theirs and blaming it on you,
If you can trust yourself when all men doubt you,
But make allowances for their doubting too:
If you can wait and not be tired by waiting,
Or being lied about, don't deal in lies,
Or being hated, don't give way to hating,
And yet don't look too good, nor talk too wise:

If you can dream—and not make dreams your master;
If you can think—and not make thoughts your aim;
If you can meet with Triumph and Disaster
And treat those two imposters just the same;
If you can bear to hear the truth you've spoken
Twisted by knaves to make a trap for fools,
Or watch the things you gave your life to, broken,
And stoop and build 'em up with worn-out tools;

If you can make one heap of all your winnings
And risk it on one turn of pitch-and-toss,
And lose, and start again at your beginnings
And never breathe a word about your loss;
If you can force your heart and nerve and sinew
To serve your turn long after they are gone,
And so hold on when there is nothing in you
Except the Will which says to them: "Hold on!"

If you can talk with crowds and keep your virtue,
Or walk with Kings—nor lose the common touch,
If neither foes nor loving friends can hurt you,
If all men count with you, but none too much;
If you can fill the unforgiving minute
With sixty seconds' worth of distance run,
Yours is the Earth and everything that's in it,
And—which is more—you'll be a Man, my son!

The message the poem brought was a pattern Jack would aim to follow the rest of his life. When he finished reading, he put the book back in his pocket and stared out of the train window but saw nothing. He was sick with grief.

Chapter Eleven

WRECK! TRAIN WRECK!

It was late afternoon when the train arrived in Cumberland. Jack went directly to Riley's Boarding House.

"Why Jack you're back zo zoon! Did you have a nice rest?" Gretchen was surprised to see Jack.

"NO!" Jack snapped and brushed past all his friends and Gretchen on his way up stairs to his room.

"Whew! What's with him?" asked one.

"Zumpthing is very wrong! Let him go, Davey will find out zee trouble later." Gretchen was wise.

Jack was not aware that he had snarled. He flung himself onto the bed and sobbed.

When Big Davey came off the run, Gretchen explained what happened. Davy was very concerned and went up to Jack's room. He knocked gently on the door.

"Laddie, it's Davey."

"It's open." Jack answered.

Davey went into the room and closed the door behind him. Jack sat up on the bed.

"What's gone wrong son?" Davey turned the straight backed chair around and sat down straddle the seat and rested his arms on the back.

"OH God, Davey, she's dead!" Jack cried into his hands.

"Who? Laddie, who's dead?" Davey thought it was a family member.

"Em—Emmaline Butterfield—The Girl In The Blue Picture Hat—she died of consumption—I didn't even know she was sick!" Jack's shoulders shook with the sobs.

''Whoa son, easy now, tell me about it.'' Davey's voice was calming and gentle.

Jack told Davey about their meetings, their music and their art. Davey listened until Jack was talked out and cried out.

''You and Emmaline made more memories in your short time together than most folks make in a lifetime. Don't think of it as a tragedy, Laddie, consider it a gift. What you two shared will last YOU a lifetime. What she taught you no one can take away. It's not the END for you, son, it's the beginning of a life of beauty and joy that will ALWAYS be yours. She gave what no other could give. Be grateful for the gift and go on.'' Davey was wise beyond his own knowledge.

Jack was silent for a long while then he said, ''Davey, where do you get the strength to GO ON when something like this happens?''

''Each man has his own strength, Laddie, some less, others more. Deep down in a man's soul is a well that he draws from when the need be. Faith in the Good Lord keeps the well full. Keep the Faith, Laddie, and ya will have the strength when ya need it.'' Both men fell silent.

There was a knock on the door. It was Gretchen with a tray of food.

''Za two of you will give zee place a bad name if you don't eat zee food. I brought you zee left-overs. I'm going to bed—I'll get zee tray in the morning.'' She placed the tray on the dresser.

''Gretchen will you marry me!'' Davey teased and pinched her cheek.

''Gwan-ya beeg blow-hard! Becky will part your hair with a stove poker!'' She laughed back at him and left the room.

Suddenly Jack was ravenous. He could not remember the last time he had eaten. The talk with Davey had been more theraputic than either man knew.

The next day the men went back to work together. Jack's heart was heavy but at least he could cope with his loss. Long hard hours with no time to dwell on his problems was a big help.

Jack's life was busy. He worked and played hard. He was well-known up and down the railroad and was well-liked. He gobbled at the table of life with both hands. He joined the usual clubs; The Elks, The Odd Fellows and Big Davey sponsored him into the Mason's. He was respected by his cronies and adored by his women. He was a railroader's railroader. He looked taller than his six feet because he was lean and hard. He was what you call tall, dark and handsome.

His conversation was laced with railroad jargon and profanity but somehow his swearing was not offensive. It was as much a part of him as was his pleasant, resonant voice, which he seldom raised. He was noticably left-handed, never picked a fight or ran from one. His carnal appetite was enormous and he ate often. He had tootsies in every tank town and his affairs were easy, fleeting and many.

Jack was a natty dresser and a big spender. Away from work he was freshly scrubbed, clean-shaven and trailed a light scent of bay rum. His twenty dollar Stetson had his initials punched into the inner hat band. Fine broadcloth shirts sat off silk neckties, pearl studs and gold stickpins. Spats and a gold-headed walking stick completed the picture. Did suits come in any other color besides blue? Light blue, dark blue, navy blue and grey blue. His startling hazel eyes flashed green, blue or brown depending on his mood.

At the end of a busy run, in full railroad garb and covered with soot, he still looked quietly dignified and self-assured. He loved his work and it showed. He adored his 'iron mistress'—that coal-consuming, water swigging metal levithin—called a locomotive. His life was good.

Christmas came and went again. On April 16, 1917 the United States declared war on Germany. The heavy loads on the trains grew larger and longer. Roadbeds, equipment and men were pushed to the limit.

War! What a terrible word. Most expected it but when it came, people were shocked, bewildered and apprehensive. Men in every walk of life volunteered for the American Expeditionary Forces as did many railroaders. This left a large gap in the train crews and a shortages of men between the ages of 18 and 30. Consequently, the railroads were badly undermanned. The crews that remained worked double tricks and were shorthanded. There were more cinder dicks riding the trains than there were crew members. These policeman were guarding special unmarked crates and sealed cars for the war effort.

By late summer the men were exhausted, worn equipment broke down and accidents happened daily. What was once a joke, 'you can tell a railroad shack by his missing fingers' was no longer a sick joke but a reality. Now, if a man had a mangled or missing limb, it was even money that he was a railroader.

On a cold rainy night in September, the men gathered around the stove in the yard office to swap yarns and talk shop when Squeaky Davis burst through the door. He was the yard mud hop, dispatch runner and errand boy. He got his name from the thin, high pitch of his voice.

"Wreck! Train Wreck! Through freight is over at the bottom of 20-mile-grade!" He yelled and tried to catch his breath.

Every railroader knew where that bad grade was located and all jumped to their feet.

"Who's runnin'?" Someone shouted.

"What's he haulin'?" Asked another.

"What happened?" Quizzed another.

It was more than a mile from the depot and telegraph office to the yard office and Squeaky had run the entire distance. Between gasps for breath, he tried to answer their questions.

"D. W. Stanton, but that's not official! Nuthin' on the crew. He had 50 flats of coal, 20 of livestock, 4 boxes' of flour and the rest was secret stuff,"—cough wheeze—Squeaky gasped for breath.

Jack heard little after Squeaky mentioned Big Davey. His heart froze in his chest and his temples throbbed. Davey would never make a mistake, he wrote the book on railroading. It had to be a broken wheel or a split rail. Davey constantly urged the company to find a better steel.

Then he heard Squeaky say, "—and a nearby farmer called in and the wrecking crew called us. They want all hands—everyone. The big hook pulls out in five minutes. Come on!"

Outside the men scrambled up onto the slow-moving wreck train. Some onto the flatcars that carried the huge crane and hook that was used to right the overturned cars. Some on the flatcars that carried hand tools and others on the replacement cars used to carry rails, ties and spikes. More scrambled up the bunk cars and into the caboose.

Jack swung up onto a replacement car and found a seat on a small barrel marked SPIKES and three other men did the same. The men paid no attention to the rain that fell on them. The train gained speed.

The man seated next to Jack spoke absently, "Even at top speed, it will take this thing forty minutes to get there. Hurt and scared livestock can be scattered all over the county by that time. A scalded man can die of shock . . . " His voice trailed off.

The men talked quietly among themselves and eventually fell silent, each with his own thoughts. Jack heard their voices but little else. He was deep in his own agonizing thoughts. 'Please God, don't let it be Davey! He's like a father to me—I need him and Becky needs him. What would she do without him? Davey would never miss that curve, he's been over it dozens of times. He just would not make that mistake. It had to be a broken wheel or a split rail'———.

"There she is! Grab the flares!" Someone shouted as the train slowed to a stop and the men scrambled off. Jack hit the ground running.

The big locomotive was lying on her right side. A great cloud of steam was rising into the chilly night from the lake of hot water that surrounded her.

The wrecking train had reached her head on and reaching the engine and crew would be quick but reaching the back of the train would be another story.

"The boiler blew when she went over! That water is hot! Get it trenched away from her! Hurry up!" a man shouted.

"Flares! More flares!" called another.

Picks and shovels flew to free the water and men ran to bring more light to the workers.

"You see anybody?" Called a man.

"Not yet but don't those animals sound pitiful?" someone answered.

The wrecking crews were professionals and each man knew his job and did it. First, find the crew and care for them. Flares and torches were set up around the perimeter of the engine and ladders were dragged in to reach the cab window, now on top.

The illumination took place and a grisly picture was revealed. Smashed cars, twisted steel, splintered wood and dead livestock was a nightmare to behold.

It was an unspoken prayer of every railroader that he would live out his life and never look upon such a scene or live through a wreck like this.

Bawling cattle, bleating sheep and squealing swine sent shockwaves of death and dying into the darkness.

The tabloid portrayed before Jack's eyes seemed unreal, mechanical and hollow. It was no bad dream, it was the gruesome truth. Every railroader dreaded but accepted it as part of the life he had chosen.

Gun shots cracked ominously from the dark. Some crew members were mercifully ending the suffering of the badly injured and dying livestock.

"Over here! More light!" someone shouted and several torches were brought to the left, upturned side of the locomotive. The torches lit up a horrible sight.

"Mother of God!" Breathed one man.

A man on his hands and knees, was crawling around in about a foot of hot water. He was completely water soaked and hatless. The flesh on his face, neck and hands hung loose in strips exposing bone in many places. His tongue was so swollen it held his mouth ajar and the tip protruded grotesquely. His staring eyes buldged under puffed lids. He had been cooked alive by the steam and boiling water.

No one could speak. A man fainted dead away and three retched and vomited where they stood.

Jack sprung from the darkness into the light and plunged knee-deep into the hot water. The pain of the hot water was excruciating but Jack seemed not to notice. Running in knee-deep water requires great strength and exertion but his adrenaline made it possible and he covered the distance in several great lunges.

"That's Big Davey!" A man shouted.

"God have mercy!" The man crossed himself. The men recovered their wits and dug frantically to drain off the water.

Davey was barely alive and dazed but he recognized Jack. He reached out feebly with his right arm in a pathetic plea for help from his friend. The exertion was too much and he fell face down into the hot water and lay motionless.

Jack gently lifted him out of the water, turned him over carefully and cradled his friend in his arms. Davey emitted an errie, gurgling sound when he was moved then was silent and still.

Jack wanted to scream but the sound would not come. He wanted to cry but the salty tears that stung his lids would not fall. His head pounded and his clenched jaws ached. He held close to his heart, the only other man he would call father, except his own.

After a long moment, Jack found his voice and shrieked at the top of his lungs. ''Doc! Where the hell is the doctor!''

''Right here, son. I'm right here.'' The doctor spoke softly.

Jack had not noticed that most of the water had drained off and the doctor and the men had moved in closer to him and Davey.

''Help him! For pity sake help him!'' Jack screamed.

The doctor placed the stethescope on Davey's chest, checked his heartbeat, pulse and vital signs. When he finished, he stood up and removed his stethescope and spoke softly.

''He doesn't need me anymore, he's out of his misery. I'm sorry son.'' The doctor patted Jack's shoulder and walked away.

Jack held his friend close and cried until his entire body shook.

After a while, Jack helped the men place Davey's huge body on a waiting stretcher. The shock was wearing off and the pain in Jack's feet and legs was agonizing. The rest of his body was chilled to the bone. His wet clothes clung to him and his teeth chattered.

He stood in stony silence while his friend's body was carefully loaded aboard the work train. The doctor threw a blanket around Jack's shoulders and gave him a small glass of liquid. ''Drink this, it will ease the pain. Better go aboard where it is warm.''

Jack downed the bitter liquid and boarded the train. He sat down on an empty bunk in the caboose and carefully removed his wet shoes from his smarting feet. He pulled the blanket around him and sat huddled alone—so alone.

Jack had fallen sound asleep and when he awakened, he sat bolt upright and could remember nothing or where he was. After a few moments it all came rushing back to him. The remembering was terrible.

Jack saw that he was not alone. Several other men and the doctor sat nearby on bunks and chairs and the train was moving.

''Feeling better, son? The drink I gave you contained a drop of laudanum to ease the pain and make you sleep. While you slept I treated your burns. They are painful but not serious. We are on the way home now. The preli-menary work is done. The track is passable and the secondary crew has taken over. I'm sorry about your friend, back there. The men explained how close you were. How Stanton gave you your start on the railroad and all. There wasn't anything I could do for him. He was scalded beyond my help. The cab of the engine was blown away when she rolled over and your friend was thrown out. How he survived the explosion or how he got around the engine will never be known. When the water hit the firebox the whole thing went up like a powder magazine. The fireman died instantly and how your friend survived as long as he did is a miracle."

"Thank you, I'm much obliged. I know you did what you could." Jack drew the blanket up around him, laid back on the bunk and listened to the wheels on the rails. The sound played a constant staccato that kept repeating; Davey come back; Davey come back; he won't come back; he won't come back; he's gone forever; he's gone forever; gone forever; gone forever; gone, gone, gone. The affects of the laudanum took over again and Jack fell asleep.

A pall had fallen over the Cumberland yards. Instead of the usual teeming behive of raucous men and noise it was strangely sluggish and hushed. When the railroad loses one of it's own, it's like a bit of her heart is gone. No one talks about it but all feel the pain.

In the yard office, Jack asked the clerk, "Has Mrs. Stanton been told?"

"Yes, as soon as the word came over the brass, two men were dispatched from the Tygart Lake depot to her home. The company has arranged for everything. The service for Davey and his fireman will be held at 11:00 AM day after tomorrow at the Old Stone Church—it be'in the biggist—the fireman will be buried here and Davey goes to Tygart on the afternoon passenger. Mrs. Stanton requested he be laid to rest in the church yard, there. The company is keeping a room at the Regancy Hotel for her when she arrives tomorrow." The clerk explained.

"I think she would rather stay at Riley's. She will have to to pick up his things there, anyway. Can you fix it?" Jack asked.

"I guess so—sure, I'll see to it." The man realized it was important.

Jack thanked the clerk and went directly to Riley's. It was the hour before dawn, dark and chilly.

He opened the hall door at Riley's and there was no one around. He was grateful for that. Jack could smell the cooking and knew Gretchen was up. She heard the door and went to greet him. They clung to each other and tears glistened in her eyes but there was no words. After a long moment, Jack went up to bed.

He slipped out of his damp clothes, crawled into bed and faded into the blessed darkness of sleep.

Jack stirred when the big bell in the hall sounded breakfast. He took his watch from the bedside table. 12:00 noon! What happened to breakfast? He bathed, shaved and dressed as quickly as possible but he could not drop down the stairs, two at a time because his feet were too sore.

In the dining room, he was solemnly greeted by his friends. To Gretchen he said, ''What happened to the breakfast bell?''

''I deed not reeng it. I knocked on zee doors, quietly, zooz not to wake you. For you, sleep eez better zan food.'' She hugged him.

''I'll meet the East bound and bring Becky here. I thought she'd rather be with friends than in a hotel. That way, she can collect his things in private.'' Jack explained.

''Of course, I will take goot care of her.'' Gretchen agreed.

''The company has arranged a car and driver for her. She will be picked up from here between 8:30 and 9:00 AM in the morning. I'll be around if she needs me.'' Jack explained.

The East bound had just arrived at the depot and Jack searched the crowd for Becky. She stepped off the train and looked tiny and helpless. Jack's heart twisted in his chest. What would become of her, now?

''Becky!'' Jack called and pushed through the throng.

''Jack, Oh Jack, how will I live?'' They clung to each other without words. She sobbed softly and Jack choked. The people bumped and jostled them.

When Becky regained her composure, Jack said, ''There's a car and driver waiting for you. There are somethings you have to attend to at the office this afternoon. Later, Gretchen is expecting you to stay there but the company has a room for you at the Regency if you want it.'' Jack explained.

''Gretchen has a kind heart, I'd like to stay there. David was very fond of the Rileys. Please Jack, don't make me go alone, I can't pick out a casket and do what has to be done without you! Please! I'll never get through it by myself! You are all I have left.'' She begged.

''Uh no I don't—I'd rather—don't ask——.'' Jack hated funerals and dreaded this one most of all.

''PLEASE! Jack! I have no one! PLEASE!'' She insisted.

''All right Becky, I'll do what I can.'' Jack agreed but his stomach tied into a knot. Becky pulled him into the waiting chauffeured car, by the hand.

''Mrs. Stanton, I'm Will Adams. I'm terrible sorry about your Mister. I'm s'posed ta take you anywhere you want to go as long as you're here but first, I have to take you to the Main Offices. After that to Martin's Mortuary.'' Will was uncomfortable and wrung his hat in his hands. He closed the door after Becky and Jack got in and drove the car away from the depot.

At the offices, Jack helped Becky out of the car and Jack said, ''I'll be right here when you come out. The business in there is private between you and the company.''

''Promise you will be here? Promise?'' Becky pleaded.

''I promise.'' Jack patted her hand and she went into the building.

Jack looked around for a saloon. Down the street a sign read Mory's Place, Spirits'.

''Will, I could use a snifter about now, how about you?'' Jack asked the chauffeur. Jack looked around the city and inhaled a huge gulp of fall air. It smelled of damp earth and burning leaves. Fall was his favorite season of the year, but this season had a blight on it.

''A pint would be jake with me, thanks.'' The man answered and they both went into the saloon and stood at the bar.

''I'll have a double shot of good rye and a rollin' rock beer. My friend will have a pint of what ever is on tap.'' Jack told the bartender and dropped a coin on the bar.

''Here's mud in your eye and thanks.'' The chauffeur drank long from his glass of beer.

The men finished their drinks and went outside to wait for Becky.

She came out and they drove directly to the mortuary.

After the gruesome details were taken care of, Jack and Becky got back into the car and they were both visibly shaken.

''Where to, folks?'' Asked the driver.

''The Riley's Boarding house on second street, please.'' Jack instructed.

''Sure thing, I know the place.'' Will answered.

The three rode to Riley's without words.

''Mrs. Stanton, I'll be here to pick you up at 8:30 AM.'' Will said.

''Thank you, Will.'' She answered.

Jack and Becky went inside. Gretchen was waiting in the hall and hugged Becky.

''Gretchen, do you have a glass of sherry or something for Becky, She needs a rest before supper?'' Jack asked.

''Zertainly I do. You go right up and I weel breeng eet. Davey's things are just as he left zem.'' Gretchen's heart was breaking and she wiped red eyes on her apron.

''Jack, if you don't mind, I'd rather not go down to supper. I'm so tired I just want to go to bed.'' Becky was weary.

''Becky, you have to keep up your strength. When was the last time you ate something?'' Jack asked.

''Uh, I can't remember.'' Becky answered.

Gretchen brought a half-full bottle of sherry and a small glass on a tray and placed it on the dresser in Davey's room.

''How stupid of me! After you have rested, I weel breeng you a zupper tray.'' Gretchen said.

''Thank you both.'' Becky closed the door.

''Oh Jack! I'm zo zorry for her.'' Gretchen cried on Jack's chest.

Later in the night, Jack could hear Becky weep softly through the thin walls. He cried too. He had no idea how he would be able to get through tomorrow's ordeal much less help Becky. He would not go at all if Becky had anyone else.

The morning arrived grey and dismal. Why does it always rain on a funeral? Jack did his best to buck up and hold a pleasent face for Becky but his chin was on his chest and his stomach ached.

Will Adams arrived at the set time and all were ready. Will dragged Jack's and Davey's heavy valises to the car.

''You steel have zome money coming to you, Becky.'' Gretchen said through her tears.

''Thank you for having me. It's so little, keep it and feed someone who is hungry, David would like it that way.'' Becky hugged Gretchen.

The three got into the car and drove away.

Jack and Becky arrived at the church at the proper time but the rest of the service was blurred and hazy. The eulogies were heartwarming and true but long. D. W. Stanton and his firemen had dozens of friends and co-workers with much to say about them. The service was ceremonial and restrained. The voices and sounds faded in and out. Nature has a form of anesthesia that allows the human body to endure calamity. More than ever Jack was certain a funeral was a paganistic ritual that is torturous to the living and inconsequential to the dead and should be abolished.

Eventually it was over. The crowds moved out into the street for the procession to the cemetery and in Davey's case, to the depot.

One thing Jack remembered vividly was the line of automobiles that ran around the block. There were more than he had ever seen in one place in his entire life. And more varieties than he knew existed. There were Maxwells, Mercers, Elmores, Pierce—Arrows, Studebakers and dozens of tin Lizzies. Strange what is remembered in a crisis.

Becky clung to Jack's arm in the car and wept under her black veil. At the depot, Davey's coffin was loaded into the baggage car. Jack and Becky went aboard and found seats.

They rode in silence for a long while then Becky dug into her purse.

''I want you to have David's Masonic watch fob and his worry stone.'' She laid them in his hand.

''His worry stone! You mean he didn't have it with him?'' Jack was shocked.

''Yes, he must have forgotten it. I found it on his dresser where he left it. Maybe if he'd had it in his pocket it would have saved him.'' She said it but she did not believe it.

"I can't take his fob, you gave it to him—for a birthday—I think." Jack said.

"Please, he'd want you to have it." Becky insisted and fell silent again.

Jack had no words and she expected none.

He turned the fob over and over in his hand. It was beautiful. It was red and black inch and a half wide strip of fine silk grosgrain about six inches long with the Masonic Keystone in ivory at the end. A treasure indeed, for Jack. Davey carried the fancy fob only with his best suits for dress. At work, he used a chain as did most railroaders.

They rode in silence. At Tygart, arrangements had been made and the coffin was taken to the small church yard for burial.

A few neighbors from the village gathered at the graveside and the Reverend said some nice words about Davey. Becky dropped a handful of dirt on Davey's coffin and it was done.

Later at the house in the pine grove, Becky stood staring out of the window overlooking the lake.

"Becky, I have to tell you something." Jack began.

"I know, you have to deadhead back." She said flatly.

"No, there's more. Last night I found what happened to Davey's train. After everyone had gone to bed at Riley's, I went to the yard office. I couldn't sleep. The investigation was over. They found a split rail where he went over. He was right! Their bad steel killed him! He said the rails were widow-makers and I laughed at him. I quit my job last night Becky, and I'm on my way home. Soon as I feel better I'm going to join up. I hear they need engineers OVERTHERE." He gestured with his left hand.

Becky stared at him for a long moment then said, "Go with God, my son." She kissed his cheek and turned back to the window.

Jack suddenly realized the little person he was speaking to was not the Becky of old. The shell was there but the heart was gone. There were no more tears and nothing more to say.

Jacked backed out of the door and closed it softly. In the cool evening air, he turned up his collar to ward off the chill and walked to the depot.

He caught the next train to Parkersburg and the packet boat to his home. . . .

Chapter Twelve

TWO ON THE SEAT BOX

After a few comforting weeks at home, Jack's mind and body recovered. With the help of Ma'am's cooking, his appetite returned and his gaunt cheeks filled out. His father's council eased his mind and steadied his confidence. With time, he would recover from the deaths of Em and Big Davey.

He tramped the hills with Duke and clowned with his sisters. On the first of November, 1917, he joined the U.S. Army.

''I'm sorry I won't be here for your wedding, Leone, but if you're a good girl, I'll bring you something from 'Overthere'.'' Jack teased his sister.

''Gwan! Ya scalawag! I can still take the wooden spoon to ya! Keep your head down and wear dry sox'', she hollered, then she stuffed a pair of sox into his pocket that she had made especially for him, hugged him and wiped her eyes on her apron.

''Sen, my Seneca, be sure to keep up the family history and write to me.'' He hugged her and she nodded. Seneca adored her brother but said nothing.

''Keep safe, my son.'' Tears glistened in Ma'am's eyes.

''I will Ma'am. I have your little testament right here.'' Jack patted his front shirt pocket. He held his mother for a long moment.

''Son.'' Jimmy had no words but they were not necessary. The bond between them was stronger than words. They shook hands and Jimmy thumped Jack's back and squeezed his shoulders.

Duke dragged his brother's bindle along and at the end of the lane, Jack turned and looked back at his home and family. They waved to each other and hot tears stung his eyes. When they would meet again was known only to God.

"It's up to you to look after the family now and I'm sure you can do it."

"I will until I join up and you keep your powder dry." The brothers shook hands.

Jack watched from the train until Duke and the station were out of sight.

Jack's heart was heavy yet he was filled with anticipation. He had turned one more corner in his life and was about to embark on another great adventure.

Cantonments sprung up in nearly every state for housing and training The Great American Army. Camp Perry was big; acres and acres of tents and barracks lay as far as the eye could see.

The new recruits were lined up according to height. Jack wished for an explanation but dared not ask. The Army explained nothing to it's raw recruits, however, it was apparent that dispensing uniforms and gear in this manner was more expedient.

He deemed himself fortunate to be assigned a bunk in a wood floored structure with 49 men rather than to a tent on the ground with 5 other men, with winter approaching. This would prove to be academic. Any bunk anywhere was paradise at the end of a grueling day.

In his uncomfortable Army brogans, Jack walked his blisters into hard calluses. He was classified 'Sharpshooter' for his marksmanship with a rifle but had to learn to use both hands with equal skill. A lefty was at a disadvantage as everything was designed for the right-handed.

The men dug, hauled and marched—and marched—and marched—and marched. They fell onto their bunks exhausted at dusk, to drag themselves up again at dawn. The rigorous training improved their stature, hardened their muscles and honed them into a precisioned fighting regiment.

At the end of his basic training, he was sent to Fort Dix, New Jersey for maneuvers and mock war. Dix was the same barracks-and-tent town as Perry only larger—much larger. It was huge tracts of land full of shell craters, strung barbed wire and miles of trenches all to simulate war.

The staged gas attacks were the worst for Jack. He was more sensitive to the gas and took longer to recover than the other men. He was certain the real thing would be a disaster for him.

On the whole, Jack found Army life different and exciting. He observed, listened and learned. He adapted easily to the not-always-pleasant routine because he never took it or himself too seriously. He was intelligent, obedient and rolled with the punches—all vital to army existence.

The United States sent hundreds of locomotives and equipment to France and laid hundreds of miles of standard gauge tracks. The French were unfamiliar with our equipment which meant thousands of railroaders were sent to teach them. Jack was assigned to the 33rd Transportation Company and embarked on a ship for England.

Aboard ship, his bunk buddy was hogger from McComb, Mississippi, by the name of Shirly Haas. Southerners often gave their firstborn son the mother's maiden name. She was Agatha Shirly hence, Shirly Haas. With what some thought a girl's name, he had to fight his entire life. He went by the name of Shel but sooner or later it slipped out and the fight was on. By the time the ship landed in Liverpool, the two men were good friends.

The troops were bivouacked outside the city. In a nearby pub the English soldiers learned Shel's name.

"Blyme! This Yank's name is Shirlee! Now ain't ya the PRETTY one!" The soldier curtsied and pulled at his trousers as if he had on a skirt.

"Ya think it's funny do ya? Well what do ya think of THIS" Shel slammed his fist into the soldier's jaw and sent him flying over a table. The Yanks lined up opposite the Limeys and the melee erupted. The American Revolution was revived and diplomatic relations between the two countries was set back fifty years.

There were too many men involved to lock them up so some received L D—latrine duty and others got K P—kitchen police. Jack and Shel peeled potatoes and emptied garbage for a week. They fought together back to back and were trounced but it cemented a long-lasting relationship.

Later Jack and Shel wangled 72 hours liberty and decided to go fishing, a favorite sport of both. They were informed fishing was not allowed in the Duke's private trout stream but elsewhere was permissible.

With a picnic of bread, cheese and wine, the two men sped off on rented bicycles to find a spot.

Having no idea which was the Duke's stream, the men settled down in a shady glade by a stream and cast in. The fishing was excellent and they lazed in the shade for several hours. They ate the food, drank the wine and basked in the quiet countryside.

Suddenly, a fat little man appeared who scolded them and gestured menacingly with his riding crop. His girth was covered in a riding habit and he muttered, mumbled and grunted from under a huge handle-bar mustache that was joined on each side with pork chop sideburns.

After a few minutes of the noisy annoyance, Jack and Shel suggested—not too politely—that the little man go away and stop scaring the fish. A few more mutterings and the man left.

The day was fading and the food was gone. The calm was broken by the squeal of brakes on a paddy wagon that ground to a halt near the men. Without a word, Jack and Shel were roughly thrown into the back of the of the Black Maria along with their bicycles and fishing equipment.

They tried to laugh off their bumpy ride to the pokey but the humor was hollow.

In the village, they were manhandled and shoved into a dark, dank dungeon. When the great iron door slammed shut Jack's heart leaped to his throat and his temples throbbed. Caged! He was caged like an animal, in a strange country and an ocean from home.

Shel noticed the color drain from Jack's face.

"Easy Pal, it's just a mistake. We didn't do anything wrong. The C O will get us out." Shel was not reassuring.

"We're out of uniform! How will they know we're soldiers? They didn't ask!" Jack could hardly breathe. There was little light and less air. Jack made a silent vow that if he ever got out of that place, he would never—but never be put in jail again. The thought of a life in a cell so terrified him he felt faint. He paced back and forth to get enough air and choked down his panic. It was so quiet the men's breathing sounded loud.

After what seemed a lifetime but had only been hours, voices were heard and the iron door clanked open. In the doorway, stood Sergeant Hines, arms folded and scowling at Jack and Shel. He was the platoon top-kick, tough as nails and mean as dirt. To Jack, he looked like 'Gabriel come to the rescue!.

"You Mugs did it this time! You roughed up the Old Duke himself! Had a Hell-of-a-time springin' ya.' You'll pound the ground plenty, for this! Come out of there! Where's your uniforms, ya flea-bitten hog heads? Don't ya know nuthin'?" He snorted.

The two men tried to explain but the Sarge had none of it.

Back at the camp, on the carpet in front of the C O, Jack and Shel were given a scathing reprimand on the protocol demanded while in a foreign country. They were also reminded of the high plain on which the British people regard their Royalty. The real punishment was five miles around the parade grounds with full equipment, at double time.

Later in the barracks, where they soaked their blistered feet and rubbed their cramped arms and legs, Jack told the story to their buddies. He was a great storyteller and mimic and soon had the men howling with laughter when he imitated the portly Duke's mumbling.

Two weeks later the two men were sent to France.

Shirly (Shel) Haas was sent to Amiens and the Central Supply Company, there. Jack was sent to Nancy and the Hospital and Supply Company along the North lines and the front. Although their paths crossed occasionally at a coal tipple or a water tower, they would see little of each other in the next two years.

The trip by train to Nancy through the devastated land was horrible. The once-green landscape was pockmarked with craters, the earth was churned into knee-deep mud and the once-beautiful trees stood as broken, naked sentinels of destruction.

At Nancy, Jack was to find a small hotel operated by a widow named Fleur Rambeau. Here, he and his crews were to be billeted until further notice. Since the Americans worked side by side with the French, their orders could come in French or English, Fleur would translate. Besides, there was no camp nearby and the hotel rates were cheaper than building one. Fleur was instructed to house and feed the men and she would be reimbursed by the U.S. Army.

The Hotel La Blanc was on the corner of the square. It was neither white or large. It was a two-story walk-up with half a story below ground. It had a side entrance as well as the main entrance.

The hair stood up on the back of Jack's neck. He had never been here before but he recognized the place. He had seen it before. Nonsense, it was not possible and Jack dismissed it.

The large wood and glass door was ajar and Jack went in. Straight ahead were the stairs; one set went up and one set went down. To the left was the proprietors desk and to the right was the dining room and kitchen. There was no lobby and everything was on a small scale. It was very different for Jack but the cooking food smelled inviting. Lately he was always hungry.

From the steps to the lower level, came a beautiful lady in a brown shawl over a dark green dress. She had shiny auburn hair, green eyes and she was fine-boned but well-rounded. She moved in a cloud of delightful perfume. When she reached out her hand to him, Jack went weak-kneed.

''Ah Monsieur, you are my American Railroad man, no?'' Her voice was musical and pleasant and except for the French accent, her English was excellent.

''Oh yes, I'm Jack Lansure, U S Army Engineers.'' He took her hand for a moment.

''You may have a room down, a room up or a room up-up. What will it be.?'' She lifted the hinged desk top, went inside and replaced it. The back wall was covered with room keys and she pointed for Jack to select. ''The Army man said there would be thirty two of you. That is more rooms than I have but some rooms have two and three beds. He said they would double up. He also said, they would be coming and going at different hours and the Army could manage. He will also send food and supplies as we have very little. Have you a choice of rooms?''

''Not really but I'd rather be up than down.'' Her perfume made Jack's ears ring.

''In that case, I have selected a tiny room on the top with easy access to the doors. You will be alone and the necessary is on the floor below. Is that satisfactory?'' She lifted the desk top and came out.

''Fine, that's just fine.'' Jack was in a delightful fog.

''This way please, by the way I'm Fleur Rambeaux.''

''How'd ja do.'' Jack followed Fleur up two flights of stairs and into a tiny room.

''It is small but it is always light. See?'' The windows were in the right slope of the the ceiling. Fleur pulled a hanging cord and the drape drew away from the windows and sunlight flooded the room.

''I like this.'' Jack looked around the room. The bed was big but the small room still had space for a bedside table, a battered armoire, a washstand and a faded chair.

''It is often too warm in the summer but it is always cozy in the winter. Your key, Monsieur, come now I will show you the dining room.'' Fleur led the way down stairs. Aha, that perfume. Jack bathed in it's essence.

The dining room had six small tables and a pass-through to the kitchen as well as a cafe swinging door. On each table there was a threadbare checkered tablecloth and in the center, a wine bottle held a large candle with hundreds of drippings solidified to the sides.

Fleur noticed Jack's curiosity when he fingered one of the bottles.

''We use many candles here because the—how you say—electricity is unpredictable, the War you know.'' She teased him good naturedly and they both laughed.

Jack would come to find that Fleur was a courageous, hard-working French patriot. The longer he knew her, the more he liked her and oh, her perfume. The men filed in by twos and threes and she assigned them rooms. As time went on, she thought nothing of being awakened in the middle of the night to feed five or six hungry railroaders. Their hours were as unpredictable as her electricity. She had two kitchen helpers, an old man and a woman and they often grumbled but she was philosophical and would say, ''When the war is gone, all will be good again.' She managed to squeeze all thirty two men into that tiny hotel and fed and cared for them as if they were family. She had three other women to help with the scullery and housework.

The men teased her and she loved it. She even enjoyed a friendly pat on the rump from her guests. One by one she learned their favorite food and arranged the cooking, from time to time and availability, so each man received his favorite. How she obtained some of the goodies would forever, remain a mystery. A favorite with many was bread pudding. When flour, eggs, milk and sugar was available, she served it—sometimes with raisins or vanilla.

When she was complimented on her thoughtfulness and ingenuity she would beam with pleasure but never revealed her source.

The La Blanc Hotel became the home-away-from-home for those homesick Yanks and War became a bit easier with Fleur's help.

The weeks ran into months and the months into a year. Jack and the crews worked hand in hand with the French who were completely unfamiliar with the U S equipment and the language barrier made things worse. Try as they would, they had great difficulty with the locomotives. They were heavy-handed on the throttle and jerky with the brakes. In making up the trains, they caused damaged equipment, breakdowns and unthinkable delays. Besides teaching operations to the French, the Yanks had to make their scheduled runs to and from the front. The trains hauled men and supplies all along the lines and to the front. They carried the sick and wounded from field hospitals to base hospitals. The hours were long and exhausting and Jack often fell into bed too tired to eat.

The Germans were fighting for their very existence and often fought fanaticly to hold their ground. The Allied forces were just as determined to push them back. Often a town or village would change hands three times in a week. The devastation was unimaginable.

The road crews were often laying rails in front of Jack's engine to repair the torn up tracks caused by the German's Big Bertha. The huge cannon, mounted on a railroad flat car, could fling a shell 20 or 30 miles and caused a crater in the ground large enough to swallow a two-story building. Some of the towns were reduced to nothing but burned out skeletons; a stack of charred timbers here, a pile of rocks there or half a brick chimney still standing.

Jack's heart broke when he thought of his own family in these conditions. He gave what food he had to the starving women and children who came begging to the train. All the Yanks gave what they had. The children's misery could not be measured.

After one particularly bad run in the late summer of 1918, Jack and his crew dragged themselves to Fleur's. Most staggered to the dining room but others like Jack, plodded to their rooms and bed, too tired to eat.

Fleur fed her charges, saw to those who had not eaten and finally, she took a tray up to Jack.

He only grunted when she knocked and entered with the tray.

"Drink this, mon cher." She said and lifted his head to take the thin rich soup from the bowl. He drank the warm liquid and rolled over.

"Not yet, mon amie, take this." She instructed Jack. She rolled him back and forced a cup of coffee to his lips. The coffee was notoriously bad because it was mostly chicory root but it was warm and Fleur had laced it with cognac.

''Ugh,'' he muttered his thanks and went back to sleep.

When Fleur peeled off his dirty shirt, pants and sox, he simply groaned. She took the tray and dirty clothes and left the room.

Jack slept around the clock. When forced out of bed because his bladder was bursting, he decided to shave and clean up since he had to go to the floor below for both and he smelled a bit gamey.

Later he fell back on his bed and slept.

Jack's latest orders arrived for him and the crew so Fleur delivered them to his room.

''Jacque it is Fleur, may I come in.'' She knocked gently. ''I have your orders.''

''Sure, I'm awake and I want to give you a big kiss for feeding me and putting me to bed.'' He enjoyed teasing her.

''It was not important but when you work hard you must eat. You only have three hours to report to the yards with the crew. The man who delivered the orders was very excited. He said the Borsch were on the move again.''

Fleur sat down on the bed beside Jack and he gave her a big, noisy smacker.

''Hurry now, the crews are gathering in the dining room waiting for you.'' She patted his cheek and left the room. Secretly, she loved this yank, who was half her age.

The orders were urgent and specific. All American railroad personnel were to report for duty in full Army uniform. Each work train was fully supplied with food and water and had one additional car specially designed for stretcher cases.

In the dining room, the men spoke to Jack. ''What do you make of this, Jack?'' Asked one.

''Looks like we are to move a field hospital. One that is close to the front. Why no work clothes—I don't know—unless the Big Brass don't want us to be mistaken for spies.'' Jack played it glib for his friends but underneath he was puzzled and apprehensive.

''You think the Jerries have broken through again?'' Said someone.

''Will this be a long trip?'' Asked another.

''You fellas know as much as I do, let's make tracks out of here.'' urged Jack.

At the yards there were additional instructions for Jack and the other engineers. Their orders read; make top speed to Rheims but bypass Suippes and Verdun. Both towns were under siege and the Germans were fighting fiercely.

The trip to Rheims should take twelve hours but this time it took three days. Jack and his crew arrived in the middle of the night, exhausted and out of food and water. It had rained continuously since they left Nancy and the entire countryside was a sticky mud hole. All they had to sustain them and ward off the October chill was half a case of table wine scrounged up by one of the French crew members.

Jack and his fireman, Alaburton Green—Al, for short—drank a bottle from the case and stretched out on the floor of the cab to sleep.

When they woke up at dawn they were cold, hungry and hung over. The cab's iron deck was torture for their bodies and they were stiff and cramped. A thick fog with mist hung over the place and the heavy canvas gangway curtains did little to keep out the damp chill.

Al staggered to his feet and opened the firebox door. It was the first warmth they had all night. The warm glow heated the cab. Al gorged the iron behemoth with coal and the men studied the gauges. Jack began the routine to move the train. He tapped the glass of one gauge and looked at his reflection. He saw a dirty face, bloodshot eyes and a three-day beard. Aloud he said, "I look a fright!"

"How's that, Jack?" Al heard him speak but could not make out the words.

"It's nothin', I saw my face in the glass and I look-a-booger." Jack replied.

"Don't we all. Here, have a drop of the hair-of-the-dog. Ya can't feel worse and who knows, ya might feel better." Al gave Jack the wine.

The first swallow went down like coal oil but the second was not as painful. Jack placed the bottle in the case and the men went back to work.

The sporadic distant heavy gun fire caused the pace to quicken along the train's length. After the train arrived, the doctors, nurses, orderlies and civilians worked through the night to get the wounded aboard. Jack's train would take the evacuees eastbound, to Nancy and the westbound would go to Compiegn.

An ambulance ground to a halt in the mud, near the engine. A man emerged, plowed through the mud and scrambled up into the cab. Jack and Al stared at him.

His too-long chestnut colored hair framed his lean face. He stood ramrod straight and glowered at the men. His tattered shirt and breeches dived into muddy boots. A blood spattered clinic coat hung loosely from his shoulders.

It was difficult to tell how long he had been on his feet or in his soiled uniform. He had dark circles under his eyes and his face was grim.

"I'm Henri Du Lac, Surgeon with the Imperial Forces under General Foch. This is my hospital and we must evacuate at once! The Borsch have broken through near here. Who are you and who is in charge here?'' He scrutinized Jack and Al and the inside of the cab, noting the case of wine.

''Guess I am.'' Jack admitted.

''You are—that's impossible—you're drunk! You can't operate this train! You're not suitable for this mission!'' His anger turned to despair. ''Do you know what they are loading back there? Five hundred seriously wounded stretcher cases; internal bleeding, brain injuries, compound fractures and those too badly injured to stand a jolting ambulance. How could they send me such dregs as you.'' He was distraught.

Before Jack could speak the doctor's orderly popped up at the gangway. He spoke excitedly in French to the doctor and disappeared as quickly as he had come.

''Monsieur, you are not suitable for this mission but I have no one else and we must leave quickly.'' The doctor spoke to Jack. ''The cargo you carry is human life and some is hanging by a thread. Most will survive if you don't kill them in your drunkenness. Everytime you jerk this train, men will die. Each time you stop too fast, more will die. When the car sways too much around a curve broken bodies will scream in agony and die because you were drunk. Hear me, wastrel, at the end of this trip, I will have you removed from the Army and my countrymen will have you publicly disgraced because, monsieur, you are a disgrace''!

Without a backward glance, the doctor dropped to the ground, slogged through the mud to the ambulance which promptly drove away.

The doctor's unfair verbal barrage left Jack and Al stunned. The skin on the back of Jack's neck began to creep and a hot ball of frustration, humiliation and anger began to choke him. The blood rushed to his hairline and his eyes flashed. Through clenched jaws, he began to swear. ''That son-of-a-bitch! In all my 26 years nobody ever laced me so bad! Who the hell does he think he is! That god-damned pill-pushing Frog! What does he know about what I can or can't do! Nobody can talk to me that way—nobody!'' Jack growled.

''Easy Jack, he doesn't know what he's talking about. He'll calm down when he learns the truth—when he finds out we drank the wine because there was no water. He doesn't know your the best hogger around.'' Al did his best to console Jack.

''I'll show that saw-bones who can run this engine, I'll fix him!''

Jack was still muttering to himself when Charley Beaman, the brakeman called up to Jack's side of the engine.

''Hey Jack!''

''Yea Charley.'' Jack called back and poked his head out of the cab window.

"Let her roll, we're all loaded back here and some of these men are badly hurt."

Jack was calmer now and the doctor's stinging words were still ringing in his ears, but he had a more important job at hand.

Al nodded that he was ready, Charley had time to get back to the caboose so Jack pulled on the whistle cord that hung above his head. The sound sent screeching shock waves into the clinging mist. He looked out the cab window for the green light. The signal arms swung and the light turned green. He released the air and nodded for sand. Very carefully, he eased her over and took up the slack. The steaming smoking beast shuddered and moved. The locomotive had to drag ten cars, a bunk car and a caboose plus a full load. Every nut, bolt and timber strained when the big engine tried to move the train. Jack inched the throttle over more and more. The big drivers caught and caravan moved out of the town. It was 8:05 AM and no sign of a weather break.

"I'm so hungry I could eat dirt, wish Charley would come with the java." Al said, after an hour or so into the run.

"I'm hungry too but I can't go much more canned bully beef and beans," Jack answered.

The two men worked well together. Al kept the fire box full and the water up. Jack strained to see the right-of-way ahead. The fog had lifted a little but it rained intermittently. So far, the trip was uneventful. The big engine belched a huge festoon of grey smoke from her stack and the wheels made a rhythmical staccato on the rails below. The speed was slow but steady.

As if by magic, Charley appeared on top of the tender. He was a good-natured Irishman who came from a long line of railroaders. When teased about his Jewish sounding name, he would bark 'Me family was in Ireland long before there was a Mc anything!" He was big and strong and his blarney was as thick as his brogue.

He scrambled down the coal pile into the cab. He carried assorted containers of food with tin plates and cups.

"Here it is me buckos, no bully or hardtack—food-real-food! He opened a container and gave each man a half a loaf of freshly baked bread. He lifted the dividing compartment and revealed a pot of stew. "See, real bread and stew like me mother used to make!" He closed his eyes and sniffed the air which was filled with the aroma cooked food and coffee.

"Oh Jack, smell that—real grub and hot java." I could eat a horse!" Al drooled.

"You might be doing just that! Where'd you get the fixens, Charley?" Jack teased.

Charley dished out the food to the hungry men.

"One thing for sure, the people in that hospital ate real good. The storeroom was full and I figured they wouldn't miss a bit-o-this-and-that." Charley confessed.

"Carrots, genuine, garden fresh carrots and potatoes, even Fleur couldn't find carrots! Charley, you sure can cook up a storm when you have something to cook." Al managed to say all that with his mouth full of food.

The men wolfed down the delicious meal and Charley filled the cups with more coffee. They ate ravenously but were not once distracted from the engine or the job at hand.

"Charley you saved my life." Jack thumped him on the back and returned his cup and plate.

"I feel almost human again." Al patted his full stomach.

"Wait a jiffy boys, there's more!" Charley fumbled around in his coat pocket and extracted a huge chunk of sweet chocolate, broke it in two and gave each man half.

"Jeeze, Charley, where did you find CHOCOLATE! Al was delighted.

"Some things I NEVER tell. By the way every time we stop, that nasty saw-bones is all over me like a dirty shirt so please, keep moving." Charley said and packed up his trappings and went back over the tender and disappeared.

Both men were refreshed and their work seemed easier. They made the routine stops for coal and water and all appeared normal.

At dark, it was still raining and they were less than half way home. All engines ran without lights as the blackout was strictly observed along the railroads. To guide the trains forward, there was a network of civilian spotters with lanterns and torches about every 60 rods—1,000 feet—or so. The engineer was signaled to pass, slow or stop by the spotter. At night, they were the eyes of the railroads because torn up tracks and shell craters were commonplace.

The hours dragged by and once more exhaustion and cold tested Jack and Al. Jack's eyes burned from squinting down the tracks for spotters and his body was cramped and aching. Al was bone-tired from shoveling tons of coal and mopped his grimy, sweating face with a dirty handkerchief.

Suddenly, Jack felt crowded on the seat box, as if someone had set down behind him. He looked but there was no one. Jack glanced at Al to see if he had noticed anything unusual but he was busy with his work. The crowding persisted. Jack stood and shook one leg at a time to relieve his aching joints and swung his head from side to side to ease the pain in his neck and head. He sat down on the seat box again and again he was not alone. He was positive his imagination was playing tricks on him.

Without warning, a warm hand clasped his right shoulder. Instantly, his exhausted, cold, cramped body was relieved. A wave of warm comfortable, sense of well-being spread over him. He felt rested and clear-eyed. He had never had such a feeling. At the same instant, a warm hand covered his own on the throttle and gently but firmly closed the throttle and slowed the train to a stop. Jack automatically set the brakes.

Al was quick to react to Jack's strange behavior. "Jack! What the hell—why'd ya stop here?"

Al's voice jerked Jack back from wherever he was and he said, "I'du know—it was—I think there is something wrong here—I missed two spotters." How could he explain another presence in the cab when there was no one to be seen.

Instantly the men dropped to the ground on his side of the engine. It was pitch black and still raining. Jack felt his way along the engine to the front and took a step forward. His way was blocked at eye-level by a large piece of cold metal. He felt along the metal and followed it to the ground. It was the rail. It had been been curled up by a great force. Al and Jack met at the rail, at the same time an excited French spotter began to shout from far up the tracks.

"I'm sorry! I'm sorry!" He cried as he ran to the engine. "The Borsch have broken through with their big guns and there is destruction for five miles along the line. There are so many dead and wounded in the village. My family." He sobbed into his hands.

The crew and hospital personnel had gathered and tried to comfort the distraught man.

Soon lanterns and torches illuminated the entire area. A small group stood at the front of the engine in dumb silence. There was a crater in the earth large enough to swallow the locomotive.

The force of the blast threw the left rail into the weeds of the right-of-way and curled the right one up into a half circle less than a foot from the front of the engine. Inches more and the train would have derailed and wrecked.

The entire tableau took but a moment. Al stared at Jack and said, "How the hell did you know that hole was there? I couldn't see a thing! Another foot and we'ed been spread all over the countryside!" Al's eyes probed Jack's face.

"I REALLY don't know, it was kind of strange; if I told you, you wouldn't believe me." Jack stammered.

The astonished doctor stared first at the crater them at the men. He could barely comprehend what he saw. His voice croaked when he said, "How could you know? How could you see in the dark? The wounded men back there, all of us, you saved our lives. This thing you have done is a miracle! A miraculous thing!" His voice trailed off.

Others had heard what he said and echoed his words. "IT's a miracle! It's miraculous how he saved the train! It's truly a miracle!" They cried.

A crowd swarmed around Jack and Al and their voices raised to cheers and excitement.

The sound of heavy gun fire erased the euphoria from the crowd and the war was back again. It was 3:00 AM and they were 20 miles from Nancy with no track in front and the Germans threatening their back. What now? Jack wondered.

"Tell Charley, Doctor Du Lac, and the French spotter that I'd like to talk to them. We've got to get cracking." Jack instructed Al.

They gathered around him and he said, "We have no choices. The wounded men can not be dragged around, the track is out in front and the Germans can be here anytime. If you will help me, we'll get out of this mess.! Spotter, what's your name?" Jack asked.

"Louis, monsieur."

"Louis you know these parts and the people. We need as many hands as you can find with picks, shovels, hoes, crowbars, wheel barrows and carts and all the rope there is. Can you manage that?" Jack asked the French patriot.

"Yes monsieur, I can do it. I will bring my people. I go now." The spotter left.

"Doctor, will you and your medical staff help?" Jack asked.

"Yes of course, anything, but first I must apologize. . . . . " The doctor tried to apologize.

"Never mind that now, we have work to do." Jack interrupted the doctor. "We have to fill in that hole with enough dirt and stones to lay track over it. We will take ties and track from behind us to replace what is blown out allowing us to go on. I figure we can fix it faster than help can get to us, if we get the people. Charley, you shinny up that pole and click our location to Nancy. You got your spare key?" Jack asked.

"How'd ya know I was a sparks, Jack, I never told a soul." Charley grinned.

"A good hogger knows all about his men besides, your bunk buddy says you talk in your sleep." Jack winked and pointed two jaunty fingers at his friend.

Charley climbed the telegraph pole and attached the wire to his key then slid down.

"Al, you and a couple of the crew set your Rosalies (affectionate name for a bayonet) and stand guard up ahead and behind the train. It will be light soon and I don't want any surprises." Jack explained.

"Right O." Al answered.

"Charley, you getting anything?" Jack called to Charley who was kneeling in the weeds pounding his telegraph key.

"It's coming in now. Yes, they got me and will stand by." Charley called back.

From the distance, came the sound of voices and commotion. Louis was as good as his word. He was followed by about 30 people carrying picks, shovels and tools of every kind.

"Monsieur, more will come soon. Tell us what to do." The men asked.

Jack explained what was to be done and the good-natured men, women and children began to fill in the crater. The ground was heavy with water and slick but they worked without complaint.

At dawn, the rain stopped and the sun came out. The people lugged, dragged and carried the heavy ties around the engine to the new roadbed they had built of dirt and stones. The heavy rails were the biggest problem but all pitched in to help. They grunted and sweated to fit them in place on the ties. Pulling the spikes was much harder then pounding them in. If the repair would hold for the weight of the locomotive to pass over, chances were good it would hold for the rest of the train at very low speed.

The exhausted people sat down to watch. They had to lay twice as many ties in the repaired area to support the rails in the soft earth.

Jack, Al and the crew prepared the engine to move. Jack took up the slack and eased the throttle over. Slowly the train moved. The ties sunk some under the engine's weight but the mend held.

The group of weary workers cheered with delight and ran to the cab of the engine when the train stopped on the good track beyond the repair.

After the congratulatory bedlam subsided, Jack thanked the people for the help and asked Al to stoke her up for the end of the trip to Nancy.

The trip back was routine but Jack was so tired he remembered little about it. At the yards, other crews took over and Jack and his men dragged themselves to Fleur's and sleep.

The next thing Jack remembered, it was dark and Fleur was there with a tray of food. She drew the ceiling drapes for the blackout and lit a candle.

"You must eat, mon amie." She urged.

"I'm not hungry—just sleepy." He sat up and tasted the coffee. "Umm good." He said.

"Eat something and sleep more." She urged.

Jack folded the bread, dunked it in his coffee and ate his food.

"You'll make somebody a great mother Fleur, but I already have one." He teased her and she swatted at him. He ducked and they both laughed.

When he finished the food, she took the tray, snuffed the candle and left the room. Jack slept again.

He opened his eyes when he heard pounding on the door and Al's excited voice.

"Yea, what is it, Al?" Jack inquired sleepily.

"Get up, get dressed, hurry! We're heros, Jack. We made all the papers! See!" Al held up a newspaper and the headlines read: YANK'S MIRACLE SAVES HOSPITAL TRAIN.

"That's a lot of bunkum. We did nothin' of the kind." Jack muttered and rolled over.

"Oh, but we did! We not only saved the train from wrecking into the shell hole but the Jerries were right behind us. We tore up the tracks so bad behind us they could'nt get their guns and supplies any further and the battle line held right there. The Yanks and the Frogs pushed them back from St. Mihiel and now they are on the run. If you had not asked the people to move the track so we could go on, the Jerries would have caught the train and who knows what they would have done with the injured men and us. That reminds me, how DID you know that crater was there? The people say it was a miracle." Al went on.

"Enough of THAT talk, it was no miracle! I admit it was sort of creepy but it was just a lucky break—a hunch—and nothing to get all het up about." Jack tried to sound nonchalant in front of Al but down deep, he was puzzled about the strange phenomena.

As the men spoke, a figure appeared at the door. It was Doctor Henri Du Lac. He was hardly recognizable as the hostile, disheveled man on the train. His long hair had been trimmed and he was clean. He wore the full dress uniform of an officer in the French Medical Corp. He tucked his swagger stick under his arm and removed his hat.

"Pardon me gentlemen, Miss Fleur said you were here and allowed me to come up.

Jack and Al stiffened because they thought they were about to be set upon again.

"Please, I'm not here to offend. I have come to shake your hands and beg your forgiveness." The Doctor moved closer and extended his hand.

"Well in that case—." Al took a step toward him and took his hand.

"If you don't mind the way I look." Jack stood up from the bed in his dirty underwear and held out his hand.

"Monsieur Lansure, you look like a Prince to me and my people. For what you did out there, we have no words but you will have our grateful thanks forever. That's what I'm here for. The people of the village are having a festival in your honor, by proclamation of Mayor Francois Daru. Colonel Louis Jognac will bestow the Medal of Merit upon you and your crew for your heroism and courage. Now gentlemen, I have much to do. It is 12:00 noon. We will expect you on the square at 2:00 PM. My eternal thanks." The Doctor bowed at the waist and backed out of the room.

For an instant Jack and Al were struck dumb and rooted to the spot.

"What the hell do ya make of that!" Al said under his breath. "That sawbones wants to give us medals! The other day, he wanted to give us tar and feathers!" His voice rose to a shout.

"Count me out! I'm not much for all that hoopla." Jack said thoughtfully. He had plans of his own.

"Oh come on, get cleaned up and we'll have some fun. I'm fed up with this war stuff." Al urged.

"You go ahead. After I clean up, I'll go down and eat. I'll see you later." Jack said

"Okay." Al agreed and left.

Jack bathed and dressed. When he approved of his image in the mirror, he went down to the dining room and trailed a scent of bay rum.

The lunch crowd was thinning out but there were several of his crewmen still eating.

"Hey Jack! What do ya think 'o that! They're going to give us medals!" shouted one.

"Glory Be! If only me sainted Mother was alive to see it! May she rest in peace." Charley Beaman gushed in his Irish brogue and crossed himself.

"They're makin' a big party on the Square! The people are making pancakes and sausage outside and they rolled out a big barrel of wine!" The man was excited.

"That's a crepes-au-carne, ya stump-jumper, have'nt ya learned nothin' about this country yet?" One man corrected and scolded his friend.

"Ya should see all the flowers and colored streamers! It's really pretty!" voiced another.

"They put decorations on the bandstand and set up chairs for the ceremony. It's gonna be a fancy party, alright." Said another.

"They say, the French Brass will be here." Said someone.

"You guys go ahead and have fun, I'll be out after I eat." Was Jack's response.

The men finished their meal and left by twos and threes.

Sitting alone, Jack stirred absently in his cold coffee. Fleur came to his table and said, "Mon amie, you are so sad when you should be so gay—so happy!" She said lightly and swung her arms about.

"Sit down please, Fleur, I need to talk to you." He was troubled.

"But of course, mon cher, what can I do for you?" She was concerned for him.

"Fleur when I first came here, something odd happened. Something real queer. I'd never been here before but I knew what it looked like. I'd seen it before. The village, the square, your hotel, the little church were just as I'd seen it. I don't know how but I've been here before. Out there, I knew something was wrong. I didn't know what but I knew something was wrong, I just knew it. I can't explain any of this! Maybe I'm going crazy!'' Jack's voice rose.

''Don't be silly mon amie, it happens to we French all the time and we call it 'Deja vu'. We can not explain it either but why bother? It happens—so it happens. It is nothing to worry about—it's just life.'' She dismissed it lightly.

''Deja vu, huh? Well, what about this miracle and hero stuff? You know very well it was no miracle and we're a far cry from heros! We were just mugs doing what we had to in a pinch. Call it what you like but this big party for us is all wrong.'' Jack was agitated.

Fleur dragged her chair closer to Jack and took his hand in hers.

''Mon cher, listen to me. What you did out there may have been just good judgment and luck to you but to those war-weary people, it was a miracle! They have had years of war and killing and are sick inside. Anything that stops the killing is a miracle. You saved those injured men from certain death in a train wreck and from God know's what, at the hands of the Borsch! What is a miracle? Who knows? Who's to say? To those simple people, any relief from the slaughter is a miracle. To you, maybe it was chance or fate. Perhaps, it was a coincidence but to them, it was a miracle. They desperately need a reason to cheer, to laugh and dance. They need music and laughter, flowers and food and they need to drink wine and sing. They are showing their joy and gratitude to you the only way they know how. At the same time, they are healing their own wounds. Doctor Du Lac suggested they give you medals and the French Army agreed. He feels horrible about the things he said to you. Yes, he told me all about it. You must not deny these people a chance to forget their troubles and be happy for a little while. Don't you see, it's as much for them as it is for you and your men.'' She patted his hand and stood up.

''But Fleur, I——.''

''No, no! Don't talk, just sit here and think about what I've said. I'll be back later.'' She interrupted. Fleur went into the kitchen and left Jack alone with his thoughts. He sat alone a while longer, then went out the hotel side door to the street.

The village square had a festive air. The shop-fronts were decorated and all the merchants displayed their wares. Children ran and laughed with excitement and the band members tuned their instruments. The people gathered, stood in clusters and chattered happily.

Jack leaned on the hotel doorjamb and watched. Perhaps the things Fleur said were true. Maybe they did need to escape from the war and any excuse would do. Any light is welcome when one is lost in the dark.

A French Army Motorcade drove into the square and stopped in front of the Mayor's office. Assorted Army Brass emerged from the cars and paraded into the building. The General was particularly imposing-looking with a four inch handlebar mustache.

With the Army Brass, came the crowd of people and more were coming. A wave of people pushed Al into the doorway with Jack.

"Hi ya Buddy, I been lookin' all over for ya!" Al had been drinking his way around the square with the people. He hugged Jack's shoulders. "This is gonna be some shindig! Did you see the big Brass?"

"Yes I did, specially that General with the handlebar mustache! You know those generals kiss you on both cheeks when they give ya a medal?" Jack was emphatic.

"Naw!" Al was disbelieving.

"It's true! And I'm damned sure I'm not going to let that General kiss me! Why, if he came at me with that big mustache, I'd laugh right in his face! That would put the kibosh on the whole shebang! Ya wouldn't want me to mess up the party now would ya?"

"But Jack ya gotta come, you did the most!" Al insisted.

"No I did not! You fellas did all the work. Now git up there and step smartly for all the Yanks in this country. Git!" Jack pushed Al out into the crowd.

The Army General and his entourage came out of the building and up onto the bandstand followed by Jack's crew who had gathered nearby, as instructed.

The ceremony began with a drumroll followed by a long-winded speech by the Mayor. The crew stood ramrod straight and polished inspite of the fact they understood very little of what he said. After some time, Charley Beaman whispered out of the corner of his mouth to Al. "Where's Jack, he's going to miss the whole thing."

"He's not coming." Al whispered back.

The ceremony went on as scheduled. The men received their medals and were kissed on both cheeks by the General.

Jack made his way through the crowd to a small church nearby and went in. It was almost empty. He sat down in the rear and looked around in the dim light. Candles burned and flickered at the alter and it smelled of wax, flowers and old wood. He did not know what a miracle was, but he was about to ask 'Someone' who did know. We will never know if he received an answer or not but when he came out of the church later, he smiled.

By now, the ceremony was over and the party was in full swing. The men displayed their medals proudly. Al pinned Jack's on him without kisses and the fun began.

The men danced with the pretty girls and soon all were dancing including Jack and Fleur. He was no longer sad and the celebration went on into the night. The pent-up emotions of the war-ravaged people burst out in rollicking song and dance and swept away their troubles if only for a moment. . . .

In November, the Armistice was signed and the shooting war was over. Jack and his crew moved rolling stock from one place to another as it was needed. They taught the French how to operate the big locomotives.

By June 1919, the men were assigned to Le Havre, to a troop ship for home.

Far up on the ship's railing, a soldier shouted to the men coming aboard.

"Hey! Dirty neck! Dirty neck Lansure!" Shirly (Shel) Haas had found Jack at last. He had been searching in the new arrivals for his friend. A steam locomotive engineer has a dirty neck more often than any other vocation except his brothers in the coal fields. Engineers often call each other 'dirty necks' in camaraderie and fun.

"Hey Reb, I thought you went back to Dixie!" Jack shouted back to his buddy.

Aboard ship, the two men threaded and pushed their way through the sea of soldiers to find each other. When they met, they hugged and thumped each other's back.

"Damn! I'm THAT glad to see you. Why'd you stay so long?" Jack asked.

"Well, I checked to see if you were still here. When they said you were I decided to stay too. Besides the Frogs had a time catchin' on to our big hogs. You look great—no nicks?" Shel was delighted to find his friend.

"Nary a scratch—unless you call a lopsided tattoo—a scratch. The tattooman was soused worse then I was!" Jack bared his right forearm and displayed the Masonic Emblem of the Square and Compass tattooed on the inside.

Shel looked at the tattoo, it was anything but square but it was colorful. Both men roared with laughter.

The officers called roll but they did not separate Jack and Shel. They inched their way into the hold of the ship and found bunks.

"Up or down, Jack?" Shel asked.

"Machts Nichts." Jack answered.

"Where'the hell did ya learn the Jerry talk?" Shel cried.

"Oh that, we carried prisoners once in a while. One of them gave me this ring." Jack held out his right hand. It was a gold ring set with the head of a knight in armor carved from a piece of cream and brown quartz. It was a beautiful ring.

"The rest of this stuff, I just gathered up from anyone who was looking for a few dollars. Draggin' it around with me has been a real pain-in-the-neck. Where's you get all yours?" Jack explained.

"Here and there. I swapped for most of it; A blanket here and mess-kit there—you know." Shel answered. "Can't we go up on deck? It's hotter than hell in here!" Jack wiped his sweating face. The tight soldiers quarters filled with men and the heat increased.

"Somebody said we had to stay down here 'till the ship clears the harbor and we are out at sea. The sailors say we get in the way. Them swab-jockeys got a lot o' nerve if ya ask me.'" Shel observed.

At sea there was little to do but laze on the decks, read on your bunk, or stand in endless lines for meals, showers and toilet. Card and crap games floated around the ship in spite of the warning orders against it.

Jack had played lots of Poker in his time, but never a game called Euchre. The sailors were masters at it. It was a game where Jacks, in both suits, were higher than any Ace. The game was confounding and quick.

In the time it took the ship to cross the Atlantic Ocean, Jack lost all his war trophies and $1,700.00 dollars in back pay. Shel lost $1,000.00 and all his souvenirs. The sailors on board, wiped out half the Army on board the ship.

Jack silently vowed he would never play any kind of cards again. This lesson was a bitter pill, indeed.

"How the hell did that happen?" Shel puzzled.

"I can't tell ya for sure, but one thing I CAN tell ya, it will never happen to me again! I promised my sister I'd bring her something from over there for a wedding present. It's the first time I ever went back on my word and THAT will never happen again, either." Jack was filled with regret and remorse.

Jack and Shel hung over the ship's railing and watched while the ship pulled into New York harbor.

"Look Jack! Ain't she a beauty? Shel cried and pointed.

"She is that!" Jack exclaimed.

The men stared in silent wonderment. Suddenly the entire ship load of soldiers gave out a cheer heard all over the harbor. There she stood, the sign of refuge, peace and home. It was the Statue of Liberty.

The two men were separated on the dock and assigned different trains for home. It was a sad good-bye.

"I'm gonna see my folks first, but I'm heading West as soon as possible. I'll let you know where." Shel's voice croaked.

"I'll be at home for a while but I got to go to work. Those sailors cleaned me out. In a few weeks I'll be down to my uppers." Jack declared. "Drop me a line to let me know you're alive and I'll do the same.'' He added and fought back the lump in his throat.

The men hugged, thumped each other's back and went their separate ways to catch their trains.

Jack got off the train in his hometown at 10:00 AM. He was worn out from traveling but the smell of the cool mountain air filled with pine trees and honeysuckle, refreshed him. He stepped off the distance to his home quickly.

He stopped at the end of the lane, to study once more, the home of his youth and sanctuary.

Ma'am was hanging wet wash on the line. Paap was hoeing in the garden. The three saw each other at the same moment. Ma'am dropped a wet shirt, paap dropped his hoe and Jack let his gear slip to the ground. They all ran together and hugged.

Home! Jack was home from the War. . . . .

Chapter Thirteen

FANNELLA

Jack basked in the welcome warmth of his family once again. The family get-to-gethers restored his strength and renewed his vigor. He delighted in his nieces and nephews; Bruce had two girls and Lu had two boys. They all enjoyed the antics of their Uncle Jack. He took them for walks, romped with them in the grass and searched in the 'crick for crawdads'. Leone had married and moved to Clymer but had no children. Jack missed her but not like he missed his Sen. She met and married Samuel Elkhorn on the Seneca Reservation where she was teaching and her absence left a great void in his life. He tried to fill the void with fun with the children.

Jack had become quite a good storyteller and thought nothing of taking a child onto his lap and gathering the rest around him to spin what he called, a yarn. On the whole, the stories were true but with the children, he omitted the profanity, unseemly situations and drunkenness.

''Tell us about your tattoo Uncle Jack,'' begged young Freddy.

''Oh yes please do, Uncle Jack,'' cried little Elizabeth.

''I've told you that story three times already,'' Jack insisted and laughed.

''We know but we like it,'' said shy Roxie.

''Alright just one more time,'' Jack agreed. He enjoyed the wide-eyed wonder on their faces as they listened to every word. His voice was resonant and pleasant.

''Far across the big ocean is a country called France, there was a big war. War is sort of like baseball; they all choose up sides and each tries to win. I was over there runnin' an engine for our side. One day I went into a place they called a CAFE to get a cup of coffee. Inside, a man was having coffee and we talked. I told him I was an engineer and he told me he was a tattoo artist. That's a man who paints pictures on people. Well not exactly ON people but in such a way that the pictures can't wash off.''

''Never-ever wash off!'' Piped up tiny Roxie.

''That's right honey, never-ever. Well, the man and I drank an awful lot of coffee that day and you know coffee isn't good for ya and it fills ya up. We got too full. He was fuller than I was but he wanted to paint a picture on me and I said yes.'' Jack went on. ''He didn't know what kind of picture to paint. When I told him I was a Mason, he said he had painted lots of those emblems on people and painted one on me. Here it is!'' Jack bared his right forearm and expose the slightly lopsided compass and square. The children squealed with delight and ran their fingers over the tattoo. They were always amazed they could feel nothing but his arm. It was there but could not be felt.

''Now you young'ins run along and let me read.'' Jack stood little Roxie on her feet from his lap.

''Thanks for the story Uncle Jack,'' she said shyly. All the children ran off to play.

The summer passed quickly and by fall, Jack was eager to go to work. In his search, he found the Baltimore and Ohio had just completed a subdivision in Akron, Ohio. New roads meant new jobs and that seemed a good place to start. The automobile industry was growing by leaps and bounds and the tire and rubber business grew right along with it.

Near the railroad yards in East Akron, Jack stopped in a tavern to lift one and chin with the railroaders.

He told them about himself and asked about jobs and lodgings. They informed him that the Akron, Canton and Youngstown Railroad was about to expand by buying the nearly-defunct bridge line called the Northern Ohio.

They directed him to the main offices and the Flat Iron Hotel, where many of them stayed. The tavern was called the Cork-N-Bottle but affectionally named the Plug and Jug by the railroaders. It was a mom-n-pop operation who catered to the railroaders. The food was good and the prices reasonable. Jack ate a hearty meal, thanked the men and went to the hotel.

Jack had been assured it was clean, bug-free and the food reasonable, if not up to the quality of the Plug and Jug, under the skills of Ned and Mable Louis. He took a room at the Flat Iron, unpacked his valise, read up on railroading and went to bed early.

The next morning he dressed in his best. Paap said, 'If you want to sell something, package it nice.' His suits were a bit tight at the shoulder because he had filled out in the Army. He trailed a light scent of bay rum when he dropped his key off at the desk and went out into the sunny, brisk, fall morning.

He turned and looked back at the five story building he had just stepped from. It had very small frontage on the main street but fanned out half a block back into a huge wedge shape. It truly was shaped like an enormous flat iron—hence the Flat Iron Hotel.

Jack hopped a trolley in front of the building and rode to downtown Akron. When he reached the railroad building, he stepped off and went into a diner for coffee. He stirred his coffee and collected his thoughts. He was too excited to eat. After a bit, he dropped a coin on the counter and left.

He crossed the street, went inside, stated his business at the reception desk and sat down.

After having been passed from one to another well-tailored executives, he was asked to fill out some papers. When he was about finished with his paperwork, a huge carved oak door opened into the room. Out stepped a tall, harried-looking man in his shirt sleeves with his necktie askew.

"You John C. Lansure?" He asked and held out his right hand. He took the papers in his left.

"Yes sir, I am." Jack took the man's hand. "Most call me Jack."

"I'm Bart Stewart." He muttered and scanned the papers before him. "B & O, huh? Cumberland Division. Veteran. Umm. They tell you what we plan here?" He asked of Jack after some muttering.

"Yes they did. From what I've read, a bridge line through there is not only a good idea but necessary." Jack was glad he had read up on things.

"It's a hell of an undertaking on not much but guts and spit. Think it would work—do ya?" Stewart asked.

"Yes I do, but you can't tell much by me I'm a hogger, not a line boss." Jack stated flatly.

"Modest too, I like that. I can't promise we'll last the year out. The equipment is worn out and we've not much money but we do need good workers. Tell you what, if you take a chance on me, I'll take a chance on you. We need dozens just like you. Is it a deal?" H. B. (Bart) Stewart, President of the A C & Y Railroad held out his hand again to Jack.

"Yes indeed, it is!" Jack pumped Bart's hand.

"One more thing, you'll be assigned here until I get this End unraveled, then we'll see. How's that?" inquired Bart.

"That's jake with me." Jack said.

"This is Thursday—you mark up at the yard office on Monday. The paperwork will be done by then. Now, about your wages. . . . ." Bart went on.

"What ever you decide will be fine. I'll be there Monday and thank you very much for the chance." Jack interrupted.

"You're welcome." Bart smiled when Jack pumped his hand and left the railroad building.

Outside, Jack was so excited he thought he could fly. Instead, he jumped, clicked his heels and hopped the trolley back to the Plug and Jug. He was hungry as a bear and he knew Mrs. Louis would have something on the back burner. Besides, he wanted to tell the other railroaders he had been hired and would be bunking at the Flat Iron. They chewed the fat on into the evening and Jack got acquainted. Sooner or later, every Floozy around made it into the Plug and Jug. Jack learned all their names; Maudie, Jozie, Willy—short for Wilhamina, Sally, Irma and Kate. Sooner or later, he would be seen with anyone of them. He never showed partiality but he abhorred public displays of affection and if it occurred, he was never seen again with the 'lady'.

Emmaline had taught him appreciation of the classics; music, opera and symphonies. The big city afforded much of this and he went to these affairs as often as work allowed. Many times he could not arrive until late, still pay full price and stand in the back for the last half hour of the performance. It was enough, it filled his needs and added to his pleasure and knowledge.

The few times he could sit through an entire performance of a traveling opera company, or Shakespearean troup was a delightful bonus. Occasionally he took a companion but was annoyed by the lack of interest and idle chatter, therefore he usually went alone. To Jack, it was a private time with his Em.

At work, H. B. Stewart was right, the equipment was worn out. The locomotives broke down, accidents were prevalent and the hours were long. By the spring of 1920, the A C & Y was a full-fledged railroad, not just a switching line. Alas, the rail bed between Akron and Delphos was so bad, the maintenance track car often fell off between the rails. Equipment, road beds and locomotives had to be replaced. The locomotives were purchased from the Nickel Plate and the Big Four.

One year ran into another. The railroad prospered, the cities prospered and the country prospered. Late in 1922 Jack was transferred to the West End; Plymouth to Delphos. That was jake with him but he would miss all the things the big city had to offer. Change was the spice of life and as a rule, it was for the best.

Jack said goodby to his friends in Akron; his gals moaned and rolled their eyes and some even cried a tear. At the Plug and Jug, he told Mable Louis he was healthy because she was such a good cook. He teased Ned Louis by saying the Plug and Jug was the only DIVE he had ever been in where the whiskey wasn't watered.

He gathered up his belongings and caught the morning flyer to Delphos.

It was late afternoon when he marked up at the yard office in Delphos.

"I'm Jack Lansure, hogger from the East End." Jack said to the yard agent-in-charge.

"Oh yes, some of your new crew has already marked up. Shacks, Brubaker and Richardson; Squawk Moore. Shack Buzzard and Bakehead

Vause will round out your crew. They are all 'right guys'.'' The agent was reassuring.

''Thanks. I need a flop and chink.'' Jack said.

''Flops are kind of scarce around here—the railroad expansion and all.'' He took a piece of paper from the spindle on his desk and offered it to Jack. ''Maybe this will help. A woman left it here earlier. She said she was a widow and had rooms to let above the dry goods store. It's on main street you can't miss it.'' Jack took the paper and it read: 'Hazel Metz, Rooms to let. 10 N. Main, Up.'

''We don't have a laundry here but you might ask the Widow Metz. Sometimes these rooming houses do laundry, too.'' The man was encouraging.

''Thanks for you help.'' Jack stuffed the paper into his pocket.

''The best hash in town is Molly's Place on the square. Ya can't miss it.'' The man called as Jack left the office.

Jack found the address easily and the stair door on the street was open.

''Hello!'' Jack called up the stairs.

''Hello.'' Answered a woman's voice and the up-door opened.

''I'm Jack Lansure. I've been bumped here on the railroad from the East End and I need a room.''

''Come on up. I'm Hazel Metz.'' She wore a gingham dress and a flowered apron. Her honey colored hair was coiled at the neck and covered with a blue bandanna. Tiny wisps of hair crept from under the bandanna and fell around her pretty face. Large, quiet gray eyes studied Jack carefully. She had been cleaning and the place smelled of Fel's Naptha soap and furniture polish.

''You're staring at me Mr. Lansure, is there something wrong?'' She asked calmly.

''Er, no, that is 'course not, but they said the Widow Metz and I expected someone older.'' He blushed and stammered.

''Widows come in all ages Mr. Lansure. This way please.'' She smiled and showed him down a long hallway. ''This room is for the part-time roomers who don't mind the street noise or the light from the windows. Off the hall, are two large rooms on the left and a small one on the right. There are no windows but they are clean and quiet sleeping rooms. You may choose as you are the first.'' She showed him around the sparsely furnished but spotlessly clean rooms.

''I'll only be here three or four days a week. The small room is fine. I'm told there is no chinaman in town and I need laundry done.'' Jack explained.

''I'm new here too, but for 50¢ more, I'll do your laundry.'' She said. ''The room is 50¢ a night and I'll make your breakfast and pack your pail. Is that too much?'' She looked guilty and anxious.

''That's just jake with me.'' He answered.

Before they could say more, a baby began to cry in another room off the kitchen.

"A baby!" Jack was surprised.

"I promise, I'll keep them quiet! They will never spoil your sleep! I'll keep them still!" She appeared frantic while she led Jack through the kitchen and a small sitting room to a bedroom beyond. Standing there in a rickety, iron crib was a pair of twins. They stopped crying when they saw their mother and smiled.

"This is Paul and this is Patricia—I call her Patty. They are nine months old. We live back here off the kitchen, so we won't disturb the roomers." Hazel explained. "They won't be any bother, I promise!" She was very frightened.

"It's all right! I love kids!" Jack read the panic in her voice and understood she had to make a living. "I'll tell the other guys you have rooms. Can I stay tonight? I'll get some supper and be back later." Jack hoped to calm her.

"Yes sir, that will be just fine." She was relieved.

"I'll pay a week in advance." He handed her a bill.

"Five dollars! You only owe me three!" She was delighted and astonished.

"I eat a lot!" Jack lied but he knew she needed the cash.

Jack put his valise in the small room and went down stairs to eat. . .

At Molly's Place, he kidded with her and chinned with the other railroaders there. Molly had been up north in Yankee Land most of her adult life but her southern drawl was still as thick as gumbo. She enjoyed the attention and the men.

"I was fourteen years old before I knew DamnYankee was two words." She would drawl and laugh impishly. No one went hungry at Mol's. She would feed a hungry person if they had the price or not. Her heart was as big as her frame.

"See ya later, Mol." Jack called and left the place. He had made another friend.

He went up the stairs at the widow Metz's and opened the door to her kitchen.

She was having a cup of coffee at the big table and stood up.

"I was waiting for you, Mr. Lansure, would you like some coffee?" She asked.

"No, thanks I just ate, but I'll set a bit." Jack pulled out a chair, turned it around, straddled it and sat down.

"I forgot to give you a key to the up door. At 11:00 PM, I close the street door to the stairs and bolt it from the inside. There is no lock or key just the big bolt. Anyone who comes later will have to use the brass knocker on the door. If I know in advance, I'll leave it open.''

Jack hooked the key to his watch chain and said, ''Thanks, guess I'll turn in. Good night.'' Jack went into his room to sleep.

''Before I forget again, does this town have a morning paper?'' He called from the hallway.

''Yes, The Toledo Blade and The Lima Daily. I'll see to it you have one at breakfast.'' She called back.

Jack settled in at the Delphos end at Metz's and did the same at the Plymouth turnaround.

In Plymouth, he took a room with board at Hattie Sutton's. She was also a widow with a 15 year old grandson to raise. She and her husband, Alfred, had operated the boarding house business right up to the time of his death recently. Her cooking was the 'stick-to-the-ribs' variety with no frills.

The best food in town he was told, was Beckridge's Bakery, Confection and Restaurant. It was primarily a bakery but served meals also. Their Friday Fish Fry was known all over the country and their daily specials were very popular.

If short orders were preferred, Rudy's Bar and Grill was the place. Long after Beckridge's was closed, the lights glowed cheerfully from Rudy's.

Jack went inside at Rudy's, put his foot on the brass rail and ordered a double shot of rye and a Rolling Rock beer. He chinned with the barkeep and ordered a hot dog. He also ordered a pickled egg from the beet jar and a dill pickle from the pickle crock. Both jars sat invitingly on the bar near him.

He talked to those around him and got acquainted. The atmosphere was warm and the people were friendly. Jack always did his best to fit in no matter where he was.

After he ate, he went outside and walked around the square. He noted the location of the hardware and tack shop, the bank, the drugstore and ice cream parlor, barbershop, meat market, grocery and millinery. Even at night, the town looked prosperous.

He lived at Sutton's and worked hard. It was always the same run, Delphos to Plymouth, Plymouth to Delphos. The trip was the same but the daily workings were different from hour to hour. The days ran into weeks and the weeks ran into months. Jack liked his new crew and they liked and soon respected him as a topnotch hogger. The hours were long and demanding but Jack was in his element and loved the life. The crews were pleased with the new locomotives and the Lansure-Vause team made them hum.

In the early spring of 1923, certain events transpired that would change Jack's life again.

Jack was 30 years old, traveled, experienced in the ways of the world, a natty dresser and a confirmed bachelor. His liberal, loving, hill-country upbringing by adoring parents, gave him the inner strength, security and self-confidence needed to make his way in life and he enjoyed it.

He was born in November, a Scorpio and more or less true to his sign. Darkly handsome, investigative, intelligent, honest, soft-spoken and thoughtful but he was never sullen or brooding. He was highly idealistic and had a strict code of rules he lived by and woe to those who broke them. He was of good humor and laughed readily.

If he had any extremes, it had to be his carnal appetites. Jack fed this propensity as often as possible with an assortment of willing women, careful to avoid any permanent entanglements. He was a railroader with a 'gal in every town.' He was footloose and fancy-free and liked it that way.

On a quiet street in Plymouth lived Fannella Jane Effie Ellen Saddler, (always called Fan), she was born in May, a Gemini, the sign of the twins. She had not only two sides to her personality but three. One was her outward self—pretty, appealing, obedient and obvious. The second was short tempered, sulky and rebellious. The third and the one to yet be awakened, was her lusty, sensual, passionate side. That-not-yet-defined thing was slowly growing inside her—waiting. She felt and heard its murmurings from time to time but could not find the meaning or understand the stirrings.

She was very pretty, small and petite with dimpled cheeks and enormous hazel eyes that smoldered with intensity as if hiding acute pyrotechnic energies. Her wavy, chestnut colored hair was long and caught at the back of her neck. Six Mary Pickford long curls fell over her shoulders and the smooth, silky skin of her face glowed bright pink when she blushed at the slightest thing.

Fan Saddler was the overly sheltered 19 year old daughter of a north central Ohio minister. She had never been more than twenty miles from her home in any direction. Her father was a stern fire-and-brimstone disciplinarian and her mother was timid, withdrawn and submissive. Although, her mother was attentive and solicitous, Fan secretly resented her mother's passive ways. She understood them because her own apprehension of her father's stern and gruff ways also made her reticent and shy in his presence.

Fan had two older brothers who treated her like a toy or a pet and protected her as if she was an object of art. None of her family took her seriously or accepted her as an individual.

In her secret place in the attic, Fan read and dreamed of adventure and romance in the arms of a tall dark stranger, on a great white steed in a far away land. She was generally bored with her humdrum existence although she had a persistent beau, she vaguely rejected him as uninteresting and dull.

One moment Fan was doll-like, playful, appealing and loving; the next, she was hostile, resentful and angry. She would throw a hateful temper tantrum, wretchedly fling herself onto her bed in waves of crying and sobbing as if there were no limits to her grief and misery.

She was coddled, soothed, and cajoled but never once told to stop that unacceptable behavior. The outbursts, personality changes and frequent poutings were passed off lightly by her family and no one took her seriously. Eventually her 'spell' would pass and was soon forgotten. The telltale signs of immaturity and irresponsibility went unnoticed or ignored.

Since Fan's high school graduation, she worked steadily as a teller in the local bank. It was mentally stimulating and interesting at first but that too, became monotonous and unchallenging.

Often, for a change of pace, Fan worked in the bakery of the Beckridges, Saddler's longtime friends. She worked mornings in the bakery or evenings in the dining room.

Occasionally, Jack would take a meal at Beckridge's as a change from Hattie Sutton's plain fare. On that fateful day, Jack came into the place when Fan was helping out.

He slid onto a stool, took a menu from the rack behind the sugar shaker and scanned the list.

Fan came from the kitchen to take his order, pad and pencil in hand. It was lightning at first look.

''Why hello there, Dolly Dimples. I'll have two dogs on a load of hay and let them ride—some flour pie—java—light and sweet and for later—a slab of custard pie.'' Jack could feel his body over-heating.

The meeting and conversations were awkward but when his hand brushed hers as she took the menu, the electricity between them started a fire that was unmistakable.

Fan fled to the kitchen. She had written down all that he had said but understood none of it. The cook, Bert Wells had overheard the conversation and saw her surprise.

''I wrote it down Bert, but I don't know what I wrote!'' Fan was confused and flustered.

''It's all right Fan, I heard him. He's one of those railroaders and they speak a language all their own. He wants the sauerkraut and weenies with dumplings—custard pie for dessert—coffee with cream and sugar.'' The cook saw her agitation.

''Well, why didn't he just say that, the smart aleck!'' she sniffed. She did not understand her uncalled-for disdain or the throbbing in her throat. He was so handsome she could hardly breathe and his eyes—they seemed to look right through her. She tried to compose herself.

Jack realized this was not one of his chippys and he wished he had not been flip with her. Stirrings welled up in him that he thought he had long buried with his first love at 15. So taken was he with that little slip of a girl, he could feel the panic growing inside. This was a forbidden relationship—one which leads to marriage, a home and children. The kind he had spent his entire life trying to avoid. He left the restaurant with no intention of ever seeing her again or falling into the 'tender trap.''

Fan had found the man of her dreams but had no idea what to do with the knowledge. He did not ask her name or ever come back into the restaurant.

Weeks went by and Fan was devastated. She had told no one of their meeting and began to believe he did not exist at all, perhaps he was just another of her dreams. Her turbid world became more flavorless than before.

Jack made friends wherever he went and spent most of his free time with the other railroaders or taking his carnal pleasures on the seamy side of town.

Try as he may, he could not drown the image of her in a sea of other women's faces or erase the touch of her hand in the arms of any.

One day, Jack had just cut out and was about finished for the day when he spotted the hostler who was trying to ignore a persistent young fellow. Jack had seen the husky, barrel-chested, sandy haired kid around there before. This time with hat in hand, he was pleading for a job from the railroad hostler. The enthusiastic boy was not having much luck when Jack intervened.

''What's the beef, Browny?'' Jack asked of the hostler.

''Hi Jack, this here kid is plaguing me for a job and he ain't dry behind the ears yet.'' Browny was emphatic.

''I am too and I'm strong too, I worked on the highway gang for two summers, I'm a vet and I'm almost 23. Please just give me a chance, I'll prove I'm a good worker.'' The boy pleaded.

''Browny, the last time we talked, you said your lumbago was acting up and you could use some help around here. This young lummox looks strong enough to turn a saw mill with a crank—what have ya got to lose? The kid has to start somewhere. I think he would make a good fireman—look at those arms!'' Jack pointed out to Browny.

''I will be a fireman too, you'll see! Please try me Mister Browny.''

''What's your name kid?'' Browny asked.

''Harry Andrew Saddler, sir but everybody calls me Andy.''

''You got any overalls—a tweed suit won't do.'' Browny asked.

''No sir, I don't but if you hire me, I'll have a pair in an hour.'' Andy was so eager.

''Well, Jack here, talked me into it. But I'll tell ya this boy, you will work harder for me than ya ever have in the past. Now go to the yard office and tell the man there, Browny Ames sent ya. He'll tell ya what to do.''

"Thanks Mister Browny, thanks a lot—I'll do just what ya say. Ya won't be sorry—I promise. And thank YOU, Mister—Mister—." Andy said.

"Jack Lansure, howdy, Andy." Jack held out his hand and Andy pumped it vigorously.

"I'm much obliged to you Mister Lansure and I'd like to thank you proper. Will you come to dinner Sunday, aweek? I'd like for my family to meet you?"

"I guess I can, that's right neighborly of you. A man can always do with a little home cooking. What's a good time?" Jack was pleased to be asked.

"My dad's the minister here and we eat about 1:00 PM. Everyone knows where the parsonage is on High street. We don't have much money but we eat good. See you then." Andy waved his hat and ran down the street toward his home to tell his family of his good fortune.

It was customary for one of Fan's brothers to call for her when she finished work at Beckridge's and walk her home. It was Andy's turn and he ran all the way from the railroad yards to tell his sister of his new job. She came out of the building just as he arrived.

"Fan! Hey Fan, I got it! I got it!" He shouted when he saw her.

"You got what, Andy?" Fan asked.

"The job! The railroad! I got a job on the railroad! A nice fella helped me and we talked the hostler into it!" Andy was breathless and excited.

"Easy Andy, you'll snap a hame." She said calmly.

"But don't you see—I got a JOB on the RAILROAD!" He thought she did not understand his words.

"I heard you. I think it's very nice and Mother and Dad will be pleased. You don't have to shout." She replied calmly. His news did not help her tepid existence. Her lack of enthusiasm dampened his spirits.

"There's more! I asked the nice man who helped me get the job to come to dinner Sunday, aweek. He said he would and I gave him the directions to our house!" He watched for her reaction.

"A stranger is coming to OUR HOUSE for dinner? Someone we don't know! Oh! I'll get to wear my new patent leather shoes! Wish I had a new dress. You sure we don't KNOW him? He's not from around here?" Fan quizzed her brother.

"Honest, Sis, he is a stranger to these parts. You think Mother will mind? Will you help her fix something special? I know lots of folks come to dinner because Dad's the preacher but this is important." Andy was apprehensive and Fan noticed.

"Of course we will and I'll make my baking powder biscuits that you like so well—with lots of honey or maybe some of mother's peach butter." Fan was delighted at the prospects of someone different coming to dinner. Any change in her lackluster world was welcome.

As the time drew near for Andy's special dinner, the parsonage hummed with activity. Fan and her mother, Matilda, cleaned, polished and dusted to be sure all was spotless for their guest. As the time came closer, the more excited Fan became at the prospects of something different and the anticipation made her squeal with pleasure. She childishly begged for a new frock but had to settle for a bit of lace and ribbon on an old one. The family could manage a good meal from a donated chicken or ham but a new dress was out of the question. Fan pouted but accepted the trimmings instead.

The appointed day arrived. The guys at Sutton's boarding house razzed Jack about going to the parsonage for dinner. He took it all in laughing good humor. Hattie Sutton inspected him carefully and straightened his necktie.

''Now you be on your best behavior, you scalawag, or ya will be answerin' to ME! We wouldn't want the railroaders to get a worst reputation than they already have! Mind you—watch your table manners!'' Hattie patted Jack's cheek and everyone laughed. She took a grandmotherly interest in all her boarders.

Indeed, Jack looked the elegant gentleman and trailed a light scent of bay rum. His usual railroad garb had given way to tailor-mades and a gray felt Stetson. His grey-blue suit covered a starched, white broadcloth shirt and an unusual gold stickpin held his navy blue silk necktie in place. Grey spats and gloves completed his attire. A gold headed walking stick gleamed in the sun as he walked away from Sutton's. He resembled a rich merchant or wealthy banker passing and tipping his hat to the local gentry while making his way to the parsonage. Most were startled when they realized it was the railroader they usually saw in porched cap, pin striped denim and gauntlets. He doffed his hat, smiled and walked on briskly. Leaving them to guess and gape.

Jack turned the corner at High Street and Andy spotted him from the front porch of the parsonage.

''He's here! He's here! Dad and Mother, he's here!'' Andy called excitedly through the screened door.

''Hi Mr. Lansure, how are ya?'' Andy pumped Jack's hand.

''Fine Andy and Jack's the name. We're buddies now that we're in the Boxcar Brigade together. I appreciate the invite to dinner.'' Jack got a kick out of the eager young man.

''Come on in, I want ya to meet my family.'' Andy opened the door.

Andy led Jack down a small hallway past the parlor on the left, to a large room that served as dining room and sitting room. On the right was a doorway to other rooms in the house and along the wall, near the kitchen door, stood a huge sideboard. To the left, stood an elegant barber's chair in front of a rolled top desk. Other furniture included a Morris Chair, a large leather couch and a crystal radio set, atop a small table. In the center of the room, a great, round table and chairs had been carefully set for company.

The Reverend Saddler struggled to find his footing from the pivoting barber chair.

"Please Sir, don't get up, I'm Jack Lansure." Jack shook the elderly man's hand.

"Welcome to our home and thanks for helping Andrew." George Saddler had a pleasant face and a bald head.

"This is my brother, A. B.". The big burly man stood from the Morris Chair.

"He's a Richland County Deputy Sheriff," Andy went on with pride.

"Howdy Jack." A. B. took Jack's hand and dwarfed it with his own. He was no taller than Jack but he was twice as wide at the shoulder and barrel chested.

"A. B.—a Lawman—that's the best business I can think of—next to railroading—of course. Good to see you." Jack shook the huge hand and they both laughed.

"And this is my mother." Andy beamed when Matilda Saddler came in from the kitchen with a dish of food in each hand and put his arm around her small shoulders.

She placed the food on the table and wiped her hands on her colorful apron. Her greying blond hair was coiled on top of her head and her plain brown dress was brightened only by her apron.

"Thank you for having me to dinner Mrs. Saddler, I seldom get a home-cooked meal." Jack took her small hand in both of his.

"You're most welcome. We're grateful to you for helping Andrew. He's very excited about his new job. Dinner will be ready shortly," she said.

In the kitchen, Fan placed a dozen piping hot biscuits in a clean towel and set them in a wicker serving basket. She heard voices and knew their guest had arrived.

With the basket of biscuits in hand, she stepped through the kitchen door. It was HIM! It was the man in the restaurant! It was HIM! She had not spoken aloud she had only drawn in her breath. She sagged against the wall because her knees had turned to rubber. Her grip on the basket in her hands failed and slowly it began to slip from her grasp.

Andy leaped to catch the falling basket of biscuits and shouted, "Whoa there girl! Don't drop my biscuits, they were made special!"

Fan fought to regain her composure and felt her face burn red. "Sorry Andy—I—er—that is—uh," she stammered.

"Sis, this here's Jack Lansure—Jack this is my sister Fannella—we all call her Fan."

"How do you do Miss Saddler," Jack said in the most proper manner and took her hand in his. He never blinked or hinted that they had ever met before. Suddenly his collar was too tight and when he took her hand, the blood roared in his ears. The sensations he was feeling were overwhelming.

"Hullo," was all Fan could muster. Her hand in his sent waves of excitement through her. She was speechless and rooted to the spot.

"Please be seated, we will have Grace," shy Matilda spoke softly and all sat down.

Reverend Saddler asked the Blessing and the meal progressed. The Saddlers sat in their usual places. George at the head of the table and Matilda opposite him. A. B. sat on his father's right and Fan and Andy on his left. Today, Jack sat at A. B.'s right, diagonally across from Fan. When their eyes met, she was seized with a new pleasure that confounded and embarrassed her. She blushed continuously. The food was tasteless and she heard only bits and pieces of the conversation.

The men talked about everything; their work, the War and baseball. Andy chattered the most. "Gee, Jack, that stickpin is a humdinger! It looks like a big ruby 'till ya get close up then ya can see it's a little rose carved out of metal! Amazin' what jewelers can do today." Andy exclaimed.

"My sister, Rose, gave it to me for Christmas one year," Jack explained. "She told me she found it by accident somewhere but decided it was a good way for me never to forget my Rosie. She hated to be called Rosie and I did it to tease her." Jack explained.

"What a nice thing to do. She must love you a great deal." Matilda said thoughtfully. "Perhaps the name Rosie, doesn't suit her."

"You're right Mrs. Saddler, my sister, Rose is no Rosie. A. B., what's that short for?" Jack asked A. B.

"His name is Absolum Brock but it didn't fit in the Army and it doesn't fit a deputy," Andy interrupted, "he signs it A. B. but most think it's Abbe. Sis you really outdid yourself this time—these biscuits are the best yet!"

"I think you're right, Andy. Mrs. Saddler, your peach preserves are as good as my mother's and her's is the best." Jack seldom admitted that anything was as good as Ma'am's—but this was.

When the meal was finished the men took coffee, brandy and cigars in the parlor where Fan placed the large tray containing everything. The men served themselves and talked. Fan and Matilda cleared the table and washed the dishes.

When Fan went to the parlor for the coffee tray, Jack was cording on the upright piano and the three men were singing while Reverend Saddler puffed his pipe in a nearby rocking chair. All were war veterans; Jack, in the Army Engineers; A. B., in the Army Cavalry Military Police and Andy in the Marines. They sang at the top of their voices: "Over there! Over there!———" and "Pack up your troubles in your old kit bag and smile, smile, smile.———" "It's a long way to Tipparary! It's a long way home!————" They sang loudly.

When Fan walked down the hall from the parlor with the coffee tray, her brothers stopped singing and Jack began a solo. He corded the piano and sang;

"She took me to the parlor and cooled me with her fan,

I heard her whisper to her Maw, I'm gonna marry this Railroad Man——!" All laughed.

Fan fled to the kitchen and to her mother who saw her tears.

"There, there, little one, the men must have their little jokes. Pay no mind to it." Fan was flustered but now she was angry at her mother's submissiveness.

"Pay it no mind? He's laughing at me! Making fun of me!" she raged.

"Now, now, I'm sure it's not that way at all," Matilda tried to soothe Fan.

Later Fan could not face Jack when they said their 'Goodbys' and only grunted when he was leaving.

On his way out the door Jack called back, "Mr. and Mrs. Saddler, may I call again?"

"Anytime, my boy, anytime," George Saddler answered. Jack liked the family and they liked him.

The weeks turned into months and Jack visited the parsonage as often as his work would allow. He had become good friends with A. B. and Andy and he was accepted into the family.

Jack and Fan got to know each other on long walks and began to understand the raging inferno within themselves. Jack had never been in love before—not the 'I can't live without you' kind of love but with Fan, he was. He adored her outrageous childishness, naivete and blatant immaturity. He thought she was cute and laughed off her temper tantrums and spoiled antics. She was, for him, as no other.

Fan, on the other hand, saw different things in Jack. She saw money, plenty of everything, travel, adventure and fun. Oh, she loved him in her own way but it not as it should have been. He was her escape from a sparse, rigid, lackluster life that she hated and did not understand the stirrings within her.

From time to time, on his calls to Fan's family, Jack would take small gifts. To Matilda, a fancy sewing basket as thanks for a button sewn on. To George, a bottle of Napoleon brandy that was his favorite but could ill afford. To A. B., an ivory Keystone for his watch fob because they were both Masons. For Fan, from a dry goods store window, a bolt of cream colored silk pongee. Jack's generosity made Fan squeal with delight. For Andy, a pair of leather gauntlets.

When the word got out on the railroad that Jack was seeing the Preacher's daughter, there was no end to the raspberries. He would smile, give a left-handed salute and go on about his business.

His regular 'cuties' sniffed the air in resentful scorn. "That slick one will NEVER marry her, he's got girls all up and down the line and will never settle down to one—so-called 'lady' or not!" chided one of his disappointed gals.

At the 4th of July Celebration, Jack proposed to Fan on a picnic blanket in the park. She snatched the diamond ring from his fingers and thrust it on her own, threw herself into his arms and toppled them both into the grass. Fan jumped to her feet and shrieked with delight. "Hurry Jack, I must tell mother!" she cried.

"Fan, we haven't had our picnic or seen the fireworks yet," Jack laughed at her.

"Of course, Jack, how silly—but I can't wait to show mother how big the diamond is." She was a greedy, incorrigible child.

"When should we get married, Fan? I get two week's furlough the last of October and I'd like to take you to Denver, Colorado. The fall is my favorite time of the year and the Rockies will be in full color. If you'd rather, we can go to Niagara Falls."

"Oh Jack, that will be wonderful! I'll have time for Mother to make my dress and coat out of the pongee you gave me! I'll need lace for a veil—some pearl buttons, new slippers—Daddy will marry us in the parlor—we will serve tea and cakes——" Fan chattered.

"Hold it! hold it, which will it be, Denver or Niagara? I have to arrange passes and pullman reservations," Jack called to excited Fan.

"Oh, I'm sorry Jack, but I have never been anywhere far away and I'd love to go out west! What a wonderful life we will have! Will we have our own place? Do we have LOTS of money? I've never been on a pullman train before." Fan stopped to catch her breath.

"Easy now, one question at a time!" Jack delighted in her childish chatter.

"I know where there is a furnished flat for rent and I know where there is a house being built on the edge of town—both in Carey. As of November

1st, I'm being bumped there. I've been keeping it a secret in case you wouldn't marry me.'' Jack couldn't resist teasing her.

''You knew all the time I'd say yes! A real flat of our own! A new house soon! I can't believe it! You really are my knight on a white horse come to carry me off to wondrous places!'' She flung her arms around his neck.

They kissed in the half-light of the evening just as a huge rocket burst over head.

''Look Jack we set off the fireworks!'' Fan laughed impishly and they kissed again. . . . .

The wedding was set for the morning of October 17th 1923. It was a sunny but cool day. Fan and Jack took their vows in the parlor and Reverend Saddler officiated. Close friends and family crowded in to see the bride and groom. Fan was lovely in a creamy silk pongee street length frock with her Mary Pickford curls spilling over her shoulders. Her veil was more hat than veil. The creamy French lace was gathered high on a cap of silk pongee. Later, it will top her coat of matching fabric as a traveling ensemble. Her nosegay of fall flowers would be arranged into a corsage for the shoulder of her coat. She was enchanting.

Jack wore a navy blue suit with grey accessories, his fancy stickpin and spats. Although pleasant and smiling he appeared reticent and uncomfortable, as if a very personal and private event in his life was being intruded upon by others.

The ceremony was short but wonderfully personal and warm. Fan was given by her father, to the man of her dreams and Jack received the love of his life. Their age difference seemed unimportant.

Outside the parsonage they walked through a hail of rice and confetti, to the waiting car. A. B. and Andy would drive them to the train station in the rumble seat of his roadster. The boys put Fan and Jack on the B & O noon flyer for Chicago.

Aboard the train, Fan was like a wiggly child. She stood by her seat and tried to keep her footing while the swaying, lurching train gathered speed. When she was tossed into her seat she would laugh with childish delight, ''Oh, Jack, this is fun!''

''Sure honey FUN, but if it knocks you down and you break something it won't be so funny.'' Jack was concerned for her safety.

'' I never dreamed it would be so exciting! Tell me about Chicago and all the things we will see,'' she begged.

''Well, Chicago is a very big place and the stock yards is one of the largest. They call it the meat market of the world. From a hotel window in Omaha, Nebraska you can see for miles in any direction on the Great Plains and Denver, Colorado sits in the Rocky Mountains.'' Jack gestured with his left hand to accentuate the story.

''Oh don't stop, tell me more,'' she said sleepily and nuzzled comfortably on his shoulder. The day's excitement was taking a toll on her and soon she slept soundly.

Jack held Fan, watched her sleep and toyed with the lovely soft curls that lay around her face while she slept. Perhaps he dozed off also.

The train jerked to a halt and awakened them with a start. ''Chicago! All out! Chicago! Change here! All out!'' The conductor's loud call sent the passengers to scrambling for their belongings. Each time Fan and Jack moved, rice and confetti fell from their clothes. A worldly, wise pullman porter rubbed several of the fallen rice grains between his fingers, rolled his eyes and laughed out loud. Newlyweds have no secrets and are easily spotted anywhere.

Jack and Fan were to change trains here, for the Rock Island line's Rocky Mountain Limited for Denver. Connections were notoriously bad. The 'Limited' departed at 7:30 PM, and this allowed Jack and Fan time for sightseeing. Fan ran to each window and pressed her face close to the glass to see inside.

''Oh look Jack, perfume and toiletries! Lady Esther Face Cream and Powders, Cara Nome Perfume! Jack, let's go in—Please!''she pleaded, ''I never saw so many in one place! Our drugstore only had a few things at Christmas but nothing like THIS!'' Fan pulled Jack into the beautifully lighted, sweet-smelling retail store.

''Umm it smells so good!'' A patient saleslady allowed Fan to spray, sniff and apply dozens of aromatic liquids, Fan was fascinated.

''Pick something you like and we'll take it with us.'' Jack knew she would want a fragrance for herself.

''Could I—really—could I! Cara Nome is my favorite but Lady Esther is better for my skin. Help me, Jack which do you like best?'' She held up two bottles for him to smell.

''Very nice. Why don't you take them both and there won't be a problem.'' He knew she would be delighted. ''Both! You mean I can have TWO kinds! All to myself! At once?'' She was astonished at his generosity. Before in her life, she could afford none now she was allowed two.

''Wrap them both please,'' Jack spoke to the clerk and gave her some money.

''Oh, thank you, dear Jack, thank you——'' Fan tried to hug Jack's neck but he held her arms and gently pushed her away.

''Not in public please, Fan,'' he whispered through his teeth. He hated public displays of affection—married or not.

Fan stared at him, ''But you let me hug you in the park.''

''We were alone there.'' He smiled and tweeked her cheek. He hoped he had not hurt her feelings.

''Thank you for coming in,'' the polite saleslady handed Fan the fancy wrapped packages and gave Jack his change. Fan took Jack's arm and her packages and the incident was forgotten.

Outside, Fan proceeded to investigate her new surroundings. Jack enjoyed watching his child bride explore everything. They picked a restaurant and went in. A gracious maitre d' seated them. Fan gazed at the beautiful drapes and furnishings and gaped openly at the lovely high fashions worn by the other diners.

A tuxedoed waiter gave them huge menus, filled their water goblets and disappeared. Fan studied the menu a few moments and said softly, ''I don't know what all this means, you order please.'' She looked baffled.

''What will you have, chicken, steak or fish?'' Jack asked quietly.

''May I, the steak, please?'' Fan noted that even the soup was expensive.

To the returning waiter, Jack said, ''We will have one order of Blue Points on the half shell, two Vichyssoise, two Delmonicos—medium, twice-baked, house greens and coffee now, please.'' The waiter nodded and moved away.

''What does all that mean—what are we having?'' Fan giggled with anticipation.

''Oysters, potato soup, steak, potatoes, salad and coffee.'' Jack said with a smile.

''Oysters! I never ate them before! Why not just say 'potato soup' instead of that other?'' quizzed Fan.

Jack tried to explain it to her and they laughed, talked and had fun over a sumptuous meal. Fan declined the oysters but ate hungrily of all else. The flaming 'Cherries Jubilee' was phenomenal to Fan and she ate hers and half of Jack's. . . .

Later, on the pullman train, Fan was a playful child in their 'roomette'. She ran the water in the tiny sink and bounced on the berth. They had comfort and privacy. She changed behind the drape into her new nightgown and peignoir. It was made of soft, pink gauze, trimmed in lace and ribbons. In spite of her childish gushiness, she was painfully shy. She brushed out her long curls and allowed her silky, shiny hair to fall over her shoulders.

She was so lovely in the soft light that Jack could hardly breathe. He realized she was all he would ever want in a woman. He took her gently into his arms and they loved. . . . .

While she slept in his arms, in the dark, he raised the window shade. There was enough light for him to see a damp curl on her cheek and he moved it away.

He was pleased and surprised at her eager response to his kiss and his touch. He had no way of knowing that he was satisfying those strange stirrings that had been plaguing Fan for years. Her carnal appetite was growing.

She stirred in his arms and murmured, "Oh, Jack, love me again." She snuggled close to him.

The huge locomotive dragged the long train over the gleaming rails and the staccato of the wheels orchestrated their love making and eventually lulled them into deep sleep. . . .

When the train pulled into Denver, Fan hung out the window and called, "Jack! Look! It's so beautiful! The mountains look like a painted picture.!"

"Isn't THAT something to see!" Mountains anywhere, to Jack, were the happiest of creations.

The newlyweds were met by a representative from the resort hotel where they had reservations.

"How 'do, folks, I'm 'Ole Bart come to fetch ya. Sorry I'm late, I had another flat tar' on the dang thing, AGAIN. Don't know why horses won't do anymore!" The aging man grumbled and took their luggage to the open automobile nearby.

The trip to the lodge was lovely and Fan chattered about the scenery, the thin air and the weather. Jack adored her nonsense.

Their cabin at the lodge was picturesque, quaint and had a huge fireplace with complete privacy. Fan examined and poked into everything.

The next week was everything that all newlyweds expect. The couple walked, hiked, rowed on the lake, ate fancy meals in the great dining room of the main hotel and sat in the warm sun of the veranda. At night, they loved eagerly.

One afternoon near the end of their stay, Fan and Jack were rowing on the lake. Fan had a bad habit of twirling her wedding rings on her finger. She was not accustomed to them and she constantly fiddled with them. Suddenly she screamed, "My ring! Jack my ring!" And flung herself into the cold lake water. She screamed again and went under. Fannella Jane Effie Ellen Saddler Lansure could not swim a stroke and was terrified of water.

Jack dived in after her. He brought her to the surface, gasping and sputtering.

"My ring! I lost my ring!" She screamed and clung to Jack.

"You nearly lost your life, ya little fool, hold on to me!" Jack scolded.

The attendants heard the commotion and were rowing at top speed to reach the pair clinging to an overturned boat. They dragged the shivering couple out of the cold water, covered them in warm blankets and hurried to shore. ''Oh Jack, I've lost my wedding ring! I'm so sorry!'' She cried softly in his arms, with chattering teeth and shivering body. She showed him the diamond engagement ring, alone on her finger.

''You are more important than a ring! What ever possessed you to jump into that cold water? You can't swim a lick and that ring went straight to the bottom! We can always replace the ring but I CAN'T replace you!'' They clung to each other and shivered. The attendants hustled them to their cabin for hot baths and warm, dry clothes.

Under the circumstances their food was trayed in and served. They lazed by the fire and sipped the Irish coffee prescribed by the helpful waiter, who discreetly disappeared. Fan continued to weep.

''Come on now honey, don't cry anymore. I'll buy you a new one as soon as we get home.'' Jack cuddled her in his arms.

''No! No! I'll NEVER have another one! You gave me the most important one and I lost it! My punishment for losing it is, NEVER having another. It's absence on my finger will always remind me of my carelessness!'' She stated firmly.

''Hey, Hey, That's pretty drastic! It's only a ring.'' He was surprised at her decision.

''No, that's the way it is. My father would agree the punishment was just!'' she declared.

''What's your FATHER got to do with THIS?'' Jack was astonished.

''Father always said, the bigger the crime, the harder the punishment.'' She was resolute.

''That's probably true sometimes, but not in this case—you're joshin' aren't you?'' Jack asked.

''I am not and that's final. No ring is what I deserve.'' Fan was resolute.

The subject was closed but Jack had much to think about while he sipped his coffee and held her.

The time passed and Fan's carnal appetite grew daily. Jack was delighted but at times, overwhelmed. Never had there been such demands on his body. Perhaps all new husbands felt as he did and perhaps it would pass.

The trip home was fun but uneventful. A. B. and Andy were at the station and took them to the parsonage for a short visit. Fan chattered incessantly. She told her family of Chicago, the luxurious railroad pullman, the mountains, their cabin and how she jumped into the lake after her ring.

''And I'll never have another ring. That's right isn't it father?'' She did not give him time to answer but went on chattering. ''Smell my wrist, mother, isn't it nice? I have two kinds to choose from!'' Fan held out her hand to Matilda but not long enough for her to inhale the scent. ''Come on Jack, it's getting late. I'm anxious to get to OUR home.'' She babbled on and ran to A. B.'s roadster and waved back. The whirlwind visit to the parsonage was over and they drove away leaving Fan's dumfounded family standing on the porch.

Fan was happy in the furnished flat on the second floor of a great Victorian home. It had an inside and outside entrance, the use of a washing machine in the basement and all the usual household accruments.

Fan planned elaborately for their first Christmas. They selected the tree together but before the trimming was complete, Jack had to leave for work. Fan was annoyed and would pout each time he had to leave her. Jack's job often interfered with Fan's plans and became more and more an aggravation to her.

''That old railroad! You love it more than ME!'' She would pout and Jack would console her as best he could. He had a job to do and he did it.

Jack had many friends and they became Fan's friends. She loved to party and delighted in her newfound freedom. In one of the many speakeasys they frequented, Fan met and became good friends with Saddie Ross. She and her husband, Mort, ran the 'Happy Hour Cafe' now a speakeasy, together until he was killed in France. She operated it alone with the help of homeless Mushy, the swamper, who slept in the storeroom. Sade, as she liked to be called, was a good friend of Jack's long before he met Fan. Sade was glamorous. She rolled her silk stockings below the knee, wore jeweled clips in her bobbed hair and used a long cigarette holder. Her dresses were of the highest fashion and fabric and Fan admired her. Sade took Fan under her wing when Jack was at work and Fan spent much time in the 'Happy Hour'.

Jack quietly disapproved but set no rules.

When Fan was sure she was going to have a baby, Jack did set down the rules; No more drinking, no more late hours with Sade and no more parties. Fan agreed, reluctantly but knew it was best for the baby.

Fan concentrated on their new home. She plagued the builders and haunted and hurried them constantly. She ordered furniture, drapes, glassware and dishes. Finally it was finished and they moved in bag and baggage. It was a cozy French bungalow on a large lot at the edge of town. Fresh air and green grass—perfect for the new baby, although it was still winter. . . .

Chapter Fourteen

SENECA RAINDROP

Fan poked at the fire in the fireplace with an iron and added another chunk of wood.

"I can't ever remember when winter was so cold," Fan said as Jack bounded down the stairs, two at a time and into the room. He had finished his 'trick' at work, shaved and cleaned up. He trailed a light scent of bay rum, when he crossed the room to Fan and cradled her in his arms in front of the fire.

"Not much snow just wind and cold," he answered and held her close.

"Umm, you smell good. Oh, I almost forgot! There's a little package for you from Ma'am on the stair-table," she said into his shoulder.

He released her and went to the half-moon shaped table near the foot of the stairs. He picked up the small package read the writing and shook it. "Wonder what this is all about." he said.

"Well, open it for pity sake!" Fan pleaded.

He opened the small box and a beautiful ring fell into his hand. He unfolded the tightly wedged letter and began to read. After a few seconds he dropped into his armchair by the fire. He handed the letter to Fan, put his head in his hands and began to cry silently.

"What's wrong Jack?" she gasped and took the letter. She read the words and under her breath said, "May the good Lord help us!" Aloud she said, "Oh, honey, I'm so sorry—I know how close you were." She hugged his shoulders and when she could recover her wits she said, "Come on put your feet up here and I'll make you a hot toddy before supper." Fan slid his footstool near him and placed his feet on it then fled to the kitchen. She wasn't very good in a crisis and had a tendency to prattle on and move about nervously.

Jack rolled his sister, Seneca's wedding ring over and over in his hand. His hot salty tears fell and splashed on the gleaming silver ring. He leaned back in his chair and closed his eyes. "Sen, my sweet Seneca," he whispered softly and allowed his mind to wander back to his earliest recollections of Seneca Raindrop. . . . .

. . . . .When Ma'am's buggy rolled into the lane, that cold September night in 1894, all the Lansure family ran to meet her. Sixteen year old Leone took the tiny bundle from Ma'am's arms, from the buggy and Paap helped her down. Thirteen year old Bruce took the horse and buggy to the barn. Ten year old Lu and six year old Rose squealed with delight, "A baby! Ma'am brought us a BABY!" They cried and crowded to look at it. In the house, Ma'am took the baby from Leone and said," Leone, you warm some baby clothes by the stove while I make a proper dressing for her navel. Lu, warm some fresh milk and barley water on the stove. Rose, you fluff Johnny's rocker-bed and put on clean sheets and blankets. There is room for them both, for now, until we get things sorted out. Johnny, what do you think of the baby?" Ma'am asked of little Johnny.

"It's so little!" exclaimed the not-quite-three year old tot.

"You may touch her hair and her hand if you wish—gently now, she's just a baby." Ma'am instructed.

Very gingerly, Johnny touched the baby's head and smiled. When he reached for her hand, the baby latched onto his index finger and clung fast.

"Look Ma'am, she's got me! She likes me! She's got my finger!" Cried the excited boy.

At that instant, a bond was sealed between Johnny and Seneca that would be forever. The bond was unspoken and invisible but it was always there.

After that night, Ma'am and Paap never again discussed 'arrangements' for Seneca. She was woven into the family fabric as a precious member.

After all the excitement was over and the baby's needs were tended, Jimmy and Agnes Lansure looked in on the two sleeping in the little rocker-bed. Tiny Seneca was holding onto Johnny's index finger and both were sleeping soundly. Johnny had been placed at the foot of the bed but had squirmed and wiggled his way up close enough to Seneca to reach her hand.

Jimmy and Agnes hugged each other and smiled. Agnes was expecting another child of her own in March but it seemed to make no difference at all that she would have two babies in diapers, come spring.

Seneca was a happy baby and cried very little. She would coo and try to catch her own fingers. If she fussed at all, Johnny would hold out his finger and she would grasp it tightly and smile. She whimpered and coaxed only if she needed fresh linen or food and soon her tiny, undersized body grew healthy and strong.

When Dudley was born the following March, Ma'am had two in the cradle and diapers or nappes. All pitched in and the children grew rapidly. Time passed quickly and soon the infants were toddlers and the toddlers became happy children.

Seneca enjoyed her brothers and sisters but more often than not, she would be with Ma'am. She was near Ma'am in the kitchen, in the vegetable garden and at quiet times on the porch in summer or by the open fire in winter.

In Ma'am's role as a midwife, she used many herbs, berries and plants in her apothecary of compounds and medicines. Seneca trailed along in the woods and meadows while Ma'am gathered. By the time she was twelve, Seneca Raindrop could recognize all the herbs, what they were used for and had a keener eye than Ma'am's at finding them.

Seneca was very artistic. From a bundle of grasses, blossoms, vines and twigs, she could fashion the most beautiful wreaths, garlands and table arrangements. She had an inner view of style and beauty that manifested itself in everything she fashioned with her hands.

She was a gifted student and spent long hours reading and writing. At fifteen, she made regular trips with Ma'am on house calls, when not in school. She looked and acted like Ma'am and her calm, comforting presence at birthings was invaluable as was her skill with the newborns. Seneca was adept at midwifery but it was not to be her calling.

At seventeen, Seneca Raindrop Lansure was a beautiful young woman. Her girlish, loosely-flying pigtails gave way to a black, shiny, thick braid that hung from the nape of her neck to the center of her back. She combed her hair straight back exposing her ears and displaying the lovely gold earrings given her by her brother, John, now called Jack. She treasured the earrings highly and was seldom without them.

When Seneca was old enough to understand, Ma'am and Paap explained to her the circumstance of her birth and that she was chosen out of love, to be their very own and would always be their child. They also told her of her Indian ancestry and opened the way, if she wished to search for her 'other family'.

She regularly took flowers to her mother's grave and read all that she could find about the American Eastern Indians. All through her teen years, she wrote letters of inquiry to government agencies, Indian agents and dozens of historical societies in the search for her family background and kept a running journal of her findings, which had not been much.

She graduated from Teacher's College with honors in two years instead of the usual three. Ma'am had more and more paper work to do as more birth records were required with larger case histories. The ledger Ma'am kept with 3-line entries had become full pages. Seneca kept most of Ma'am's records and did it with ease and accuracy.

One day when Seneca was eighteen, Roger Beasley, the postman, drove his new motor car into Lansure's lane. Although Mr. Beasley was aging, his taste in motor cars was up to date. The letter he carried was for Seneca.

To her delight, it was an answer to one of her inquiries. The letter was from an Indian Agent from upper New York State who had found a living relative of Seneca's. According to him, the immediate family to the tribal chiefs were recorded. After much digging into old archives, he found that Seneca's mother's older sister was still alive.

The letter also stated that 'Small Bird Seen Flying' could neither read or speak English, was very suspicious of white people and was old and sickly. What is more, the only reason she had consented to see Seneca was that her birth coincided with her sister's disappearance from the tribe and Seneca's Indian name.

The next weeks were busy ones. Arrangements were made through the Indian Agent for Seneca's visit to the reservation in New York State. She had to make the train trip alone but Ma'am and Paap were assured by the Agent that she would be met at the train, escorted to the reservation and be well-chaperoned at all times.

The day of departure arrived cold and sunny. Duke, Seneca's brother, pulled Ma'am's horse and buggy to the front hitching rail. All the family gathered to see her off. Seneca was lovely in her navy blue, silver fox fur trimmed bonnet and cloak with muff to match. Ma'am looped a small lunch basket over her arm and kissed her cheek. "Keep safe, my dear, the world out there can be big and frightening. Take firm steps, walk tall and be calm." Ma'am said.

"I'll remember, Ma'am." Seneca heeded her mother's words.

Paap hugged her and pressed a few dollars into her hand along with one of Jack's worry stones from the old Seneca Indian, out west. "She will give you a gift and you must give her one. Give her the worry stone first then if it seems right, give her some money. You wouldn't want to hurt her feelings. Tell her we understand about the worry stones but little else and tell her we send greetings." said Paap.

Paap placed her small grip in the buggy and helped Seneca in beside her brother. She waved from the buggy as they road away and tears glistened in all their eyes.

At the station, Dudley now called Duke, hugged his sister, put her bag on the train platform and helped her up. The train pulled out and Duke watched until it was out of sight.

The conductor put her luggage on the overhead rack and punched her ticket. She was too shy to talk to strangers but she remembered her manners, whispered her thanks and sat down.

Seneca had been away to boarding school but this trip was different. She had a loving family but now she was to see blood relatives and a completely strange world.

After a long while of staring out of the train coach window, she nibbled on a butter and jelly biscuit from her lunch basket but she wasn't very hungry. She couldn't be called 'afraid' but the lump in her stomach lay heavy.

She left the train at Buffalo and boarded the packet boat up the canal to Rome. She stepped onto the dock, which was piled high with bales of cotton, hay and straw and stacks of sacked grain and flour. She turned around and around searching the faces of all for the one who was expecting her. She found no one so she sat down on a clean sack of wheat and waited.

After a bit from behind her, came a deep masculine voice. "Are you Miss Lansure?" he inquired.

"Yes, I am." She jumped up and turned to see who spoke.

Seneca was looking into the face of the most beautiful man she had ever seen. Yes, beautiful to her. He was clean-shaven with a strong chin and black hair that covered his ears under his high-crowned, broad-brimmed hat. His large black eyes appeared to look deep into her soul. They both blushed beet red.

He was flustered too, and when he could speak, he said, "I'm Samuel Elkhorn. I teach at the settlement and I'm sent to fetch you. Hello." He held his hand out to her.

"Hello," she whispered. When they clasped hands, the heat and chills coursed through her body in waves. She felt her knees buckle and his strong arms circled her with support.

For an instant, he held her. The sweat beaded on his upper lip as if the winter day had turned to summer. When he recovered and steadied her on her feet he said, "The buckboard is over there." He pointed to a heavy-laden wagon and horse tied to a hitching post nearby.

She smoothed her clothing and straightened her bonnet. He helped her up with her baggage, untied the horse and climbed up on the seat beside her.

Seneca had a million questions to ask but dared not. She studied her companion from the corner of her eye and tried not to be obvious. The electricity between them charged the air and he could feel her eyes. He smiled and exposed a row of beautiful white teeth. She smiled and blushed at being found out which showed the dimple on her cheek.

''I understand you have no knowledge of your Aunt or the Indian people although you are an Indian Princess,'' he began.

''That's true, my mother died when I was born and Ma'am and Paap--I mean—a white family raised me,'' she answered.

''I'm a Lenni Lenape—Nanticoke, what white people call Delaware. That's a misnomer. The Walum Olum and the Lenni Lenape Nations have been here for centuries with their tribes like mine—The Nanticoke. The first governor of Virginia, Thomas West was titled Lord De la Warr and he called the people 'his Indians' so came the name. After I finished college, the government sent me here to teach mathematics and manual training at this settlement school. Do you know ANYTHING about us?'' he asked.

''Only that you carry worry stones for good luck, never tell lies and can pass through the woods unheard and unseen,'' she giggled.

''Are you laughing at me?'' he said, sternly.

''Oh, no I'm NOT. Laughing helps keep up my courage,'' she explained.

''Would it help if I fill you in on a few things as we ride along? He inquired.

''Oh yes, please do, there is so much I need to know!'' She felt better.

''The story goes, that your Aunt walked here from her home more than one hundred miles to the south. She wandered into one of the longhouses of the village and asked to stay in one of the unoccupied booths until she died. She was very old, half-starved and sick. The women of the tribe asked the elders to allow her to stay and promised to feed and care for her—which they have done to this day. They beg her to tell them of her past but she says nothing, other than she came from far away. We found her, for you, completely by accident because she is a stranger to this tribe. They also say that she is cranky and disagreeable and will often chase them with a stick to be left alone, when they try to comb and clean her but they accept her as she is.''

''What a strange story. Why do you suppose she will see ME?'' asked Seneca.

''No one knows and everyone was surprised when she said yes. There are a couple of other things you should know. In the longhouse, never walk between the people and the fire—always go behind. Never speak until you are asked and when asked to sit down, do so on your knees and heels with the legs to the right or left. Only men sit cross-legged. If you are accepted, she will give you a gift. You then, give a gift to her. Have you something?'' Sam asked.

''Yes, I have a worry stone that came from far out West and my Paap gave me money to see to her needs.'' Seneca said.

''The worry stone is fine but don't offer money unless I say so.'' Sam warned.

''Thank you, Mr. Elkhorn, I'll remember.'' She was grateful for the information.

''You can call me Sam, if I can call you Rainy—which it is,'' he pointed out.

It was true, it had begun a cold drizzle but neither had noticed and both laughed out loud while the creaky wagon bumped over the dirt road.

She agreed he could call her Rainy and she would call him Sam. In a very loud voice he said, ''Miss Seneca Raindrop Lansure—welcome to our world—Rainy.'' He looked at her and smiled and she blushed again.

They rode in silence for a bit then Sam spoke, ''I'll take you directly to the Reverend Ezekiel Fletcher and his wife, so you can dry out. You will be staying with Zek and Maude who are the missionaries here and they asked to help. After breakfast in the morning, I'll take you to the settlement.'' Sam said.

Before dark they arrived at the Fletcher's. Zek was tall, gangling and bald and Maude was plump, good-natured and warm. They showed Seneca in to a plain but comfortable bedroom with a roaring fire. Zek took her cloak and Maude said, ''I'll bring ya a bit of bread and cheese and a cup of hot tea before you sleep, ya look plum done-in.'' Maude turned down the bedcovers and went on, ''We put in a hot brick to ward off the night chill.''

''Thank you both, you're most kind.'' Seneca was weary.

''Good night and Bless you,'' the Reverend said and closed the door behind them.

Seneca loosened her clothes, stretched and stepped out of her petticoat. The buckboard ride had put a kink in her spine and she was bone-tired. She was warming herself at the fireplace in her under-drawers and camisole when Maude knocked and entered. She placed the tray on the dresser and said, ''Now you eat a bite, child and we will talk in the morning when you're rested. Good-night.'' She stepped out and closed the door.

Seneca stared out the window into the rainy darkness, nibbled at the cheese and sipped the tea. She thought about the wonderful adventure she was having. She rummaged through her grip for her journal and wrote in it. Later she slept.

The morning was bright, sunny and cold. The rain had stopped and Sam arrived early. Again he helped Seneca on to the buckboard for the trip to the settlement. They chatted as they rode and got to know each other.

Seneca had lots of partners for school affairs, square dances and ice cream socials but she could never talk to any of her companions and of course, after the small talk they lost interest. With Sam, it was different and easy. They talked about books, music and teaching. They had much in common and he was not like anyone she had ever met before, besides they liked each other. Sam was dedicated to his teaching task and said so. He was positive the future existence of the Indian people was education. Ignorance had already caused the demise of many nations and tribes.

When they arrived at the settlement, she expected dozens of neat wigwams and tepees all in rows. Beautiful women in beaded buckskin, carrying healthy, happy babies in ornate back-boards and handsome warriors in colorful, feathered headdresses, skin moccasins and robes with sheaths of arrows and bows. She expected it to be as it was in the books she read.

It was heartbreakingly untrue. In a large clearing in the woods stood two big dilapidated longhouses and several shabby wigwams. There was no one in sight and the only sign of life was smoke curling from the rundown dwellings.

Sam reigned up and a pitiful looking man emerged to take the horse and wagon. He was barefooted, his man-made shirt and pants were in tatters and his dirty, matted hair had been cut short. Seneca tried not to stare.

Sam helped Seneca down and they went into the largest longhouse. Seneca was not prepared for what they found.

It was dark, smelled of dried meat, sweating bodies, damp earth, dog and human excrement and the smoke from the fires burned her eyes. A few steps inside, she hesitated and stepped backwards. Sam was behind her and stopped her. For an instant he held her in his arms and whispered in her ear.

''An Indian may be afraid but must never show it to others.''

Seneca remembered Ma'am's words, drew herself up to full height, straightened her bonnet and marched directly toward the open fire in the center of the huge building, passed all who stared at her from the dark recesses.

Sam and Seneca stood by the fire and looked about. From a dark booth in the corner, a woman spoke in the Seneca language.

Sam said, ''Small Bird Seen Flying says come closer.''

''Should I?'' asked Seneca.

''Yes,'' Sam answered.

Seneca's eyes had become accustomed to the dim light and she could see well. She moved closer to the corner and the old woman who sat there. The woman spoke again.

''She says take off your hat.'' Sam whispered to Seneca.

Seneca loosened the ties, slid the bonnet off and smoothed her hair. The old woman spoke again and the attending women helped her to her feet then she promptly chased them away with her walking stick. The old woman came close and studied Seneca. She smelled of old flesh, rotting teeth, tobacco, filth and smoke.

Seneca stood motionless for her inspection. The Ancient One, as those people called her, touched Seneca's hair, eyebrows, skin and moved her chin from side to side. The other women gathered to touch her clothing, long braid and high-top button shoes. When they lifted her skirts, Seneca struck them away and stepped back.

"Courage, they only want to see what you are wearing—underneath." Sam whispered.

The old woman growled a few words, brandished her stick and they moved away from Seneca and helped her sit down.

"She says she's weary of standing and wants you to sit with her and tell her about yourself." Sam translated to Seneca.

"Sam! How can I? What should I say?" She pleaded.

"Steady now, you're doing fine. Begin at the beginning and I'll translate to her." he said calmly.

Seneca took a deep breath and began. She told them of her birth in a boxcar, how she got her name and the death of her mother. She told them about the white family who loved, raised and educated her and of her white brothers and sisters. She told them that she learned at an early age that she was an Indian Princess. She explained how she wrote many letters in effort to find her mother's family and of the long journey to find 'Small Bird Seen Flying,' now called 'The Ancient One.'

When Seneca stopped talking and the translation was finished, all was quiet.

Small Bird Seen Flying—'The Ancient One,' began to speak and Sam translated:

"The Great Manitou made the Seneca a great people. He taught them to approach like the foxes, fight like the lions and disappear like the birds. He has now granted my last wish when I thought he had forgotten me. Many years ago when I was young and beautiful, I had a mother, father, a young husband and son, also I had a sister. It seemed at that time, all the tribes were at war with one another. By mistake, our warriors attacked a peaceful Abnakie village they wrongly thought to be Huron and slaughtered many. The Huron were our enemies. The Abnakis were usually gentle and peaceful but if attacked they become savage, vengeful adversaries. They blamed my father most of all since he was the Chief, it being his fault or not. They slowly tortured him to death. My mother simply died of the shock of having to watch. My small son age 4 years, was swung by his ankles against a big tree and his little head burst like a ripe melon." The Ancient One lost her composure and began to sob. Out poured all the agony she had stored within herself for years. After a while, she wiped her face on a bit of cloth and began again. "My husband and my sister's husband were tortured together and eventually burned at the stake. The Abnakis grew drunk on whiskey and needed to sleep from their murdering. They decided to keep me and my sister until the next morning because they had special plans for her as she was heavy with child. They bound us with rawhide thongs and threw us into a dirty tepee.

My sister, 'Painted Turtle,' gnawed, chewed and strained at her rawhide bounds until her wrists bled. Eventually she was free and she released me. My sister loosened a stake in the floor of the tepee allowing space enough to squeeze through. She begged me to go quickly but I said no. I told her she must go and save her child. If the Abnakis had me, they would not follow her. She did not want to go but she had no choice, the child must live. She removed the necklace from her neck and placed it around mine. She slipped away and I never saw my sister again. The Abnakis were busy with me and did not follow her.'' The old woman stopped talking, turned her back to all and slowly allowed her shirt to fall to her waist. The whole group of people gasp in horror. Her back was a mass of terrible scars. She pulled up her shirt, turned back and began to talk again while Sam translated. ''The front of my body is worse but you must not see. After hours of torturing me, I did not die but I begged Manitou to carry me on the Great Wind but he did not. They tired of their sport and threw me into the tepee to die. I crawled out on my hands and knees and reached the river. The cold water soothed my cut and burnt body and the cool drink gave me strength. I tied myself to a floating log and drifted and dreamed and dreamed and dreamed. I know not how long I floated. When my senses returned I was in a lean-to covered with a deer skin. Sitting near me was a huge, frightening, white, mountain man. He was covered all over with hair and bearskins but his eyes were soft. I tired to run but he held me and said, ''You are alive but by the Great Manitou and I'll try to keep you so. Your injuries are many and terrible. Did the Huron do this?'' I said, ''No, Abnakis. How is it that you speak my tongue?'' He told me he was a trapper, spoke many tongues and his name was Jed—Jedadiah Jones. I told him my name and I recovered. Jed and I spent many years together. We trapped the streams and rivers and had a good life. Then came the white-man's sickness called cholera. I nursed him but he died. Again I was alone so I walked here. I asked only one wish of the Great Manitou and that was to see my sister once again. He never granted my wish until now. This young woman is the living image of my dead sister, 'Painted Turtle.' I recognized her at once.'' The Ancient One coughed, shuddered and tears rolled down her cheeks. The women covered her with a blanket and one brought broth.

''Oh, Sam, what can I do? She needs a doctor and a home. She wouldn't allow them to care for her because she was ashamed of her scars and there was nothing to be ashamed of. Those scars are her triumph over her horrors!'' Seneca sobbed.

"Now that they know her story, they will tend and treat her in private." Sam assured her.

The Ancient One spoke again, "Now that my eyes have seen you, Raindrop of the Seneca's, the Great Wind will carry me away soon. Sit closer, that I may touch you." Sam translated and Seneca moved closer. "I have not as many years as they think but my body is crippled and worn-out. 'Painted Turtle,' my sister, gave me this necklace at our parting and I give it to you at our parting." The 'Ancient One' hung the necklace of bits of stone, glass and wood on a thong, around Seneca's neck.

Seneca drew her close, held her in her arms, rocked her gently and cried. Quietly she said to Seneca and Sam translated, "Hoka Hey—It is a good day to die. Now I fly away." 'Small Bird Seen Flying' sighed softly and died. Her face was content and beautiful in death.

The women chanted in mourning and Seneca stayed for the burial. She was certain that her life was part of a Grand Design that led her here to help the Indian people. Determined to return to teach, she made arrangements with the Fletcher's to stay with them. After a brief visit with Ma'am and Paap she planned to return.

Sam took her to the boat and while they rode along he revealed his affection for her, "Seneca Raindrop—my Rainy—you have filled a long-empty place in my heart and I wish you to marry me." He said simply while they stood on the dock and waited for the boat.

"Oh Sam!" Seneca completely forgot her shyness and flung her arms around his neck. "I think I love you too, but I don't know what love is—do you?" She said, trying to breath. When she realized what she had done, she gathered her composure, released him, straightened her bonnet and blushed beet red.

"We will find out together," Sam said softly and kissed her tenderly.

The shrieking whistle sounded the boat's departure. Sam helped Seneca aboard and watched the boat move slowly away from the dock. . . . .

Seneca was home with Ma'am and Paap only long enough to arrange her move to the Indian Reservation. It was a sad time indeed, especially for Ma'am. She grieved when any of her children left the nest but with Seneca it was different, somehow, more final—what it was, Ma'am was not sure but the pain was great.

Sam, the Indian Agent and the Fletcher's made all the arrangements for Seneca to teach on the reservation and have lodgings until she and Sam were married and their little home was ready.

Age and poor health kept Ma'am and Paap from being at Seneca's wedding but when she left home they sent their blessings and prayers with her.

At the station, Ma'am choked back the tears and smiled when she kissed her beloved Seneca goodby. Paap pressed a few bills into her palm and hugged his daughter. Duke hugged his sister and wiped his nose. There were just no words.

Seneca stood on the train platform and waved until she could no longer see the only mother and father she had ever known. . . . .

Again at the Reservation, Seneca Raindrop Lansure settled in at the Fletcher's and got acquainted. She was shown around the dilapidated school house and introduced to her students. She and Sam mended, repaired and furnished their modest house. Seneca was cheerful and bubbly, she and Sam worked well together and were best friends. When they completed their task, the house was sound and cozy. No matter that it had an inside pump but an outside privy, it was their home.

Their wedding was humble but meaningful. Sam and Seneca were very much in love. Zek officiated and Maude pumped the organ and cried. Seneca had borrowed her sister Rose's lace veil and fashioned a new garland for herself. Her dress was wheat colored broadcloth, a gift from Ma'am and Paap. The Indian people gave her a beautiful deer skin beaded belt that circled her waist and hung almost to her knees. The pattern in the design told of her history including her marriage to Sam. It was a touching tribute to her and she was moved to tears. Even more remarkable was Seneca's wedding ring, which she had not seen until the ceremony. Sam had fashioned it from a single piece of silver. He had punched and pounded out a unique latticework of gleaming metal, an inch in length on the top and a quarter of an inch band. It was an outstanding piece of artistic metal work. There was one thing however, the ring was just a bit too large for Seneca's finger. She adored her new treasure and would laugh and say "I'll grow into it" and would never take it off her finger or allow Sam to alter the size.

They had no honeymoon per se, but they did have what the locals called a 'Serenade' or 'Belling'. Friends and family would gather around the newlyweds at their home and sing, play music, beat drums, ring bells, shoot guns and fireworks and serve food and drinks. It was a noisy tribute to the couple if they wanted it or not. Sometimes the pair was whisked into an open wagon or truck and driven around the countryside on unpaved roads to give them their 'Dusting'. This was the traditional, well-meaning, good natured way to keep the married couple from their nuptial bed and have a lively party at the same time. At the end of the festivities, the group passed the hat for the couple and that was the most fun of all. Anything could be in the hat; a shotgun shell, a horseshoe nail or a bottle cap along with a pile of assorted coins and a few paper dollars. When all were exhausted, the merrymakers would depart and the harried couple was alone at last.

The years passed but Sam and Seneca had no children of their own. It was not known if Seneca was barren or if Sam was sterile but no matter, they had their hands happily full with the children in their charge. 'Two Moons', a Seneca woman, was the local midwife and Seneca helped in many deliveries just as she had helped Ma'am. She and Sam worked tirelessly during epidemics of influenza, diphtheria, typhoid and through dozens of contagious children's diseases. The antiquated clinic was pitifully understaffed and overcrowded.

Seneca wrote dozens of letters, talked to many government officials and plagued the local agents to do something about the deplorable conditions on the reservation. Sometimes it worked and some improvements were made but usually her pleas fell on deaf ears. She and Sam did manage to obtain better textbooks, reference books and a much needed encyclopedia. The new schoolhouse never materialized. The centrally heated, water-bucket-on-the corner-shelf, the smelly, tilted, leaning outhouse and the old, rickety seating benches in the old school remained the same. They patched the roof, wired the stovepipe and propped up the listing outhouse.

After a particularly bad epidemic. Seneca found she had become surrogate mother to a three year old boy named, Alvin 'Small Tree Stump' or 'Stumpy' for short. His parents had died and Seneca had comforted the child. Stumpy's distant relatives saw to his basic needs but he preferred to be near Seneca. He would huddle on her porch when she came home from teaching or he would be sitting outside the schoolhouse waiting for her after class. He was quiet, well-behaved and so alone. Seneca would often take him in for a good scrubbing and some food or Sam would take him to the manual training shop and allow the interested boy to watch while he made a shelf or a footstool. On the way home, Sam would give the sad boy a 'horsey-back-ride' just to see the waif smile, which was seldom.

Stumpy was too young for school but during inclement weather, Seneca would place a pallet under the water pail shelf where he could sit or nap as he chose. The children's drinking water was fresh daily, per Seneca's instructions and the older children took turns each day filling the pail from the pump outside. From Stumpy's place, on his bed under the shelf, he could hear and watch Seneca teach and listen to the children recite. He enjoyed the activity and was content. At times, Seneca would glance from her teaching and see the motherless orphan sleeping peacefully. She adored the little fellow and would smile to herself. Sam and Seneca became very attached to the boy and he thrived.

The following winter was very cold and it made unusually heavy demands on the old potbellied stove in the center of the schoolroom. It was made hotter and hotter each day to furnish enough heat for the large room and the children. On many days, Seneca urged the children to remain in their coats and hats to ward off the chill.

This was one of those bitterly cold days. Sam built the fire in the school on his way to his work to allow it to warm up for classes. When Seneca arrived, she smelled something hot but could find nothing burning or smoking.

About midmorning, Seneca sent one of the older boys for firewood from the shed outside. When the boy opened the door it caused a huge back draft and the ceiling burst into flames. It had been smoldering in the rafters, for hours and when the air hit, it erupted.

Calmly, Seneca herded her children outside; the older ones helping the younger ones. When about the half the children were out, a big timber fell and barred the door with flames.

Quickly, Seneca smashed out the window with a footstool and passed the remaining children out to Sam and others who had come to help. It was but a few feet to the ground and all escaped. When it was Seneca's turn to leap to freedom into Sam's arms, she heard a sound. She turned back to peer through the heat and smoke toward the sound and saw Stumpy. He was huddled in his corner on his pallet, paralyzed with fear and choking from the smoke.

''Sam! It's Stumpy!'' she screamed and raced to the boy, snatched him up and fled to the window. When Seneca passed the frightened child to Sam, his hands passed over hers and her loose wedding ring fell into Sam's hand.

''Hurry! Rainy, hurry! Sam shouted.

''Sam! My dress!'' she screamed and turned to beat out the flames on the hem of her skirts. That instant the flaming ceiling fell in on Seneca.

''Sam! Sam!'' She shrieked as the inferno engulfed her. There was no rescue and no escape.

''Rainy! Rainy! Sam screamed and tried to climb into the window. Men outside held him tight. They knew it was futile and dragged him away from the fire engulfed building.

''Rainy! Rainy!'' Sam screamed over and over. When Sam Elkhorn stopped screaming, he looked as if his very soul had been snatched from him. He looked tired, old and beaten. He stood and stared while the blazing inferno destroyed his love and his life. Stumpy clung to one of Sam's legs and cried.

The Indian people who had come to love their Princess, knelt in the snow and wept and chanted.

A few days later, Sam gave the keys to their home to Zek and Maude and hugged little Stumpy. ''Please distribute our things among our people, Rainy would want that and will you send this package for me? It's for Rainy's mother.''

''Of course, Sam. Where will you go—what will you do!'' Maude cried and hugged the weeping boy in her arms.

''Nothing—just nothing,'' Sam answered and walked away down the road into oblivion. . . . .

. . . . Jack was stirred back to the present when Fan brought him a cup of coffee laced with Old Grand Dad and placed in on the table beside his armchair.

''I brought your coffee in a while ago but you were sleeping,'' Fan said softly. ''I wasn't asleep, I was thinking about Seneca, my Sen.'' Jack choked back his grief.

Jack had not been sad or melancholy since he had met Fan. Suddenly, as if by some evil trick, he had been placed back into that dark time when he had lost his favorite cousin, Li'l Dan. Again, he felt abandoned—deserted. The bond between Jack and his sister, Seneca, was an intangible, invisible but an undeniable fact. So personal and deep was it to Jack that her death left a gaping hole in his soul. From the first time she grasped his finger as an infant, she held a special place in his heart. Although he saw little of her after they grew up, she was always with him. Her death made a change in him and Fan could feel it.

''You never talked much about her but I know you two were very close. I'm so sorry, honey.'' Fan was not good in a crisis and poked nervously at the fire.

''I remember she was terrified to sled ride down the big hill up on 'Gobbler's Nob' but she would ride down with ME. She would get me around the neck so tight that I could hardly breathe and she would squeal like a banshee. At the bottom we would roll off into the snow and laugh. . . . . .'' Jack put his face in his hands, held Seneca's ring and sobbed. . . . . . .

Chapter Fifteen

23 SKIDDOO

Fan noticed that Jack was never quite the same after his sister, Seneca, died in the fire. He was calmer, more withdrawn and reticent. Fan did what she could to please him and take his mind off his grief. She showed him the baby clothes she made, played the piano and sang for him and cooked his favorite foods. When he had time off from work, she dragged him to an endless string of outings. They did not 'hit the joints' anymore because Fan was 'showing' and booze and long hours were taboo.

Jack was happy to go to work and the long hours kept him occupied. He concentrated on the railroad and the new baby. The thought of a child of his own, gave him great pleasure. He liked children and looked forward to having a family.

Jack worried about Fan because she grumbled and complained constantly about being alone. She whined that all her pretty clothes did not fit, she was tired and she hated the railroad. To amuse herself, she played endless games of 'Solitaire', drummed the piano and studied Astrology, which was all the 'rage'. Fan's friend Sade, read the Tarot cards and Fan hung on every word as if it was the gospel truth. Since she seldom saw Sade, now that she was carrying a child, Fan decided to teach herself to read the cards. She learned quickly and it was exciting for a time. When she ran out of people to read for, she got bored and lost interest. She had become acquainted with her neighbors and it helped. They all had children except Fan and they had oceans of advice for her. The Ripleys lived on their right and Liz had two boys. The Bells lived on their left and Ada had one boy. Across the street was Sy and

Stella Cronen, they had the most children—seven and one coming. Sy's health had been broken by a bad case of pneumonia last year and he had never completely recovered. This was a major disaster for the Cronen family since Sy was a brick layer and mason who would never be able to stand the rigors of the work again.

One day, on his way home from work, Jack stopped at the nearby dairyman to pay his milk bill. The dairy house and barns sat beside the railroad tracks and his pasture lands followed along the back end of Jack's lot. Joe Porter sold his fresh milk from cow to customer on the spot. The sign on the side door of the Porter house read WALK IN and Jack did. A small room off the hall in the house was Joe's office.

''Hello Joe! Anybody here?'' Jack called from the hall.

''Come on in, Jack.'' Joe was an ordinary man of forty or so who stood from his roll-top desk and took Jack's hand. ''How are ya these days?''

''First rate Joe. I'm able to eat regular and pay my bills—that's why I'm here.'' The men shook hands.

''Well, now let's see, here we are.'' Joe took a stack of papers from a spindle on his desk and thumbed through them. He selected one and said, ''That'll be two dollars and ten cents, if ya please.''

Jack stuffed the bill in his pocket, paid the man and said, ''That's quite a stack of unpaid bills, Joe.''

''Sure is, there's been a lot of sickness around but ya still have to have milk and groceries and the bills pile up. Speakin' of sickness, did ya know that Sy Cronen hasn't worked in six months? He owes every body in town and he owes me seven dollars. Don't know how much longer I can afford to 'carry' him,'' Joe said thoughtfully.

''Has it been THAT long? I know Stella is having another baby about the time we are—soon. Ya can't stop their milk Joe, those kids need it!'' Jack pleaded.

''I wish I could Jack, but I got bills too,'' Joe explained.

''Tell ya what, Joe, ya say Sy owes seven dollars, well I'll pay six dollars of his bill. When Sy comes and asks how much he owes you tell him, one dollar. Put what ever else he owes on my bill. Now Sy's a proud man and you must never tell that I paid the bill. When he finds full-time work, you and I will talk again. Here's the six bucks and don't forget, he only owes you one dollar and it's our secret. Agreed?'' Jack cautioned.

''That's mighty generous of ya Jack, one dollar and mum's the word.'' Joe agreed.

''Mum is right! Sy is my friend and I wouldn't hurt his feelings for the world. In the same fix, he'd do the same for me. He's an honest man and he will catch up on ALL his bills as soon as he can. In the meantime, you and me—we're just helping him a little and remember—not a word.'' Jack was emphatic.

Joe, the dairyman, scratched his head and watched Jack walk down the street whistling to himself and said, ''Nice fella, that Jack Lansure, NICE fella.''

At home half a block away, Fan was preparing a meal in the kitchen.

''How ya feel'in, honey?'' Jack asked and kissed his wife.

''I'd feel fine if my back would stop aching—Oh, feel THAT! It's a real prizefighter!'' She placed Jack's hand on her swollen belly.

''Jesus! That feels funny! I think it's trying to get OUT of there!'' They laughed and hugged each other.

The changes on the railroad were encouraging, jobs were plentiful and everyone prospered. Some of the trains that Jack 'made up' and 'hauled' were almost a mile long and growing. There seemed no limits to the strength of the big 'Lima's (locomotives) and the West End was as busy as was the East End. The little switching line had become a full blown railroad.

On the morning of July 16, 1924, Jack was dressing for work and Fan was trying to make her awkward, swollen body comfortable with a cool, wet washcloth. ''My back is killing me this morning, I wish you would stay home with me,'' Fan grumbled.

''So do I honey, but I have an engine to run,'' Jack tried to comfort her.

''That old engine, it comes before ANYTHING!'' She pouted.

''Now you know that isn't so and now that the baby will be here soon, we need all the dough we can scrape together.'' Jack tried to be reassuring.

''Doc Caine says it can be anytime—wish it was soon—Oh, my back!'' Fan flinched.

''I'll be home as soon as I can. Maybe if you sat on the porch swing, you would be cooler.'' Jack kissed Fan's cheek, took the stairs two at a time and bounded out the screened door.

About an hour later, Fan began her labor pains. She called Doctor Caine and he said he and his nurse would be over shortly. Fan called her mother, Matilda Saddler, who would arrive on the afternoon train. She called Liz Ripley from the front porch and she was there.

Shortly thereafter, Doc Caine arrived with his nurse. A quick examination revealed that Fan's water had broken prematurely and this meant a more difficult first birth, added to the fact that Fan was tiny and the baby was large. A 'dry birth' was always more lengthy and with more complications.

The pain was excruciating, Fan ground her teeth together, bit her lip and writhed in a soggy bed of her own perspiration.

The hot day wore on toward noon with little progress. There was no breeze outside and the bedroom was stifling, although there were two open windows.

"Misses Ripley, can you get word to the railroad for Jack. I think he should be here now." The doctor spoke softly to Liz who had been bathing Fan's face with cool water and a cloth.

"Sure, Doc, I'll go myself—it will only take a jiffy." Liz was a pretty, good natured, redheaded, Irish lass who hurried out of the room.

"Nurse, how close now?" The doctor asked the nurse who had been monitoring Fan's pains.

"Every six minutes or so." She said.

"Prepare the chloroform, I'll have to 'take' the child," he said resolutely and shook his head.

"Yes, doctor." The nurse prepared a cupped screen and gauze and opened a small can of chloroform.

The doctor applied the liquid chloroform to the gauze on the cupped screen and placed it over Fan's mouth and nose. Immediately she breathed in great gulps of the pain deadening fumes, relaxed and lay still.

"Now when I tell you, add more chloroform, one drop at a time," the doctor instructed.

"Yes sir," the nurse replied.

Fan groaned and stirred.

"Now nurse, two drops," were the doctor's instructions.

"Yes sir," she replied and dropped more chloroform on the gauze.

The doctor worked the tiny head out and Fan screamed.

"Two more drops." He said.

"Yes sir." She answered.

The tiny shoulders appeared and Fan cried out again.

"Two more drops, it's the shoulders," he said.

"Two more, yes sir," she answered.

The baby fell into the doctor's hands, Fan groaned and lay still.

The sweating doctor held up Fan's tiny son and patted him lightly. No response. He patted him again, more forcefully. No response. The child was alive but would not breathe.

"Quick nurse, prepare a bath of very warm water." The doctor directed and she obeyed. They tested the water, that it not to be too hot and gently immersed the baby into the water. No response. They repeated it. Nothing.

"Nurse, cold water—hurry. I must attend to her." He gave the limp child to the nurse and turned to Fan who lay motionless and pale.

"Fannella can you hear me," the doctor gently slapped her wrist and lifted her eye lid. "My God, Alice, it looks like anti-tolerance to chloroform for both of them.'' Alice Turner was her name but he only called her by name in a crisis. ''How are you coming with the little one?'' He asked while he finished his work on Fan.

''I get no response at all, sir.'' She heaved a great sigh, wrapped the infant boy in a blanket and gave him to the doctor.

''She will be all right, I think, but we can't give up on this child.'' The doctor said.

The doctor and the nurse did everything they knew to revive the baby but to no avail. When the infant's body temperature dropped, it was hopeless. The tiny life came but never lived.

The exhausted doctor was coming out of Fan's room and rolling down his shirt sleeves when Jack leaped up the stairs, still in his soot covered work clothes.

''Doc! Doc! I couldn't get here sooner! I was switching at the stone quarry and they couldn't reach me! What happened? How's Fan—the baby?'' Jack was frantic.

''Hello Jack, glad you're here. She's fine but we just don't know about these things son. We don't know why chloroform affects people differently but it does or why some require more and some require less.'' The aging doctor wiped his swetty face with his handkerchief.

''I don't understand—just what does that mean? I want to see Fan!'' Jack reached for the doorknob.

''Wait son, Fan won't know you yet. We must talk. Your son was born alive but the chloroform had an adverse affect on him and he wouldn't breathe. We did all we could but he would not respond. I'm sorry Jack, the baby did not survive.'' The exhausted doctor patted Jack's shoulder.

Jack seized the doctor by the front of his clothing and hissed through his teeth, ''What do you mean—he didn't survive—you're saying my son is DEAD?''

''I know how you must feel son, but we did all we knew how.'' The doctor gently extricated Jack's hands from his clothing. ''The birth was difficult for Fannella and the chloroform we administered to ease her pain, caused a malfunction in the child's lungs and heart. We don't fully understand what happens but it is almost always fatal. I'm sorry Jack, I will take the child to Horace Redman and tell him you will call later to make the funeral arrangements. You may go in now.'' The doctor was very distressed.

Jack sagged against the closed door and looked as if someone had struck him a mortal blow. He opened it and the nurse uncovered the tiny lifeless body and Jack saw his son for the first and last time. The infant was perfectly formed with a thatch of black hair and appeared to be sleeping. Jack took the tiny bundle in his arms and cried out in his misery. After a time, he returned the child to the nurse and bent over Fan who lay still and pale, on the bed. Jack knelt beside her and took her hand and kissed it.

"Fan, Fan, honey, can you hear me?" Jack said softly. She stirred, murmured something and lay still once more.

"Doc! Doc!" Jack cried.

"It's alright son, she will sleep off and on for the next 24 hours. It's best she does, the more rest she gets now, the faster she will recover." The doctor explained.

At that moment Matilda Saddler, Fan's mother, appeared in the door way. She removed her hat and placed it on the dresser.

"Oh 'Tilly', we lost our son," Jack wept and held her in his arms." Fan's sleeping but she will be okay."

"There, there, my boy. You two will have lots more babies." Matilda glanced at the doctor for reassurance and he nodded, 'yes'. "Now, you get cleaned up and I'll fix some supper. Doctor, there's fresh coffee on the stove and Liz has fixed you a sandwich." Matilda was a comfort to everyone and the good neighbor Liz, knew just what to do at trying times.

A few days later, Jack stood alone at the graveside where he laid his son, John Clellend Lansure Jr. to rest. Fan was too ill to join him so with hat in hand, Jack stood in the warm July sun and cried.

In the weeks that passed, there was a steady stream of visitors and friends. Fan recovered slowly but enjoyed being the center of attention. Matilda waited on her daughter, hand and foot. She brushed Fan's lovely hair into thumb curls, cooked her favorite foods and in general, answered her every whim.

Fan recovered from her loss without much physical or emotional damage but with Jack it was different. He had not recovered from the sudden death of his sister, Seneca and now the death of his son appeared to have delt him a fatal blow. Matilda observed that he seemed to be 'bleeding internally', theoretically, but she had no idea how to ease his pain.

Jack concentrated on the railroad and his work. The long hours kept his body busy and his mind occupied. His railroad buddies knew of his tragedy and their kind condolences, although well-meant, were a constant reminder of his loss.

When she had completely recovered, Fan resumed her social life with gusto. She spent more and more time at Sade's Speakeasy. The Jazz Age was her 'cup of tea'.

Her life was one party after another and she spent Jack's money as fast as he earned it. She often forgot to tell Jack that she was having a house party until he came home from work, tired and dirty and opened the door to find a houseful of people carousing to the blare and scratch of the Gramaphone or the thumping of the 'Upright'.

There would be coarse men with slicked-down hair in gaudy suits with loud women in 'bobbed' hair, rolled-down stockings and rouged faces. In the center of the fracas was Fan, having the time of her life. She had learned to dance the 'Charleston', 'The Black Bottom', 'The English Quick Step' and the 'Fox Trot'. She delighted in dancing and her capacity for alcoholic beverages was astounding.

Jack was mildly, rightfully annoyed but said nothing. He would bathe, rest a bit and join the festivities. He enjoyed watching Fan laugh and have fun with her long curls bouncing as she moved.

Jack's solace was found in the cab of his engine. The more he worked the better he felt. The more Jack was away, the more Fan turned to her new-found friends for fun and gaiety. When he was home, she devoured him with her sexual appetite. So great were her demands upon him that at times he could not function. When this happened, she would beg, whine and pout. Often, her vicious side would appear and she would be hostile and verbally abusive. Her outbursts were beyond destructive. Jack would not fight back. He simply put on his hat and went for a walk, leaving Fan to sputter and rage alone. When he returned, she would be in another mood. She would beg his forgiveness, promise never to be mean again and of course, Jack would forgive her.

One day, Jack came home from work to find Fan posing on the front porch, twirling around, flinging her arms in the air and calling to him. "Don't you think I'm gorgeous?" She would whirl and giggle.

"Your hair—you've CUT your HAIR! All the curls are GONE!" Jack wailed, "How COULD you do that? Any other woman would give her eyeteeth to have hair like that!"

"Bobbed hair is the style now—I thought you'd like it," Fan said softly and cowered under his wrath. She did not understand his tirade and had no idea that she had done anything wrong.

When Jack saw he had crushed her to tears, he took her in his arms and held her. "Well I suppose if YOU like it, I'll get used to it. In time, it will grow out again." He consoled her but he was trying to console himself.

"Sade took me to her beauty parlor. It was fun! I'd never been in a beauty parlor before," she giggled, "and there were all those machines that curl you hair PERMANENTLY! The lady had a hard time making mine lay flat. She sold me this hair clip—isn't it pretty?" She pointed to the metal clip above her left ear that held her hair in place.

"Sade—I might have known! That woman has some very BAD ideas." Jack said thoughtfully.

"But Jack, I thought you liked Sade. She was YOUR friend first," Fan looked puzzled.

"True but Sade doesn't influence me and she does work on you," he said.

"Are you hungry? I made 'hunter's dinner' especially for you." She ignored his remark and changed the subject.

Fan's flighty extravagance continued until several bouts of unexplained nausea sent her reluctantly to Doctor Caine. It was true, she was to have another child. Jack was delighted and immediately set down the rules; no booze, no wild parties until all hours and no more Sade's Speakeasy. Fan agreed willingly, this time and vowed never to allow them to administer any chloroform to her no matter how painful the birth might become. Instead, she took long healthy walks, ate a balanced diet and obediently took any and all the pills the doctor prescribed. She vowed to have a healthy baby and a live one.

In mid-April, Jack had a few days off to go fishing with three of his railroad buddies and planned a weekend of fly fishing. Fan was not due until the end of April and Jack did need a rest from his job. In late afternoon, April 24, the men dressed in fishing gear, took their tackle, tent and cots including a big number 0 iron spider for frying the catch. Also, they took assorted tin cups and plates with a huge coffee pot. Like four small boys on a great adventure, they loaded into Rich Richard's old fliver and chugged away. They planned to camp along the river bank and do nothing but fish, eat and tell lies about ones that got away until Sunday night.

Fan watched the jolly bunch drive away. It was lovely spring weather and Fan took her evening walk in the fresh air. Her Saturday was uneventful and humdrum. She did her usual shopping, after which, she stopped to have a cup of coffee with Sade, whom she had not seen in a long while.

"For Christ's sake, 'Fancy' girl, you're as big as that new house of yours, how the Hell are ya?" Sade was loud and crude but she had a heart of gold. She had called Fan, 'Fancy,' since their first meeting years before. She gave Fan a big bear hug. "Take a load off and we'll chin awhile. Those packages are bigger than you are!" Sade pulled a chair from a table for Fan and sat down on one beside her.

"Oh, I'm fine Sade, except that I'm awkward and clumsy and I get tired too soon. What's new with you? You look great." Fan sat down heavily on the chair. "Thought I'd talk to you and rest before I start home." She said breathlessly.

"Mushy, two javas and a couple of those sticky buns from the kitchen," Sade called to her helper.

The women ate, drank the coffee and talked together. After a rest, Fan took her groceries and walked home. After a nap in Jack's easy chair, she went out on the porch to swing and to watch the evening fall into night.

The Sabbath dawned fresh and sunny, but Fan was sick at her stomach and cramping. She was sure it was her time but it was too soon. This was the 26th and she wasn't due for a week or so. She called the doctor, her mother and good ole' Liz—always-when-ya-need-her—Liz.

The doctor and nurse and Liz arrived and Fan explained that Jack was away. Matilda's arrival would be later as she would arrive on the afternoon flyer.

Fan paced the floor. It was easier for her to walk off her pain than it was to lay in bed. The doctor thought it strange but allowed it. When Fan thought it time, she laid on the bed. Marrilla Elsa Lansure came screaming into the world at 2:30 PM Sunday, April 26, 1926. She was much smaller than her late brother but she was perfectly healthy and squalled mightily.

The doctor gave the tiny bundle to an exhausted but happy Fan just as Jack burst into the room, still in full fishing garb and waders. He kissed his Fan and held her.

"Oh, Jack, I'm so glad your here! I didn't expect you until night. How did you know?" She was delighted but puzzled.

"I didn't. Rich slipped on a rock and fell in this morning. Without dry clothes, he figured to catch his death so we came home. Sure glad we did! How do you feel?" Jack explained.

"I'm fine but look at her! She's perfect but she's so little!" Fan uncovered the infant and Jack beamed with pleasure. He snatched a pillow from the bed and made a soft cradle to help him hold his tiny prize.

"Doc, I want to show my buddies downstairs, is it okay?" Jack asked.

"Sure son, just keep her warm," were the doctor's instructions.

"I'll be right back!" Jack called over his shoulder.

Down stairs, Jack's friends were having a drink in the kitchen and attended by ever-helpful Liz. She had thrown a warm blanket over Rich but he was still wet and shivering.

"Look at her guys, isn't she beautiful?" Jack glowed with pride. Newborns are anything but beautiful but they agreed anyway. He uncovered the wiggling infant and when Jack touched her hand, the baby clung to his left forefinger with much more strength than he ever imagined an infant could evoke.

"Look at that! She's got me! I didn't know babies were that strong!" Jack gushed. Years ago my sister, Seneca, held on to me that way.

"She's a cutie, alright." Rich shivered through clicking teeth.

"Hey, thanks for the trip, it was a welcome change but you better get Rich home and into some dry duds. Here's mud!" They all downed another slug of Old Grandad and left.

Jack took his precious bundle up to Fan.

''You want me to settle up with you now, Doc? I'm sure much obliged.'' Jack was very grateful to have a sound child.

''No son, I'll send you a bill the first of the month. What are you going to call her?''

''Fan and I have already talked it over, she will be Marrilla Elsa Lansure.''

''That's a mighty big name for that little young'en!'' The doctor chuckled, took his black bag and his nurse and left.

Liz saw them out just as Mrs. Saddler arrived.

Elizabeth, you are always there when we need you! Thank you. How's Fan—the baby. . . .''

''Oh Mrs. S., she's fine and you have a healthy granddaughter! No problems at all,'' Liz was excited.

''Lord be praised!'' Matilda said under her breath and hurried upstairs. There were tears of joy and relief among the family.

Later Jack had spring bouquets delivered to Fan with love for their first child, to Matilda in honor of her first grandchild and to Liz in grateful thanks for her unfailing devotion to his family.

Summer followed spring and Fan appeared content. She doted on the infant and complained less about the railroad or being alone. Each afternoon, weather permitting, she would push Marrilla in the baby buggy to the depot to meet Jack at the end of his day's work.

For the first time in a long while, Jack was happy and content. He adored Marrilla and his relationship with Fan smoothed out but was far from perfection.

Fan's preoccupation with her baby was as a child playing with dolls. She bathed, dressed, undressed, fed, played with and watched it sleep. She often left the beds unmade and the dishes in the sink but she was an exceptional mother and Jack deemed that more important. He would go quietly and pay the mortgage or the grocery bill that she had 'let slide'. She was 'too busy' or 'forgot' or could not remember the 'due date'. Since her time was spent with the child, Jack made no demands.

The railroad prospered. Business doubled and tripled. Yard crews, section crews, bridge crews and train crews worked long hours while gandy danders (trackmen) and nut crackers (machinists) worked around the clock. The little bridge line was rapidly becoming an important railroad. Nearly any man who wished to work could find it on the AC&Y. The bonanza drew men from everywhere. Among the job seekers was Jack's younger brother, Dudley Clayton, always called Duke.

Jack arranged with Fan that Duke would stay with them. Fan was not happy about the additional laundry and cooking but she was happy to have company when Jack was expected to work night trick. The house was large and although Fan and Duke had never met, he was family and all was ready for his arrival.

The doorbell sounded, Fan set Marrilla in her bassinet and opened the door. Neither was prepared for the other.

Fan drew in her breath and stared. Duke was a beautiful man, like her Jack, but different. He stood at least six feet, three. His thick shock of black curly hair needed trimming and his cornflower blue eyes riveted Fan to the spot.

Duke stared at the slip of a girl before him. She was the loveliest thing he had ever seen. He felt his body temperature rise and the sweat beaded on his forehead. When he could regain his voice, he said in deep baritone, "I'm Duke Lansure."

"Yes—of course—won't you come in—I'm Fan." She blushed beet red and stammered, "Jack will be home soon."

"May I hold the baby? I'm good with kids." He moved to the bassinet.

"Sure her name is Marrilla," she sputtered and felt ridiculous—he knew THAT—she was embarrassed.

His enormous hands lifted the tiny baby into his huge, muscled arms. His back and shoulders rippled with strength under his shirt, from years of working in the coal mines.

The baby drooled on him and he threw his head back and roared with a booming laughter that shook the glassware. The noise startled Marrilla and she began to cry.

"I'm sorry, I didn't mean to scare her. My sister, Leone and I are the loud ones in the family." Duke was nervous in Fan's presence and did not understand why.

"It's alright, she's probably wet. I'll show you to your room. When Jack comes, we will have supper." Fan was calmer now and she liked this 'gentle giant' that she led up the stairs to his room. "Make yourself ta' home. I have to change her and finish supper." Fan left him to his own devices.

Fan changed Marrilla and put her down for a nap. In the kitchen, she basted the roast and sliced the bread.

Jack burst through the front door and clapped both his brother's shoulders, after having seen Duke's old secondhand 'wreck' in the driveway.

"Damn, it's good to see ya Duke, how the hell are ya?" Jack cried.

"Fit Jack, fit. Ya sure got a nice family. Fan showed me around but I laughed and scared the little one. I forget how loud I am, sometimes." Duke explained.

"Come on, let's have 'one to cut the road dust'." Jack retrieved his bottle of 'Old Grandad' whiskey from the end of the buffet and found two

'Rolling Rock' beers in the ice box. The bottles were warm because there was no ice.

"Guess Fan forgot to order ice," Jack was embarrassed and laughed nervously.

"I knew there was something I forgot." Fan said, thoughtfully.

"Don't matter to me I drink it anyway I can get it." Duke said and laughed again until the glassware clanked.

The three laughed, talked and got acquainted again. Jack had not seen his brother in a long while and it was all new to Fan. After the hearty meal, Fan served the coffee in the living room. Duke took his guitar from the case and Jack sat down to 'cord' on the 'Upright'. After a bit of 'tuning up, the house rocked with music; 'Ida, Sweet as apple cida'—'How ya gonna keep um down on the farm'—. Duke handed Jack his guitar and took his banjo from its case.

"Fan now you play the piano." Duke suggested.

It was the beginning of a harmonious threesome. Their music would drift out the open windows and off the porch in summer and ricochet from the ceiling and walls in winter.

The men worked steady and Fan cooked, cleaned and tended the baby.

Duke paid room and board but miserly salted away every extra penny to buy a new car. He wanted a shiny new roadster with isinglass windows, a convertible top and a rumble seat. He would like yellow but would take black. Duke was very popular with the ladies but had no serious attachments. His musical abilities made him the center of attention wherever he went. Usually, he was found alone strumming his guitar under a tree in Jack's backyard or on the front porch swing. In winter, he sat by the fire and played. Duke was what most called a 'loner'. Marrilla was almost one and toddling about she enjoyed a seat on her Uncle Duke's lap while he played her a tune on his harmonica. At nap or bed time, it was her favorite way to go to sleep. When he was home, she always got her wish.

Duke's birthday fell in March of the spring of 1927 and Fan went all out to have a nice party for him. She invited all their friends and his. She cleaned, baked and made fancy hors d'oeuvres. On the morning of the party, Jack announced at the breakfast table that he had to work unexpectedly. Fan flew into a rage. "How could you do that to me! After all my WORK! I hate that railroad—I hate you—you always go away when I need you!" She screamed.

"Fan, I'm sorry but I can't help it. I have to work when they call me." Jack explained.

"You always say that! You are NEVER here when I need you!" She raged.

Marrilla began to cry in her high chair and Duke stood up to take Marrilla from the room.

"Don't go Duke, you may as well know that he cares more for that railroad than he does for me!" Fan raged, "I hate him!"

"Fan, I'm sorry. I'll be home at 4:00 PM but I have to be back at work by 10:00 PM. I'll stay at the party as long as I can." Jack tried to soothe her.

"Do you realize your brother hasn't had a birthday party since he was twelve years old! How could you not be here for his 32nd?" She raged.

"Stop that, you two, I haven't had any parties and I don't need one now. I won't have you fightin' about me." Duke said while he held Marrilla who was busy chewing on his watch that he had given her to play with.

"It's not about YOU, it's about that awful RAILROAD! It's first in Jack's life and it always has been!" Fan slammed the dishes into the sink.

"Duke, I just can't make her understand that I have to go WORK! I run an engine for a living! It's what I do!" Jack looked at his watch, from the front of his bib overalls, took his railroad cap and gauntlets and left for work.

"See! See! He just goes to that engine and LEAVES me!" Fan cried through her tears.

"Easy now, I can't see that's altogether fair. A man has a job and he gets his orders. I get mine and Jack gets his." Duke tried to comfort her.

"That's different, you are always home at night and he's away half the time! I hate to be alone at night!" Fan would not be consoled.

Duke's birthday party was a grand success until Jack had to leave for work. Although Fan said nothing, her anger was felt by all because she was seething inwardly. A few at a time, the guests thanked her for inviting them to the party and left.

Fan stood in the center of the rooms and cried, "Look at all this food! They didn't even stay to see you cut your cake! I hate them—I hate Jack—It's all HIS fault! He ruins all my fun!" Fan threw a fit of temper. She stamped her feet, flailed her arms and sobbed like a child.

Duke put his arms around Fan to calm and steady her. She pummeled his chest and screamed, "I hate him! I hate him!"

"Easy girl easy, I'm not the enemy." He held her firmly in his arms to stop her flailing.

Fan's anger subsided and she could feel his muscled body and his strength. Her soft body molded to his. She slipped her arms around his neck and clutched his thick hair. They kissed. Silently, her body begged and pleaded for his. His body answered quickly and strongly to her pleas. He gently lifted and carried her up stairs to his bed. Her clawing, scratching, writhing sort of love making aroused passions in Duke heretofore unknown. Her demands upon him were met over and over as if she would devour him until they both laid exhausted and spent . . .

The party was forgotten and it was as if Fan and Duke's night of love never existed. The only apparent change in the Lansure household was in Duke. He spent more and more time away from the house with his friends. Fan and Jack seemed the same because Jack wanted his marriage to work. He was with Fan as much as possible.

In June, Fan was certain she was going to have another child in December. Jack was delighted but Duke looked as if he had been struck. He took his guitar and went out to the porch to play in the soft summer night.

Months passed without incident except that Duke bought his bright, shiny new black roadster. Jack bought a new Stutz Bearcat and Fan made him return it for a Sedan. On December 19, 1927, Jason Clive Lansure was born. He was a big baby at nine pounds. Jack had a son. His pleasure in the boy was boundless. Jack had a boy and a girl and his life centered around them. Fan was an excellent mother and the children grew healthy and strong. At six months, Jason weighed as much as Marrilla who was just over two years.

That same June, Duke Lansure quit his railroad job, loaded his musical instruments into his new Ford roadster and with all he owned, left town. Rumor had it that he headed West for the Texas oil fields but no one knew for sure. Jack and Fan never spoke of him.

Christmas of 1928 was a disaster for the Lansure family. Jack's aging father, Jimmy, died December 1, and his beloved sister, Rose, age forty, died suddenly on the 16th. Jack despaired. In spite of the fact that Jack's mother, Ma'am, had come to stay a while, their Christmas was a sad one. The only happy faces in the household belonged to the children, Jason and Marrilla. Jason was toddling and learning to talk. He could not say Marrilla, it was 'Rilla' and 'Rilla it became to all, from then on.

Ma'am stayed until spring then returned to her home in the Pennsylvania hills.

Fan and Jack worked at the marriage and watched their family grow. 'Rilla was a precocious child and chattered like a magpie. She often used big words that did not fit or she did not understand. When her antics brought laughter, she would be most indignant. For example, 'Rilla dragged a chair to the sink to help Fan with the dishes. 'Rilla was washing them but not too thoroughly. After Fan had returned several still-messy items to the dishwater, 'Rilla said impatiently, "Mother, don't be so 'perpendicular'." Jack bought 'Rilla a pair of roller skates for her third birthday and she delighted in the sport so she learned quickly. Weather permitting, she rolled up and down the sidewalk with her friends, constantly.

Jason on the other hand, was more reticent. He had a big voice for a little fellow and he spoke in one or two word sentences. At times, it got him into trouble. For instance, the gas station across the street, had a glass case full of penny candies and he and 'Rilla made a purchase anytime they had the price. This day, Jason selected something pink, black and gooey. When Fan asked what he bought, he answered, "Horse Feathers."

"Jason what did you buy with your penny?" Fan repeated.

"Horse Feathers."

"Jason, don't SASS me." She was losing patience.

"Awh gee, Mom, Horse Feathers." he repeated and held up the wrapper.

In large black letters HORSE FEATHERS was printed on the wrapper.

"Oh I'm sorry, honey, THAT is the name of the candy. I thought you were being a naughty boy." Fan hugged her sticky son and he proceeded to enjoy the goo.

When ever possible Jason was found at Joe Porter's dairy barns. The courageous little fellow had already tried to climb Joe's silo. He had climbed up three or four rungs and fell. Joe found him unconscious and carried him home. The doctor could find nothing wrong with Jason and when he regained consciousness, he was fine.

This day, Jason had spent most of the morning tagging around after Joe while he milked, cleaned stalls and dropped hay. For Jason to reach the barns, he walked the path along the pasture line fence behind Jack's back yard. Suddenly, it began to cloud up and thunder crashed. Jason was terrified of electrical storms and began to race down the path toward home. The pasture fence was made of barbed wire. Jason tripped and fell head first along the fence. The barbs caught his head as he fell. Great gashes were torn into the flesh of his forehead at the top of his left eye and ran to his left ear.

Joe Porter had seen the child fall and ran to his side. Jason was covered with blood and was trying to wipe the blood from his left eye so he could see. Joe lifted the boy in his arms and ran, calling to Fan to get the doctor. She heard Joe shout and rang the doctor's office.

"Here Joe, lay him on the table and I'll get water and towels." Fan said calmly—she usually fell apart in a crisis.

"I think his eye is okay but that wire tore him up good. He got scared when the storm started the cows milling around." Joe said after a quick examination.

"Doc is on his way." Fan said and blotted the blood that flowed freely from Jason's wounds. The little one had stopped crying and sat quietly on the table while his mother tended him.

"In here Doc," Joe called out when he heard the doctor's car drive in.

Doctor Caine examined the boy and said, "Three of these tears are bad ones and I will have to clamp them. Lay him on his back and hold him still."

The patient child cried out only once while the doctor worked over him. The wounds were carefully sterilized, 15 shiny clamps closed the gaping cuts and over all, was placed a large dressing.

''Mix these powders in his milk twice a day and keep the bandage dry and clean. Tetanus—lockjaw, that is—can be dangerous and a rusty fence is a likely place to find it. I'll be back day after tomorrow to change the dressings. If he develops a fever before that—call me.'' The doctor's instructions were simple. He washed his hands, placed his surgical equipment in his bag and left.

Jack arrived at that moment from work.

''What is it Doc, who's sick?'' Jack was anxious.

''It's Jason, he fell along Porter's pasture line fence and tore himself up some. Don't worry, I clamped him up and he should be okay if infection doesn't set in from that rusty fence. I'll see him in a couple of days.'' The doctor got into his car and drove away.

Jack found Fan, Jason and Joe Porter at the kitchen table. Jason was having milk and cookies, as if nothing had happened and Fan and Joe were nervously trying to steady the coffee cups they were holding.

''Hey there, Buddy, the Doc tells me you got bunged up some.'' Jack knelt down beside his son at the table.

''See daddy, bannage!'' Jason was proud of his bandages.

''That's a lollapalooza!'' Jack exclaimed, ''How'd you get that?''

''I go home.'' Jason spoke well enough for his age, but he was more interested in the milk and cookies before him.

Joe Porter stood up and Jack took his hand, ''I don't know what to say, Jack, I feel real bad about this. He was around the barn with me all morning then I see him high-tailn' it up the path for home. A storm was brewing and the thunder cracked. He fell head long and when I got to him, he was covered with blood—I didn't know where he was hurt!''

''Don't worry, Joe, Doc says he'll be fine. He shouldn't be plaguing you at the barns anyway.'' Jack tried to erase Joe's misgivings.

''Oh, I like having him around but I guess a dairy farm is no place for a little one. I'm real sorry, Jack—Fan.'' Joe left by the back door.

''How bad is it Fan?'' Jack asked Fan. He noticed her hands were trembling.

''Doc says the barbs missed his eye by a fraction. He put 15 clamps in the worst cuts and said the rest would heal on their own. Oh, Jack he's so little and he's hurt bad.'' Fan reached for Jack and he held her.

''Don't cry, honey, kids get a lot of bumps before their grown. Doc says all we have to worry about now is Lockjaw. Joe stretched that fence last summer so I doubt is there is much chance of that.'' It's the old, rusty ones you have to be careful of.'' Jack comforted her but he was trying to reassure himself.

''I put half a teaspoon of the powders in his milk and he drank it all so I guess it doesn't taste bad.'' Fan was still weeping.

"Come on, son, lets go sit on the porch swing. I think you could do with a yarn and a nap." Jack took the child in his arms and went to the front porch and sat down on the big wooden swing. Still in his work clothes, Jack held and swung his precious boy back and forth in the swing. "A long time ago, there was a little fellow who stumped his toe on a BIG rock. . . ." There was no point to continue. The pleasant sound of Jack's baritone voice and the gentle swinging had lulled the small child to sleep. . . . .

1929 was another turning point in Jack's life. In October of 1929, the stock market crashed. Usually sane men leaped from tall buildings, off high bridges and under fast-moving trains. The country went mad. For the next few months, most of the people held their breath and marked time.

The AC&Y did it's best to hang on. Layoffs were many and crews were shifted from one place to another. Those with the most seniority held their jobs. Those with little, lost theirs. Jack had nearly ten years and it was enough to keep his job but not enough to keep him from being 'bumped'. A man with more years than Jack requested his job and got it and this 'bumped' Jack to another location. In turn, Jack 'bumped' someone elsewhere and so on. Jack 'bumped' into the East End and got the Akron yards.

Fan was inconsolable. That beautiful French Bungalow was her dream house and she refused to move. When told that she must move, she would throw outrageous temper tantrums. Besides, she would argue, who would buy their house, nobody had any money. Her argument was valid but Jack must find a way to sell and move his family by September of 1932 because 'Rilla would start school and they must be in Akron before then.

Jack knew Fan was right about folks having no money. Those who had managed to save a few dollars, lost it when the banks closed. Others had worthless passbooks to money they could not retrieve. Jack had friends and ideas.

Jack surmised that Sade had ready cash and planned to ask her if all else failed. Sidney Glasser was the local bootlegger and Jack knew he had a quick eye for a fast bargain.

Jack had already been 'bumped' and was gone most of the time. He and a real estate agent were scouring East Akron for a French Bungalow for Fan. A similar house would make the move less bitter for her. Since he had to be away, Jack gave Fan instructions to see Sid and explain the deal to him.

Fan was reluctant but realized she had no choice. Jack said they must get $1700.00 dollars and not a penny less. Fan made arrangements to meet Sid at Sade's for lunch to talk business.

Fan was a beautiful woman and her beauty never went unnoticed especially to Sid who had seen her several times before at Sade's. He was astonished when she called for the lunch date to talk. Sid was a rumpled fat man with hot hands, greasy hair and a stale cigar protruding from his flushed face. He watched Fan enter the speakeasy with hungry eyes.

"Fan you're more beautiful than ever. Motherhood agrees with you." Sid held her hand too long.

"Sid, I have a business proposition for you—just business." Fan withdrew her hand.

"Business—what kind of business? Have a chair." He held a chair for her at one of Sade's tables.

"I want to sell you my house." Fan said.

"Your HOUSE! Why?" Sid was flabbergasted.

"Because you are the only person in town with any cash." Fan stated flatly.

"Cash—me—what makes you think that?" He quizzed.

"Transactions in your business are always done in cash." She said.

"Pretty smart, aren't you." He remarked.

"No, just desperate. Jack was bumped to the East End and we have to sell out and move. We're asking $1800.00. I have the deed here and Jack has already signed. All it needs is my signature and the date." Fan showed him the paper.

"$1800.00! You only paid $1200.00 when you bought it. I remember when Bud Barkley built it!" Sid was surprised.

"That's true but real estate has gone up and we made a lot of improvements. We put in the lawn and trees, laid the driveway and planted all the hedges. Then there was all the curtains and blinds for the whole house and we paid extra for the fireplace." Fan remembered all that Jack had told her to say.

"Well it might be worth $1500.00 but no more, mind you." Sid was weakening.

"If we weren't in such a hurry, I'd ask around but we have to move by Labor Day and that's only two weeks away. We have to be in Akron when school starts because of 'Rilla." Fan explained.

"She's school age—already—'magine that! How about $1700?" He asked.

"$1800.00." She replied.

"$1750.00! Not a penny more—that's my last offer!" He was emphatic.

"DONE!" Fan held out her hand to Sid and he took it in both of his.

"Now we will have a nice lunch and I'll pay you later." His eyes gleamed.

"You pay now, Sade and Mushy can be our witnesses and we will have lunch after." Fan nodded to Sade and she agreed.

Reluctantly, Sid counted out the money on the table and Fan signed the deed. Sade and Mushy witnessed the transaction and Fan put the stack of bills in her purse.

"What's the special today, Sade and thanks for helping me." Fan said.

"My pleasure, Fancy Girl, it's roast of beef and the wine is on the house—or should I say—under the table. I think this is a celebration but I hate to see you move away." Sade said.

When the lunch was over Sid said, "May I drive you home? I'd like to SEE what I bought!" Fan knew the sleazy man had ulterior motives and it made her sick.

"No thanks, Jack will be home Saturday—come then. Besides I need the exercise." She said her goodbyes and left. . . .

Chapter Sixteen

THE DEPRESSION

The moving van was ready to roll. Jack loaded Fan and the children, Jason and Marrilla, into his Dodge Sedan and followed the van. Fan was depressed but the kids were excited.

''Fan, I'm so proud of you! You beat that slicker at his own game. You got $50.00 more than I asked you to get. I really only expected he would give you $1550.00 tops, the market being what it is today. When the chips are down—you're a real humdinger, honey!'' Jack's accolades were not having much affect on the disappointed Fan.

''Honey, when we get to Akron, I have a BIG surprise for you!'' Jack went on.

Fan acknowledged Jack's remarks but said nothing. She was one step from tears and continued to look back along the road that was taking her away from her dream home.

The big van rumbled over the road. It eventually lumbered across the Main street in Akron and pushed East.

''I found this nice house in East Akron. It's close to school, church and groceries and not far from the Yards. It's on a side street with lots of room for the kids to play. There are two bedrooms up and one down. The kitchen is smaller than you like but it has a breakfast nook and a big dining room.'' Jack tried to peak her interest but she just stared out of the window.

The moving van stopped and Fan drew in her breath. ''Is this it? It is almost like the Carey house!'' She cried.

''I knew you'd like it. I can't help that it's been painted brown instead of white, it is still a French Bungalow.'' Jack glowed with pride.

"Oh Jack, how did you ever find it! Let's go inside," Fan was her usual childlike self again.

"You go in, here's the key. I'll help the van get backed in." Jack was a happy man when Fan was pleased. There was one big difference between this house and the Carey house as this one was not for sale. It was rental only.

The house was more than Fan expected and the fact it was rented made no difference to her. The family settled in comfortably. The children made friends and all fell into a normal routine. Jack liked being back in Akron among his old friends. His new crew worked like a well-oiled machine.

Marrilla enjoyed school and did well. Jason dragged his stake-sided wagon everywhere. Fan made friends with the grocer's wife, the butcher's wife and the preacher's wife. Their lives were better than most.

The hard times caused the most suffering among the children. One evening, after Jack returned from work, 'Rilla ran to him. She threw herself into his arms as was her habit, with this quiet man she adored. "Daddy! Daddy! Look what I got!" 'Rilla held up two large, one-buckle-type overshoes.

"Where did you get those?" Jack was calm but surprised.

"A man came to school and he and the teacher gave them to me." She gleefully put them on.

"Why would they give them to YOU?" Jack asked of the happy child.

"They gave them to EVERYONE, silly. The man asked if I had any overshoes and I said 'NO' so he gave me these!" She was delighted with her prize.

Fan had overheard the conversation between 'Rilla and Jack and interceded.

"Jack, I tried to explain to her that the man was from the Welfare Board and those overshoes were for the needy children but she doesn't understand."

Jack took his seven year old daughter onto his lap and said, "Sweetheart, do you understand that when daddys don't work that sometimes there isn't enough money to buy all the things a family needs and some children have to 'go without'?" Jack asked.

"I remember Imogene Kronen's daddy didn't work—he was sick. Imogene could have peanut butter on her bread, or jelly on her bread or butter on her bread but not all three at once. She liked to come to our house 'cause Mom always put all three on our bread." So sheltered and protected was young 'Rilla that this was her idea of deprivation.

"Well, that's pretty good," Jack hugged his child, "but there are children who's daddys have no money to buy overshoes so charity buys them. Tomorrow you and I will take the overshoes back to school so some needy child will have a pair."

"Then I won't have any and I'll be needy." 'Rilla's eyes filled with tears and Jack's heart broke.

"First, I promise we will go to the shoe store and buy you a pair just like these—then we will go to school and give them back." Jack could not bear to see her cry.

"Oh daddy, I love you!" Rilla hugged her father's neck and slid from his lap. "Momma, daddy's gonna buy me another pair just like these and I won't be needy anymore!" The happy child ran off to play.

Fan leaned on the doorjamb and said, "Is there ANYTHING you will deny that child?" She was pleased at Jack's decision to buy the overshoes and smiled.

"Nope!" Jack stated with finality and grinned.

The next morning, Jack and 'Rilla went into the shoe store for the overshoes. They bought the exact style, the exact color and 'Rilla beamed with pleasure. Outside on the street, 'Rilla clung to Jack's forefinger with one hand and clutched her prize with the other. Jack gave her his exaggerated eye wink that drew up the side of his lip and smiled. It was the loving assurance the small child lived for. His approval was the most important thing in her life. It gave her strength, courage and purpose. Jack adored the curly-headed, moon-faced child at his side and he let her know it.

At the school 'Rilla took her seat among the other children and Jack talked to the teacher, Miss Johnson, who was a dead ringer of our perceptions of a school teacher. She was bespectacled, neat, clean and lean.

"I've come to return these overshoes. Marrilla did not understand that they were for more needy children. Please excuse her. I bought her a pair and these belong to you." Jack handed the overshoes to the surprised teacher.

"That's very nice of you, Mr. Lansure, but it wasn't necessary. We had enough pairs to go around." Said the teacher.

"It was necessary for ME. I always 'haul my own freight." Jack stated flatly over a firm jaw. Jack was a proud man and silently prayed he and his would never need charity. He studied the children in the room that surrounded his daughter.

Miss Johnson noticed his preoccupation with the children and asked, "Is there anything wrong, Mr. Lansure. You seem worried." She asked with concern.

"In all my life, I have never seen such a group of pale, undernourished children." He said.

"Yes, it is disturbing. In hard times, the little ones suffer the most. Many of the father's of these children have no work and their children can't eat properly. All the milk they receive in a day, was what we used to provide for them." She explained.

"The milk you used to provide—why not now?" Jack inquired.

"The milk fund has run out. There is just no money anywhere now. We gave each child milk twice a day. A ½ pint in the morning and a ½ pint in the afternoon. Growing children need more than that but most of them got little or none at home. Their resistance is down and many suffer from colds, diarrhea and rickets. They have little vitality or learning capacity. I expect this Depression will get worse before it gets better and their suffering will go on." She said softly and shook her head.

"Who's in charge of the milk fund—who started it? Jack asked.

"The Welfare people and now they are strapped, too. The overshoes came from a private donor—not the Welfare." She said.

"A private donor—that means the people raised the money by having a bake sale or fish fry—like that." Jack persisted.

"Yes, some kind of fund-raiser or perhaps a gift from a wealthy philanthropist." She said.

"Thank you very much Miss Johnson, you'll be hear'in from me." Jack gave a left-handed salute to 'Rilla and left the school.

Jack had a couple of hours to kill before he must call for 'Rilla again so he went directly to the church rectory and Reverend Morton Armbruster.

"Mort, how are ya?" Jack asked.

"Good Jack, good. How are you? You're not laid off are you?" Asked the concerned clergyman.

"Naw, nothing like that. I just take a couple of days off now and then, to give another engineer a chance to work a few days. Many of my friends are out of regular work and working the extra board can't hardly feed a family." Jack explained.

"You should be commended for that, son." The aging preacher clapped Jack on the back.

"I didn't come here for THAT. I have a problem that I think you can help me with." Jack answered.

"I'm always willing to help where I can." The preacher said.

"Did you know the school milk fund has run out and those half-starved kids get no milk at all?" Jack asked.

"I heard about it—some time ago—I think. There is no money anywhere." he stated.

"Well, Mort, I got an idea how we can replenish the milk fund if you will help. The church basement will seat fifty people—that right?" Jack asked.

"More like seventy five at one time." He stated.

"What's the most the Ladies Aid Society has ever cooked for?" Jack inquired.

"Why 500 I think it was. For a Labor Day Celebration. We made wieners, sauerkraut and dumplings—that was two wieners a plate—and white sheet cake for dessert." Mort said.

"How many pounds of meat did you need?" Jack quizzed.

"If I remember correctly somewhere around one hundred pounds. Butch Walters made them up special and gave them to us at his cost. Just what are you getting at, Jack?" He asked.

"Will your Ladies do a lot of cookin' for a good cause?" Jack went on.

"Sure, they always pull together when the need arises." The Reverend was confused.

"Great! Hunting season opens in two weeks and that will give me just enough time." Jack seemed pleased.

"Enough time to do what?" The impatient man asked.

"If I can gather up EVERYTHING you need to make a plate dinner for 500 people will you cook and serve it?" Jack still evaded the question.

"Well, I suppose the Ladies would agree, for a good cause. Is this for the milk fund? What do we cook? It would have to be cafeteria style." The Reverend was still confused.

"Venison! A venison dinner fund-raiser to replenish the milk fund. Cafeteria style will be 'jake'. I'll go down to my home in Pa. and get the deer. I'm sure Butch Walters would dress and cut it into roasts for us. I'll bet Sam Collins would supply flour, sugar and maybe, canned goods. Barney Otis will give ya the shirt off his back, if he's got it. He will find onions, potatoes and greens from his produce market. I'll ask the B of L E (Brotherhood of Locomotive Engineers) for a few dollars for coffee, tea and spices." If I ask, my Mason brothers will furnish apples for the pies. If my luck holds, the dairy will supply the milk, cream and butter and maybe, ice cream for the pie. I'll let you know how I make out. You pick any date after deer season, for the dinner. Thanks Mort, I'll be seeing you." Jack shook the Reverend's hand and left the rectory.

Jack went to everyone and explained his plan. All the merchants and organizations were generous. He even got ice cream for the pie. When the local newspaper heard the plan, they ran the announcement and the menu, free of charge:

ROAST VENISON DINNER

$1.00 Mashed Potatoes and Gravy $1.00

Vegetables Greens Rolls

$1.00 Apple Pie A la mode $1.00

Coffee and Tea

Serving Saturday from 3:00 PM until gone.
Food donated by local merchants and organizations.
Cooking and Baking done by Ladies Aid Society.
Located in Brethren Church Basement

When hunting season opened and Jack was about to leave for Pennsylvania and his home, 'Rilla was the most excited. Jack loaded his gear and guns into his car, kissed Fan and Jason and explained he would be gone only as long as it took to get the deer. 'Rilla hugged his neck then watched him drive away. She understood what he was doing for the children and she nearly burst with pride.

At home, in the hills of Pa., Jack hugged his mother and they talked. He explained what he was doing. She cooked him a meal and saw him up to his room to rest.

Before dawn, he was hiking the woods. It was windy, raw and cold but there was no snow for tracking. He roamed the familiar hills until dark and went home. The next three days were the same. No tracks—no deer. He called Fan and told her to call the Yards and mark him off for a couple of more days. Fan was worried because Jack had caught a bad cold.

Two more days passed and no deer. Jack was desperate. Many people were hungry and the hills were hunted out.

Late afternoon of the last day, Jack had tramped around for what seemed endless hours with no sightings. Suddenly, he found himself in his very own 'Quiet Place'. Naw, can't be, that's miles from here, but it was. He had walked much further than he realized. How strange he felt, in this treasured place of his youth. Li'l Dan's tree stump had long since decayed but Jack looked for it anyway, for reasons he could not explain.

It began to snow great fluffy flakes of white that quickly covered the ground. As if by apparition, a huge buck deer stood forty feet away, about on the place where Li'l Dan's stump used to be. The magnificent animal stood stalk still and stared at Jack through the falling snow. So surprised was Jack, to see the deer standing there, he almost forgot to fire. Jack regained his wits, in an instant and with one shot through the shoulder, the animal fell where he stood.

Where had the deer come from—which direction—there were no tracks in the snow from any direction. Again, Jack wondered if this was a magical place that he thought of as a boy.

His heart pounded happily as he field dressed the deer. This huge animal would, indirectly, restore many frail children to health. The big buck was a perfect specimen with ten points. Jack staggered under it's weight and half dragged and half carried the deer out of the woods. The day had grown much colder but Jack had not noticed. He sweated from the exertion of his task. His chills and exhaustion vanished the instant he saw the deer. Accomplishment and success are the world's best tonic.

Ma'am had the evening meal ready when Jack returned and marveled at her son's appetite. All week he had just picked at his food. He ate like a starving man but declined another night's stay. His mission was accomplished and he must return to family and job. Ma'am understood and hugged her son, goodby. She watched with pride and happiness as he drove away with his prize deer tied securely to the fender.

The trip back to Akron was uneventful but tiresome. At home Jack put his car in the garage. He left the unloading for tomorrow except for his guns. The deer was perfectly safe on the fender because it was frozen stiff from the long ride in the cold.

He crept into the house and upstairs as quietly as possible but Fan heard him. She raised up on one elbow and called, "Oh honey, I'm so glad you're home!"

"Shush, I don't want to wake the kids to see the deer 'til I get some shut-eye, I'm bushed." Jack whispered and touched his wife.

"Oh, you're cold as a clam! Get in here and get warm." Jack slid into Fan's arms and nearly as soon as his head hit the pillow he slept soundly.

The next morning Jason was so excited about the deer he went to the garage for a peak in his pajamas. Fan snatched him back inside for clothes and breakfast. 'Rilla was more interested to see her father. She opened the bedroom door a crack to see her sleeping hero. He got a deer for the children. She closed the door ever so quietly and went softly down stairs. Jack had heard her and smiled. He rolled over and fell back to sleep.

Later Jack took Jason and 'Rilla in the car to deliver the deer to the slaughterhouse and to the railroad yards to mark up.

'Rilla stood close to Jack while the butcher hung the big deer on a chain hoist that moved from place to place and weighed it. She found this place smelly and unpleasant. On the other hand, Jason was fascinated by the busy men there, skinning, cutting and slicing. He inspected everything.

"He's a beauty Jack." Butch Walters said to Jack after a quick examination. "He weighs 160 pounds gutted and probably weighed 200 on the hoof. He will make a lot of roast venison. I'll bring you the rack but what about the extra bones and hocks?''

''Give them all to the church, they will see it gets to the soup kitchens around here.'' Were Jack's instructions.

The day of the dinner arrived. The Ladies had worked for three days to bake pies, make rolls, prepare vegetables and roast huge pans of venison.

Jack loaded Fan and the kids into the car to go to the church and 'buy' their share of the dinner. People had gathered around the church and the basement was full. Fan and Jack stood in the cafeteria line and paid the same as everyone. All children paid less than the dollar expected. Fan and Jack lingered over their coffee and talked with friends.

Reverend Mort spotted Jack and Fan and waved. He stood at the end of the long table where Jack and Fan sat and shouted ''Ladies and gentlemen, may I have your attention! I want to thank you for coming and tell you that we have taken just under $200.00 and there IS more venison to sell!'' The bones made 20 gallons of soup for the kitchens. The noisy crowd clapped and shouted. ''Now I want to introduce the man who made all this possible! He shot the deer you are eating!'' The crowd roared again. ''Ladies and gentlemen—Jack Lansure and his family—stand up Jack and take a bow!'' The Reverend shouted and the crowd gave Jack's family a thunderous standing ovation. Jack blushed red and wished he could hide, he hated such whoopla. Fan was in her glory, she loved all the attention and dragged Jack to a stand. He nodded to the people. 'Rilla was the proudest of all. Her daddy was a great man and she beamed. Jason enjoyed the whole show and bowed from the waist. As soon as possible, Jack dropped into his chair and told Fan it was time to go. He wanted out of the limelight. It was not easy to move through the crowd of well-wishers and away from the accolades. Jack had done a fine thing for his community but to him it did not require all this fuss.

There was a nice write-up in the paper and the milk fund was restored for two more years. The needy children would have milk again and that was what Jack thought important and it made him happy.

Time passed. The cold Jack caught while hunting for the deer, got worse. He coughed incessantly and he lost weight. When Jack caught a cold it hung on for weeks.

Fan tried to comfort him but she was depressed. She missed her Carey friends and found difficulty keeping friends here. She did not know the reason but she did not fit in.

In the spring, Fan knew she was going to have another child in October. She was neither pleased or displeased but complained that no doctor would be as good as Doc Caine.

Jack was delighted at the thoughts of another child but was troubled about his finances. It cost much more to live in Akron than it did in Carey and Fan still spent his money as fast as he made it.

The local doctor was adequate but this time Fan had serious complications. Kidney problems plagued her along with weakness and stomach upsets. Drake Glen Lansure was born October 9, 1934. Little Drake was a very difficult birth with long painful hours and much bleeding. Fan was bedridden. Jack hired a woman to help with the house and the children but the bills skyrocketed.

By Christmas, Fan was better but not well. Fortunately with the bedroom downstairs she could rest and still tend to 'Rilla and Jason as well as little Drake. Come spring Fan was recovering although little Drake was a colicky baby and sapped most of her regained strength, but the family managed. When the infant slept Fan could rest. 'Rilla now nine, was a big help to her mother and seven year old Jason was more or less, self-sufficient.

One warm day, Fan lighted the oven to prepare a meal. Suddenly, little Drake began to cry in the bedroom and Fan went to tend him. She breast-fed him and changed his nappes.

From the kitchen Fan smelled something hot. Oh God she thought—the skillet in the oven—she forgot to remove the iron skillet she kept there when she lighted the oven. She put the baby in his crib ran to the kitchen and threw open the oven door. She grabbed the smoking skillet dropped it into the sink and turned on the water. The grease exploded! It flew onto the walls, cupboards and the curtains burst into flame at the window over the sink! Fan screamed in pain and terror!

A neighbor outside in his yard heard her screams and saw the smoke. The quick-thinking man grabbed his fire extinguisher and raced to Fan's aid. He put out the fire quickly. The woodwork around the window, on the cupboards and at the sink was scorched and blistered. The curtains were completely destroyed but there was no serious structural damage.

Fan had several burn spots on her arms and face from the flying grease and was hysterical and frightened but otherwise unharmed. The kindly man tried to calm her and explain that water is the worst thing to put on a grease fire. Use table salt, play box sand or even flour but never water.

All that Fan gained health wise was lost with the fire. Shock and guilt put her back in bed. Jack was devastated, he could have lost his whole family. His financial status fell again with the house repairs and more doctor bills.

When Jack went to pay the rent at the end of the Month, the landlord informed him that he had one month to get out. His reasons were that Fan was too sick and too irresponsible to tend the house and children. Jack and his family were being evicted! What would he do—where would he go? Rentals were very expensive and there was little to choose from. Be out in one month—impossible! What would be the next calamity? The whole world was mourning the death of Will Rodgers and Wiley Post.

Jack posted an ad in the yard office and asked his railroad buddies to look around for a house that he could afford. Again they came through for him. They found him a house on Graham Avenue a few blocks away and still within walking distance to school for the kids.

It was near 'Dead Man's Curve' so named for the bad curve in the main thoroughfare where so many had lost their lives in automobile crashes. At normal speed, it was impossible to negotiate the sharp turn and there was inadequate warning.

'Rilla and Jason enjoyed the change but for Fan and Jack it was chaos. The little house had only two bedrooms—both up. The packing had to be done by the movers because Fan was too ill and Jack could not afford to miss work. They broke her dishes, cracked the bedroom mirror and damaged her precious piano. Some of her furniture had to be stored in the damp basement because it would not fit in the tiny house.

The family managed the winter but Fan was miserable. Little Drake was frail and cranky and absorbed most of Fan's time. She regained her health reasonably and Jack was keeping his head above water financially.

The news came without warning; Jack was 'bumped' again to a place called New London. Fan shrieked!

Once again Fan and Jack had to pack up and move. This time Fan had to do the house hunting. Grandma Saddler came for a week to watch the children while Fan went to New London to search.

Rent was cheaper in New London but rentals were scarce. With help from the local people, Fan found a house for rent on Park Avenue. It to, was too small for the family—with only two bedrooms—but they made do. When 'Rilla and Jason were out of school the Lansures moved to New London.

Just when things seemed to straighten out and get better, Grandma and Grandpa Saddler had to move in with Jack and Fan. Hard times had closed the church and they were both in poor health. Again, the little house was much too small. Temporarily, the Saddlers slept on a bed in the dining room. Again Jack and Fan looked for a larger house. They found one on Third Street and moved again.

This time, things were better. The house had several bedrooms up, a privacy stairs, a formal dining room, a bedroom down and the most beautiful woodwork Fan had ever seen. It was not a French bungalow but it was close enough and Fan loved it. There was space for a garden and the outbuildings could house a milk cow. The Saddlers were comfortable, Jack had lots of friends around town and Fan was content. This was important since she was carrying another child. All went well until the spring of 1936.

Jack's sister, Louisa Eunice Lansure Montgomery, died of Consumption (Tuberculosis). Jack took 'Rilla and Jason and went to the funeral in Pennsylvania. Fan was too ill to travel and remained behind with Drake.

Jack faced his grief alone. Lu had been sickly all her life but when death comes, it is never welcome. Ma'am's health was poorly also and it added to his worry.

At home once more his spirits lifted. Jannell Agnes Lansure was born June 20, 1936. He loved his children above all things and let it be known. Tiny Jannell was Fan's smallest birth. She was a quiet, happy baby with auburn curls and soft eyes. Jack was delighted, he had two boys and two girls.

Up to this time, 'Rilla had several attacks of appendicitis and Doc Jones advised surgery to remove her appendix. While 'Rilla was in the hospital, Fan ran back and forth to look after 'Rilla and to breast-feed Jannell at home. Fan's physical health was only so-so but her mental health and depression was a serious worry to Jack. Simply being alive placed a strain on her. To Jack, she was distant, vague and detached with fits of uncontrollable weeping. Everyone assumed it was a bad case of the 'After Birth Blues' and overlooked it.

'Rilla's recovery was a constant concern to Doc Jones. She walked bent over from the adhesions and was pale and listless. Doc spent a month each year on his yacht at the Vermilion Lagoons and the time was now. Doc and his wife Hortense, agreed to take the ailing ten year old with them rather than delay their vacation. At the end of a week 'Rilla had progressed enough to return home but her recovery was unusually slow. Jack's bronchitis was no better and the Doc worried about them both.

The nation-wide drought continued and again the country mourned the loss of one of her greats. Amelia Earhart was lost at sea.

One day, Jack came home from work all excited. He told the family that there was a 17 acre farm for sale about two miles northeast of town and it was in his price range. Jack explained the country was the place for folks to grow old and for children to grow up. He also explained there was no electricity, no running water and the outhouse was some distance from the house. At the time, those things seemed unimportant if the family could own their home again and the authorities promised the electric 'was coming' but no one knew when.

Fan and her children had never been without a bathroom, electric lights or a furnace. With four children and four adults to cook for, clean up after and wash by hand for, Fan was overwhelmed. The cistern was low and water had to be carried from the barn to the woodshed for washing. Fan's electric stove and her electric washing machine sat idly by gathering dust while Fan labored over a washboard and tub.

Frail Drake fell seriously ill. His symptoms were vague and Doc Jones was perplexed. 'Rilla lost weight, coughed and could keep nothing in her stomach. Jack's bronchitis grew worse. Jack and 'Rilla had been exposed to the disease when they attended Jack's sister, Louisa's funeral. They had tuberculosis. Both were in the early stages and contagion was possible but unlikely, fortunately none of the other members of the family contacted the dread disease. With rest, special diet and treatment, the doctor assured Fan and Jack that 'Rilla would recover. For Jack it may be another story. He had to work and could not go to a dryer climate or stay home and rest. He did however, take as much time off as he dared, followed the treatment instructions and made the best of it.

The railroad had it's problems also. It was plagued constantly by theft, vandalism and arson. The hobos, bums and free-hitchers broke the seals on the 'reefers' (refrigerator cars) causing thousands of dollars in waste and spoilage. They set fires in cattle cars for warmth, that ultimately went out of control and destroyed the entire car.

In spite of the great numbers of 'Cinder Dicks' (Special Railroad Detectives), the losses to the railroads were huge in addition to the hard times and the depressed economy.

The train crews were given special orders to discourage the bums, hobos and free-riders at all cost, although many were not low-lifes but desperate men going from town to town in search of work.

One afternoon while Jack was dragging his local from Delphos to New London and outside of Plymouth, he saw a trackman signaling frantically for him to stop. Jack let his train roll to a stop and set the brakes.

"What's up, Bob?" Jack called from the cab window.

"Somethin' bad Jack, real bad! A new shack (brakeman) on the East bound Freight spotted a 'bo (short for hobo) hitchin' a ride on the rods. (The under braces of a railroad car.) He let out a tie spike, knocked the guy off the rods and the train cut him to pieces." Bob Grafton was a shack on the East bound also.

"Holy Hell Bob, who'd use that Devil's Iron on a human?" Jack shouted and dropped to the ground from the engine cab.

A tie spike also called a 'Bo Knocker', a ' 'Lynch' Pin', a 'Bum Club' or a 'Dead Beat Duster'. What ever it's name, it was a lethal weapon. It was a twelve inch long, two inch thick solid iron bar with a hole in one end to attach a long rope. The devilish device is let out under a moving train to bounce up and down on the ties underneath slamming, banging and leaping as it bounced along with the ferocity of a ball peen hammer.

A poor unsuspecting man clinging to the rods, was unprotected and would be mercilessly pummeled by the iron bar. At best, the vicious blows would break a man's bones as he hung precariously to the undercarriage. At worst, it would cause a man to lose his grip and fall under the moving train wheels to his death.

The two men hurried to the scene of the tragedy. Many trainmen and curiosity seekers had arrived and stood around talking in hushed tones.

"What the hell happened here, Claudy?" Jack asked of the freight train conductor Claude Long, called Claudy.

"New man—terrible Jack, terrible. Nobody knows the 'bo and he had nothing on him to tell us. You want to have a look and see if you know him? It's ugly."

"All right, the railroad had to know who he is." Jack steeled himself for the horrible sight under the cover. "AAAAGH!" Jack threw his head back and wailed like a banshee.

"My God Jack, do you know this man?" Claudy cried.

"Hell yes! And so do you!" Jack struggled to get a grip on himself. It's Hattie Sutton's grandson, Oliver! Olly's just a kid—you hear? Just a KID!" Jack's grief overcame his composure and he shook with pain and anger.

"Oh, for Christ's sake—I didn't recognize him!" Claudy groaned.

"How could you—how could anyone? Where's the brainless bastard that did this?" Jack raged.

"The 'Cinder Dicks' took him into custody until this mess is cleared up. Jack, he was just follow'in orders. The company don't want the 'bos on the trains." Claudy tried to explain.

"Orders—orders! That's not an order, it's a death sentence! That boy was on his way to Celeryville to take a job with the harvest. He told me about it a couple of weeks back when I saw him at the water tipple. He just turned sixteen and he's all Hattie has left. How in the hell are you gonna' tell her THIS?" Jack whispered. Jack's voice had dropped and was hardly audible. He wiped his face with his bandanna, "That kind of news could kill her—she's up in years." Jack gathered his composure, drew himself up to his full height and growled, "If I ever hear tell that any member of MY crew uses that cursed weapon on MY trains, I will PERSONALLY crack their skulls with it! You men hear me?" Jack snarled. He was sick with rage and frustration.

"Jack, ya can't mean that! These guys have orders to keep the 'bos off anyway they can. It's terrible but it's a RULE." Claudy's words fell on deaf ears.

The crew members muttered, shook their heads and went back to work. The wrong person overheard Jack's threat and the repercussions were yet to come.

The more the story was told, the more it was exaggerated. 'Jack Lansure won't take orders.' 'Jack Lansure can't take orders'. 'Jack Lansure disobeyed orders!. 'Jack Lansure wants to run the railroad his way,' and so on. By the time the tale reached the higher-ups in the main office, he had been made out to be a 'Rogue Engineer'. When the story reached the Trainmaster, A. W. Harnsberg, Jack's goose was cooked. A. W. hated everyone and delighted in hurting those who worked under him.

In spite of the fact that Road Formen, J. W. Kersey and F. D. Small and Train Master, W. E. Rauls went to bat for Jack, the wheels of insubordination began to grind. There was a set progression of steps that led to formal disciplinary action and it had been set in motion. A hearing date had been set for August 16, 1937 and Jack was suspended from his job until further notice. At that time, a month without pay alone was bitter punishment. With a family to feed and himself and two children sick, it could mean his financial ruin. The widespread drought continued and the heat was debilitating.

At home, Jack tried to rest and enjoy his children. He adored his flock and they gave him will and purpose. For the first time in a long time, Jack could take his children for walks in the woods, tell them yarns and help Fan with the sick ones. His own health improved with rest and quiet.

Generally, the farm work and the livestock was tended by Grandpa Sadler. Now, there was nothing to share-crop because of the long drought and the hogs and sheep had been sold off. The beautiful matched set of Belgian horses were gone and all that remained was a brood mare named June Rose and a milk cow called Daisy. By fall, the last of the animals would be gone including the children's pet buck sheep called Dunny and a pet pig named Honey. Nothing grew in the fields and little in the garden. The kids did not want to part with their pets but understood it was necessary. Their sale would provide hay and grain for the cow, coal for winter and school clothes for Jason and 'Rilla. June Rose was about to foal and that money would help Jack pay the huge doctor bills.

Just when Jack thought that nothing else could go wrong, Grandpa Sadler rushed in to tell the family there was something very wrong with June Rose. Quickly they summoned the best veterinarian in the county, Glasco Jenson. He doctored all of the family's livestock over the years, although he drank heavily, it never interfered with his work. After several frantic telephone calls to Glas, Jack jumped into the car and drove to his home/office. The usually brilliant vet was in a drunken stupor and was of no use to himself or anyone.

By the time Jack found another vet it was too late. Although he worked over the mare for hours, the foal was born dead and a short time later June

Rose died. The family grieved as if they had lost a family member. June Rose had been with them for years. Jack had lost a prized animal and the financial boon he expected.

The day before Jack's hearings, Fan and the kids took him to the station to catch the East bound passenger and saw him off. 'Rilla was too old to cling to his finger but she stood close and her eyes filled with tears. Jack smoothed the curl from her temple and twisted it around her ear as he had often done before. He gave her that exaggerated eye wink of his and smiled. To 'Rilla, it meant all would be well. She and Jason hugged Jack's waist, watched as he tossed his old valise onto the train platform and climb up after it.

No one knew how long the hearings would take and the family went back to the farm to wait. 'Rilla was gaining her health back but Drake was losing ground.

In Akron at the hearings, Jack listened to all that was said about him good and bad. There was not a breath of air outside and the heat in the room had reached the nineties.

One of the Three-Judge-Panel spoke, "John Clellend Lansure, you have heard all that has been said in these proceedings, do you have anything to say in your own behalf?" The Judge said without emotion.

"Yes sir, I do." Jack stood up at the table where he had been sitting and faced the Judges.

"The Defendant may proceed," added the Judge.

"Well Sir, I never disobeyed an order in my life and I've never knowingly killed a man," Jack began and a murmur went up in the room.

"Order! Order in the court!" The Judge shouted and banged his gravel.

"All my life I've tried to haul my own freight, keep my nose clean and try not to judge others too quickly. I know what it is to feel responsible directly or indirectly, for another person's death. To feel the pain and misery that comes with guilt because your actions caused a death, even if you were far away and did not know it 'til later. To know, in your heart, that if you had done things differently, that person might still be alive." Jack paused and tried to swallow the lump in his throat. The pain of Jenny's death never left him. "I could never allow that to happen to me again. As sure as I'm standing here, the use of a deadly tie spike would make ME responsible for the death of a man if it was used by one of my CREW. I understand that the bums and 'bos do a lot of damage and we chase 'um when we see 'um but to use that iron club would be the same as killin' 'um. I can't do it—I can't kill a man. I thank you for listen'in to me." Jack sat down and a murmur went up again.

"Order! Mr. Lansure you may go home now. The findings of this board will be sent in writing to your home by registered mail in a few days. Thank you." The Judge said.

"Thank you, Sir." Jack said and left for home.

What Jack did not know and could not see was a lone spectator at a door in the back of the great room. Just as Jack was about to speak, the President of the AC&Y, Bart Stewart, who had hired Jack, had stepped into the room and heard all that Jack said. He slipped in and out and Jack never knew he was there. He would not know until much later that Bart had saved his job and his career.

The city heat drained everyone and the air was thick enough to slice. Jack caught the West bound passenger train home and was relieved to get out into the country again. It was beastly hot but there was a slight breeze.

He dropped off the train when it slowed at the edge of town and walked cross-lots through the fields to his farm.

Fan knew when the passenger was due and watched for Jack each day. She saw him coming and was relieved.

"Rilla, run see if there are any ripe tomatoes in the garden, your Dad is coming!" Fan called.

"Jason, gather what eggs there are!" Were her instructions.

The two screamed with delight and ran to see if they could spot him across the fields. When they saw him, they ran to do their assigned chores.

"Oh Jack, I'm so glad you're home, it's Drake, he's so sick. Doc said he would talk to us both soon as you got home." She was too preoccupied with the sick child to ask about Jack's hearing and went to use the telephone.

Jack sat down on the big swing in the cool shade of the porch. Jason and 'Rilla finished their tasks and ran shouting and laughing onto the porch and into their father's arms.

"Daddy! Daddy! They shouted.

"I got two tomatoes for you and Mom saved the lemons for your lemonade." 'Rilla held up her prize.

"Here's four eggs for ya Dad," Jason shouted. He was careful not to crush them.

"Well, look at that! I thought there was nothin' left in the garden or in the hen house. We'll eat good tonight! Here you two, sit by me and cool off." Jack said to his children.

"Tell us a yarn Daddy, please," 'Rilla pleaded.

"Yea Dad, tell us one." said Jason.

"Well now, let's see. It was hot like this one day, when I was about your age, Jas——————" Jack began the tales that held his children spellbound.

Fan came out onto the porch with Jannell in her arms, very quietly as not to break the spell, to sit in the big wicker rocking chair and rock the toddler.

Before the story was quite finished, a dirty, torn, rusty, old black roadster rolled into the driveway and ground to a stop. A tall, painfully thin, aging man got out. He looked around and smiled at Jack and Fan.

"Duke!" Fan whispered and drew in her breath.

"Jesus! What now?" Jack hissed softly.

They were not prepared for what they saw. The brand new, shiny roadster was a wreck. Duke himself was an old man. He was bone thin with a weather-beaten, lined, pale face and his gorgeous black curly hair was streaked with white and bushy-looking. Jack and Fan stepped off the porch to greet him.

"It's been a long time, Duke," Jack spoke and they shook hands.

"Ten years" Duke said, "Fan, you both look well and this sure is a nice farm." Duke observed.

"Duke, you remember 'Rilla and Jason. Kids, this is your Uncle Duke he's been away." Fan's mouth was cotton dry.

"Hi Uncle Duke." They shook his hand and ran off to play.

"This is Jannell and Drake is inside, he's real sick, mother's with him." Fan tried to be gracious.

"Come up and set a spell out of the hot sun. You on your way home? Mother is poorly and she will be glad to see you." Jack was ill at ease.

"Thanks, I'm just passen' through. I stopped to see Joe Polo and he told me you lived out here. He asked me to supper and spend the night with him. I used to work for him, years ago." Duke looked tired.

"Yes, I remember." Jack said thoughtfully.

"You two talk, I'll make some lemonade." Fan fled into the house with Jannell.

"You say mother's poorly—I didn't know that. I've come home because I'm all burned out myself. They told me I should go to a Vet's Hospital and find out what ails me. I can't shake this cough and at times I'm too weak to sneeze. The oil fields are a hell of a place for weak lungs." Duke said thoughtfully. "Jason is a strappin' healthy kid. It's good to see him—all of you." Duke went on.

Fan brought the lemonade, set it on the table for the men and went back inside. The men drank the lemonade and talked for some time then Duke said goodbye to them and drove away.

Fan and Jack watched him drive off and Fan said, "Doc Jones will be here as soon as he closes his office for the day." They said nothing about Duke's unexpected visit.

They went inside to spell Grandma Saddler who had been sponging the small, wasted body of the little boy. The child was in and out of consciousness and was being fed intravenously through his ankles. The little thing had been rolling his head from side to side for so long the hair was worn from his head and there were sores on both ears. His condition was critical.

When Doc arrived, he explained to Jack and Fan that the child needed a pediatrician, a child specialist. Doc did all he knew to do but it wasn't enough. The best one was a Doctor Mills of Cleveland and it would cost one hundred dollars for the Doctor to come this far regardless whether the child survived or not.

Jack and Fan were stunned at the cost but asked Doc Jones to bring him as quickly as possible. They would scrape up the money somewhere.

Three days later the Doctors Jones and Mills arrived with a nurse, to treat Drake. They brought equipment and instruments and set it all up in Drake's room.

It was only ten A.M. but it was already °80 degrees. Fan and Grandma Saddler made fresh cucumber sandwiches, new buttermilk, custard pies and tea for the guests and placed them in the fruit cellar to cool. Doc Jones said the treatment would take several hours and Fan would serve what she had.

The three worked over the sick child behind closed doors. The nurse came out to the kitchen pump for water several times, otherwise the family saw no one.

The family sat on the porch and waited and waited and waited.

Fan fed Jannell and put her down for a nap. 'Rilla and Jason ate and went back to the river to swim. No one else could eat.

Shortly after two P.M. the three came out of Drake's room and washed up at the pump. Doctor Mills began, "Mr. and Mrs. Lansure, I've done everything I can for your child. He's been sick a long time and I don't know if he has the strength he needs to fight on."

"What are his chances? Please Doctor, we have to know." Jack pleaded.

"His bowels have been paralyzed for at least ten days or two weeks. What we did today was to try to get them to move again; to stimulate his intestinal tract. It looks to me that nothing in that little boy is functioning and we have to change that. If we did our jobs, this is what will happen. Watch him constantly, get him to take water and juices—no milk—no food. Sponge him from time to time and keep him comfortable. About ten forty five or eleven tonight, you will hear a rumbling—a gurgling from the boy. This is good. About midnight his bowels will move. He will eliminate diapers full of very unpleasant, smelly, black feces and his urine will be dark and rank. This is what you must do. Do not use diapers. Use clean rags, torn sheeting, shirt tails, underwear legs or anything that you can burn. As soon as he eliminates, remove the makeshift diaper and burn it at once, being careful not to touch the matter inside. To answer your question Mr. Lansure, about fifty-fifty. If his bowels move by midnight, chances are good that he will live. If they do not, he won't last 'til morning. He will sleep now.'' The exhausted Doctor wiped his sweating face with a white linen handkerchief.

''Thank you, Doctor Mills. Will ya have a bite to eat? Fan made sandwiches and buttermilk.'' Jack asked.

''Buttermilk—fresh churned buttermilk? I'd be delighted! I haven't had any in years.'' The doctor was pleased.

They all gathered around the dining room table and ate. Later, when they were about to leave, Jack said, ''I'm sorry that I can't pay you all at once but I will pay you ten dollars a month until it's paid. Is that okay with you?'' Jack gave the doctor a ten dollar bill.

''That will be fine, thank you.'' The doctor put the bill in his pocket and they drove away.

The evening was cooler and a thoughtful neighbor, Mable Kelly, came to visit with the family and offered a prayer for the sick baby.

Jack and Fan took turns sitting with the child. Grandma and Grandpa Saddler went to bed. Fan laid down with 'Rilla and Jason and Jack sat with the sick child. The hours dragged by and Jack paced the room. The parlor clock struck ten P.M.. The child hardly breathed and did not move. Jack was frantic. The silence was maddening.

Jack heard something. The sound was coming from Drake. His insides were rumbling—gurgling just like the doctor said it would. His joy brought tears to his eyes.

''Jack ran to the stair door, flung it open and shouted, ''Fan! Everybody! It's Jake! Everything's Jake!''

All the family was awake and they did all the things they were told to do by the Doctor. Grandpa built a big fire in the lane and Grandma tore clean rags for diapers. Fan sent 'Rilla to make coffee and Jason to stir up the fire in the cook stove. Fan and Jack held each other and stayed by the baby's side.

''Everything's Jake, is it? Well, little Jake it is.'' Fan said.

''Yes sir, he's Jake alright!'' Jack repeated.

It happened just as the doctor said it would. The tiny boy passed diaper after diaper full of horrible, putrid feces which contained huge white worms that was quickly burned in the hot bonfire. The baby took water from a spoon and Fan continued to sponge him. Once, little 'Jake' opened his eyes and smiled at Jack and Fan. Their joy made them cry and cling to each other.

By dawn, everyone was exhausted but happy. Drake now called Jake, would live.

The last days had been so hectic that Jack almost forgot about his hearing. The postman rolled into the driveway and honked his horn. Jack and the kids went to investigate.

''Registered mail for ya, Jack,'' the man called from the car window.

''Thanks Wally, I've been expecting it.'' Jack's finger shook as he signed the clipboard and took his letter.

''See ya later.'' The postman said and drove away.

''Fan! Fan!'' Jack called to his wife who ran into the yard.

''You open it! I can't!'' Jack gave the letter to Fan and she tore it open and began to read.

''What does it say for Christ's sake, tell me!'' he shouted.

''Nothing—I mean—you still have a job—they dropped the charges for lack of evidence—no insubordination—look for yourself!'' She cried and gave Jack the letter.

''My pay—they reinstated me and gave me my back pay! Fan look, it's RAINING! Feel it? WATER! The drought is over!'' Jack and Fan were like kids again. They laughed and cried while the cool water drenched their faces and clothes. Jason and 'Rilla splashed around in the down pour but little Jannell understood none of it.

Chapter Seventeen

LIFE AND WAR

The rains broke the back of the long drought and the country slowly limped back. The railroads hauled more scrap metal, iron ore, coal and slag than ever before. The A C & Y was getting orders that usually fell to the New York Central or the Nickelplate Railroads. The 'laid off' crews went back to work and Jack's family flourished.

One day Jack came home to find Jason, now ten, and 'Rilla, now twelve, having a loud squabble.

"'Rilla's got a boyfriend! 'Rilla's got a boyfriend!" Jason jeered.

"I do not! You're a dirty rotten sneak and a brat!" She shouted.

"Here! Here! What's this shoutin' match all about?" Jack stepped between his children and held them apart.

"This is their third quarrel this week. They usually get along fine, I don't know what's got into them." Fan said and shook her head.

"'Rilla's been acting dippy ever since that bum was here! She's no fun anymore! She spends hours fixin' her hair and scribbling in her DIARY! She won't even help me milk anymore! She's just plum coo-coo! She thinks she's Mrs. Roosevelt writing 'My Day'. 'Rilla wrote 'My Day of The Traveler' in that silly book of hers! And ya know what else! She wore my best pants to go blackberry pickin' in! She says her poor legs get scratched! Gone coo-coo! That's what she has!" Jason was upset and mystified at his sister as he explained to his father.

"HE is not a BUM and that book is my personal property. My legs DO get scratched and you're a low-down, dirty skunk!" Jack had never seen 'Rilla so angry.

"Hold it! Hold it! That's enough from both of you. I won't have such goin' on. Jas, fetch me a 'Rollin' Rock then go do your chores. You and I will talk after bit." Jack was concerned. "'Rilla, get my 'Old Grandad, I need to cut the dust."

"I'll fix you a 'Dust Cutter' and you talk to her. Jason do your chores, now." Fan instructed and went to the cellar for beer and to the end of the buffet for Jack's whisky bottle.

"Now, sweetheart, tell me what this is all about. What BUM does he mean?" Jack asked of the weeping 'Rilla.

"A man came here and asked to do some work for some food. He was NOT a BUM, he was a stage actor from New York. He said his name was Julius Garfinkle but he would rather be called Jules. He said he had taken acting lessons from a European actress and teacher named Madame something-skaya and she told him that a good actor had to know life and people and must 'suffer.' He's working his way across the country to California to be in the MOVIES! He told me he was born in a place called 'Hell's Kitchen' and lived all his life in New York. He's traveling to learn things and to 'suffer.' In an hour's time, he chopped all those old tree trunk rounds into kindling. He was so strong. At one time, he was a Golden Gloves Prizefighter! Oh Daddy, he was so handsome! I wrote about him in my diary and Jas read it all! Now he teases me about it! He's just awful!" 'Rilla had no idea that the teacher and actress was the world renowned Madame Maria Ouspenskaya or that she was having her first real crush on a man.

"I see. Well don't let him discourage your writing. You are a good writer and someday your scribl—writing will be important. I'll talk to Jas about it. Now you run along and help your mother." Jack had not noticed until now, the little changes in 'Rilla as she grew toward womanhood.

After supper Jack and Jason took a walk. "Now tell me about 'Rilla. You know that you aren't supposed to snoop in each other's things. You both know better than that. Your personal things are private and no one is to cross that line. You have never done this before—why now?" Jack asked his son. "'Rilla's been writing in books ever since she could spell." Jack went on.

"She's different now, Pop, she never wants to climb trees, go fishing or help in the barn. She doesn't want to help me milk. She says she doesn't want to smell like a cow anymore. You know you have to lean your head on Daisy's flank to milk her, otherwise, she steps and switches her tail until you do. 'Rilla says Daisy smells. It didn't used to bother her. Now, she moons around and daydreams all the time when she's not hiding in her room. She's gone coo—coo!" Jason scratched his head.

"She's not coo-coo Jas, she's just growing up. Soon, she will be a pretty young lady. Her privacy is very important now, so no more peeking. Ya got that?" Jack explained.

"Awh gee Pop, I didn't mean nuthin' by it. Ya mean she's gonna git worse?" Jason was puzzled.

The two went on with their walk in silence, the subject was closed . . .

The next few years were uneventful, quiet, happy years. Jake (Drake) grew healthy and strong and was a good student. Jannell was a pretty, quiet child that would start to school in the spring. 'Rilla graduated from the eighth grade and made a place on the marching band majorette team. Jason loved the out-of-doors and football but book learning was not his forté. For years, he and 'Rilla had been the same size and weight and wore the same size shoe. Suddenly, he shot up rapidly growing into his big voice.

Fan's outbursts were more and more frequent. The more independent the children became, the more detached she became. Again she forgot to pay a bill and when Jack questioned her about it one evening when they were preparing for bed. She flew into a rage.

"So I forgot! I'm sick and tired of having to do everything! You never do anything! You're always gone on that railroad of yours! I have to tend the kids, run the farm, pay the bills and everything else! I'm going to have another baby in December!" She shrieked at him.

"Another baby! Doc said you shouldn't have any more—I thought we agreed—I didn't know!" Jack was dumfounded.

"Don't look so surprised! It isn't YOURS and neither is Jannell! You old fool, I need a man! A real man! You are always away, too sick or too tired! I can't stand to be alone and you know it but you still leave me alone! Well, say something—don't just stand there and stare! Go to that old railroad and see if I care!" Fan flounced out of the bedroom.

Jack was rooted to the spot. He felt as if someone had kicked him in the stomach. When he regained his senses, he tossed a few clothes into his old valice and headed for the door.

Jason and 'Rilla knew something was very wrong this time, but did not know what to do about it.

"Don't worry sis, he'll be back, you'll see." Jason tried to console his weeping sister.

Jack caught the West bound freight to Delphos and bumed a ride in the 'dog house' of the engine. The little compartment on the tender of the engine was too low to stand in and too short to lie in but it was better than walking and Jack slept fitfully all curled up.

In Delphos, he knew Hazel would have the street door bolted at this hour but he would have to wake her anyway.

He banged the brass knocker and the piercing sound echoed all around the quiet village square. The upstairs light went on and Hazel opened the door.

''Jack! I didn't expect you until tomorrow night—anything wrong?'' the sleepy lady asked and led him up stairs.

''Plenty! Hazel, plenty!'' Jack looked awful and she could see his agitation.

''Ya want to talk about it? There's some coffee in the pot—I'll heat it.'' She was awake now and lit the gas under the coffee pot.

''You don't want to hear my grief, do you? I sure would like some java, it's been a long day.'' Jack sat down at the kitchen table as he had done hundreds of times before.

''What are friends for? We all got problems and sometimes it helps to spread them out and look at them—talk about them.'' Hazel served the coffee and sat down at the table.

Jack poured out his miserable tale to Hazel who said nothing but let him talk. She made more coffee and he talked. He was full to the 'running over' and it all flooded out to his friend. After a long while, he put his head in his hands and cried. He cried as if his heart would break. Hazel stood up, moved closer to him and cradled his head to her waist. She smoothed his hair and patted his shoulder. He cried and cried.

Her body was warm and comforting. Eventually, he dried his eyes with his handkerchief. He looked up at her and said, ''Ain't this a hell of a way for a grown man to act?'' His eyes were red and he grinned sheepishly.

''Ya feel better, don't ya? That's what counts. Jack, what are you staring at.'' She was puzzled.

''You. I don't think I ever really LOOKED at you before. I've known you for years but I never SAW you.'' Jack stood up and studied her carefully. The honey-colored hair that she wore bound at the nape of her neck, now fell beautifully over her shoulders. The starched housedress and apron gave way to a peach colored, gauze and lace nightgown that peeked out at the throat, from a soft seersucker housecoat. The soft fabric molded to her find boned, slim body and fell to her ankles. Her soft face smelled of castile soap and her hair smelled of lemon. Jack fingered her silky hair and kissed her cheek. ''You're lovely,'' he breathed on to her skin.

Suddenly there was hunger in her eyes and his own needs began to churn. Her arms slipped around his neck. He lifted her light frame and carried her to his bed.

Their love making was sensitivity releasing, softly throbbing and exquisitely fulfilling. So gentle and restoring was their 'moment,' they felt they would drift into another dimension.

Jack awakened alone to the smell of bacon frying and coffee perking. He never felt so good. He shaved and dressed quickly. His head was full of millions of agonizing thoughts of what had happened. He went to the kitchen.

"Good morning Jack," she said as if they had never loved and this was just like any other day in their lives. Her hair was coiled on her neck, as usual, her dress and apron were starched, as usual and she had packed his pail, as usual.

" 'Mornin' Hazel. About last night, I. . . ."

"Sit and eat your breakfast. I want to talk to you," she interrupted, "sit-sit," she ordered and sat down at the table with her coffee. He ate and she talked.

"I'm going to tell you a story that no one knows. I was raised in the slums of Toledo by a drunken father and a frightened mother who he beat regularly. When I was seventeen, I met and married Ralph Metz. He was so unlike my father. Ralph was sober, loving, gentle and hard working. I adored him and we were deliriously happy. Not too long after the twins were born, I noticed a change in him but I couldn't put my finger on it. One night he did not come home at all. The morning I found out, was the day I came here. Ralph told me he had fallen in love with a MAN. I screamed him out of the house. What was I to do? I couldn't go to MY family and I had no friends—what was I to do? Our sugar bowl contained a few dollars and I took it. I bundled the twins into the baby buggy and went to the train station. With half the money, I bought a ticket to anywhere out of Toledo that was ready to roll. The day I got here, I had nothing. No supplies for the babys—not even diapers. I went into the dry goods store downstairs to buy flannel and Goldie Roseburg was there. She saw I was in trouble and helped me. She owns this building and this flat. Her brother was in the secondhand furniture business and gave me credit. The first day you came here, I had six cents left. In all these years, I haven't looked at a man. When I do, I see my old man and his drunkenness or I see Ralph and my betrayal. I had begun to think I was dead. That I was nothing but a burned out shell, incapable of passion, of wanting, of needing a man. Last night, you brought me back to life! You made me whole again. I'm a complete woman again, thanks to you. Your needs were different. You were crushed, full of despair and anguish, even doubtful of your manhood. We repaired each other in the only way we know how. It was just something that happened. It never happened before and it will never happen again. You go back to your wife and kids and we will be better people for our 'moment.' She stood up and touched his cheek.

"How can I go back after she tells me Jannell is not my child or that the one she is carrying isn't either? How can she say that?" Jack's anguish was back.

"Hold it—wait just a minute! What are the most important things in your life? Your kids, of course. How can she hurt you the most? Through your kids. She's mean and spiteful and wants to hurt you. How does she do it—the kids. She's carrying another child—it's risky and it makes her crazy. I'm sure it isn't true and in your heart, you KNOW it isn't true." Hazel was wise.

"Because of the danger to Fan, we weren't going to have anymore." Jack explained.

"Well, so you two 'slipped up', it happens all the time. Now go to work and go back to your home and kids. SHE may not be worth it but THEY ARE." She laughed, gave him his pail and shoved him out the door.

Hazel had given Jack the strength he needed to go home and search for a solution to his problems.

Fan, with 'Rilla and Jason, met his train at cut out time. The two ran to meet their father.

"You're coming home aren't you, Daddy?" 'Rilla's eyes brimmed with tears and Jack brushed her hair behind her ear as he had done millions of times.

"Yea Dad, if you don't come home, there won't be no home!" Jason kicked the street curb with his shoe and tried not to cry.

"Can we talk this over Fan?" Jack asked of his wife.

"I 'spose so." Fan was at a loss of words.

Jack winked at 'Rilla and they piled into the car and drove home. The children were delighted but they knew all wasn't settled.

Grandma and Grandpa Saddler had recovered more or less, from their financial problems when the Social Security plan went into effect to help the elderly. Since there was to be another baby again, the house was too small. Grandpa had a small stroke and could no longer work on the farm, so the Saddlers took an apartment in town where they could walk to everything.

Fan had great difficulty carrying the baby as the doctor had predicted. She spent much time sitting and resting which placed much on Jason and 'Rilla. There was no livestock except the milk cow and Jason tended to all the chores. He saw to Daisy's feed and water, did the milking twice a day and cleaned barns and stalls. 'Rilla bathed and fed her siblings, helped with the cooking and laundry and washed and dried hundreds of dishes. It was a big responsibility on both the youngsters.

One Sunday in December, Fan felt better than usual although the baby was due any day. Fan and Jesse Moss had been good friends for years and went back and forth a lot. Jack and Marvin Moss both were away from home much of the time on their jobs.

The two mothers decided to pool their Sunday dinners and eat at Jesse's. 'Rilla and Julie Moss, Jesse's daughter, were best friends. They spent long hours together learning to twirl their batons. 'Rilla was a drum majorette and Julie was an alternate in the high school marching band. The girls would practice in the front yard and Fan and Jesse would sew and talk or do needle work. Many times they would play cards with other members of Jesse's family. Jason would go exploring down by the creek or bounce a ball off the barn to strengthen his throwing arm for baseball or football. It was too cold this December day, so all agreed to play cards after dinner.

The ladies were clearing the table when the news came over the radio. Everyone was stunned and no one could speak. President Roosevelt said the Japanese had bombed Peal Harbor in Hawaii and it was WAR! What ever happened to 'Peace in Our Time'?

None of them could grasp the full meaning of WAR. They could not even imagine Assembly Lines, Lady Riveters, Car Pools, Shortages, Ration Books or War Bonds. Who ever heard tell of Civil Defense, Blackouts, Fifth-Columns or Espionage? The War years would grow into an exciting, baffling, anxious and horrible time.

Fan's physical condition worsened and she was two weeks overdue. Exactly what was wrong was unknown. Happily on January 1, 1942, Perry Blain Lansure weighed in at nine and a half pounds. He was big, strong, cried very little and was the first baby born in Huron county that year. Fan, on the other hand was weak, weepy and out of sorts. She barked at the children, scolded the temporary housekeeper and whined. The doctor said she had a bad case of 'Afterbirth Blues' but would need an operation as soon as she was strong enough. Her recovery was painfully slow and dragged through summer into fall.

Jack was gone more and more. Along with his regular engineer's job, he often acted as 'Pilot' for other railroads who wished to use the AC&Y. Many times it was faster and easier to allow the other companies' trains to pass over their lines than it was to cut and switch cars in the usual way. The National Defense Program demanded everything 'yesterday'. The War Effort had everything but time.

The day after Thanksgiving, Fan went into the hospital to have her operation. If all went well, she would be back home in a week or ten days.

Grandma and Grandpa Saddler kept little Perry as he was a tiny baby and still nursing part-time. It was just a few steps from the Saddlers to the hospital. A temporary housekeeper was caring for the other children.

It was a terrible cold winter. The furnace in the Saddler's apartment building overheated and started a fire that burned down an entire city block. The water froze as it came from the hoses and the firemen were helpless. Grandma Saddler was rescued but several attempts to locate the baby in the smoke failed.

Thanks to the heroic efforts of one man, Perry Black, little Perry Lansure was rescued. Black knew the apartment layout and risked his life to feel his way in the thick smoke to the sleeping child that was near death. It struck everyone profoundly that the child and the hero both shared the same name, Perry. Fate? Providence? Or just a strange coincidence?

Little Perry recovered quickly in the hospital and in his mother's arms. Grandma Saddler never fully recovered. Grandpa was away at the time and they lost all they owned. Precious antique furniture, heirloom jewelry and even Grandma's dentures that were in a glass of water on the night stand. She lost all her hairpins including the six gold ones her father gave her when she was just a girl, for her pretty sandy hair. She lost a lifetime of treasures and nearly lost the greatest treasure of all, her eleven month old grandson, Perry.

Again the Saddlers came to live with Jack and Fan but again, the house was too small. The farm itself, had become too much for the family and again, the Lansures moved. They found a nice big house on West Hooker St. and settled down again. The children could walk to school and attend school activities. Grandpa could have a small garden and Grandma could rest, she was bedridden often.

'Rilla worked the switchboard at the telephone office afternoons and made popcorn and ushered at the local movie theater, evenings.

Jason worked part-time for a local farmer operating the combine or hauling wood.

One day after the Saturday Matinee, 'Rilla burst into the house so excited she could hardly breathe. "Mom! Daddy! It's HIM! I saw HIM! He's in the MOVIES!" She cried.

"Who's in the movies?" Fan asked.

"Take your time and tell us." Jack tried to calm her.

"Hurry! You have to come to the first show! You have to see HIM!" She panted.

"Go to the show to see who?" Jack asked again.

"My friend! The man who came to the farm a long time ago. My Julius Garfinkle! It's him I swear, it's him but his name is John Garfield now.

Hurry! You have to come and see and I have to go back to work. I just ran home to tell you. If you don't SEE him no one will believe me! Hurry!'' 'Rilla pleaded.

The family hurried to the theater, bought their tickets and went inside. Sure enough, 'Rilla's friend was John Garfield and he was in the movie called, 'Four Daughters'. 'Rilla was ecstatic and the family could not believe their eyes. Jack was not at home that fateful day but they confirmed that 'Rilla's Julius (Jules) Garfinkle and John Garfield were one and the same.

''Oh brother! I thought 'Rilla was coo-coo then, now she will REALLY be off her rocker!'' Jason had to see it to believe it and whispered to his father in the darkened theater.

''It's true Jason, that's him alright.'' Fan said and could hardly believe her eyes.

''She was right—he wasn't a BUM.'' Jack said quietly while they watched.

Later, after the showing of 'Four Daughters', 'Rilla gushed, ''Oh, Daddy, isn't he WONDERFUL!''

'Rilla watched the movie over and over and plagued the theater owner to find out more about her John Garfield. Her 'Traveler' was a real movie star and she had pages and pages to write in her diary.

Jack and the railroad were busier than ever and the railroad employees got worse and worse. One by one the best men went into the service until there was nothing left but the young and untrained, the old and worn out and the misfits who could not get work until now. For example; The local switch engines, at the end of each work day or run, are placed on sidings to be readied for the next work day. The big locomotives were turned over to the hostler for refueling and preparation for the next shift. This stupid man not only dropped the ashes from the firebox but all the coals and fire. The fire is never fully extinguished from the firebox because it takes hours—even-days to rebuild the bed fire.

With the heavy wartime schedules to keep, Jack was furious at such incompetence. There was nothing to do but wait for the fires to be rebuilt. A day's delay in the schedules was a week of snarled production and so it went.

'Rilla enjoyed her high school days with her friends. Her sophomore year, she became the head drum majorette in the NLHS Marching Band. Although her friend, Julie Moss was an excellent baton twirler, she was a natural gymnast and tumbler. Julie tried out for the cheerleading team and made it. She and Billie Ann Giles were to become accomplished cheerleaders, gymnasts and tumblers. Their 'jumps', 'flips' and 'stands' had never been done up to now and they set a precedent for NLHS cheerleaders.

'Rilla's friend, Phoebe David, played the clarinet and with the help of the drummer, Bo Blanchard, 'Rilla put the band through it's paces and formations at football games, local parades and celebrations.

The friends 'Rilla made in school were long lasting, including, Flora (Duchess) Yurley. She was the refined lady of the group and kept the clamoring teenagers in line. She quieted them when they were too noisy, calmed them when they were too raucous and always reminded them of their manners. The group of five girls were often referred to as the 'Five Musketeers'. Later, Billie Ann Giles and Shane Roberts were crowned 'Homecoming King and Queen'. She was 'Miss Personality' and he was 'Letter Man' and star athlete. Julie Moss had the title lead in the class play, 'Aunt Tillie Goes To Sea' and 'Rilla was the maid who lost her dentures over the side of the cruise ship.

When 'Rilla burst onto the stage with all her teeth blacked out with spirit gum, Jack roared with laughter until he shook and smashed his new Stetson flat on his knee. Fan laughed until she cried. The play stopped for several minutes while the audience thundered with laughter and applause. 'Rilla was a very funny sight with what appeared to be, no teeth in her mouth. The play was a big success.

In spite of their differences, and as often as possible, Jack and Fan attended school functions that involved their children. They encouraged them to study, read and apply themselves.

In the spring of 1944, 'Rilla graduated from high school and went to Cleveland to further her studies.

Jason worked for the Railway Express but it was only temporary until he could volunteer for the armed services. He applied for the Army but chose the Navy. This was a first for the Lansure's immediate family because their ancestors were Army men. The Lansures were decorated heroes as far back as the Norsemen or Vikings who were also well-known as seafarers. Beginning with the French Revolution, the Lansures were great horsemen when they began to keep accurate records. Later, during the American Revolution and through the American Civil War, their standard of Army leadership was unequaled. In the First World War, many distinguished themselves as did Jack. During the Second World War, the pendulum began to swing back to the ancient Viking seafarers. Surprising what can be found in tracing a family tree to it's roots.

Jack never worked so hard or was away from home as much as now. To add to his burden, he was bone tired and there was no time to rest.

One rainy, foggy night in the fall, Jack eased his big locomotive into the Akron Yards to feed the iron behemoth coal and water. As usual, he dropped down with his tallow pot (lubricating oil can) to grease the necessary parts.

The cliffs of Good Year Heights rose straight up from the AC&Y yards and was covered with big trees. The rain fell silently and the thick fog shrouded everything down to the ground.

Suddenly out of the fog, a faint voice called, ''Hello, there.'' The sound drifted in and out and there was no way to tell where it came from. ''Hello, there!'' Jack heard it again. Jack answered in a loud voice, ''Hello, there!'' He repeated it, ''Hello, there!''

Two of his crew members heard Jack call and went around the engine to him. ''You want us Jack, we heard you call?'' They said.

''No, but LISTEN, there's somebody up there calling 'Hello, there.' '' Jack insisted.

The men listened for a long moment and heard no sound. The two men eyed each other but said nothing.

''I don't hear anything do you, Joe?'' Asked Bill.

''No, I don't.'' Joe answered.

''Well, I HEARD it!'' Jack was certain.

The two men walked back along the train to finish refueling. When out of ear shot, they thought, Joe said, ''Bill, I'm worried about Jack. He's worn out. He puts in hellish hours to make sure all this war material moves along to the other carriers and to the coast.''

''I know he's tired but ya don't think he's beginnin' to 'hear things', do ya?'' Asked Joe.

''When a man is about to crack, he does strange things. There he goes again.'' Said Bill.

From the other side of the train, Jack called again, ''Hello, there!''

''Yea, I hear him but do ya think THAT means he's going NUTS.'' Joe wondered

''Search me! It just seems funny to hear a grown man talk to himself.'' Declared Bill.

The men finished their work and 'cut out'. Jack went to the Plug & Jug for a 'road dust cutter'. The tavern had changed hands but the food was still good. Jack downed his rye and sipped his beer. He scanned the menu and made a mental selection.

When the waitress came to take his order he said, ''Evenin' Alice. I'll have the Number 2; Grunt Slabs with 'sas, smashed Maine, punk with grease and sweets, java, light and sweet and a slab of custard.''

The waitress wrote his order on her pad and went to the kitchen. Jack sipped his beer.

When the waitress brought his meal, it was Number 3; Sausage with horseradish and hash browns, greenbeans, rye bread, black coffee and apple pie.

''Alice, I ordered Number 2, the pork chops. . . .'' He explained.

''You ordered Number 3, I have it right her!'' She interrupted and laid his check on the table.

Too tired to argue, Jack ate the sausage dinner, paid the check and went to his hotel room to bed. Perhaps he did order the sausage—maybe he was about to 'cave in.' He was not sure.

When Jack arrived at his hotel room, his evening paper was not in front of his door as usual. Why not? Had he forgotten to order it? Jack was uncertain. Perhaps he was falling apart. Too tired to think, Jack cleaned up and fell into bed.

The next morning, he was awakened by a loud banging on his door. Jack opened the door a crack, since he was still in his underwear.

''I'm sorry, Mr. Lansure, it's me Freddy, the paperboy. I forgot to leave your evening paper so I brought you the morning edition. I'm awful sorry Sir, will that be okay?'' The apologetic boy explained.

''Sure kid, no harm done. What do I owe you for next week?'' Jack asked.

''Let's see, that'll be 24¢, Sir.'' The boy counted on his fingers.

''Here ya go.'' Jack tossed him a half a dollar and closed the door.

Inside the room, Jack unfolded the paper to the front page. It read:

LABOR DAY BALLOON ASCENSION FAILS!

Balloonist Down In Heights Trees—Called 'HELP' All Night

Stranded man saw lights and trains below him but no one heard his calls.

* * *

Jack dropped onto his bed and began to laugh. He was NOT crazy! He did hear VOICES calling! The fog and rain muffled the sound but there was a MAN hanging in the trees, overhead calling for help. What a relief!

Jack dressed quickly and went to breakfast. His step was light and he felt better than he had in a long while.

The waitress, Alice, met him at the door. ''Oh Mr. Lansure, PLEASE excuse me! I DID serve you the wrong dinner last night. I'm so sorry. After you left I found YOUR check. It had slipped off the counter onto the floor and I found it later. To make amends, your breakfast is on the house. You name it—anything you want—you name it!'' Alice confessed.

''That's not necessary, I like sausage.'' Jack would not hurt her feelings.

''Oh yes PLEASE, my boss will be all over me like the pox, if you don't.'' The anxious girl urged.

''Well in that case, I'll have; Tom juice, Two Headlights—dimmed a little—with a String of Flats, Burnt Punk with the Works and Java, light and sweet.'' Jack said and sat down on a stool at the counter.

''Hey George,'' Alice called to the short order cook. ''Bacon and eggs—over easy—toast with B & J.'' She called. ''Mr. Lansure, what kind of potatoes do you want? Hash browns, home fries or shoestring?'' She went on.

''Surprise me.'' Jack liked them all.

''George, shred some,'' she called to the cook.

Jack was feeling better and better. He finished his food, thanked the nice folks, left Alice a tip and went outside.

When his crew spotted Jack they ran to him shouting.

''Hey Jack, ya DID hear voices! That balloonist was hanging right above us in the trees!'' They all talked at once. They were ashamed and foolish.

''Yea fellas, I saw it in the morning paper. You birds thought I was a goner, didn't ya?'' Jack smiled and they were relieved that he was not angry. All the men had a big laugh over it and spoke of it often to friends.

The War finally came to an end August 15, 1945.

Jack and Fan were too busy to fight. 'Rilla graduated from the Cleveland Academy of Cosmetology and went on to study Journalism at The Newspaper Institute of America. Jason was to make a career in the Navy. Jake and Jannell did well in school and frisky Perry was a wiggly preschooler.

On August 25, 1946, 'Rilla walked down the flower-strewn church isle on Jack's arm to the organ strains of Lohengrin and Liebestraum to marry the love of her life, Halcey Bogard Evans, (Hal). Hal and 'Rilla were raised in different worlds but their ideals, attitudes, tastes and goals were the same.

Hal was a city boy to the core. He thrived on metropolitan life, the bright lights, traffic and congestion spurred him on. Farm life, on the other hand, was dirty words. To him, it meant backbreaking work in the fields, questionable income and dirty fingernails. The only taste of farm life that he ever had was picking beans, all summer, for the local grower for spending money and helping in his mother's vegetable garden. He found both painful drudgery. He had no idea what farm life was all about and drew the wrong conclusions which added to his apprehension and insecurity. 'Rilla often called him 'Hayseed' because he was anything but. She would tease him about his lack of farm knowledge and he would grin good-naturedly.

'Rilla, on the other hand, was raised in the country and through her eyes, it was wonderful. She was secure, self-reliant and adapted to city life with vigorous confidence. She enjoyed the Opera, Symphonies and the Theatre and in her spare time, she took many roles in 'Little Theatre' productions. She found city life glamourous, exciting and opportunistic. She thrived on the busy pace, pretty fashions and the social life.

The wedding was beautiful. She was lovely in white satin and he looked strained in a black tuxedo.

It was the only time anyone could remember seeing Jack a bit tipsy. By the time he had a drink with everyone at the reception, to toast his 'Rilla and his new son, he was willing to make a SPEECH. This was very out of character as he always shunned the spotlight. The wedding went off without a hitch and Jack had the most fun of all.

For their honeymoon, 'Rilla and Hal took an automobile trip out West. They were driving along one early morning and Hal spotted a farmer in his field doing something strange.

"Look 'Rilla, look at THAT!" Hal exclaimed and slowed the car to a stop.

"Look at what?" She asked.

"Over there—in the field! Look at that machine!" Hal was excited.

'Rilla began to laugh so hard she could not speak.

"What is it? What's so funny?" He was surprised at her laughter.

When she could regain her composure a bit she said, "You don't know what THAT is—you never saw a machine like it before?" She laughed more and he was indignant.

"Of course not, I'm not a farmer! What's so funny?" He was bewildered at her laughter.

"That's a manure spreader. The farmer is fertilizing his field for planting. The wagon bed is full of horse or cow manure. A conveyor belt in the floor of the wagon moves the dung back to that wheel-thing on the back and it throws the dung out into the field. MANURE SPREADER, understand?" 'Rilla cradled her man in her arms and said, "My dear city boy, will I EVER make a 'Hayseed' out of you?".

'Rilla and Hal received a letter from Jason, somewhere at sea, that instructed Fan to give the newlyweds $50.00 dollars from his savings account. Jason had been sending allotment checks home to Fan for her to bank. When it was discovered that there was no SAVINGS and Fan had spent the allotment checks as fast as they came to her, Jack raged. That was the last straw—the one that finally broke Jack's back. To squander his money was one thing but to squander Jason's money was something else again.

Jack knew he had to do something for himself and Fan with regards to their finances. What to do, he had no idea. There were no marriage counselors, per se, or support groups, only lawyers from which to seek advice. After much deliberation and self-examination, Jack went to see the Company lawyer.

Jack explained to the lawyer, Daniel Presser, that Fan was a good mother but had no conception of money, was child-like and immature and shunned responsibility. She could not save a dollar although Jack had a good income and the more he made the more she spent. He was getting along in life and had no nest egg or prospects of one.

The lawyer Dan, listened carefully to Jack and took notes. He told Jack he would go see Fan and speak to her about this and get back to him. Jack was relieved. Things at home were better and he felt the lawyer's talk with Fan helped the situation but he did not ask. Jack and Fan never could communicate.

Time passed. The lawyer called Jack into his office and explained that there was to be a 'hearing' in front of a Judge to help with the matter.

What Jack did not know was the fact that the lawyer had been to see Fan and had made some promises to her. When Jack got home, the night before the hearing, Fan and the three youngest children were not at home. This was not unusual, Fan often took the children on the bus to visit friends or relatives and arrived home late. Jack had never had set hours.

The next morning Hal and 'Rilla came to visit from Cleveland. They had no idea it was to be a 'hearing' day or knew of any of Jack's plans to correct his financial structure.

When Jack saw Hal and 'Rilla at the courthouse, he was delighted and relieved. The lawyer asked 'Rilla to say a few words in her father's behalf. She agreed providing she could say a few words for her mother, also. The lawyer declined and Hal and 'Rilla sat in the back of the courtroom with the spectators and listened. The purpose of the 'hearing' was still unclear to Hal and 'Rilla.

Jack took the stand and told his story to the Judge being careful not to defame Fan in anyway. When Jack finished, the Judge asked for Mrs. Lansure.

"Your Honor, I'm here to speak for Mrs. Lansure." Dan Presser began, "She will not contest the divorce. She will not demand custody of the minor children or expect alimony. She requests some small funds to take over a small business of her own with half the household furnishings and nothing more. I have granted her requests on behalf of Mr. Lansure. The funds to be allocated at a later date." Lawyer Presser sat down.

Jack was stupefied. 'Rilla jumped to her feet but Hal pulled her back into her seat.

The Judge asked a few more questions of Jack and his lawyer and said, "I can't see where a divorce is the answer to this situation but then I can't see why it isn't—DIVORCE GRANTED." The Judge banged the gavel on the desk.

"DIVORCE! I thought this was a 'hearing'!" Jack demanded of the lawyer.

''It is, Mr. Lansure, a divorce hearing and you won everything!'' The man was jubilant. ''You got full custody of the children and no alimony to pay. All she wants if $100.00 dollars to start her business! You won everything.!'' The lawyer had won his case.

''DIVORCE! I needed advice! Now I have no wife, no HOME, three little ones to take care of and an engine to run!'' Jack was in shock.

''Oh, THAT, Mrs. Lansure will send your half of the furniture sales after the sale.'' The lawyer tossed over his shoulder on his way out of the courtroom.

'Rilla and Jack hugged each other and cried. ''My God 'Rilla, what have I done.? I needed advice—not a DIVORCE! I need a divorce like I need poison!'' Jack was devastated and 'Rilla wept.

''Let's go home and see what Mom-Fan has to say about this before we panic,'' was Hal's advice.

Jack, Hal and 'Rilla went to the house to see Fan. She met them at the door, hugged Hal and 'Rilla and to Jack she said, ''At least, I thought YOU would talk to ME instead of sending your lawyer.'' Fan was not angry, just resolute.

''Fan, I swear, I didn't know it would come to this! I went to Dan Presser for advice—not a divorce!'' Jack was frazzled.

''Well, we ironed it all out and it's done. I hate to give up the kids, but I can't keep them on what I'll make in that little store. I hope I can keep myself. I'm packing now. The movers will be here Monday morning. As soon as I sell everything, I'll send your half. I'll take $50.00 now and the rest when you have it.'' For Fan, she was unbelievably calm.

''Will you be alright in a strange town among strange people? Who do we know in Youngstown?'' 'Rilla was concerned for her mother. Fan would be all alone at 43 among strangers.

''I don't know a soul except the old lady that sold me the store, but I'll manage.'' Fan was determined.

''What kind of a store is it?'' Hal inquired.

''Secondhand EVERYTHING. Mostly clothes. There is old dry cleaning equipment and a sewing machine in the back to do repairs and it has sleeping rooms. I'll be just fine.'' Fan said. ''Where will you and the kids be, so I can write to them.'' She went on.

''I don't know! I haven't had time to think! School won't be out for another month yet! I don't know what to do!'' Jack stammered.

''Well, you got a divorce and it's done. There is one more thing you can do for me, if you will. Will you see to it that I get some of your railroad retirement? I'll be old then and I will need more support.'' Fan said calmly.

"You bet I will. We've been married almost 25 years and you're entitled. I'll see to it." Jack agreed.

"'Rilla, you and I better go. I'm sure they have things to talk over." Hal was polite.

The drive home was long and 'Rilla wept most of the way. "I can't believe this is happening! How can it BE? What a terrible mistake this is for the kids—for all of us!" She wept.

Hal consoled her the best he could but the divorce was final and 'Rilla's world was crumbling away. Her security had been shattered. Divorce only happened to OTHER people—never in her own family. . . .

Chapter Eighteen

CAN'T DIE TWICE

Jack found himself at nearly 55 years old without a home, three motherless children and a third rate hotel room for accommodations. The situation was calamitous. Other times when faced with disaster, he sought solace in his ancestral home.

HOME that's IT! HOME! Brother and sister, Bruce and Leone were both still alive and she lived on the family place! Bruce couldn't help much but Leone could—if she would. She was always unpredictable but usually came through in a pinch. She had lost her only child, an adopted son, in the War and had no other children. It might work if Jack and the kids could limp along until school was out.

Jack made arrangements with Leone. When school closed for the summer, Jack, Jake, 13, Jannell, 11, and Perry, 6, went to Jack's home in the hills of Pennsylvania. Leone was nearly 70 but was happy to have children in the house to take her mind off her own loss.

For a time, things were good. The children did not understand why their mother was gone but found comfort in their Dad. They got used to Aunt Leone's barking which was much worse than her bite and they had a home and stability. They soon got acquainted and attended the same school their father had so long ago.

They also got to know their Uncle Duke who had never married and lived nearby. Duke had been alone so long he often talked to himself. The children thought that was great fun. Once, while doing some remodeling for his sister, Leone, Duke accidentally rolled the wrecking bar over his thumb. The pain was excruciating but he never flinched. Instead, he held up his painful thumb and said, "There, ya son-of-a-bitch! That will teach ya to get in the way!" Duke swore at his damaged thumb. The children shrieked with laughter from an upstairs window and Jake nearly fell out. For years, they told the story of their Uncle Duke and the wrecking bar and would roll with laughter each time.

Although Leone was up in years, she enjoyed the children and in general, their lives were good. Everything went well until Jack announced that he was going to marry the Widow Rauls. Aunt Leone went crazy. "You don't mean you are going to MARRY that 'Old Rip'! She chases anything in pants! You're too old for HER! All she sees is your MONEY! I can't believe you are that STUPID! John Lansure, you never did have a lick 'o sense and THIS proves it! You can have any woman around here—why pick the bottom of the barrel? She's ugly enough to stop an eight-day-clock! You've gone CRAZY—plum loco!" She stopped to catch her breath.

Leone huffed and scolded and ranted and raved but Jack's mind was made up. Martha Rawls had one boy Perry's age still at home but her other three were grown and married. She needed a husband for financial support and Jack's kids needed a mother. After much consideration, Jack believed it would be a good 'arrangement' for them both. Love never entered in to it. Fan was the love of Jack's life and in spite of their problems, he would never love another.

Again, Jake, Jannell and Perry were uprooted. When Jack married the woman they would call 'Aunt Martha,' their lives changed. It's true, they needed a Mother but not THAT woman. She was rude, crude and ignorant. She talked incessantly, gossiped constantly and snored like a buffalo. She was loud, boisterous, uncouth, impolite and had the morals of a billy goat.

Again Jake, Jannell and Perry felt deserted when Aunt Leone went away to live. As soon as Jake was old enough, he enlisted in the Navy. Jannell spent summers and holidays with 'Rilla but little Perry had no place to run.

He was always the 'outsider' because in all things, Aunt Martha sided with HER son, Ned.

Jack and Martha made some repairs on the old place and settled down to what was laughingly called 'wedded bliss'. To Jack, the important thing was he was back to his roots and his children had a home. Everything else was secondary. He was not happy but he was resigned to make the best of a bad deal.

After a hitch in the Navy, Jake had enough. Although he and Jason served together aboard the same ship in the Mediterranean Area, it was not his planned career. Jake was an accomplished swimmer and diver and would make beautiful but frightening dives from the 'crow's nest' of their destroyer into the sea. His timing and execution was perfect. Jason would hold his breath and watch his brother. Jake would wait until the ship rolled to the side then plummet into the sea as graceful as a bird on the fly. Jake could have easily made swimming and diving a career, but since he was a small boy, he planned to railroad with his father.

When Jake left the Navy, he put his 'separation pay' and a bit of savings in the bank, bought himself an expensive pair of leather bedroom slippers and told his sister, 'Rilla, who he always called 'Hollywood' because of her interest in acting and the theatre, " 'Hollywood,' I've got my own checkbook, a pair of slippers and now, you can call me MISTER." He would laugh impishley and hug his sister.

The day he became Jack's fireman on the engine, was a dream come true for both. They worked well together and the other railroaders called them 'Big Jake' and 'Little Jake' Lansure. In his spare time, Jake took a course in air brakes and other related subjects to qualify him for promotion to engineer when Jack retired in October of 1957. Jake studied hard and did well.

Jack had the time to spend with Jake he never had before and he was very pleased with and proud of the man his son had become. Although it was never spoken about or mentioned, all in the family knew that Jake was Jack's favorite child.

In March of 1957, there was much sickness on the railroad and they were often shorthanded. Jack and Jake were about to 'mark off' when the Agent asked if Jake would work another 'trick' (shift), because there were not enough firemen to go around. Although very tired, Jake agreed to work a second trick.

"You look done in son." Jack said to Jake.

"I'll get a sandwich at the Plug and Jug and I'll be fine." Jake called over his shoulder to his father.

Jannell had graduated from school and had gone to Akron to work. Both she and Jake stayed at Mrs. Cummings' rooming house. Mrs. Cummings was a railroader's widow who took in roomers to supplement her little pension. Jack had known the Cummings for many years and had worked with her late husband, Herb.

Jack and Jannell had been asleep for hours when the police officer pounded on the front door. Jack pulled on his pants and looked at his watch on the stand; 3:00 AM He hurried down stairs and opened the door.

"Evening Sir. My name's Olson and this is Officer Simms. Are you Jack Lansure?" One officer asked. Jannell and Mrs. Cummings crowded behind Jack at the door.

"Yes, I am." Jack answered.

"Do you know a Drake Glen Lansure?" The policeman went on.

"Yes, he's my son! What's wrong?" Jack's skin crawled with foreboding. All he could think of was TRAIN WRECK!

"There has been an automobile accident up on Dead Man's curve. Your son is in the hospital and we have come to take you there." The officer explained.

"I'm coming, too!" Jannell cried and ran to dress.

"I'll be just a minute." Jack said and took the stairs two at a time. He was relieved it was not a train wreck.

They dressed hurriedly and ran to the police car. The siren screamed through the dark and sleeping city. Jack's head pounded and Jannell cried. The officer explained that Drake apparently fell asleep, failed to negotiate the curve and hit a tree.

They arrived in the hospital corridor just as the Doctor came out of a door there.

"Are you Mr. Lansure?" The doctor asked.

"Yes I am and this is my daughter, Jannell. How's my boy?" Jack choked.

"I'm sorry Mr. Lansure, Drake has expired." The Doctor said softly.

Jack drew in his breath and sagged against the cold tile of the hospital wall. Jannell held her breath and watched her father turn into an old man right before her eyes. He was not quite 65 but he looked 80. She clung to him and wept.

When Jack could speak he said, "May I see my son, please?" Jack croaked.

"You may but I suggest you do not. His trauma is many and severe. I suggest you see him later at the Trowbridge Mortuary. Homer Trowbridge is the best in the field of reconstruction, that is, if you agree to allow him to do the work." The doctor was kindly.

"Oh, Dad, he must be smashed up terrible!" Jannell cried. "You don't want to see him like THAT."

"Yes, Miss, the damage was extensive about his head and chest." The doctor was gentle.

"There is one more thing Doctor, did my son suffer? I couldn't rest if I thought he suffered bad." Jack choked on his tears.

"No, Mr. Lansure, he did not suffer. He may have had a heartbeat for 4 or 5 minutes but he was in no pain I assure you." The doctor went on, calmly, "With trauma this extensive, death is instantaneous. Will you be alright? When you are ready, the officers will take you home." The doctor went on.

At home, Mrs. Cummings helped Jannell notify the family, Fan and relatives. The family gathered and were more or less numb but all were concerned about Jack. He had only briefly greeted the family members and went to bed.

Jannell cried in 'Rilla's arms, "Did you see him! 'Rilla, dad turned an old man right before my eyes! He wasn't old before—now he's OLD! Oh, 'Rilla, what can we do to help him?"

"Yes, I saw how he looks. Everyone grieves in their own way. Dad wants to be alone, where it's quiet, so he can sort out his thoughts. When he hurts, he wants let alone. I'll take him a 'Dust Cutter' and we will let him sleep for a while." 'Rilla was a 'take charge' type and for her Dad, she would see to things as she had always done for him.

The Lansure family was asked to arrive a half hour early for the first showing and open house at the Trowbridge Funeral Home. A young man, in a suit and tie and about twenty, escorted them to a large room full of chairs with doors at both ends. He asked the family to be seated and said, "I'm John Atkins, one of Doctor Trowbridge's assistants. Since you haven't met him yet, I will explain. The Doctor has no use of his arms and hands. Under his instruction, we do his reconstruction work. He is a Master at his craft but he has been stricken with a terrible paralysis. He creates and all we do is act as his hands. Please excuse me for a moment." He said and disappeared behind one of the doors.

The family waited. After what seemed hours, the young man returned. With him was a man in his fifties and another young man about his own age. The elderly man's arms hung stiffly at his sides and he spoke, "Mr. Lansure and ladies and gentlemen, I greet you but I can not shake your hands. John has explained my situation. Drake is ready but we have difficulty combing his hair. Can you help?" he asked.

"Oh, it's his cowlick. I can fix it." 'Rilla stood up and followed the man.

When 'Rilla saw her brother in the casket she froze to the spot. Her feet were lead weights and she could not step. The man took her elbow to steady her and said, "It's alright, just take your time." He gave her a brush and comb and moved her closer.

When 'Rilla was near enough to see his face clearly, the skin of her body crawled and the goose bumps covered her. He was NOT DEAD! He was 'playing possum'. She had seen him many times, lay on the couch and pretend he was asleep to fool the other children and then raise up and laugh at everyone who thought he was asleep. His handsome face appeared to have a faint smile and 'Rilla was sure he would sit up and laugh. She stood and expected her brother to open his eyes and laugh impishly at her.

"Please, Miss, visiting time is near." The man spoke to 'Rilla who stood trance-like by the casket.

Jake's cowlick was at the front of his hair line and would lay down only if combed in the proper direction. If not, it stood straight out like a cock's comb. 'Rilla had combed it into place many times as the boy grew up. Usually when she combed his hair, his flesh was warm and soft. This time, when she touched her brother, he was stone cold and hard. She was jerked back to the terrible truth that he was not 'playing 'possum' but that he was DEAD.

She wanted to scream at the top of her lungs and run away. Calmly, she smothered the urge to escape and combed her brother's hair into place.

The door opened and her family gathered with her at the casket.

"Jesus Christ! I can't stand this! He looks like he's 'playing 'possum' and will jump up and laugh at us!" Jason said, hugged his father and sobbed.

Jannell hugged Fan and said, "I thought he'd look—I mean—the car was so smashed——that is—." she sobbed.

"I know dear, these men are artists." Fan said through her tears.

Jack staggered under his own weight and Jason felt his father give way. He led Jack to a chair near the casket and helped him sit down. The viewing hours were torturous for the family but Jake had dozens of friends, railroad buddies and relatives. When the visitations were over, the family followed the black, flower-laden hearse out of Akron and into the country and to the family place in Pennsylvania.

Jake 'laid in state' at the family home and then, on a cold day in March Drake Glen Lansure, their beloved Jake, was laid to rest in the family plot on a beautiful tree covered hillside. Jack believed that a funeral was a paganistic ritual that should be abolished. It was torturous for the living and inconsequential to the dead. After this ordeal, he vowed to be cremated without formality.

Jack began to eat better and soon his strength came back but not his vitality. The death of his son took two things from Jack that were irretrievable, his heart and his youth. At 65 he was an empty old man. Lonely and broken, he went back to work and finished out his career as a locomotive engineer.

In October of 1957, Jack took his pension, the easy chair given him by his children and retired to the Pennsylvania hills of his childhood.

At the last physical exam by the company doctor, Jack was told he must NOT sit down and do nothing or he would die. The doctor said Jack was like the big engines that he ran, 'If you rest—you rust.' Jack took the advice and bought himself a saddle horse. He did not play golf but he loved the outdoors. He rode his gentle, black and white pinto horse named Dan all over the hills.

Jack suffered much from the cold and dampness. The first winter of his retirement he went to Florida, where it was sunny and warm and bought what he called 'his cabin in the woods'. It was a comfortable cottage outside of Deland, just large enough for himself and 'Aunt Martha'. The soothing climate eased his lung problems and he loved the heat. On the other hand 'Aunt Martha' hated the heat and isolation. She was not content to sit quietly under a shady tree. She had to be on the go and into everyones business. In Florida, she knew no one but Jack and that was not enough. She refused to go South with him again. She remained up North where she could gossip and pry about all the people she knew. Jack made the best of it and went alone.

In November of 1961, Jack was summoned to the Veterans Hospital near Pittsburgh. From a top floor window of the hospital, Jack stared through the dirty, rain-streaked pane onto the soggy city below. He had known for half his life that this day would come.

He turned and looked at the wasted form on the bed. In the half light and accentuated by the glaring white sheets, the man already looked touched by death. The labored rattle of his breathing indicated that he was alive. The ravages of disease, neglect and time took a terrible toll on the human body. Jack shuddered. It was impossible that this gray, feeble, emaciated choking person could be Dudley (Duke) Clayton Lansure, Jack's younger brother. Duke was 66 but looked 80. Jack remembered when this tale of misadventure began so long ago. . . .

In Carey in 1926, Duke was staying with Jack and Fan. Jack had made arrangements with the section boss to give Duke a job as a section hand or 'gandy dancer'. Duke was well suited to the job. He was a hulk of a man, heavy-shouldered and thick through the rib-cage. The rest of his body was slender and lean. He stood six feet 4 and his big frame was topped with a shock of black, curly hair. His face was handsomely chiseled and rugged but brooding. His eyes were cornflower blue and soft, when he smiled they lit up like beacons. His temper had a short fuse and a blow from his sinewy arm sent many thoughtless adversaries sprawling in the dirt. Usually, Duke was a man of peace and he never 'picked' a fight but he did not run. His short, hot temper and his great size brought out the scrapping nature of some. On the whole, he was hard-working and fun-loving. The girls flocked around him which surprised him and caused him to blush beet red from shirt collar to hairline. By choice, he was a loner and preferred to sit alone and make his music. He played the guitar, banjo, violin, accordion and piano. He had no formal training but played well. He was the center of attention at gatherings and parties.

It was good times for Jack and Fan with Duke. They would play and sing around the fire in winter and in summer, their music drifted from the porch. Fan played the piano and Jack strummed the guitar.

Jack's life fell apart six months after the birth of his son, Jason Clive in December of 1927. On a warm June day in 1928, Jack came home early from work. Duke and Fan were having an argument in the parlor. Duke was holding Fan by the shoulders and his strong fingers were digging painfully into her flesh.

"Tell me the TRUTH!" He rasped through clenched teeth.

In panic and fear, Fan shrunk from his biting grip.

Applying more pressure with his hands he demanded, ''Tell me the TRUTH. He is mine, isn't he? He is MY son. Say it!'' Duke growled.

Fan cried out in pain when Jack came through the parlor door. She ran to him and sobbed in pain and terror.

Duke turned to Jack and snarled, ''I'm glad you're here. It's time you know the TRUTH, about her and about us and Jason. You left her alone once too often. She begged you not to go but you had to go out of town again, for weeks at a time. She pleaded for you to stay but you went. Remember? The spring of '27, I hardly worked at all because the weather was so bad.'' Duke reminded him. . . .

. . . Jack's mind flashed back instantly, to that miserable March. He was on nights and started at 4:00 P.M., of course he remembered. The section gang hadn't worked for days because of cold and snow. Fan had pleaded with Jack to stay home from work.

''Please Jack, not today, don't go stay home with me, please I need you, lay off and stay home. You have been gone all but three nights this month. I hate that railroad, you're always gone. I never see you. Please don't go and leave me again,'' she had begged.

Jack remembered how she had clung to him and cried.

''You know I can't stay honey. I'd like to but I just can't. We are short-handed. It's my job, it's what I do. Duke will look after you and 'Rilla like he always does when I'm gone.'' . . . Jack remembered well. . . .

''Well,'' Duke growled, ''You went off once too often and left her alone to cry. I was there to listen to her and dry her tears. She hated to be alone and you knew it. I was THERE and you were GONE. I have loved her from the start and I will always love her. It happened, I didn't plan it but it happened. Fan if you don't tell him, I WILL.'' Duke's voice was rising.

The look of terror was gone from Fan's face replaced by woeful resolution.

''Tell him I said!'' Duke shouted.

With tears streaming down her cheeks she screamed, ''YES! YES! It's TRUE!'' She clung to the front of Jack's clothing. ''You always went away and left me! I could not stand it any more!'' She released her grip on Jack and dropped into a chair, put her head in her hands and sobbed.

Jack stood motionless as if struck dumb. His eyes went from Fan to Duke.

''You mean you, you and Fan,'' The idea that Fan and Duke would have an affair boggled his mind and he was speechless. When he could compose himself, he went on, ''You are not trying to tell me Jason is YOURS and NOT MINE?'' Jack's voice rose, ''Fan! Fan say it's a LIE! Tell me it's not true! Fan!'' Jack's voice broke.

Fan did not look up or answer but sobbed into her hands. Through her tears she said softly, ''I'm sorry Jack, I'm sorry. I couldn't help it. You went away and left me and I could not stand it. I needed you, I needed SOMEBODY. You were gone.'' Her voice trailed off into muffled sobs.

For a long moment Jack stood stupefied. When he could speak his voice was stone cold and guttural, ''That's a rotten, dirty LIE. Don't EVER say that again! Jason is MY son and will always be so. NOTHING or ANYONE will ever change THAT. Do you BOTH understand that?'' He moved quickly to Duke and grabbed his shirt front. ''Do you understand? Jason is MINE!'' Jack snarled. ''You wife-stealing bastard! I ought to SHOOT you where you stand! I got you a job, put a roof over your head, food in your mouth, now THIS! You get your gear and haul your stink'n carcass out of here before I KILL YOU!'' Jack loosened his grip and pushed Duke backwards and left him flailing to keep his balance. The bigger man did not fight back. He was astonished at his brother. Jack's eyes were dark and menacing and he was so unlike the usually soft-spoken, gentle brother Duke knew and understood.

''I love her Jack. I have always loved her.'' Duke whispered. He wanted to tell Jack that he had loved Fan from their first meeting but could not. He wished he could say that it broke his heart to see her cry everytime Jack went away on another road trip. There would be no reasoning with Jack so Duke backed out of the parlor and went up stairs to his room.

Jack snatched Fan out of the chair by her upper arms and shook her like a rag doll bruising her flesh while she hung limp in his hands.

''I can't believe you would do this! How could you? Why woman, why? I love you. I give you all I can! Why for God's sake?''

Fan stared at Jack wide-eyed and trembling. Suddenly Jack realized that Fan did not understand the situation or that she was at fault so he released her.

Duke came downstairs and paused at the parlor door.

''I'll be back! I'll be back for the rest of my stuff and I'll be back for my boy!'' Duke was angry. He went out the front door and slammed it hard.

Jack and Fan could not communicate or talk to each other. They lived the next weeks with their predicament festering between them like a boil. They waited.

Fan cleaned, shopped and played with 26-month-old 'Rilla and 6-month-old Jason. She took the children for long walks by placing 'Rilla in the open end of the baby buggy at Jason's feet. She kept away from the house as much as possible to avoid Duke's return. When Jack was away at night, Fan played endless games of solitaire and jumped at every sound.

Jack went through the mechanics of operating the locomotive. His expertise was so great that in spite of the thundering emotional hammer in his brain, his steady, cool, professionalism, never wavered. Inside however, Jack was sure he would erupt like a suppressed volcano and fly to pieces.

The dreaded day arrived. Jack came off the run to find Fan and the children waiting in the railroad yards. He turned the final switching over to his fireman and crew. He slid down from the cab to Fan below. Jason was asleep in the buggy. Jack kissed his cheek and snatched 'Rilla out of the pram. She had been pleading with out-stretched arms from the moment she saw her daddy.

Jack flung her into the air until she squealed with glee, then nuzzled her to his face. He ignored the fact that his soot-grimy face was smudging her pretty pink and white coat and bonnet. How they loved each other.

"Give daddy a kiss," Jack said with pride. Instantly, little chubby arms circled his sooty neck and the child kissed his cheek. Jack's heart swelled with love and happiness for his little girl.

The worried look on Fan's face brought Jack to the dreaded reality at hand.

"He's back, isn't he?" Jack asked.

"Yes, he picked up his clothes but refused to give me his key. Oh, Jack, it was awful! I thought he was going to take Jason! What are we going to do?" She whined.

"Be quiet. Don't let 'Rilla see that you are upset," Jack instructed firmly. He sat 'Rilla back in the buggy, gave her his gold railroad watch and chain to play with to soothe her objections and pushed the carriage toward home.

Fan took a deep breath and told Jack what had happened.

"Duke arrived shortly before noon and let himself in with his key. Jason was asleep but Duke demanded to see him. I allowed him in the nursery but told him not to wake the baby. He touched Jason's hand, watched him sleep for a long moment, then he left. When I asked for his key, he said he would be back later to talk to us both." Fan was unnerved.

"Did he say when?" Jack asked.

"NO! No he didn't. I'm so afraid. What if he tries to take Jason?" What will we do?" Fan was panicked.

"It's a little late to worry about that now, lady." Jack was constantly confounded by Fan's child-like response to problems. The fact she had committed a sin in the eyes of God and man never crossed her mind. She over-responded to attention and coddling and gave herself with careless abandon, never once considering the dire consequences of her actions. Fan had no idea this family crisis was mostly her fault nor did she have any sense of wrong-doing. She was only aware of the threat to her own little world and her Jason. She was a frightened child.

Jack would have liked to shake her, but when he saw her tears and the fear in her eyes, he could not. There was no point punishing a child that did not understand why it was being admonished. He loved her so he chose to make the best of it. Jack realized the terrible price he might pay for laughing off Fan's childish antics and irresponsibilities as comical and cute. Her naive immaturity was no longer amusing.

"If Duke gets mad enough, he can tear this place down. I don't know what he will do. Did he say where he's staying?" Jack said.

"Mrs. Purdy's maybe, that's where most all the railroaders stay. We didn't talk about that." Fan went on absently while they walked. "I wish he would go away and never come back. Just get in his roadster and GO!"

They were almost home and Jack did not answer the foolishness—or was it?

At home, Jack washed up and Fan finished preparing dinner. Jason banged his highchair with a teaspoon and 'Rilla tagged around after her father. When they sat down to dinner, Fan took Jason on her lap and placed 'Rilla in the highchair. The food was on their plates but before they could take a bite, a key was heard in the front door lock.

"DUKE!" Fan gasped.

"Sit still and feed the children!" Jack exclaimed calmly.

"You CAN'T ask him to eat with us." She croaked inaudibly.

Jack took a plate from the shelf, silverware from the drawer and set another place at the table. Duke's frame filled the kitchen doorway.

"Have a seat there's plenty and we have to talk." Jack pulled out a chair for his brother.

"Thanks." Duke was surprised but sat down at the table where he had many times before.

Jack emptied the meat platter onto Duke's plate. It contained three large pieces of browned home-made link sausage, a favorite of both men. Jack passed the home-fried potatoes and apple sauce to Duke along with fresh horse-radish. The men ate heartily, including several slices of Fan's fresh bread with butter and jelly.

The air was so charged with strain and tension that Fan could not eat a mouthful. It was if an invisible hand was gripping her throat. She fed and tended the children but her hands trembled and her mouth was dry.

The babies had no knowledge of the drama around them and went on eating, playing and jabbering as tots do. Jason began to squirm and fuss on

Fan's lap when he was given bits of bread or potatoes instead of the sausage that he liked. There was no more sausage except one bite-size piece on Duke's plate.

Jason, now standing on his mother's lap facing the table, leaned over and snatched the sausage from Duke's plate. With baby-like delight, he gnawed and chewed on his prize.

When the baby took the meat, Fan's heart stopped. This would be the flame that would lite the explosion she and Jack were expecting. Nothing happened.

Duke patted Jason's head affectionately and smiled.

Jack leaned back in his chair, took the coffee pot from the stove and poured a refill for Duke and himself. Fan had not touched her cup.

The silence was deafening and Fan could stand it no longer. She stood up, with Jason in her arms and announced it was bath and bed time. Jack kissed and lifted 'Rilla from her highchair to the floor and she took her mother's hand. Fan all but dragged her from the room. When she reached the front stairs, Fan snatched 'Rilla around the waist, ran up the stairs with both children in her arms and fled down the hall to the bathroom.

She closed the door behind her and sagged heavily against it. She heard the muffled voices of the men below, but could not hear the words. The ominous sounds beat upon her ears. She quickly turned on the water faucet full force in the tub and the painful pounding in her ears stopped.

At the kitchen table Duke was talking. "But Jason is my son, not yours."

"That may be a biological fact but I doubt it. For all intents and purposes he is MY son. He was born to MY wife, in MY home, by our doctor, and I intend to raise him as MY SON." You got that?" Jack growled.

"But he looks exactly like ME. You can see that." Duke insisted. "He has my black, curly hair, blue eyes and is big boned, like me!"

"All babies have blue eyes at his age." Jack growled. He was angry. "Fan has curly hair but that's beside the point. Jason is MY son and from now on, I never want to hear otherwise from you or anyone. There is nothing you can do about it. Furthermore, if you ever try to claim him or make trouble for us, I'll charge you with kidnapping. If he hears the black secret from you, I'll see to it he learns to hate you. Now get your home-wreckin' ass out of here and don't come back!" Jack was cold and menacing.

Pain and grief tore at Duke. He could not believe it was his brother speaking. The sibling bonds between them were nearly severed when Jack learned about the affair but Jack's cruel and vengeful ultimatum was the final destruction. The two brothers were strangers.

"Jack you don't mean that. You can't—you wouldn't. I know I did you wrong and you got the right but not that way. Not let me see him! It's inhuman. He's my boy, I need to see him. You wouldn't do that please, Jack.'' Duke's eyes brimmed with tears and his voice choked.

Jack's eyes were dark and his voice cutting as cold steel. He wanted revenge. ''Get out of here, NOW, and don't come back. Your duds are in the hall closet.''

The babies were in bed and Fan had descended to the landing, half-way down the stairs and sat down on the steps. She had heard most of Jack's words and said, ''His things are in the closet.'' She spoke softly.

Duke ran to the foot of the stairs and pleaded, ''Did you hear? You can't let him keep me away! I love you and that baby! You got to help me, PLEASE! Fan.'' Duke cried.

Fan sat ridgidly on the step and wept. She said nothing.

Jack took the suitcase and coat from the closet and placed them at the door.

''Now get the Hell out of here!'' Jack snarled.

Duke's body sagged. He knew he had lost. He picked up his things, dropped the door key on the table and said, ''I can't believe you could do this. I know I've hurt you, Jack, but have I made you so hard and cruel? You are not my brother anymore and for this evilness I swear, I'll make you pay!'' Duke took his belongings and was gone. . . .

Back in the hospital room, Jack stared out the window. Many years had passed and there was no longer hate between the brothers but there was no forgiveness either. If they had an inevitable meeting, a truce-like silence prevailed.

Jack bitterly remembered how his hate and revenge had sent his brother to his ruin. Shame and guilt rolled over him in waves. He recalled Duke had been gone for nearly 10 years. By bits and pieces, the family learned that Duke had been in Texas, Oklahoma and many places in between. Times were hard and he worked where he could find it. There was much speculation about what happened to him but from sketchy information and hearsay, the puzzle was loosely pieced together:

During the War, Duke was a Chauffeur in the 1103 Aero Squadron. He could drive any kind of 'Gas Buggy' and enjoyed being at the wheel. He drove trucks, lorries, ambulances and staff cars of all descriptions. After the calamity with Jack and Fan, Duke loaded his musical instruments and all he owned into his bright shiny new roadster and headed West.

He traveled until he ran out of gas or money. Sometimes he would stop to chat with a group in a general store, gas station or saloon. He was strong as an ox and could do any type labor but as a rule, he could raise the price of a meal or a tank of gas by playing a few tunes on the guitar or banjo.

In saloons and taverns, he would be tossed a few coins. Occasionally, he stayed and played as the 'main attraction' for a week, a month or several months but eventually he was back on the road, moving on.

Smoke-filled barrooms, bathtub gin, cheap booze, ladies-of-the-night along with poor diet and little sleep, took a devastating toll on Duke. He was a chain smoker and his lungs were the first to go. He was restless of mind and body and moved often, resulting in perpetual exhaustion.

Duke's love for Fan was slow to die. He tried to drown her memory in an ocean of other women. From that sea of different faces, hers shown the brightest. It haunted him.

He wandered the West for years, one saloon after another, one oil field after another, one woman after another. A few weeks here, a few months there.

After a local doctor told Duke his rambling days were killing him, Duke started his long trek East.

One day in late summer, Duke drove into the lane at his brother Jack's farm. Duke let the engine die in his now old, delapidared fliver.

Duke was greeted by several children playing in the big yard.

"We got company, Mama," 'Rilla called to the open kitchen window.

"It's some man!" Jason shouted.

"Man! Man!" Drake squealed in gleeful baby fashion.

Fan recognized Duke at once and her heart stopped. She snatched the apron from her waist, dried her wet hands on it and tossed it aside. She kept a watchful eye on the children in the yard because tiny baby Jannell was on a blanket there in the shade of a tree.

Fan hesitated at the door, smoothed a damp curl from her forehead, straightened her dress and stepped out. She took baby Jannell from the blanket on the ground and went to greet Duke.

Duke was out of the car and when he saw Fan he took a few steps toward her and hesitated. He ached to hold her in his arms and kiss away the years.

Aloud he said, "Fan, you—you're—how well you look." She was so lovely to him and he was embarrassed by his stammering. "Nice family you have." He said and gestured to the children.

"Hello Duke, it's been a long time." Fan fought to keep her composure. "Thanks. This is 'Rilla, she's 11. Jason is 9. Drake is 2 and the baby, Jannell, is 1. Children, this is your daddy's younger brother, Duke. He's been away." Fan's mouth was dry. She was as shocked at his appearance as by his unexpected arrival.

Duke was devouring her with his eyes and Fan could feel her face flush. She could avoid his stare but not his presence. He had aged so. His big shoulders drooped and his black hair was streaked with white. His face was lined and leathery and he was bone thin.

Duke studied Jason carefully. Their resemblence to each other was striking. Duke wanted to hold the boy in his arms and glory in his warmth and youth. He did nothing but speak to the boy.

"Big for your age, aren't you?" Duke asked and patted the top of Jason's head.

"Yeh, I guess so, I'll be 10 this winter. The man next door, lets me ride his combine, I'm big enough for that. My dad takes me on the engine with him too." Jason drew away from the stranger's touch. Heartbreak was written on Duke's face.

"You help your mother?" Duke inquired softly.

"Sure sometimes—here comes my dad! Hey! Look who's here!" Jason ran to meet Jack. "Dad, are you two brothers like me and Drake?" He did not wait for an answer. "Can I go ride the combine now, please, Dad?" Jason begged of Jack.

"Be careful and be home for supper." Jack instructed.

Jason ran down the road and over his shoulder, he called back, "'Bye, Uncle Duke."

Duke watched the boy trot down the road.

"Duke it's been a while." Jack extended his hand, "Come up on the porch out of the sun. It's cool there."

Duke was surprised but willing and grasped Jack's hand firmly.

"Yes, a long while. You look the same Jack." Duke said.

The brothers took seats on the comfortable porch furniture and said nothing.

Fan set the baby Jannell on the blanket and instructed 'Rilla to keep a watchful eye on her siblings, "I'll only be a jiffy. I have to make fresh lemonade." Fan hurried into the kitchen. Her mouth was dry and her head pounded.

If Jack noticed Duke's frail appearance and shabby clothes he said nothing. Duke began to cough and Jack spoke.

"That's a bad cough, guess we all have weak lungs. You on your way home?" Jack was concerned.

"Yes, I am. I'm tired to death and I want to see Ma'am. I've been poorly and the Doc out there said I better get checked up at the Vet's Hospital." Duke stated flatly.

"Ma'am will be glad to see you, she hasn't been well and can use your help." Can you stay for supper and rest the night before you go on?" Jack asked.

"Thanks, but I ran into Joe Polo and he asked me to eat and bunk with him. I worked for him once." Duke said.

Fan brought the lemonade and cookies on a tray and served. They ate and drank in charged silence.

Duke broke the quiet. "He looks just like me, all that black curly hair and those big blue eyes. At least you can give me THAT. I stayed away and didn't make any trouble. I have to have SOMETHING. I got nothing. Can't you bring him down home once in a while, so I can watch him grow? Is that too much to ask? Fan?" Duke's eyes pleaded with her and his voice quivered.

You're his UNCLE. I'm his FATHER and he's our SON. I won't have his life spoiled in any way. It's better if you don't see him at least for now. Maybe later. I'm sorry it's the best for everyone." Jack was gentle but firm.

Fan sat quiet and downcast with nothing to say.

Duke stood to go and his big body sagged. He looked even older than before.

"I guess you're right at least for now, but later when I'm fixed better and not so tired, we will see. When Jason is bigger things will be different. This is a nice farm and a good place to raise children. Goodbye, Fan, Jack." He said.

Duke wanted to say more to the woman he loved but dared not. He waved to them and got into his old car, they waved back and he drove away.

Years later when Jason was a teen-ager, there had been several trips to see Duke. A strong bond had grown between the boy and his UNCLE. Jason enjoyed visits to the old homestead and his uncle. There were several nieces and nephews but it was known to all that Jason was Uncle Duke's favorite. Duke kept the dark secret to himself. . . .

Jack was drawn back into the dim hospital room by a stirring on the bed.

"Jack, glad to see you. Pull up that chair." Duke reached out a claw-like hand and pointed to a straight-backed chair by the bed. His voice was choked off by a fit of violent coughing.

"Don't talk—just rest." Jack urged. He sat down and took Duke's outstretched hand.

The coughing spasm subsided and Duke went on, "I must, there is little time and much to be said. Open that drawer." Duke gestured toward the bedside table. "Take those papers out and put them here," Duke tapped the bedding under his fingers.

Jack complied and one by one, Duke gave Jack the papers to read. When he finished reading, Jack said.

"Duke I want you to know. . . ."

''Never mind that now, Jack, it's long in the past and there is no time left.'' Duke interrupted. His voice was husky and his breathing more and more labored but he continued. ''You and Fan did a good job of raising my boy. He grew up strong, independent and honest. You can't ask more. He loves the woods and HE LOOKS LIKE ME. He's big like me and he even laughs like I did. It pleasures me just to look at him.'' Duke took the papers from the bed and gave them to Jack. ''These papers transfer everything I own to Jason. All he has to do is sign them. You see to it.''

''This is everything you own, all your. . . .'' Jack began.

''Yes, yes.'' Duke interrupted again. ''Now there is one more thing. Jas is due home in about two weeks on 'leave from the Navy and I want to see him. I want to tell him myself, that I'm his father. You were right about it Jack, all of it. You and Fan raised him right. He came to see me often when he was grown and we would talk. Jas loves and respects you and that's the way it should be, him thinkin' you're his daddy and all but he loves his old uncle a little too. You did a good job of raisin' him. I couldn't—not without Fan. I always loved her you know, she spoiled it for me with other women and there were lots of other ones but I loved her and she gave me a son. I knew she never felt anything special for me. My loving her and the boy gave me strength—kept me going when I thought I could not. Times were hard and I had nobody. It's not easy to explain I. . . .'' Duke's voice was choked off by a coughing spasm that wracked his body.

''Shush now, don't talk. Save your strength.'' Jack soothed his brother and hot tears of shame and regret stung his eyes.

''I must. Did you know that I got to be known as the town's Character? I'm loud and gruff like Leone and I often talk to myself. The kids used to mock and laugh at me. I didn't really mind, it was sort of a game we played. I'd scowl and holler and they'd run and squall. Then we all laughed, it was kind'a fun. I delivered the GRIT for many years and they called me the old Paper Man. When I got too feeble, I had to give it up. I missed it and the little ones. It made me feel closer to Jas. After that, all I had was my music and I soon got too weak to hold my accordion and all that was left was my guitar. I could still strum a little. Jas brought me new strings for it once, you know that? He never laughed at me. 'Rilla neither, but she was a bit shy of me and my big voice. Not Jas, he'd come right in and make himself 'ta home. He sent me a letter once, all the way from CEYLON. I never forgot that. I read and re-read that letter 'til the writin' faded and the paper split.'' Duke went on.

Jack could no longer hold back the sobs in his throat and his tears fell on the white sheets. He mopped his face with his handkerchief. Duke seemed not to notice and went on talking.

"Once I wanted to tell him I was his real Pa, but I couldn't do it. He was so happy to have you for his daddy. It was best then, but now, he's a man full grown and I want him to know I'm his Pa before I die. Bring him here as soon as possible. Promise you will. I want to tell him myself! Promise me!" Duke's voice rose and he began to cough. Blood gushed from his mouth and nose. "Promise me!" He croaked.

"Yes! Yes! I promise. Oh God! Nurse! Nurse! Where the Hell is everybody?" Jack shouted helplessly.

A white-clad nurse stepped in the door followed by two doctors dragging machinery.

"I'm sorry you will have to leave now," she said crisply and moved quickly to Duke's bedside. "Please, we will call you if there is any change." She ushered Jack out of the room.

Jack stood numbly in the corridor clutching the papers Duke had given him. Time crept.

In the room, the life-support team worked to save Duke's life. It was hopeless. The doctor who had been monitoring Duke's heartbeat removed his stethoscope, switched off the machinery and drew the sheet up over the lifeless form. Duke was still and silent forever in death.

When the doctor came out of Duke's room, Jack knew. The next hour was a slow motion blur for Jack. He made his brother's funeral arrangements more or less, in a stupor.

His head did not clear until he stepped out of the hospital into the cold rain. He drove home in the cold November drizzle. Mile after mile he wondered how he could explain all this to Jason. How do you tell your son that you are not his father. After all these years how do you do that.

Jack was so troubled by his brother's death and the situation with Jason, he had to talk to someone. 'Rilla. He would talk to 'Rilla. He could depend on his 35 year old daughter from whom he had few secrets.

They discussed the matter thoroughly. The secret, true or not, must be buried with Duke. For all concerned the matter was suppressed.

It was common knowledge that Jason was Uncle Duke's favorite nephew. When Duke's legacy was bestowed solely upon Jason, no one questioned the bequest and reguarded it as the natural procedure. The enigma was never disclosed. . . .

Time marched on. Jannell married Jake's best friend, Ross Weston. They knew each other casually, before Jake's death. Afterwards, they clung to each other in their misery and grief. Their need for solace blossomed into love and they became a perfect match.

Perry enlisted in the Navy. He found it lonely but interesting and challenging. His expertise with explosives, rifles and small arms was remarkable. For the Navy's use in Greece, he designed and built a rifle and gun range that won him a Navy Commendation.

Jason's career in the Navy was very successful. He went from Apprentice Seaman to Chief Petty Officer in just a few years. He married a local girl and started his family.

Jack's great joy in life was his children. Many years ago, his father told him that a man's wealth is his children. Jack was very proud of his children and loved them dearly. In later years, he visited them often and enjoyed all his grandchildren.

Jack's health was failing. 1965 would be his last winter in the South. He went down to say goodby to his old friends and sell his treasured 'cabin-in-the-woods'. To complete his business affairs he took up residence in Deland, at Mrs. Page's Boarding House. Mr. and Mrs. Page were Michigan folks who went South for the winter and stayed. All who lived in their boarding house were 'retired something or other'.

Jack found his fellow-residents colorful and interesting; they included a retired Army Colonel, a school teacher, a New York policeman and a vaudeville actor and his wife. Each had his own story to tell.

The best tonic for Jack or 'Rilla was a visit with one another. 'Rilla's professional life was rewarding but demanding and her health was shaky at best. She had owned her own beauty salon for years but her speciality was hair color. Her expertise was in great demand. During the Beauty Trade Show season, 'Rilla demonstrated her special artistry on the platform, representing a large hair color company. All over the country, huge crowds of hairdressers gathered at those shows to learn her techniques. So great were her accomplishments that her biography appeared in three volumes of The American Marquis' Who's Who For Women and several volumes of The International Who's Who of Cambridge, England.

Her strenuous schedule took its toll on 'Rilla's health. Hal, her husband, was aware of her exhaustion and arranged a rest and a visit with her beloved father in Florida. 'Rilla took a plane to Daytona and Jack met her flight.

She was delighted but flabbergasted when her father met her plane with a car and driver. He never took a car South with him, much less a driver. Jack noticed 'Rilla's surprise but said nothing except the introductions.

"'Rilla, this is my friend Weaver, he and I bum around a lot. He's a retired Detroit auto worker and he and his wife Arliss live here in Deland. Weaver and I go fishing all the time and we never run out of talk." Jack explained.

"It's very nice to meet you Mr. Weaver and I'm delighted to know Dad has a buddy here." 'Rilla shook his hand.

"Weaver, Mrs., just Weaver. Mr. Jack and I share a lot. Both our lungs are poorly from the smoke and cinders of our work. I poured pig iron and he ran a 'smokin' horse! We enjoy a nip o' liquor and good fishing. You sure are pretty, Mrs., I jes' love red hair. Can't hardly figure you're kin to Ole Mr. Jack, him bein' as good lookin' as a mud turtle." The black man chuckled, put Jack and 'Rilla in the back seat and drove away from the airport. Jack laughed and said, "Can't say you're a John Barrymore." The banter went on.

After several days of sight-seeing with Weaver, Jack said, "Honey, today we do something different. After breakfast we're going to sit on the porch swing and chin. You and I have lots to catch up on. Then we are going to walk down town and have a genuine, truly Southern meal, complete with grits. Then we go to the park for the band concert and fireworks. How's that sound?" He winked his usual exaggerated wink and 'Rilla's heart swelled with love and pride for this aging marvel she called father.

They sat in the swing after breakfast and 'Rilla said, "Dad what ever happened to Aunt Nancy Maborn's left-handed water dipper? The one carved out of a laurel root. I haven't seen it for years. And that Mini ball from the Civil War, the one Uncle Tom Hobson dug out of a tree. It was almost cut in two because another ball had passed through it. Aunt Leone had them all put away carefully at home. Does Aunt Martha have them now? Are they safe in your care?" 'Rilla asked.

"Now that you ask, I don't know where those dear old relics are. When I get home I'll try and find out. If I can find them I'll get them to you for safekeeping." Jack said thoughtfully.

"Those family treasures must be cared for. We have very little of the past and what we have must be looked after. Another thing Pappa, when are you going to put your 'yarns' down on paper? They will be lost like everything else if you don't." 'Rilla noted.

"Daughter, you know I'm no scribe. Nobody can read my left-handed scrawl as it is, besides who would be interested in the life of a country boy turned railroader? We're a dime a dozen." Jack reasoned.

"We would—your family. Anybody—everybody. You've been places and done things that books are made of. Your life is a fabulous story. Don't waste it! Write it!" 'Rilla urged. Some people from the boarding house came out onto the porch and the conversation was closed.

Later, Jack and 'Rilla walked around town. They ate a tasty meal at Aunt Ida's Cupboard and 'Rilla ate grits for the first time. Jack had many friends there and would nod and greet them. The friends would nod and stare at 'Rilla and Jack would hurry past and walk on.

After they had met and passed several of his friends, 'Rilla said, "Dad why don't you introduce me to your friends. I never knew you to forget your manners but you rush me past and I can't speak.

"Oh, I could NEVER do THAT!" He said and his eyes twinkled.

"Why not, I'm your daughter". She said.

"That's the point, I can't tell them THAT. It would ruin all their fun!" He said.

"What fun? I don't get it." She puzzled.

"If I tell them you're my DAUGHTER, it would ruin the whole thing." He laughed.

"Ruin what?" She asked again.

"You see, the old folks around here don't have much excitement and there isn't a whole lot to talk about. Their seeing ME with a pretty redhead, half my age, will give them something to talk about all winter. They don't know you are my daughter and I ain't about to tell them. See?" Jack was having fun.

"You Rascal you! Still up to your old tricks, aren't you." 'Rilla teased.

"Just because I'm old doesn't mean I'm senile and can't have a bit of fun." He said.

'Rilla and Jack continued to walk and laugh at the strange stares and whispers. Now that 'Rilla understood it was a prank, they had a great time at the band concert.

They returned to the boarding house and Jack had great time telling the folks there, how he and 'Rilla made the eyes pop of the people they met. He was having the most fun of all.

The precious time 'Rilla had with her father was soon gone. The week went very quickly. Before they left for the plane 'Rilla asked, about a suitable tip for Weaver.

"No, you can't offer him money it would hurt his feelings. Tell you what you could do, if ya want to. His car needs new tires and I know where we can get two good recaps for five bucks apiece. Can ya go a tenner-a sawbuck? I'll see to it and he'd be much obliged." Jack explained. "He lets me buy gas and oil but he won't take money." Jack explained.

"Of course but it seems so little for the great time we had." 'Rilla left ten dollars with her father, departed for the airport and boarded the plane to the North. . . .

In the year that followed, Jack was less and less able to travel but he wished to take one more trip. He had not seen his beloved pal, Shel (Shirly

Haas) since they had served in France together, in the First World War. They kept in touch loosely and Jack knew his friend and buddy was in poor health.

The trip to Winnemucca, Nevada was long but swift and in great comfort. The huge diesels flew over the rails, through great cities and past heavily populated rural areas. His trip West in 1908–9 was obliterated and Jack realized he had become obsolete. Population, roads and automobiles had filled the great, quiet land expanses and noise broke the pastoral silence. In 67 years, the past was erased. Will it always be so? Will the present erase the past? If so how sad. Is it progress or self-destruction? Jack mulled the thought while he sped over the grand open country of his youth. Something inside him crumbled.

In Winnemucca, at 120 Shadyview, he studied the neat well-cared-for Victorian home. He fully expected his rambunctious pal and friend to bounce out onto the porch and call his name.

Jack twisted the huge brass bell on the door and it was opened by a man in white hospital garb.

"I'm Jack Lansure."

"Yes, of course, Mr. Haas is in the parlor, he's been expecting you." The man said and invited Jack into the house and down a hallway. Jack froze in the doorway.

In a wheelchair, sat a badly bloated, white-headed, nearly bald, old man.

"Jack, Oh, Jack, I'm so glad to see you! Come closer old friend, I'm almost blind and I don't hear." The sick man peered at Jack through thick glasses and reached out.

"Shel?" Jack's voice croaked and he thought, it can't be. Where is my buddy of old? Jack took the man's hand.

"Yes, old friend, or what's left of him." Tears streamed down both their cheeks and Jack held Shel's hand.

"Rodger! You met Rodger, he's my 'Mother'! He hides my liquor and cigars and pokes me full of pills! Rodger! Bring my Old Grandad, two beers, two glasses and then get lost! Jack sit here." Shel wheeled his chair to a small table and chairs near by.

"But Mr. Haas, the doctor says. . . ." The attendant began.

"The Hell with the doctor! I want to have a drink with my friend." What can it do? Kill me? I'm mostly dead as it is! Hurry, man." The disapproving man left the two friends to talk.

Jack stayed a few days but the visit was not what he had expected. He was glad to see his friend but resented seeing him in such a deplorable condition. Jack would have preferred to remember his friend as the raucous, tempestuous pal of old rather than the pitiful remnants of a man before him. Jack had forgotten they were both old men now.

The trip home was uneventful but disheartening. Jack's family was surprised he had not stayed longer as planned. When asked, Jack would shrug and say his friend was ill. Nothing more.

It is said 'You Can Never Go Back' and Jack learned that blatant truth to his chagrin. A bit more of him crumbled away.

In the spring of 1967 Jack's condition worsened. He was very short of breath and his medicine had little effect. Jack and Jason had gone to visit friends and Jack could not walk from the car to the house without sitting down to rest.

''Dad, how would it be if I take you into the hospital and get you some oxygen? I'm sure it would help you. I know you hate hospitals, so do I but in this case, I know they could help.'' Jason urged his father.

''Jas, I think maybe you're right. I just can't get my wind anymore and I'm weak as a cat. Let's go.'' Jack agreed.

Jason was astonished his father agreed so readily. Usually Jack would have to be 'dragged, kicking and screaming' to ANY hospital. This worried Jason. Jack's immediate agreement to go to the hospital was a certain indication that something was drastically wrong.

Jason delivered his father to the hospital and to the doctors and nurses there. With great misgivings, he summoned his brother and sisters home at once. The family gathered at Jack's bedside. A great oxygen tent covered half his body and all of his pillow.

''Hey you guys! Haven't ya ever seen a man in an oxygen tent before. Come closer.'' He wheezed and tried to make light of it. ''Now they are gonna' fix me right up and I don't want no long faces, lip shooten' or bawlin'. Ya got that?'' Jack lovingly admonished his children. ''I'm so glad you're all here.'' Jack continued and squeezed their hands one by one. The oxygen tent prevented him from hugging them.

So they would not tire their father further, Jason said, ''Dad, we're going down to have coffee and we will be back later. You rest now.''

''Good idea but I want a word with 'Rilla first.'' Jack said softly.

''I'll meet you in the coffee shop later.'' 'Rilla said and her family left the room.

''What is it, Pappa?'' 'Rilla asked and shuddered when she took his icy cold hand.

''Couple of things but first come closer to my hand. I want to smooth a strand of that pretty red hair behind your ear once more.'' He said.

'''Rilla bowed her head and once again, as he had done thousands of times before, Jack directed her hair behind her ear with his left hand. Hot tears stung her eyes and fell on the white sheets.

''Now none of that.'' He said, ''First take my watch and chain off that table and keep it in your pocket for me.'' Jack directed.

''Pa, I can't do THAT! Your railroad watch hasn't been out of your hands in—in sixty years! You are NEVER without it! How will you tell the time? The doctors here will have you up in no time. You will need it then.'' 'Rilla said softly.

''You and I both know that won't be so. It's curtains for me.'' He said.

''Don't say that Pa. If it will make you happy, I'll put it in the drawer for now and take it home later.'' 'Rilla choked on her tears.

''Now the other thing I want you to do for me.'' Jack said.

''Sure, Dad, anything.'' 'Rilla agreed.

''You remember a long time ago when we were in Florida?'' He asked.

''Sure do! I had a ball! Trailing around after you was more fun than I had in a long while.'' She remembered happily.

''You asked me why I didn't write down my yarns, remember? He asked.

''Sure, I've been at you for years to do it.'' She replied.

''Well, you're the only scribe in this family and I want YOU to do it. Will you do it for me?'' He asked.

''Of course, I will but you will have lots of time when you get out of here.'' She said.

''We both know I won't be goin' out of here. I know when the 'jigs up'. Now don't fuss. I don't mind going at all. I'll be glad to see Jake, Big Davey and Emmaline. There ain't nothing to dying, if your conscience is clear. Besides, I died as much as a man can die and still exist, when Jake died. You can't die twice. All I want to do now is to be with my friends who went before me. I want to join the Boxcar Brigade in the sky. Where they have no train wrecks, no death and all the trains are on time. You must remember daughter, old engineers don't die, they just throttle back and if you think you're at the end of your rope—just tie a knot and hang on. Now promise me you will write my yarns.'' Jack was weaker.

''I promise, Daddy, I promise!'' 'Rilla sobbed and kissed his hand.

''Now go have coffee with the gang. I want to take a nap.'' Jack whispered. He gave her his exaggerated wink and closed his eyes to sleep.

In the early morning hours of June 8, 1967, John Clellend Lansure, (Jack) age 74 died peacefully in his sleep. He quietly joined his son and friends in the heavenly Boxcar Brigade. . . .

THE END

ABOUT THE AUTHOR:

Mary Ellen Ester was born in Carey, Ohio and raised in New London, Ohio. Married Henry Ester 1946. Two children: One daughter and one son (Deceased). She is a Cosmetologist, Esthetician, Educator and Writer. Studied at The Cleveland Academy of Cosmetology. Has Ohio License, 1945 and Pennsylvania, 1955. Graduated Realtors Institute of Michigan, 1975. Certified by Newspaper Institute of America, 1980. Owner/Manager of Fair Lady Beauty Salon, 1960–1970. Real Estate Sales Person for Martin, Ketchum and Martin, Inc. 1972–1976. Esthetician and consultant for Adrien Arpel Skin Care and Cosmetics, 1977–1985. Adult Educator, Lakewood High School, 1979–1985 and Rocky River High School, 1980–1985. Skin Care Consultant for Halle Brothers and Marshal Field's Dept. Stores. Also, Seventeen Magazine. Contributed Skin Care Articles to Aberdeen Times, 1979. Nominated for Woman of the Year—1993 by the International Board of Research of the American Biographical Institute, Inc. Memberships: National Hairdressers and Cosmetologists Assn., Business and Professional Women's Club, Secretary, Women's Council of Realtors. A Fellow in the International Biographical Association of Cambridge, England. Biography appears in Three Editions of Marquis' Who's Who in America and Five Editions of The International Who's Who of Cambridge, England. Hobbies: Skiing, Roller Skating, Swimming and Golf. Enjoys Arts and Crafts, Latch Hooking and Quilting. Volunteers for the Red Cross.

More about the author:

Mary Ellen Ester was born and grew up when one in every ten people in this country worked for the railroads or had a family member who did.

Family life was planned around the train's schedule. They set their watches and clocks, went to work, planned their outings, took vacations, arranged honeymoons and buried their dead by the railroad schedule.

The railroads produced a language all it's own called 'railroad jargon'. Hobos and bums were a group all to themselves and the railroaders had a camaraderie unequaled before or since.

The railroads, as they were then, have all but died out except for the commuters who still live by a train schedule.

The steam locomotive began to die with the birth of the 'flivver'. For Mary Ellen's family, it was the beginning of the end. Her father, uncles, and brothers were railroaders. Now, all but one are deceased or do something else for a living.

This is but one railroader's life story. There were thousands of others.